29

Lecture Notes in Economics and Mathematical Systems 596

Michael Müller-Bungart

Revenue Management with Flexible Products

Models and Methods for the Broadcasting Industry

With 15 Figures and 28 Tables

Springer

Michael Müller-Bungart
CTcon GmbH
Burggrafenstraße 5a
40545 Düsseldorf
Germany
m.mueller-bungart@ctcon.de

Zugl.: Duisburg-Essen, Univ., Diss., 2007

Library of Congress Control Number: 2007928494

ISSN 0075-8442

ISBN 978-3-540-72315-8 Springer Berlin Heidelberg New York

Springer is a part of Springer Science+Business Media

springer.com

Production: LE-TEX Jelonek, Schmidt & Vöckler GbR, Leipzig
Cover-design: WMX Design GmbH, Heidelberg

SPIN 12058488 88/3180YL - 5 4 3 2 1 0 Printed on acid-free paper

Listen to the Water-Mill:
Through the live-long day
How the clicking of its wheel
Wears the hours away!
Languidly the Autumn wind
Stirs the forest leaves,
From the field the reapers sing
Binding up their sheaves:
And a proverb haunts my mind
As a spell is cast,
"The mill cannot grind
With the water that is past."

Sarah Doudney: "Lesson of the Water-Mill"

Preface

Revenue Management (RM) is a success story in many industries. American Airlines, for instance, estimated in 1992 that its RM system contributes additional revenues of US-$ 500 million per year. Lufthansa attributes a revenue gain of DM 950 million in 1996 and DM 1.4 billion in 1997 to RM. Since the vast majority of costs are fixed in those companies, a revenue surplus due to RM almost fully translates to additional profit. Needless to say that RM is now considered to be a key success factor for airlines, hotels and car rental companies. However, RM techniques nowadays prove to be promising in other industries as well. In make-to-order manufacturing, for instance, cost cutting has been the major means to improve profits for a long time. Having implemented tight cost controlling systems, management's focus shifted to the other source of higher profits – higher revenues – as an important, yet underused lever. This book demonstrates how to tap the potential of RM, in particular if flexible products are involved. Since the majority of products in broadcasting companies is flexible, this industry serves as an example.

The contents of the book can be summarized as follows: RM is defined in chapter 1. In this chapter, applications in a broad range of industries are presented. Chapter 2 describes two basic RM techniques: Capacity control and overbooking. Recent advances in the field are highlighted in chapter 3, namely RM in settings where customers make choices and RM with flexible products. Chapter 4 introduces issues related to the evaluation of RM techniques, i. e. the generation of test instances. Chapter 5 deals with the most important aspect of instance generation: simulation of stochastic demand data streams. Chapter 6 is based on a case study in Spanish broadcasting companies. The RM problem in this setting is thoroughly described, the importance of flexible products is clarified, appropriate models and methods are developed and tested on 18,000 instances. Chapter 7 concludes the book and outlines future research opportunities.

Writing this book would not have been possible without the support of a number of people: Alf Kimms was both sponsor and mentor of my research projects. He served as a sparring partner in many fruitful discussions. The participants of many conferences, in particular the members of the GOR group "Revenue Management and Dynamic Pricing" (chaired by Alf Kimms and Robert Klein), challenged my point of views and contributed their expert opinions. I am also deeply indebted to Yvonne Bußhoff, Julia Drechsel, Hannah Dürr, Michaela Graf and Maria Merker. The support of Kerstin Petzold was invaluable. Finally, I would like to thank my parents who made so many things possible.

Neuss, April 2007 Michael Müller-Bungart

P.S. If you have comments, questions or any kind of feedback on this book or RM in general, you can reach me at `http://www.mueller-bungart.de/revenuemanagement`.

Contents

List of Figures

List of Tables

List of Models

List of Algorithms

List of Acronyms

B&B	Branch and Bound
B&C	Branch and Cut
CRS	Computer Reservation System
DAVN	Displacement Adjusted Virtual Nesting
DB	German Railways (Deutsche Bahn)
DP	Dynamic Programming
EMSR	Expected Marginal Seat Revenue
FCFS	First Come First Serve
FSC	Full Service Carrier
HPP	Homogeneous Poisson Process
ID	Independent Demand
IP	Integer Problem
LCC	Low Cost Carrier
LP	Linear Program
MIP	Mixed Integer Program
MNL	Multinomial Logit
MTO	Make-to-Order
NHPP	Non-Homogeneous Poisson Process
NLF	Nominal Load Factor
RM	Revenue Management
SAS	Scandinavian Airlines (Systems)
SOS	Special Ordered Set

1

Defining Revenue Management

1.1 Introduction

Many readers will have noticed that the same seat on the same aircraft is sold for different prices. These differences can be quite large: Lufthansa German airlines, for instance, sells flights between Dresden and Frankfurt/Main for € 109 (return) – a special discount of very limited availability. There is no such thing like a single "regular" price for that route to compare with, but our impression is that a "usual" fare (i. e. a fare that is not part of a special discount offer) is well above € 200, fares between € 300 and 400 are still not extraordinary, and passengers even have to pay more than € 450 for some travel dates. For this (arbitrarily chosen) example the premium for "regular" tickets compared to the discount is in the order of 100 to 400 %. It is important to stress that we are not talking about different prices for economy, business and first class – all the prices mentioned above are for a single seat in the economy class compartment.

The fact that the same seat on the same aircraft is sold for various prices at the same time implies some challenging decision problems: On the one hand, it is obviously reasonable to sell seats at the highest possible prices. Demand is stochastic, though, and the bulk of passengers with a high willingness to pay (e. g. business travelers) will typically book close to departure, while other consumers who cannot afford the highest prices will submit reservation requests very early. On the other hand, a seat that is empty at the time of departure represents opportunity costs, because it may have been sold to a paying customer; and even if the fare received was low, the contribution margin would have been positive because the marginal costs of carrying an additional passenger are negligible. Given a request of a passenger with a low yield the airline thus has to decide whether to accept it (running the risk of *displacing* subsequently arriving demand with higher revenue) or to reject it – which is a bad decision if not enough high yield requests arrive in the future. In general, the question arises how the given capacity should be assigned to products (i. e. fares and passengers) such that the total revenue (profit, contribution margin, ...) is maximized. Aspects related to that general question are subsumed under the term *Revenue Management* (RM). We will define that term more precisely in section 1.2 and describe the field of RM research in section 1.4.

Much like a seat on an aircraft after the time of departure a hotel room that has not been sold at the end of the day incurs opportunity costs. A similar reasoning can be applied to rental cars, restaurant tables and capacity in many other passenger or cargo transport businesses as well as a number of non-transport or non-service industries. We will outline areas of RM applications in section 1.3.

RM has been a large success in airlines, hotels and other companies and is nowadays considered to be a key component of capacity management in many industries. Klophaus (1998), for instance, reports that Lufthansa attributes a revenue gain of DM 950 million in 1996 and DM 1.4 billion in 1997 to RM. Smith et al. (1992) of American Airlines estimate that the RM system contributes additional revenues of US-$ 500 million per year. According to Carroll and Grimes (1995), the revenue increase at Hertz (a car rental company) was up to five percent. A new RM system improved revenues by US-$ 56 million in the first year at National Car Rental and was the basis for a successful turnaround saving the company from liquidation (Geraghty and Johnson 1997). Kimes (2004) estimated that RM techniques could improve revenues by more than five percent in a typical restaurant of a US-based chain of Mexican-style restaurants.

1.2 Characteristics of Revenue Management Problems

An agreed-upon definition that characterizes the concept "Revenue Management" in one or two sentences has not yet appeared in the literature. Kimms and Klein (2005), who review a multitude of definitions in a recent survey, remark that it seems to be rather difficult to pinpoint the field of RM in a short paragraph. Instead, they study a wealth of references and compile four common characteristics of (or prerequisites for) RM problems. Before we discuss these four defining aspects in some detail we note that it is not unusual to describe RM in terms of characteristic conditions which give rise to the specific problems of the field, see e. g. Bertsch and Wendt (1998), Corsten and Stuhlmann (1998), Kimes (1989a,b), Klein (2001), Netessine and Shumsky (2002), Phillips (2005), Swann (1999), Talluri and van Ryzin (2004b), Weatherford and Bodily (1992) and Wirtz et al. (2003). It is furthermore important to stress that all these references mention characteristics that are quite similar. We therefore forbear from examining various approaches to define the term RM – the reader interested in such a discussion is referred to Kimms and Klein (2005) and Corsten and Stuhlmann (1998) – and draw on the results of the comparative survey by Kimms and Klein (2005). They compile the following four basic characteristics or prerequisites for RM from an extensive study of the literature: It is necessary to integrate external factors, the operational flexibility is limited, customers behave heterogeneously and have different valuations for products (and thus capacities), and a standardized product range is offered over a longer period of time. In the following we will discuss each characteristic aspect in detail.

Necessity to integrate external factors

To begin with the production of a physical good, the provision of a service or a combination of both, one or more *external factors* are necessary. "External" means that these factors have to be supplied by the customer. Such factors can be the customers themselves (this is e. g. the case for passenger transportation or hotels), physical goods owned by the client (e. g. cargo) or intangible items like information (e. g. the exact specification of an order). The last example shows that while the necessity to integrate external factors is considered to be a characteristic element of service industries (see e. g. Fitzsimmons and Fitzsimmons 2001, Maleri 1997, Voss et al. 1985) in make-to-order manufacturing (MTO) crucial external inputs exist as well, namely information. We thus stress here that RM is by no means limited to service companies.

The dependency on external factors implies two important features of the problem at hand: It is impossible to anticipate demand, to build up inventories of finished goods and to satisfy requests from stock; and the goods or services have to be offered before the production has begun – this is necessary to induce the supply of the required external factors by the customers. Frequently, the goods or services are even sold before the beginning of production (airline tickets, for instance, are usually paid at the time of purchase, which can be months before the departure date). This is quite a significant difference compared to, say, retailing or wholesale where it is unreasonable (or even illegal) to advertise products that are not in stock, and the goods are usually paid after purchase (especially in wholesale).

Limited operational flexibility

A limited amount of resources is given. We know (in a deterministic setting) or expect (under uncertainty) that there is a mismatch between capacity supply and demand. However, our means to increase or decrease supply or demand to overcome this imbalance are limited such that only minor corrections are possible.

Potential causes for that dilemma are that it is simply impossible to alter supply and/or demand for mere technical reasons, or that it is technically possible but economically infeasible to do so. The latter case occurs if the costs of capacity and/or demand adjustments are higher than the opportunity costs of rejecting demand (if demand exceeds supply) or the costs of idle capacity (if supply exceeds demand).

The aforementioned technical difficulties or prohibitive costs of capacity adjustments are frequently caused by the fact that the amount of capacity which can be added (or removed) from the given amount is a large multiple of the average demanded quantity. For instance, a typical request for a flight ticket will be for one or two seats, while a typical aircraft has got a couple of hundred seats. A rental car is usually hired for a few days, but given the enormous loss of value of a new car rental companies will typically keep vehicles in the fleet for some months. Since an adjustment of capacity can thus only be made in relatively high discrete amounts those decisions are rather long-term and associated with excessive costs. Consequently, we suffer from operational inflexibility in the short run.

Heterogeneous valuations and behavior

Thus far we are in a situation where there is a unavoidable mismatch between supply and demand, and external factors have to be integrated such demand cannot be satisfied from stock. If customers are totally homogeneous (i. e. their valuations of the same unit of resource do not differ, everybody demands the same amount of resources etc.) the problem can be solved easily: We just satisfy all requests as they arrive until there is no more demand or no capacity left. This is called a "first come first serve" (FCFS) policy. If the valuations and/or other aspects of customer behavior differ, the problem which requests should be satisfied becomes rather challenging.

There is an interesting link between heterogeneous valuations and behavior that is very relevant here: We can only profit from heterogeneous valuations if we are able to distinguish different types of customers. This is trivial if e. g. discounts are offered to students or senior citizens – in such cases we only have to check the respective ID cards. Typically, however, customers will not voluntarily reveal their willingness to pay (especially if it is above average), so we have to rely on heterogeneous behavior to separate customer segments. Airlines, for instance, would like to distinguish leisure from business travelers because the latter have a significantly higher willingness to pay. To discriminate those segments airlines impose a lot of conditions on discount tickets, e. g. advance purchase restrictions, cancellation and rebooking fees, Saturday night stay requirements etc. These factors make a discount ticket unattractive for most business travelers. The implementation of such arrangements which should make sure that customers with a high willingness to pay are not able to buy products or services at substantially lower prices is called *fencing*. One might say that companies induce some form of self selection by fencing. The aforementioned airline, for instance, designs its "menu of products" in a way such that business travelers (with a high willingness to pay) will automatically avoid the discount tickets.

Standardized product range

The product range consists of goods or services with given and fixed attributes in the first place, or a product is defined as a bundle of standardized goods and/or services. Furthermore, the standardized product range (or the standardized range of goods and services to create products in the sense of bundles) has to be offered for a longer period of time. Airlines (with the exception of low cost carriers, see page 21) are an example for the former: A product is basically an itinerary between two or more places, associated with departure and arrival times, conditions like cancellation fees etc. and a price. An example for the latter are hotels: The standardized service components are the single night stay in a particular room type, meals, amenities and other features like access to wellness areas. These components can be bundled by guests (according to certain rules), resulting in a price per night (which may also depend on the day). The price for a multiple night stay is then given as the sum of the daily prices. Other examples are rental car or broadcasting companies (see chapter 6 for an extensive treatment of the latter).

Both examples are admittedly somewhat ambiguous. For the airline example one might as well argue that there is a limited number of standardized services (basically non-stop flights) that can be combined to itineraries and various accompanying aspects (e. g. cancellation and refunding conditions). On the other hand, hotels may offer special weekend packages with two overnight stays, special meals etc. This would have the flavor of a product (which can only be bought as a whole or not at all) in contrast to a bundle of standardized goods and services. However, the distinction between both cases is not important in the following, and we will simply use the term "standardized product range" to subsume them.

It is important to stress here that the standardization of the product range does not imply that all features of the products are defined at the time of purchase and there are no degrees of freedom left for both the seller and the customer. At German Railways, for instance, a regular ticket does not fix the exact departure time, i. e. the passenger is free to choose between trains that depart at, say, eight, ten or twelve o'clock. Broadcasting companies, on the other hand, are typically allowed to schedule a particular advertisement freely within a certain time window (whose size is in the order of hours). The latter is an example of so called flexible products. We will introduce these in some detail in section 3.3; and the RM problem at broadcasting companies will be covered extensively in chapter 6.

The four characteristics can be prerequisites for RM problems in two different ways: Firstly, if some aspects are missing problems belonging to other fields arise, and we have lost the distinctive flavor of RM. The first three mentioned characteristics are prerequisites in this sense: If there is no need to integrate external factors we can smooth out the differences between supply and demand by building up inventories of finished goods. If we were flexible enough to adjust supply we would have to decide how much and when to (dis)invest into capacities – the resulting situation would roughly have the flavor of a newsvendor problem. Finally, we have already pointed out that if customers' valuations and behavior are homogeneous a trivial FCFS policy is optimal.

Standardization of the product range is a prerequisite in a pure technical sense – if this prerequisite is not satisfied it is simply impracticable to implement RM methods: If the product range is not standardized and not offered over a longer period of time it is impossible to forecast future demand and to make acceptance/rejection decisions in a reasonable way.

We will now finally summarize the conditions that constitute a RM problem, or, more broadly speaking, we characterize situations in which RM can gainfully be used: Since it is necessary to integrate external factors supplied by the customer into the production process satisfying demand from stock is impossible. Suffering from a limited operational flexibility we cannot balance capacity supply and demand. Customers behave heterogeneously and have different valuations for the same unit of capacity. Together with the mismatch of available and demanded capacity this implies that there are some non-trivial decisions to make, e. g. which requests to reject if demand exceeds supply. However, since we have been offering a standardized product range for a longer period of time, we are able to forecast future demand and have a basis for our decisions.

The concept of "Revenue Management" stems from the airline industry where those decisions where guided by the objective of revenue maximization – since the majority of costs in that business is fixed (this fact is somewhat related to the operational inflexibility) maximizing revenues is a reasonable approximation of maximizing profits. In MTO environments there may be substantial variable costs, and profit (or contribution) maximization – i. e. maximization of revenue minus variable costs – is certainly more appropriate, but for such problems nevertheless the term "Revenue Management" is used (for historical reasons, one might say). It is interesting to point out in this context that RM was formerly known as *yield management*. In the airline industry, however, the term "yield" signifies the average revenue per passenger. A single full fare passenger on an otherwise empty aircraft would thus represent a solution with maximal yield – this is certainly not useful, and hence the somewhat misleading term yield management was abandoned in favor of "Revenue Management".

In the following sections we will highlight RM applications in various industries (1.3) and describe various problems and methods that are subsumed under the term RM, thereby developing a structure of the field (1.4).

1.3 Revenue Management Problems in Various Industries

The aim in this section is to clarify the general set up of RM problem in various industries using the four characteristics we have just described. We will furthermore outline major features relevant for RM on a conceptual level, and direct the reader to industry specific references. This complements the expositions in Talluri and van Ryzin (2004b, ch. 11) who focus on current RM implementations in various industries, and Kimms and Klein (2005) who develop models tailored to different businesses.

Airlines

Airlines have probably been the first users of RM on a large scale. Passenger transportation by air is surely the industry that is most often referred to, and many references are explicitly or implicitly focused on an airline's business environment.

For passenger transport the integration of external factors – namely the passengers themselves – is obviously necessary. Distinct customer groups – business and leisure travelers, for instance – certainly have different valuations of the same journey, and they can be differentiated e. g. by the time of booking (leisure travelers tend to book earlier) or by their ability to comply with certain restrictions (Saturday night stay over, for instance). The product range of airlines is fairly stable over time, only prices may be a bit volatile in competitive markets. The flexibility with respect to changes in flight plans or capacities is clearly limited: Published flight plans are usually valid for six months, changes are thus only minor – for instance, it is rare that existing connections are closed or new ones are opened during that time. It is possible to lease aircrafts to increase the available capacity; however, as mentioned before the increase in capacity (a couple of hundred seats for each flight undertaken by an additional airplane) is large compared to the number of seats demanded by an average request. Other limiting factors besides flight plans and airplanes are e. g. landing slots or legal requirements like maintenance rules for aircrafts and working time restrictions for crews.

Given the amount of references that focus on models and methods for passenger airline RM problems it is certainly not useful to mention all of them here. We nevertheless like to point out some contributions by various airline practitioners that give a broader introduction to airline RM: Smith et al. (1992) describe the amazing success of RM at American Airlines. Alstrup et al. (1989) portray the situation at Scandinavian Airlines, focusing on overbooking (see subsection 1.4.1), and Klophaus (1998) refers to Lufthansa German airlines. Fuchs (1987) introduces airline RM from a practical point of view. The popular book by Cross (1998, 2001) contains a case study of People Express, a low cost carrier (LCC, see page 21) which challenged American Airlines by offering incredibly low fares. The incumbent was only able to introduce competitive fares by a carefully implemented RM system. Calder (2003) and Lawton (2002) cover the history of LCCs in great detail.

Railways and Cargo

It is easy to see that the four defining prerequisites of RM can be found in almost any transport business, let it be passenger or cargo. However, other transport industries feature quite distinctive characteristics.

At German Railways (Deutsche Bahn, DB), for instance, a regular ticket is not bound to a particular time or train. Even the route may not be fixed and can be chosen (within certain limits) by the passenger. In contrast to airlines it is thus uncertain when and on which trains a customer who has bought a ticket will consume capacity. This uncertainty is increased e. g. by special tickets for commuters, where DB does not know how often the customer will travel, and from which origin to which destination. As a consequence, almost two thirds of all passengers belong to the group of what DB calls "uncontrolled traffic" (Köhler 2005).

Other aspects besides revenue increases are relevant for DB as well. In peak demand situations, for instance, there are frequently not enough seats for every passenger, i. e. some customers will have to stand, thus suffering from a very low level of service. An obvious (but costly) solution is to increase the rolling stock when demand is maximum (i. e. adding cars or trains). By driving price sensitive customers who are flexible with respect to travel times to off-peak trains the peak level of service is increased without having to add new capacity, simply by using the existing trains more efficiently.

Treatments of the passenger railway RM problem are very rare, though. Ciancimino et al. (1999) refer to the situation of FS, the Italian public railway company, and present a deterministic and a probabilistic model and solution methods. Whelan and Johnson (2004) consider the situation in the UK and examine how fares and ticket restrictions can be used to shift demand from peak hours to times where capacity utilization is lower anyway in order to avoid overcrowding. Ben-Khedher et al. (1998) describe decision support systems at SNCF (a French railway company) including an RM system. Li et al. (2006) report on a project at Netherlands Railways dealing with pricing issues in the context of automatic fare collection systems based on so called "smart cards".

Cargo industries (regardless of the mode of transport) satisfy in general all four prerequisites as well, the major difference to passenger transportation being that the external factor is not the customer but goods owned by the customer. This difference implies some interesting unique features (see e. g. Kasilingam 1996, Slager and Kapteijns 2004): While each passenger occupies (at most) one seat, the capacity usage of cargo is frequently a multidimensional measure (weight, volume etc.). Passengers will have a preference for a certain itinerary; in particular the route, the connection times and the total travel time will be relevant. For cargo it is often sufficient if the carrier is able to deliver the cargo within a certain time window – waiting and travel times as well as the route taken to the destinations are mostly irrelevant, as long as the final destination is reached on time. Unlike passengers cargo will not travel back from the destination to the origin; in fact cargo traffic is usually asymmetric, i. e. there are many places in the world from which large amounts of cargo are shipped (but only little is received) and vice versa.

In some industries other aspects have to be considered as well: A good deal of air cargo, for instance, is not transported in dedicated cargo aircrafts but together with passengers and their baggage on ordinary scheduled passenger flights. This implies that the amount of belly space remaining free for cargo transportation is uncertain, because it depends on the number of passengers and the amount of baggage they carry with them.

References on the cargo RM problem have been very rare, but it has recently attracted some attention. Kasilingam (1996) outlines a model for air cargo RM. Models and methods for this problem are due to Amaruchkul et al. (2006), Bartodziej and Derigs (2004), Luo et al. (2005), Moussawi and Çakanyıldırım (2005), Pak and Dekker (2004) and Karaesmen (2001, ch. 2). Klophaus (1999) and Slager and Kapteijns (2004) describe the RM system at the cargo division of Lufthansa German airlines and KLM Cargo, respectively. Wendt (1991) deals with pricing of cargo plane capacity. Strasser (1996) describes rail freight RM on a conceptual level, while Campbell and Morlok (1994) indicate methods for that problem. Furthermore, there are some references dealing with so called stochastic knapsack problems. They share common features with some RM problems, in particular with simplified versions of the cargo RM problem, and there are also some loose relationships to the RM problem in broadcasting companies. We give a brief overview on the work on stochastic knapsack problems in section 6.6.

Hotels, Cruise Liners, Casinos, Tour Operators

Much like passenger transport businesses hotels, cruise liners, casinos, tour operators and other companies of the tourism industry require the participation of the customer in person. It is evident that the means to adjust capacities in hotels, cruise liners and casinos is limited: It is certainly possible to add a small bed to a room or cabin, or to accommodate a single person in a double or twin room, but only minor adjustments like these are possible in the short term. Tour operators face RM problems, too, because they rely on the operation of passenger transports, hotels etc. Cruise operators frequently bundle their journeys with trips (mostly flights) to and from the harbor as well.

An interesting aspect of many tourism businesses is that besides direct revenues associated with staying some nights in a hotel or casino or booking a cruise additional (uncertain) profits are possible. Examples for hotels include restaurants, bars and conference rooms. This extra revenue is especially relevant for casinos and cruise liners. In the former case revenues from gambling, restaurants and entertainment can be quite significant compared to those from room rents. Cruise liners profit from the fact that guests are (in a very real sense) "locked in", only being able to visit restaurants, bars, entertainment facilities, retail outlets etc. on board the ship.

While there is quite a large body of literature on hotels (see e. g. Badinelli 2000, Bitran and Gilbert 1996, Bitran and Mondschein 1995, Chen 1998, Goldman et al. 2002, Jones 1999, Koide and Ishii 2005, Lai and Ng 2005, Liberman and Yechiali 1978, Rothstein 1974) there are only quite a few scientific references on cruise liners, casinos and tour operators. Hoseason (2005) gives an overview on the cruise RM problem. Ladany and Arbel (1991) consider the market segmentation and pricing problem for a cruise liner. Lieberman and Dieck (2002) deal with the cruise operator's problem to purchase flights for guests traveling to and from the harbor by plane. Froeb and Tschantz (2003) examine the effects of the Princess-Carnival cruise line merger on competition. To analyze that antitrust case they consider a pricing problem with two competing firms and study the impact of a merger between both on prices and quantities.

Norman and Mayer (1997) survey the implementation of RM techniques in Las Vegas casino hotels. Hendler and Hendler (2004) give a very readable introduction to the casino RM problem, explaining the different sources of revenues and costs (e. g. discounts and free meals for high-yield gamblers).

Remmers (1994) presents an overview of the RM in the tourism industry in general, highlighting the differences between tour operators which bundle services to a package holiday on the one hand and providers of original services on the other. Hoseason and Johns (1998) summarize the tour operator RM problem as well. In an empirical study, Klein (2000) examines how many tour operators make use of RM and to what extent. Xylander (2003) extensively investigates the potential of RM for tour operators and develops tailored models. Würll (2004) reports on the implementation of an RM system at Thomas Cook UK. He observes that the major challenge of tour operator RM is that there is a large number of heterogeneous resources to be used (planes, hotels etc.) which are frequently purchased from a multitude of companies in long term contracts. Laws (2005) highlights some issues with respect to pricing of inclusive holidays. Oppitz (2004) of Thomas Cook points out that a typical problem of tour operators is that holidays are marked down, i. e. prices decline down to a "last minute" bargain price. He notes that this has lead to strategic behavior: Customers defer purchases to wait for discounts. Such a situation is e. g. considered by Ovchinnikov and Milner (2005) who present models and methods for last minute discounts if strategic customer behavior is to be expected. Su (2005) also deals with strategic customers and derives conditions under which markdown or markup pricing should be used, respectively. Similarly, Anderson and Wilson (2003) consider a situation where customers estimate the probability that a certain fare class which is not available now will be offered again later and defer their purchase if the chance is good enough. Wilson et al. (2006) extend this approach by also considering customers who may purchase products at a higher price (instead of strategically waiting) if their first choice product is not available.

Car Rental

The car rental industry is another area of application that has already received some attention in the RM literature. Evidently, it is necessary to integrate the customer in person for the production of the service. The product range is standardized on the basis of different types of cars, length and date of rent. It is important to distinguish between business and private customers (like holidaymakers) who have different valuations of the service. They also behave differently with respect to the time when they rent (day of week and time of year) and where they rent. We have already mentioned that there are certainly possibilities to increase the fleet by adding cars (even in the short term), but given the enormous loss of value of a car during the first months this is only profitable if there is a significant, long lasting shift in demand. Analogous arguments hold for decreasing the fleet's size by selling cars earlier than planned.

Similar to cargo transport a significant proportion of traffic may be asymmetric, because customers may rent out cars at one station and return them at another such that some stations will (on average) hire out more cars than are returned to that station and vice versa. In this case cars have to be transferred between stations (at a cost). Much like hotels where we have earlier (or later) departures and arrivals, customers may rent out or bring back cars sooner or later than expected, or cars are even returned to a station other than announced by the customer. Like in the cargo industry capacity is therefore uncertain.

Carroll and Grimes (1995) and Mayr (2005) describe the RM systems at Hertz and Sixt (a large German car rental company), respectively. Geraghty and Johnson (1997) report that the implementation of RM at National Car Rental not only improved revenues by US-$ 56 million in the first year but even saved the company from liquidation. Blair and Anderson (2002) and Anderson and Blair (2004) give an account of a system to measure the performance of RM at Dollar Car Rental.

Recently, RM applications in the rental business in general (i. e. not specific to cars) have received some attention, see e. g. Gans and Savin (2005) and Savin et al. (2005) for models and methods.

Manufacturing

Manufacturing does not seem to be an obvious area for the application of RM techniques because it is possible to stock finished goods and to satisfy incoming requests from stock. This implies that it is not necessary to integrate external factors into the production process, and albeit it is frequently difficult or even impossible to adjust capacity supply to demand, excess capacity can be employed to build up inventories which are subsequently used to satisfy requests in case of a demand surplus. This is not to say that planning aspects related to capacity usage are trivial in this setting; on the contrary this situation actually gives rise to challenging and very relevant problems, e. g. lot sizing and inventory control – but certainly not RM problems. This reasoning is however only applicable to make-to-stock production. If we consider make-to-order (MTO) environments it is certainly necessary to integrate external factors (namely the specification of the order by the customer). Since the variety of possible orders is typically large and/or the holding costs are extremely high (otherwise a make-to-order production would not make sense in the first place) inventories of finished goods are avoided. Standardization of the product range is possible by focusing on the inputs. For instance, if only a limited number of dimensions is used to specify an order, or production uses only a moderate number of machines these dimensions (or machines) form a suitable basis for forecasting and optimization models. It goes without saying that heterogeneous valuations can easily be exploited with MTO – in the extreme every order has got a uniquely determined price (and consequently, value).

Rehkopf and Spengler (2005a) present an overview on the RM problem in MTO environments and Defregger and Kuhn (2004) outline a model and a heuristic. Spengler et al. (2007, see also Rehkopf 2006, Rehkopf and Spengler 2005b) apply RM techniques to the iron and steel industry. In an empirical study Kuhn and Defregger (2005) find that many paper, steel and aluminum companies satisfy preconditions for a gainful application of RM, but actual implementations are rare. This paper also contains a wealth of references, considering as well related problems if products are made to stock.

Miscellaneous Industries

restaurant RM has recently received some attention, see Kimes (2005) for an overview. Bertsimas and Shioda (2003) address this problem in a "classic" way, focusing on whether to immediately accept demand or not (controlling for waiting times and "fairness"), while other authors consider somewhat more restaurant specific methods like meal duration control (see e. g. Kimes et al. 2002) and demand based pricing (see e. g. Kimes and Wirtz 2002).

Other areas of application include visitor attractions (Hoseason 2006, Leask et al. 2005), computing centers (Dube et al. 2004), telecommunication networks (Humair 2001, Lindemann et al. 2003, 2004), internet service providers (Nair and Bapna 2001), natural gas transport and storage (Dörband 2005, Dörband et al. 2003), golf courses (Kimes and Schruben 2002, Kimes and Wirtz 2003) and tickets for sports, entertainment and other events (Barlow 2005, Cheung 1980, Volpano 2003). In this book we will furthermore indicate applications in the health care industry (see page 82), and broadcasting companies will be extensively covered in chapter 6.

Two papers refer to somewhat special organizations as RM users: Cook (1998) mentions a project conducted with the US Navy where training facilities have to be booked in advance and it is also gainful to reserve some capacity for requests of high yield which typically arrive very late. Metters and Vargas (1999) consider a pricing problem at a child care center.

1.4 Structuring the Field of Revenue Management

Having outlined the wealth of industries that successfully apply RM techniques we will now describe the problem areas that are covered by the term "Revenue Management". We begin with capacity control (and a closely related aspect that is called overbooking), which is at the heart of RM. Sometimes RM and capacity control are even treated as synonyms. Related problems are subsumed under the term "dynamic pricing". We will discuss dynamic pricing and auctions in subsection 1.4.2. In subsection 1.4.3 we finally present various approaches from the literature to classify capacity control, dynamic pricing and the term RM itself. We will not resolve the conflicting points of view but clarify the perspective taken in this book.

1.4.1 Capacity Control and Overbooking

Capacity Control

The seminal example from the airline industry describes one of the core problems of RM: Low fare passengers book relatively early. The same units of capacity that are needed to satisfy their requests could though be used for later arriving requests of higher value as well. We thus will want to limit access of certain products to the scarce capacity in order to protect some amount to be spent for other products. This strategy is called *capacity control.*

The capacity control problem boils down to the decision whether a given request should be accepted or not. If we accept, we gain a certain amount of money (e. g. a ticket price minus a cancellation refund) and an uncertain amount of money that basically depends on requests and our decisions in the future. If we reject, the certain amount of money we get will be lower (actually zero in most cases), but our potential revenue in the future will probably increase because capacity was protected for later arriving requests of higher value. At the core of capacity control is thus the question if the revenue gain outweighs the *opportunity costs* of accepting, which are fundamentally the costs of displacing higher valued requests that (supposedly) arrive in the future.

In the current RM literature two ways of capacity control have been discussed: One option is to simply limit the number of requests we are going to accept for a certain product, i. e. for each product we decide about the amount of resources that we will (at most) dedicate to that product. This is called *booking limit* control, which is discussed extensively in section 2.2. Another option is to compute or estimate the opportunity costs of accepting a given request and to accept if and only if these opportunity costs are exceeded by the revenue gains of accepting. This can be done e. g. by estimating the opportunity costs of one unit of each resource. Such estimates are called *bid prices*. We will discuss bid prices in section 2.3.

Overbooking

We have noted in section 1.2 that some form of customer integration is a prerequisite for RM problems. As a consequence, we cannot start production of the good or service unless the customer supplies one or more necessary external factors. In some businesses it is frequently the case that the customer does not provide these factors in the way that was expected – or even not at all – with or without prior notice. There is an abundance of examples for such a customer behavior: In the airline industry for instance, passengers may upgrade from economy to business class, rebook flights, cancel their trips, or simply do not show up at check in at all though holding a ticket (this behavior is called a *no-shows*). Hotel guests may upgrade, cancel, rebook, not show up or leave earlier than planned (so called *early departures*). A rental car may be returned earlier than expected. In the following we will simply use the term "cancellation" to refer to any situation where customers change their plans with respect to capacity usage and give a (timely) notification about that change; analogously we use "no-show" to signify the same situations where the notification comes too late or not at all.

In some of the aforementioned cases customers have to pay a cancellation (rebooking, early departure, ...) fee or a no-shows penalty, in other cases they may even be refunded fully or in part (in case they have paid in advance). It is however important to stress that regardless of fees, penalties or refunds associated with cancellations and no-shows we always run the risk that scarce resource capacity is not used optimally (because we have already missed some opportunities to use the units of capacity which became unexpectedly available) or even wasted (especially in case of no-shows). It is thus reasonable to compensate for cancellations and no-shows by voluntarily accepting more requests that can be satisfied using the given amount of capacity. An airline for instance may accept request for 110 "virtual" seats albeit the respective cabin of the aircraft is only equipped with 100 "physical" ones. This strategy is called *overbooking*.

Since we accept more requests than we (in principle) can satisfy, given the uncertainty of demand, cancellations and no-shows, overbooking may lead to *oversales*. For example out of the 110 passengers who are booked on a particular aircraft cabin (economy, say) with only 100 seats, 105 might show up at check in. This is not necessarily a severe problem; if e. g. the aircraft also has a business or first class cabin which is not sold out five economy passengers will be happy to be *upgraded* and take a seat in one of the higher class cabins while having paid the economy price. If no seats are available though, airlines will frequently ask passengers to voluntarily refrain from flying (and take the next flight) in exchange of a small fee, drinks and meal vouchers etc. Finally, the airline may have to *downgrade* first or business class passengers to economy, or some passengers may even suffer from what is called *denied boarding* (or – less politely – "bumping") in the airline industry. Similar options and consequences exist in other businesses.

The downside of overbooking is thus the risk of oversales, which possibly leads to that customers experience a lower level of service than they expected – or no service at all. Both consequences will result in a loss of customer goodwill, contractual or legal penalties and compensations like hotel vouchers. The benefits of overbooking thus have to be contrasted with these costs. We will discuss overbooking in great detail and review state of the art-models and methods in section 2.4.

1.4.2 Dynamic Pricing and Auctions

Pricing as a Means to Drive Demand

The RM problem arises in the first place for the following reasons: Demand for capacity is likely to be very different from the available amount, it is not feasible to adjust this amount in the decision period and there is some heterogeneity in the demand such that the valuations of a given unit of capacity differ. Thus far we have discussed capacity control as a means to drive the usage of the scarce capacity in a revenue maximizing way. Capacity control considers demand as an exogenous force and basically our only option (yet a powerful one) is to voluntarily turn down demand in the hope to thereby protect scarce capacities for an even more profitable use later. It is important to stress that under this point of view no problem arises if demand is likely to be *lower* than capacity – in this case we will just accept all requests as they arrive, i. e. we will pursue a "first come first serve" (FCFS) policy.

Shifting our perspective, we can look at demand as a phenomenon which is admittedly outside our company, yet partly controllable by certain decisions and actions. For instance, if an airline notices that demand for a discount fare is high and seats which can be used to accommodate later arriving business passengers' bookings will be blocked by low yield requests, it can decide to stop accepting low fare requests (this would be an example of capacity control). Alternatively, it can decrease the attractiveness of the discount fare, e. g. by taking away free meals, frequent flyer miles or introducing cancellation and rebooking penalties – or simply raise the price, thereby not only decreasing discount demand, but also lowering the opportunity costs of displacing later booking high yield passengers. If we assume that demands for the low and the high fare are not independent – e. g. if we decrease the high fare customers who would have bought the low yield product will purchase the high fare instead –, it may also be an option to analogously increase the attractiveness of the high fare.

In the context of RM only the price is considered as a means to influence demand. Two classes of methods are discussed in the literature, differing with respect to the degree of control of the pricing process: Dynamic pricing and auctions.

Dynamic Pricing

Dynamic pricing empowers management with full control of the prices. Prices for products are set either choosing from a (bounded or unbounded) real interval or from a finite set of values (e. g. € 19, € 29, € 39, ...). Since every company has to set a price for any product at least once and a constant price is obviously not a very active instrument to control demand (albeit this may be reasonable or even optimal under some circumstances) we are interested in cases where the prices change over time with respect to certain conditions (remaining capacity, demand to come etc.), hence the term dynamic pricing.

A classic example for dynamic pricing is retailing of fashionable clothing. The merchandise will be practically worthless at the end of the season, on the other hand the items have to be ordered months before demand materializes and it is virtually impossible to reorder. It is thus necessary to stimulate demand by pricing decisions in a way such that the stock is cleared until the end of the season. Needless to say that this problem can feasibly be solved using a single price, but it is easy to imagine that customers who desire to purchase the clothes at the beginning of the season (when they are still "hot") are willing to pay a premium price that is well above that average. A single price policy may thus be suboptimal in revenue terms and a dynamic pricing policy can be used to drive demand in a revenue maximizing way.

It is important to stress that dynamic pricing strives for setting the prices in a way such that capacity is exhausted (on average) at the end of the decision period, yet no demand has to be turned down. Ideally, we are thus able to accept requests in an FCFS manner and the capacity control problem is implicitly solved by applying dynamic pricing. But as e. g. Bitran and Caldentey (2003) point out, this equivalence between demand and sales can in general only be created if the price setting decisions are practically unrestricted, i. e. the price can be any non-negative number, prices can be changed at any time and arbitrarily often at negligible costs. On the other hand, if prices can only be changed once a month (say) it will be difficult to control demand in such a precise way.

Auctions

If an *auction* is used to set prices, the price is more or less an emergent result of a bidding process. The total revenue and the extent to which it can be influenced by the bid-taker depend on the actual implementation of the auction and mainly on how the winners and the prices to be paid by the winners are determined. For instance, in a typical auction a single item is to be sold, the highest bidder wins and has to pay exactly the amount of her bid. Another way to auction the single item would be that the highest bidder wins but has to pay a price that is equal to the second highest (i. e. the first non-winning) bid[1]. It is obvious that the same bids will yield a lower revenue in the latter case, but we can expect the bids to be higher if the bidders can be sure that they will always pay a price that is strictly lower than their own bid (if they win). Other aspects that influence the revenue earned in an auction are e. g. reservation prices and entry fees.

It seems that auctions solve the capacity control problem as well – a request will be fulfilled and allocated capacity if and only if it is a winning one. It may be a difficult problem to determine the winners, though. To see this, suppose that winners have to pay the amount they bid and we are going to determine the winners in a way that maximizes

[1] The former type of auction is called an *English* auction, the latter is called a *Vickrey* auction. See e. g. Milgrom (1989) for an introduction to various forms of auctions.

our revenues. If we auction, say, k seats on an airplane and all bids are for a single seat, winner determination is trivial and equivalent to that the k highest bidders win. If the bids are for varying amounts of seats it is already a knapsack problem (which is NP-hard) to determine the allocation of seats to bids that maximizes the total revenue and the k highest bids are not necessarily winning. The difficulty of the problem can be attributed to the fact that the items (seats) are indivisible in this example (i. e. it is not feasible to award arbitrary fractions of items to bids). If a number of homogeneous indivisible items are sold in an auction and participants can bid for an arbitrary number of items we speak of a *multi-unit auction*. The problem gets even more difficult if bidders are presented a variety of items and can bid on arbitrary inseparable bundles of these – for instance, a passenger who wants to travel from Dresden to London via Frankfurt may bid for a bundle of two tickets, one for each part of the journey. Such a setting is called *package bidding* or a *combinatorial auction*. The capacity control problem can thus still be present in the very challenging form of the winner determination problem. The latter may be somewhat simpler, though, because it is solved after the uncertain demand has materialized fully or in part.

In the following we will use the term *pricing* to subsume both dynamic pricing and auctions.

Applicability of Pricing vs. Capacity Control

Some industries are not suited for dynamic pricing strategies, while in others it is unreasonable to execute capacity control. If the competition in an industry is fierce, we have an example for the former group – under such circumstances companies can only match their competitors' prices and it is virtually impossible to use the selling price as a control variable.

In some industries, demand may not be elastic with price for other reasons. With the words of Mayr (2005), responsible for RM and Pricing at Sixt, a leading German car rental company: "Nobody will travel to Leipzig airport and rent a car just because the local station lowers the rate at weekends." – much like demand for business air travel, demand for rental cars (at least at airports) is derived demand and thus of limited sensitivity with respect to price. This is not to say that the price of a rental car is an irrelevant attribute, but it is probably not the only one and a capacity control strategy using other control variables should be considered as well.

Even if price is a key driver of demand companies may choose to keep the price for the same product pretty constant over time for strategic reasons. German cruise liner operators, for instance, report that holidaymakers are easily annoyed if they meet somebody at the bar who has paid significantly less for virtually the same trip. These companies are thus eager to keep the prices for a given ship, length-of-stay and cabin category nearly constant over time (or even refund passengers who have paid a higher price) because the ability to differentiate the product "cruise holiday" further is somewhat limited and price changes are thus difficult to explain to customers.

Finally, the process of changing prices and communicating them may be too expensive. Klein (2005) mentions the example of package holidays, which are frequently marketed using printed catalogs. In this case, it is simply too costly to reprint and redistribute new ones after a price change. It is, however, possible to markdown these products through the world wide web or – with a rather limited scope – posters in travel agencies as "last minute" trips close to the date of travel.

On the other hand, due to the business environment in some industries it may not be reasonable to implement capacity control. For instance, reconsider a retail store selling perishable items like food, fashionable clothing or electronics. Food will have gone to waste after a short period of time. Clothing and electronics become less valuable in the eyes of customers over time and since shelf space is a scarce resource, these items will sooner or later be replaced by newer goods of higher value to the customer. In all cases the predominant aspect is not that early arriving customers purchase items that can be sold later at higher prices – on the contrary, the core of the problem is that demand may decline so fast that we are not able to clear our stocks and therefore have to bear salvage costs, e. g. opportunity costs for selling goods at bargain prices. We can summarize the difference between airlines (as typical users of capacity control) and retailers as follows: In the former case the opportunity costs of having sold a unit of capacity (a seat) are driving the problem, while in the latter the key aspects are the opportunity costs of *not* having sold a unit of capacity. The retailing setting thus clearly demands for pricing decisions, not for capacity control.

In some industries both capacity control and dynamic pricing may reasonably be implemented. We have frequently mentioned airlines as routine users of capacity control, but the advent of low cost carriers (LCCs, also know as low fare or no frills airlines) has demonstrated the power of dynamic pricing in that industry. The sales process of a typical LCC can be described as follows (cf. Dunleavy and Westermann 2005): Only one way-tickets for non-stop flights will be sold, i. e. albeit you can buy two tickets, say, one for a flight from Dresden to Frankfurt and another from Frankfurt to London, you will have to disembark in Frankfurt, claim your baggage and check in again, because the two flights are treated as absolutely independent by the carrier. In particular, you personally bear the risk of missing your connection in Frankfurt because your feeder flight is late. In contrast to a "classical" full service carrier (FSC) which certainly offers connecting flights traversing a complex network, the LCC thus basically deals with a multitude of isolated problems each related to a single non-stop flight. For each flight, there is a predefined set of prices, say, € 19, € 29, € 39, ..., € 199. Sales will start with one of the lowest prices and every now and then prices will be increased to the next-higher step. Ideally, prices will never decrease – this is called *markup pricing*. It is important to stress that the price is the only attribute of the product that changes over time – besides the price the only difference (imposed by the sales process we have just described) between the € 19 and € 199 fares is that the former will only available long before the flight date, while the latter will only be available close to departure. In particular, the same conditions of purchase, rebooking, cancellation and refunds etc. apply to all fares. LCCs therefore only implicitly segment their customers through self selection; for instance, leisure travelers with a lower willingness to pay than business travelers tend to book earlier and thus indeed encounter lower prices than the latter. Discussing the LCC business model in more detail is out of the scope of this book, so we refer the interested reader to Gorin and Belobaba (2004), who evaluate the impact of a low fare entrant to an incumbent FSC by simulation and to Tretheway (2004), who discusses the impact for FSCs in general due to the advent of the LCCs. Gillen and Morrison (2003) develop a model to analyze the competitive impact of LCCs. Forsyth (2003) studies the effect of low cost entries in the Australian market. Lawton (2002) focuses on strategic concepts for LCCs; and the very readable book by Calder (2003) covers the complete history of the low fare business.

Other examples for industries where both capacity control and dynamic pricing methods can be implemented include broadcasting, cargo and make-to-order (MTO) companies. Broadcasting RM will be extensively discussed in chapter 6, where we highlight the similarities to cargo and MTO in section 6.6.

Note that while our discussion above focused on dynamic pricing the reasoning will often not change much if auctions are considered:

In a competitive market dynamic pricing is inapplicable because the sellers are price takers – the argument obviously holds for an auction as well. If discount prices set by rental car companies do not stimulate additional demand, neither will the chance to make a bargain in an auction. If the means of communicating prices do not allow for rapid and cheap changes, there seems to be no adequate infrastructure to conduct an auction either.

1.4.3 Relationship of RM, Capacity Control and Pricing

Capacity Control vs. Dynamic Pricing

A unique structure of the RM field has not yet been established in the literature. In particular, the relationship between capacity control and dynamic pricing is viewed differently. We have already demonstrated that in very unrestricted settings dynamic pricing can be considered as a special case of capacity control where the selling prices are used as control variables. On the other hand, we might also argue that capacity control is a special case of dynamic pricing: Capacity control deals with the question if a given request should be accepted or not. This question can as well be answered by setting prices. If we want to reject a request we set the price to an arbitrarily high value such that demand effectively vanishes. The more requests we want to accept, the lower we set the price. This reasoning is as well limited to fairly unrestricted settings allowing for arbitrary price changes at any time, though. Noteworthy in this context, Klein (2007) has pointed out that if resource-specific bid prices (i. e. estimates of the opportunity costs of a unit of each resource) are used for capacity control this can equivalently be considered as dynamic pricing of resources (instead of products). Since the bid prices are only used internally for the sole purpose of capacity control, the necessary flexibility with respect to (bid) price changes can safely assumed to be given and capacity control by resource-specific bid prices can indeed be considered to be a special case of dynamic pricing. However, there are yet other means of capacity control, so this argument does not finally conclude the question.

In more constrained situations the distinction (or relationship) of dynamically changing selling prices of products and capacity control seems to be less clear. Reconsider the LCC business model: We want to use some predefined prices (like € 19, € 29, € 39, . . .) for a single seat and basically face the problem to decide when to rise the price from € 19 to 29, when to take the step from € 29 to 39 etc. This naturally appears as an implementation of a dynamic pricing policy because the only attribute of the product that ever changes is the price. However, since the prices are chosen from a given and finite set of, say, n prices we might as well consider the described procedure as a capacity control policy used for problem n (clearly distinct) products with the additional restriction that there is at most one product available at any time. This is also reasonable, because taking each price step indeed has got the flavor of closing a fare class and opening another in a "capacity control" way. It is thus difficult to tell whether the LCC way to control prices is a special case of capacity control or of dynamic pricing.

Finally, we have already mentioned various examples where capacity control is not applicable (but dynamic pricing) is and vice versa: Retailing fashionable items is a good example for dynamic pricing but clearly not suited for capacity control, while demand for rental cars, cruises and package holidays can usually not be controlled using only the price.

Classifications of the Field

In light of these arguments divergent classifications of the field of RM are not surprising. We will now present some of the major classifications and clarify our point of view.

Boyd and Bilegan (2003) claim that RM (using that term as a synonym for what we call capacity control) and dynamic pricing are distinct concepts. Their major arguments can be summarized as follows:

- Dynamic pricing is typically applied to single, isolated *products* with limited availability (e. g. a fashionable shirt), while capacity control has to deal with managing multiple products which share one or more common *resources* with limited availability. This is at best demonstrated by full service airlines which run complex networks and offer connecting flights on the one hand and low cost airlines which only offer isolated non-stop flights on the other: The former implement capacity control, the latter dynamic pricing (see our discussion of the LCC business model on page 21).
- Furthermore, dynamic pricing requires to explicitly model the dependency of demand on prices. This is possible, but not necessary for capacity control. Together with the previous observation this implies that forecasting and optimization methods for dynamic pricing and capacity control will be fundamentally different.
- Prices are often set with objectives other than demand control in mind, e. g. a company may strategically decide to keep prices lower than needed to ensure full capacity utilization in order to prevent

market entry of new competitors. Another example is given by Biller and Swann (2006), who developed a pricing method for General Motors (GM). GM's problem stemmed from the corporate average fuel economy regulation in the United States – the emissions and fuel consumption of the total number for cars sold by a certain manufacturer is limited by law. GM thus decided to increase or decrease prices to drive demand away from cars with high emissions to more environment-friendly cars.
- Pricing and capacity control are often located in entirely different departments of the organization.

However, Boyd and Bilegan (2003) acknowledge that even though *models* (and consequently, methods) of capacity control and dynamic pricing may different, both "are certainly related, and if the underlying products are identical, the *problems* are fundamentally equivalent." (p. 1379, emphasis added) – this is what we have demonstrated above. Boyd and Bilegan's point of view is shared e. g. by Klein (2005).

Talluri and van Ryzin (2004b) pick up the point that both capacity control and dynamic pricing are obviously related and differentiate the field of RM into quantity-based and price-based RM, where the former includes capacity control and overbooking and the latter dynamic pricing and auctions (see Figure 1.1).

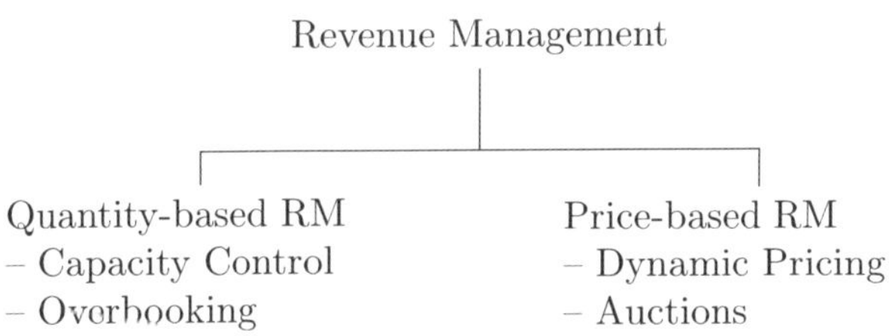

Fig. 1.1: Revenue Management and Dynamic Pricing (Talluri and van Ryzin 2004b)

The book by Phillips (2005) covers the whole field of "Pricing and Revenue Optimization", and there certainly is more to pricing in general then dynamic pricing and auctions. The book thus discusses other, more general topics, but there is as well an extensive part devoted to what Phillips calls "Pricing with Constrained Supply". The structure of that subject as given by Phillips (2005, Fig. 1.1 on p. 15) is depicted in Figure 1.2. We see that like Boyd and Bilegan (2003), Phillips (2005) basically considers Revenue Management as a synonym for capacity control and overbooking, but in contrast to the former, RM is a special case of pricing (with constrained supply). Phillips (2005) certainly notices that prices are fixed for capacity control, and demand is thus driven by controlling the availability of products (with possibly different prices). He gives an interesting argument to subsume capacity control under pricing anyway: Capacity control as a distinctive way of controlling the selling prices of products "is a legacy from revenue management's origin. The passenger airlines that pioneered revenue management in the 1980s needed to utilize [...] the booking controls embedded in their reservation systems as the primary mechanism for controlling the fares [...]" (p. 120).

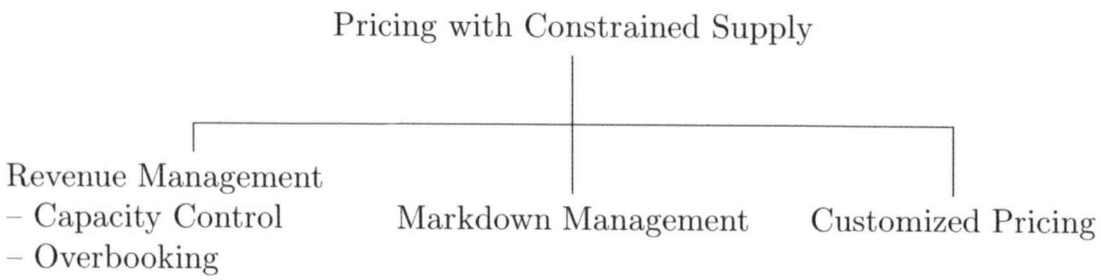

Fig. 1.2: Pricing with Constrained Supply (Phillips 2005, cf. Fig. 1.1, p. 15)

Similarly, Elmaghraby and Keskinocak (2003) also consider capacity control as a special case of dynamic pricing. Bitran and Caldentey (2003) present a "generic" conceptual model of the RM problem which incorporates price-sensitive demand and thus allows both for the modification of prices over time as well as for voluntarily rejecting demand. According to their point of view, this model basically is a dynamic pricing model, and capacity control is considered as a special case with static prices.

It remains to clarify the position we take up in this book. We have already mentioned examples where capacity control is applicable but pricing is not (and vice versa), so it seems to be important to distinguish both concepts and we can (in general) not claim that one is a special case of the other. Yet we certainly acknowledge that there are examples where a distinction between capacity control and dynamic pricing is somewhat ambiguous. In the airline industry, for example, both strategies are applicable, and the LCC sales process with ever increasing prices taking predefined steps can be seen as a special case of both capacity control and dynamic pricing.

If we consider retailing of fashionable goods as a classic example for dynamic pricing where capacity control cannot be applied we see that not all four characteristic aspects of a RM problem are satisfied, namely it is not necessary to integrate external factors. Consequently, pricing is discussed intensively for make-to-stock production as well (see e. g. Elmaghraby and Keskinocak 2003, Swann 2001 for an overview), where there is no need to integrate factors supplied by the customer either. Some applications of dynamic pricing are thus not covered by our defining characteristics while others (e. g. LCCs) are. It is furthermore interesting to note that "hybrid" problems have recently been considered in the literature where a capacity control and a pricing problem have to be solved simultaneously (see e. g. Gans and Savin 2005). We therefore consider RM (in the strict sense) as a synonym for capacity control and overbooking. RM as a broader concept subsumes those problems on the one hand and pricing on the other hand. We yet stress that mixtures are possible: Companies like LCCs solve a capacity control problem by setting selling prices, capacity control by resource-specific bid prices can be seen as pricing capacities, and simultaneous approaches to interdependent capacity control and pricing problems have also been proposed. Figure 1.3 clarifies our point of view. The upper half of that figure is very similar to Figure 1.1 (based on Talluri and van Ryzin 2004b); we only have highlighted that some authors treat RM and capacity control as synonyms, separating it from pricing, and we have avoided the term "quantity-based RM", which we find somewhat ambiguous: A price is (in a rather technical sense) also a quantity, and pricing is also concerned with matching the demanded quantities with the given supplies.

1.5 Purpose and Scope of this Book

In this book we focus on situations that satisfy all four characteristic aspects mentioned in section 1.2, i. e. we extensively cover capacity control and present the models and methods of overbooking in some detail. The reader interested in dynamic pricing is referred to the excellent books by Talluri and van Ryzin (2004b) and Phillips (2005) as well as the surveys by Bitran and Caldentey (2003), Boyd and Bilegan (2003) and Elmaghraby and Keskinocak (2003). Various aspects related to the design of auctions are e. g. discussed by Jehiel and Moldovanu (2003), McAfee and McMillan (1987) and Rothkopf and Park (2001); see also the survey by Klemperer (1999) and Talluri and van Ryzin (2004b, ch. 6). Multi-unit and combinatorial auctions seem to be es-

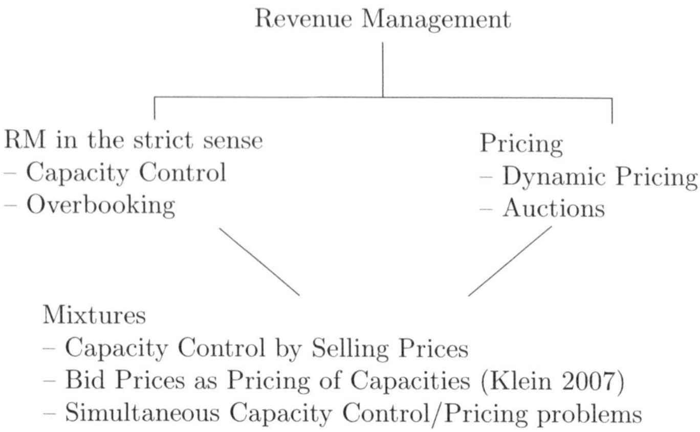

Fig. 1.3: Relationship of Revenue Management, Capacity Control and Pricing

pecially relevant in the RM context. The former are e. g. treated by Ausubel (2004) and Elmaghraby (2005). The literature on combinatorial auctions is surveyed by de Vries and Vohra (2003); see also the edited volume by Cramton et al. (2006) for an overview. Jehiel and Moldovanu (2003) also present an overview of various forms of auctions including multi-unit and combinatorial ones.

The contribution of this book to the field of RM (in the strict sense) is twofold: An established set of instances to evaluate RM techniques is not yet available. To the best of our knowledge we are the first to rigorously describe aspects related to instance generation in chapter 4. A crucial part of an RM test bed is a generator for stochastic demand data streams. We develop such a data stream simulator in chapter 5. Secondly, we cover the RM problem in broadcasting companies in chapter 6 in great detail. Broadcasting companies are rarely treated in the current RM literature. Furthermore, the business environment of TV or radio stations features so called *flexible products* which have only recently attracted attention in the RM community. A flexible product leaves the seller some degrees of freedom with respect to the production of the requested good or service. We have, for example, already mentioned cargo RM where the shipper is typically free to choose the route and travel times of the transported goods as long as the final destination is reached on time.

The remainder of the book is structured as follows: We review the state of the art of capacity control and overbooking (RM in the strict sense) in the following chapter. Chapter 3 covers recent advances of the field, in particular RM models and methods that explicitly take customer choice behavior into account as well as flexible products. Chapter 4 introduces issues related to the evaluation of RM techniques using a standard test bed of instances. A crucial part of such a test bed is a demand data simulator which is developed in chapter 5. Chapter 6 is dedicated to the RM problem in broadcasting companies. We summarize our findings and outline future research opportunities in chapter 7.

2

Capacity Control and Overbooking

In this chapter we review the state of the art of capacity control and overbooking. Our exposition is complemented by the surveys and introductory articles due to Bertsch and Wendt (1998), Boyd and Bilegan (2003), Corsten and Stuhlmann (1998), Kimes (1989a,b), Kimms and Klein (2005), Klein (2001), McGill and van Ryzin (1999), Netessine and Shumsky (2002), Pak and Piersma (2002) and Tscheulin and Lindenmeier (2003); see also the books by Daudel and Vialle (1992, 1994), Phillips (2005) and Talluri and van Ryzin (2004b). Comprehensive overviews on earlier results are contained in Belobaba (1987a), Williamson (1992) and Weatherford and Bodily (1992).

2.1 Introduction

We have noted in section 1.2 that there are four conditions which give rise to RM problems:

(1) Some form of integration of the customer into the production process is necessary.
(2) The flexibility to adjust the available resource capacity to demand is very limited.
(3) Customers are heterogeneous and thus show different valuations of products.
(4) The product range is standardized and remains unchanged over a longer period of time.

By (1), incoming requests cannot be fulfilled from stock. By (2), we may be forced to turn down demand, because the available capacity does (probably) not suffice to satisfy demand. (3) implies that the same unit of resource can be used to produce goods with different revenues (or contribution margins), therefore it is not trivial to decide which requests should actually be accepted or rejected. (4) allows us to forecast future demand in a reasonable way, and to solve the decision problem of acceptance and rejection of demand we just outlined by a suitably defined *capacity control policy.* The purpose of capacity control is to limit access of different products (with different values) to the scarce resources, especially by reserving capacity for requests of high values that (supposedly) arrive in a later point in time.

Capacity control policies can be distinguished based on the type of control variables that are used into *booking limit controls* (section 2.2) and *bid price controls* (section 2.3), where we subsume approaches based on approximate dynamic programming techniques under the latter term[1]. When we discuss these types of policies, we will assume that the capacities of the resources are given and fixed, and that we will never accept more requests than we are able to satisfy given the limited resource availability. As we have described in subsection 1.4.1 it is common in many industries to intentionally accept more requests that can (in principle) be satisfied, though. This practice of *overbooking* is discussed in section 2.4. In our exposition we will always assume that our capacity control and/or overbooking decisions do not influence customer behavior. For instance, a customer whose request for a flight at € 100 is rejected will not "buy up" and purchase a flight at € 200 instead. We relax this assumption in the subsequent chapter.

Since many references focus on airlines we will adopt three terms from that industry: Leg, itinerary and fare. We have already used itinerary and fare in their obvious meanings, it seems nevertheless worthwhile to define these three concepts more rigorously, describe their relationships and clarify how we use them. A *leg* is a non-stop flight from an origin O to a destination D such that passengers may board and disembark at both O and D. A leg is thus an atomistic resource used in the production of flight transport services. A flight network operated by an airline consists of many legs, which can be combined to a multitude of *itineraries.* Airlines charge different prices for the same itinerary, e. g. based on advance purchase or refunding restrictions. In the context of a given itinerary, these price levels are called *fares.* The terms leg, itinerary and fare can analogously be used in the cargo business or for other modes of transport, e. g. railways. A combination of an itinerary and a fare will be called a *product.* More generally, a product is designated by production coefficients $r_{ij} \geq 0$ (i. e. r_{ij} is the amount

[1] We will discuss a third type of policies (offer set policies) which are only useful for choice-based RM in section 3.2.

of resource $i = 1, \dots, m$ used by product $j = 1, \dots, n$) and a price v_j. Products may have the same production coefficients (i. e. it is allowed that $r_{ij} = r_{ik}, i = 1, \dots, m$ for $j \neq k$). In an airline example m is the number of legs in the network and if product j corresponds to a booking of one seat on a certain itinerary we have $r_{ij} = 1$ if that itinerary uses leg i (and 0 otherwise). If we discuss two or more products with the same underlying itinerary (production coefficients) which is clear from the context we frequently use the word "fare" as a synonym for product. This is especially the case for *single leg* problems (i. e. problems with $m = 1$) where there is only one itinerary.

2.2 Capacity Control by Booking Limits

In this section, we will first introduce the notion of a booking limit. Section 2.2.1 will contain some models, but we will defer the discussion of methods to the literature review (subsection 2.2.3). In subsection 2.2.2, we will discuss *nested booking limits* in great detail; but as before, methods to actually compute booking limits will not appear before 2.2.3.

2.2.1 Introduction

A *booking limit* is the maximal amount of a particular product to be sold. If n is the number of products and $b_j \geq 0$ is the booking limit of product $j = 1, \dots, n$, we will accept demand for product j until the total amount requested is greater than or equal to b_j. Denote the revenue (or contribution margin) of product j by $v_j > 0$. Let m be the number of resources, c_i the capacity of resource i, and r_{ij} be the amount of resource i consumed by product j. If we assume a deterministic setting and demand for product j is given by $d_j \geq 0$, then Model 2.1 describes a simple way to determine booking limits. This model assumes a single decision period; a multi-period model is e. g. presented by Kimms and Müller-Bungart (2003).

Model 2.1 is an LP, which can efficiently be solved using standard software. This simple structure of the model is however based on two additional assumptions:

- The amount of a product j is measured on a continuous scale, thus the booking limit b_j can be any non-negative real number. If we consider e. g. an airline RM problem, we will have to deal with integer booking limits b_j denoting the maximum number of seats on any aircraft $i = 1, \dots, m$ devoted to product j. In this case, (2.2) has to be replaced by $b_j \in \mathbb{N}_0$, and the problem becomes NP-hard.

Model 2.1: Deterministic Model to Obtain Booking Limits

$$\max \sum_{j=1}^{n} v_j b_j$$

s. t.

$$\sum_{j=1}^{n} r_{ij} b_j \leq c_i \qquad i = 1, \ldots, m \tag{2.1}$$

$$0 \leq b_j \leq d_j \qquad j = 1, \ldots, n \tag{2.2}$$

- It is allowed that requests are only partly satisfied. For example, a request of a family for three seats on an aircraft (i. e. a request for three units of a product j) can be accepted by allocating only two seats to that request, yielding a revenue of $2v_j$.

An extension of the model to stochastic demand is straightforward. Suppose that demand D_j is a discrete random variable, thereby relaxing the first of the aforementioned assumptions. As usual, we assume that the objective is to maximize expected revenues. This is formulated as Model 2.2. A similar model for continuous demand can easily be derived.

Model 2.2: Non-Linear Probabilistic Model to Obtain Booking Limits

$$\max \sum_{j=1}^{n} v_j \left[\sum_{k=1}^{b_j - 1} k P\left(D_j = k\right) + b_j P\left(D_j \geq b_j\right) \right]$$

s. t.

$$\sum_{j=1}^{n} r_{ij} b_j \leq c_i \qquad i = 1, \ldots, m \tag{2.1}$$

$$b_j \in \mathbb{N}_0 \qquad j = 1, \ldots, n$$

Model 2.2 is non-linear, though. To obtain a linear model let $\bar{b}_j$ be an upper bound for b_j, e. g. derived from (2.1):

$$\bar{b}_j = \min_{i=1,\ldots,m} c_i / r_{ij}$$

We define the decision variable:

$$x_{jk} = \begin{cases} 1 & \text{if the booking limit of product } j \text{ is set to } k \\ 0 & \text{otherwise} \end{cases}$$

$$j = 1, \ldots, n, k = 1, \ldots, \bar{b}_j \quad (2.3)$$

Naturally, we require that $\sum_{k=1}^{\bar{b}_j} x_{jk} \leq 1$ for each j and if $\sum_{k=1}^{\bar{b}_j} x_{jk} = 0$ the booking limit is zero as well. The booking limit of product j is then formally defined as:

$$b_j = \sum_{k=1}^{\bar{b}_j} k x_{ik}$$

The expected revenue obtained if the booking limit of product j is set to k is:

$$v_{jk} = v_j \left[\sum_{l=1}^{k-1} l P(D_j = l) + k P(D_j \geq k) \right]$$

Model 2.3[2] is then a linear equivalent of Model 2.2.

Model 2.3: Linear Probabilistic Model to Obtain Booking Limits

$$\max \sum_{j=1}^{n} \sum_{k=1}^{\bar{b}_j} v_{jk} x_{jk}$$

s. t.

$$\sum_{k=1}^{\bar{b}_j} x_{jk} \leq 1 \qquad j = 1, \ldots, n$$

$$\sum_{j=1}^{n} r_{ij} \sum_{k=1}^{\bar{b}_j} k x_{ik} \leq c_i \qquad i = 1, \ldots, m \quad (2.4)$$

$$x_{jk} \in \{0, 1\} \qquad j = 1, \ldots, n, k = 1, \ldots, \bar{b}_j \quad (2.5)$$

[2] A considerably simpler version of this model for the airline network RM problem is presented by Williamson (1992, p. 71).

2.2.2 Nested Booking Limits

Introduction

The booking limits obtained from models 2.1, 2.2 or 2.3 feature an interesting property: Due to (2.1) resp. (2.4), the available resource capacity is *partitioned* by the booking limits. Figure 2.1 depicts the situation for an airline RM problem with a single leg, i. e. $m = 1$. We have intentionally chosen a very simple example with just three fares $v_3 = 500, v_2 = 300, v_1 = 100$. The available capacity $c_1 = 32$ is partitioned by the booking limits $b_3 = b_2 = 12, b_1 = 8$, i. e. eight (twelve) seats are exclusively reserved for fare 1 (fares 2 and 3, respectively).

If demand is deterministic (as assumed in Model 2.1), this is clearly an optimal strategy. If demand is stochastic, partitioned booking limits are suboptimal, because the 13th request for the product with the highest fare (500 €) will always be rejected, even if seats (that were meant a priori to accommodate passengers paying lower fares) are vacant. Under uncertainty it is obviously smarter to give passengers paying 500 € access to the entire cabin and to accommodate passengers paying 300 € also using the eight seats which have initially been allocated to the lowest fare class. This strategy – which is called *nested capacity control*, or simply *nesting* – is depicted in Figure 2.2.

As we will soon see it is useful to express the *nested booking limits* as resource specific booking limits b_{ij} measured in units of the capacity of resource i. Thus $b_{ij} \geq 0$ is the amount of resource i that is (non-exclusively) available to product j. This approach is also used e. g. by Klein (2005). In Figure 2.2, we use nested booking limits $b_{13} = 32, b_{12} = 20, b_{11} = 8$.

If $m = 1$ and $r_{1j} = 1, j = 1, \ldots, n$ there is admittedly no difference between the booking limit b_j (measured in units of the product) and b_{1j}, but we will see that for $m \geq 2$ or varying r_{ij} using b_j not only complicates the notation, but also leads to wrong results. Furthermore, we can always compute b_j from $b_{ij}, i = 1, \ldots, m$ by

$$
\begin{aligned}
b_j &= b_{1j}/r_{1j} && \text{for } m = 1 \\
b_j &= \min_{\substack{i=1,\ldots,m \\ r_{ij}>0}} \{b_{ij}/r_{ij}\} && \text{for } m \geq 2
\end{aligned}
$$

Note that nested booking limits cannot be obtained using static models like 2.1, 2.2 or 2.3, because the order of stochastic arrivals is rel-

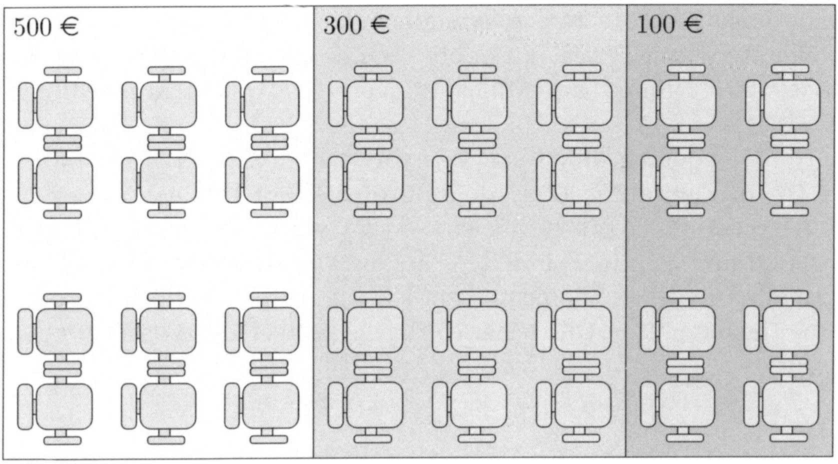

Fig. 2.1: Partitioned Booking Limits (Kimms and Müller-Bungart 2003)

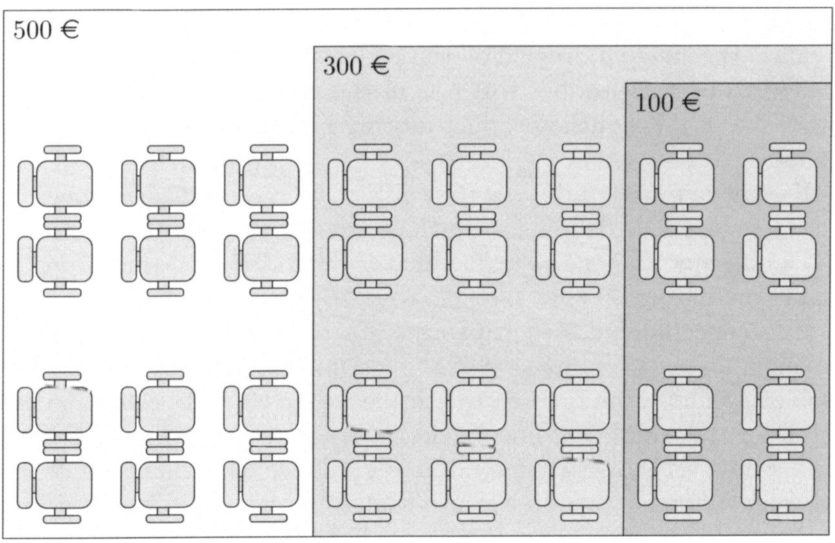

Fig. 2.2: Nested Booking Limits (Kimms and Müller-Bungart 2003)

evant in that setting, thus a dynamic model is required[3]. It is possible, though, to obtain lower and upper bounds by iteratively solving static models, see Kimms and Müller-Bungart (2004) and Müller-Bungart (2004).

Nested booking limits can be expressed equivalently as *protection levels*[4]. In Figure 2.2, 12 seats are protected for the highest fare class from access of all other fare classes, 24 seats are protected for fare classes 2 and 3 from 1, and 12 seats are protected for class 2 from 1. Formally, we define the protection level p_{ij} of product j on resource i to be the amount of this resource that is protected for other products, i. e.

$$b_{ij} + p_{ij} = c_i \qquad i = 1, \ldots, m, j = 1, \ldots, n \tag{2.6}$$

In Figure 2.2, we have $p_{11} = 24, p_{12} = 12, p_{13} = 0$.

For a nested capacity control we have to define a "ranking" of products such that product j can access resource capacity that was originally meant to be used for product k if and only if j "ranks" (nests) above k. Formally, we need a permutation π of the product indexes $1, \ldots, n$ such that j nests above k if and only if $\pi(j) > \pi(k)$. This permutation is called the *nesting order*. For the convenience of notation we define $\pi^{-1}(k)$ to be the product which is in the k-th position in the nesting order, i. e. $\pi^{-1}(1)$ is the product nesting lowest and $\pi^{-1}(n)$ is nesting highest.

If we have $m = 1$ and $r_{1j} = c$ for all $j = 1, \ldots, n$ and a constant $c > 0$ like in Figure 2.2, defining a nesting order is very simple: W. l. o. g. we can assume that $v_j \neq v_k$ for all $j \neq k$, and the nesting order π is simply increasing by fare, i. e. $\pi(j) > \pi(k) \Leftrightarrow v_j > v_k$.

The concept of nested capacity control gets more complicated if we allow for $r_{ij} \neq r_{ik}$ for $j \neq k$ and/or $m \geq 2$. We will address these problems shortly, but before we describe nested capacity control in more detail for the simple "airline single leg" case $m = 1, r_{1j} = c$ (where we can assume w. l. o. g. that $c = 1$). We will see that there are at least two very different ways to execute control given nested booking limits (or equivalently protection levels), namely *standard nesting* and *theft*

[3] It is interesting to note that the order of stochastic arrivals is not relevant if we use (nested) booking limits but also implement overbooking; see page 86. However, in this case a dynamic model is necessary as well.

[4] Note that there is a subtle difference in the wording: The counterpart of a booking *limit* is called a protection *level*. This is, however, plainly a difference in language, and there does not seem to be a particular reason not to use the word protection *limit*. This term is albeit never used in the English literature; everybody uses "protection level". In contrast Klein (2005) uses – in German – the words "Buchungs*limits*" and "Schutz*limits*".

nesting. We will then consider the "airline network" case $m \geq 2, r_{1j} \in \{0, c\}$. Finally, we will allow for arbitrary r_{ij} and deal with problems with $m = 1$ and $m \geq 2$ in turn.

Standard and Theft Nesting

A nested booking limit control seems to be as simple as its partitioned counterpart, but it is not. Consider the situation depicted in Figure 2.2 where we have nested booking limits $b_{13} = 32, b_{12} = 20, b_{11} = 8$. Under a partitioned booking limit policy, the decision rule was: "Accept at most b_j requests for product j!". If we analogously used "Allocate at most b_{ij} units of resource i to product j!" here, it would be possible to accept, say, six requests for product 1 and 19 requests for product 2. That would leave only seven seats vacant for the highest fare class, while we intended to protect twelve seats for it. This observation implies that some booking limits – or equivalently the protection levels, see (2.6) – have to be reduced in a meaningful way whenever a request is accepted. *Theft nesting* decreases the booking limits of all products, where *standard nesting* usually just decreases the booking limit of the requested product and all higher nesting products. Table 2.1 shows the behavior of both methods using the example from Figure 2.2 and a given stream of requests. We index the requests by t. The columns $c_1^t, b_{1j}^t, p_{1j}^t$ give the remaining capacity and respectively the updated booking limits and protection levels *after* the t-th request has been decided on. Note that since product 3 is nesting highest $p_{13}^t = 0$ holds for all t, therefore this column has been omitted. Decisions that differ between standard and theft nesting are marked with a "*".

The idea of standard nesting is demonstrated by the requests $t = 1, \ldots, 3$: The first request is for product 1. One of the eight seats shown in the front part of the cabin in Figure 2.2 is (virtually) used to accommodate it. The number of seats that are protected for 2 and 3, however, are unaffected, i. e. p_{11} and p_{12} remain unchanged. In $t = 2$, we accept a request for product 2. It thus seems to be no longer necessary to protect 24 seats for both 2 and 3, so we decrease p_{11} by one. Similarly, we decrease both p_{11} and p_{12} after having accepted the request for product 3 in $t = 3$.

Theft nesting, on the other hand, tries to protect the chosen number of seats for the highly ranked products as long as possible by "stealing" the seats from the lowest ranking fare classes. For instance, we see from Table 2.1 that the first eight requests (which are all accepted) are (virtually) placed in the first two rows of seats shown in Figure 2.2, thereby "stealing" a seat from fare class 1 one at a time. As a consequence, up

Table 2.1: Example: Standard vs. Theft Nesting

			Standard Nesting							*Theft Nesting*					
		accept?	c_1^t	b_{11}^t	b_{12}^t	b_{13}^t	p_{11}^t	p_{12}^t	accept?	c_1^t	b_{11}^t	b_{12}^t	b_{13}^t	p_{11}^t	p_{12}^t
t	j		32	8	20	32	24	12		32	8	20	32	24	12
1	1	yes	31	7	19	31	24	12	yes	31	7	19	31	24	12
2	2	yes	30	7	18	30	23	12	yes	30	6	18	30	24	12
3	3	yes	29	7	18	29	22	11	yes	29	5	17	29	24	12
4	2	yes	28	7	17	28	21	11	yes	28	4	16	28	24	12
5	2	yes	27	7	16	27	20	11	yes	27	3	15	27	24	12
6	2	yes	26	7	15	26	19	11	yes	26	2	14	26	24	12
7	2	yes	25	7	14	25	18	11	yes	25	1	13	25	24	12
8	2	yes	24	7	13	24	17	11	yes	24	0	12	24	24	12
9	2	yes	23	7	12	23	16	11	yes	23	0	11	23	23	12
10	2	yes	22	7	11	22	15	11	yes	22	0	10	22	22	12
11	2	yes	21	7	10	21	14	11	yes	21	0	9	21	21	12
12	2	yes	20	7	9	20	13	11	yes	20	0	8	20	20	12
13	2	yes	19	7	8	19	12	11	yes	19	0	7	19	19	12
14	2	yes	18	7	7	18	11	11	yes	18	0	6	18	18	12
15	2	yes	17	6	6	17	11	11	yes	17	0	5	17	17	12
16	1	yes	16	5	5	16	11	11	no*	17	0	5	17	17	12
17	1	yes	15	4	4	15	11	11	no*	17	0	5	17	17	12
18	1	yes	14	3	3	14	11	11	no*	17	0	5	17	17	12
19	1	yes	13	2	2	13	11	11	no*	17	0	5	17	17	12
20	1	yes	12	1	1	12	11	11	no*	17	0	5	17	17	12
21	1	yes	11	0	0	11	11	11	no*	17	0	5	17	17	12
22	1	no	11	0	0	11	11	11	no	17	0	5	17	17	12
23	2	no	11	0	0	11	11	11	yes*	16	0	4	16	16	12
24	2	no	11	0	0	11	11	11	yes*	15	0	3	15	15	12
25	3	yes	10	0	0	10	10	10	yes	14	0	2	14	14	12
26	3	yes	9	0	0	9	9	9	yes	13	0	1	13	13	12
27	3	yes	8	0	0	8	8	8	yes	12	0	0	12	12	12
28	3	yes	7	0	0	7	7	7	yes	11	0	0	11	11	11
29	3	yes	6	0	0	6	6	6	yes	10	0	0	10	10	10
30	3	yes	5	0	0	5	5	5	yes	9	0	0	9	9	9
31	3	yes	4	0	0	4	4	4	yes	8	0	0	8	8	8
32	3	yes	3	0	0	3	3	3	yes	7	0	0	7	7	7
33	3	yes	2	0	0	2	2	2	yes	6	0	0	6	6	6
34	3	yes	1	0	0	1	1	1	yes	5	0	0	5	5	5
35	3	yes	0	0	0	0	0	0	yes	4	0	0	4	4	4
36	3	no	0	0	0	0	0	0	yes*	3	0	0	3	3	3
37	3	no	0	0	0	0	0	0	yes*	2	0	0	2	2	2
38	3	no	0	0	0	0	0	0	yes*	1	0	0	1	1	1
39	3	no	0	0	0	0	0	0	yes*	0	0	0	0	0	0

to $t = 8$, $p_{11} = 24$ and $p_{12} = 12$, but the booking limit b_1 drops to zero albeit only one out of the eight requests have actually been for product 1. After $t = 9$ it is no longer possible to protect 24 seats for products 2 and 3, simply because only 23 seats are still vacant, so p_{11} decreases, while p_{12} remains unchanged until $t = 28$. Since the booking limit b_1 drops to zero so early, the requests for product 1 in $t = 16, \ldots, 22$ are rejected.

To describe standard and theft nesting in a formal and general way, let k be the product that is demanded by the t-th request. The update rule for c_i^t is easy to describe and independent of the form of nesting that is used: If the t-th request is accepted, $c_i^t = c_i^{t-1} - r_{ik}$.

If standard nesting accepts a request, the booking limits of k and all higher nesting products are reduced. However, we also have to keep in mind that the booking limit of any product is always higher than the booking limits of lower nesting products. For that reason, we e. g. also decrease b_{11} in $t = 15$. Formally, if the t-th request is accepted, we have[5]:

$$b_{ij}^t = \begin{cases} b_{ij}^{t-1} - r_{ik} & \pi(j) \geq \pi(k) \\ \min\left\{b_{ij}^{t-1}, b_{ik}^t\right\} & \pi(j) < \pi(k) \end{cases} \qquad i = 1, \ldots, m, j = 1, \ldots, n \tag{2.7}$$

This update rule ensures that $b_{ij}^t \geq 0$ for all i, j, t, since $b_{ik}^t \geq r_{ik}$ holds if the t-th request is accepted. Note that it is reasonable to require that $b_{i,\pi^{-1}(1)}^0 \leq \cdots \leq b_{i,\pi^{-1}(n)}^0$ holds for the initial booking limits $b_{ij}^0, i = 1, \ldots, m, j = 1, \ldots, n$ if standard nesting should be used, because the update rule will otherwise decrease the booking limits by the "min" operation anyway. We will see that this can be a problem if $m \geq 2$.

Theft nesting simply reduces all booking limits – we only have to make sure that the booking limit does not get negative (this would e. g. happen with b_{11} in $t = 9$). If the t-th request is accepted, we thus set

$$b_{ij}^t = \max\left\{0, b_{ij}^{t-1} - r_{ik}\right\} \qquad i = 1, \ldots, m, j = 1, \ldots, n \tag{2.8}$$

For both forms of nesting, the protection levels are given by (2.6), i. e. $p_{ij}^t = c_i^t - b_{ij}^t$ for all i, j, t.

The following table shows the performance of both methods, i. e. the number of accepted requests and the revenue, as well as the total number of requests:

[5] For these and the following formulas cf. Klein (2005, p. 178-180).

Requests	*Products* 1	2	3	*Revenue*
Standard Nesting	7	13	12	10,600
Theft Nesting	1	15	16	12,600
Total	8	15	16	–

We see that theft nesting has performed significantly better than standard nesting – in fact, theft nesting behaved like an optimal policy accepting all high value demand for products $2, 3$. This is, however, due to the fact that our initial protection levels were way too small in comparison to the actual demand – we protected only 12 seats for product 3 and 24 seats for products 2 and 3, where an optimal strategy would have protected 16 and 31, respectively. If the protection levels (or equivalently, the booking limits) are set more carefully, the basic idea of standard nesting seems to be more reasonable: If a request for product j is accepted, it is no longer necessary to protect the amount of resources used for that particular request.

The question whether standard or theft nesting performs better on average is still open: Klein (2005) develops a rather sophisticated method of capacity control (see page 76) and compares it with various booking limit heuristics from the literature both using standard and theft nesting. He finds that standard nesting performs significantly better. Bertsimas and de Boer (2005) point out that most of the heuristic methods (as those used by Klein 2005) do implicitly assume that standard nesting is used and thus may perform poorly if actual bookings are controlled using theft nesting. In their computational experiments, they agree with Klein (2005) and find that with respect to those heuristic methods standard nesting performs indeed better. Bertsimas and de Boer (2005), however, propose a very advanced method to compute nested booking limits that explicitly takes into account whether standard or theft nesting will be used to control bookings. For their sophisticated approach, they find that theft nesting performs better. The question whether standard outperforms theft nesting on average or vice versa is thus still not settled. Nevertheless, Bertsimas and de Boer (2005) are certainly right when they demand: "the operational nesting policy [...] clearly should affect the booking limits" (p. 101).

Many authors note (see e. g. Klein 2005, Talluri and van Ryzin 2004b) that standard and theft nesting are identical if requests arrive in strictly "low-to-high" order, i. e. if all requests for product $\pi^{-1}(1)$ arrive before any other request, then all requests for product $\pi^{-1}(2)$ arrive etc[6]. If demand arrives in such "blocks", i. e. all requests for product j_1 arrive earliest, and if the first request for product $j_2 \neq j_1$ arrives j_1 will never be demanded again, however, we can easily use a dynamic policy that uses only a single booking limit b, namely the booking limit for the product that is just booking. The details of such a method are given by Algorithm 2.1. Note that Algorithm 2.1 assumes that a single resource is used, but an extension to $m \geq 2$ is straightforward. We see that difference between partitioned and nested capacity control in this algorithm is minor: We are using all the remaining capacity $c - a$ in step 3, while a "strict" partitioned capacity control would only use $c - b$, thus giving away $b - a$ units of the resource.

Algorithm 2.1: "Nested" Booking Limit Control for Block Demand

1. Let j be the index of the product that is just booking and c be the remaining capacity. Initialize j = *the product to book first, whichever it may be* and $c = c_1$.
2. Compute the booking limit $b \leq c$ for product j. Set the amount of the resource a allocated to product j to 0.
3. Wait for the next request. If this request is for product $k \neq j$ set $j = k, c = c - a$ and goto 2.
4. If $a < b$ increase a by r_{1j} and accept, otherwise reject.
5. Goto 3.

The Airline Network Case

We are now going to consider nested capacity control on two or more resources. We again focus on the airline case first, i. e. we assume that $m \geq 2$ and $r_{ij} \in \{0, c\}, i = 1, \ldots, m, j = 1, \ldots, n$ and a constant $c > 0$. W. l. o. g. we may assume that $c = 1$. Figure 2.3 shows a very simple example: We have two legs (non-stop flights): one between Dresden (DRS) and Frankfurt/Main (FRA), and one between FRA and London (LHR). The former is resource 1, and the latter is resource 2. Three itineraries are possible, which are shown in the figure. For the sake of simplicity, we assume that prices are not differentiated, and we thus have three products (one fare on each itinerary). Formally, we have $m = 2, n = 3, r_{11} = 1, r_{21} = 0, r_{12} = 0, r_{22} = 1, r_{13} = r_{23} = 1, v_1 = 150, v_2 = 250$.

[6] Such a model of the arrival process of demand is called a *block demand model.* This and other demand models are discussed extensively in section 5.1.

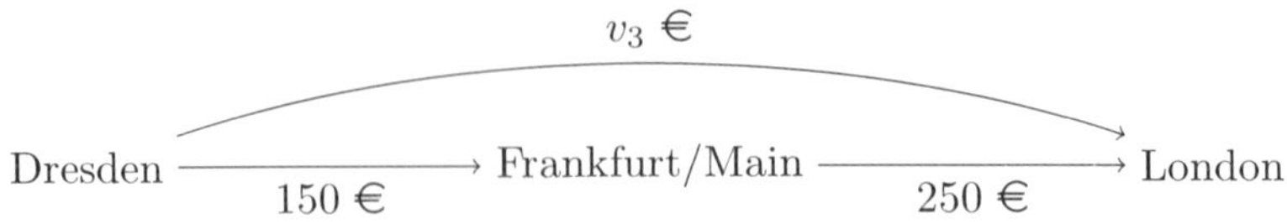

Fig. 2.3: Nesting Order on a Small Network

Standard and Theft Nesting

The implementation of both standard and theft nesting to the network case using formulas (2.7) and (2.8) is straightforward, we thus omit an example here. Some minor technical details are yet worth mentioning. Consider the simple example shown in Figure 2.3. Suppose that the nesting order is $\pi(j) = j$ and let $c_1 = 100, c_2 = 200$. Since product 3 is nesting highest, we set $b_{i3} = c_{i3}, i = 1, 2$. Note, however, that though $b_{23} = 200$ we will never use more than 100 units of resource 2 because resource 1 will then already be exhausted. It is of course possible to set $b_{23} \leq 100$, but that would require (at least if we use standard nesting) that $b_{22} \leq 100$ as well – this restriction does not seem to be necessary; furthermore $b_{22} \leq 100$ is not a very sensible booking limit for product 2, because we know beforehand that product 2 can always use 100 units of resource 2 anyway. So let us assume that we have chosen to set $b_{22} = 150$. We then simply let $b_{12} = 100 = c_1 = b_{13}$. Note that this implies that no seats are protected for products nesting higher than product 2 (i. e. $p_{12} = c_1 - b_{12} = 0$), but this is irrelevant because product 2 does not use resource 1. Analogously, we thus set $b_{21} = b_{22} = 150$. b_{11} can then be set arbitrarily as long as $b_{11} \leq 100$.

In general, it is reasonable to set

$$b_{ij} = \begin{cases} c_i & \pi(j) = n \\ b_{i,\pi^{-1}(\pi(j)+1)} & \pi(j) < n, r_{ij} = 0 \end{cases}$$

Nesting Order

Defining a nesting order for $m \geq 2$ resources is not trivial, even for our simple example. To see this, note first that the nesting order between the products 1 (DRS – FRA) and 2 (FRA – LHR) is not important, because they do not share common resources. This is a difference compared to problems with $m = 1$ – in this case, a nesting order is always a total ordering of the products; in the network case, a partial ordering may be sufficient. The relevant question is thus the position of product

3 in the nesting order. Obviously, product 3 should nest above products $1, 2$ if $v_3 \geq 400$ – given a request for the connecting flight, we will always accept it, and use seats meant to be used for products 1 or 2 to satisfy it if necessary, because the potential revenue obtained by selling those seats to local passengers is never higher. Charging a price for the connecting flight that is higher than the total price of the two local flights is, however, somewhat unrealistic, because the higher v_3, more and more passengers will choose to buy two tickets for the two local flights, claim their baggage and check in again in FRA to save $v_3 - 400$ €.

If $v_3 < 400$, the optimal nesting order is not obvious: Accepting a request for product 3 may displace two local passengers yielding a higher (total) revenue. The nesting order thus strongly depends on the distribution of demand for the three products and the amount of available capacity on the two resources. For instance, if it is rather unlikely that demand for products $2, 3$ will ever exceed the given capacity of resource 2, but resource 1 is a bottleneck that heavily constrains the number of tickets that can be sold for products $1, 3$, product 3 should nest above product 1, because the yield per seat on the bottleneck resource is much higher. On the other hand, if demand for the two local products is very high compared to the available amount of resources 1 and 2, respectively, accepting a connecting passenger will almost certainly displace two local passengers, resulting in a net revenue loss.

Formally, an optimal nesting order would be based on the differences $v_j - o_j(t, c)$ where $o_j(t, c)$ is the opportunity cost of accepting a request for product j where t is the remaining time ("time-to-go") and $c = (c_1, \ldots, c_m)$ denotes the remaining capacity ("capacity-to-go"). These opportunity costs take into account that allocating scarce resources to product j may result in a loss of revenue if future requests are blocked. If the costs $o_j(t, c)$ were given, an optimal nesting order with time- and capacity-to-go t, c would be any permutation π satisfying $\pi(j) > \pi(k) \Rightarrow v_j - o_j(t, c) \geq v_k - o_k(t, c)$. However, given $o_j(\cdot)$, an optimal RM policy is trivially determined: Since $o_j(\cdot)$ incorporates the potential loss of revenue by the displacement of *any* future request, it is obviously optimal to accept a request for product j given t, c if and only if $v_j - o_j(t, c) > 0$ – that would only be suboptimal if the potential revenue loss in the future was greater than v_j, but if that was the case, $o_j(t, c) > v_j$ would hold. It thus seems to be impossible to solve the interdependent problems of determining an optimal nesting order and optimal nested booking limits in isolation; both problems have to be solved simultaneously. Nevertheless, it is of course possible to determine a nesting order heuristically first, and to compute nested booking limits based on that nesting order afterwards. An obvious way is to use estimates $o'_j(\cdot)$ of the opportunity costs $o_j(\cdot)$. Such estimates are called *bid prices*, which are discussed intensively in section 2.3.

A classic heuristic to determine a nesting order for the network case is included in a capacity control method which is called *Displacement Adjusted Virtual Nesting* (DAVN). Before we describe DAVN, we will introduce the concept of *virtual nesting*.

Virtual Nesting

In the 80s and early 90s standard airline computer reservation systems (CRS) were only capable of implementing a leg-based booking limit control with a very limited number of booking classes (ca. four to ten) per leg (see e. g. Fuchs 1987 for an impression of the capabilities of CRS of that time). However, in a hub-and-spoke network the number of products that make use of an inter-hub leg may easily be in the order of hundreds, so it was necessary to map this large number of products into the limited number of booking classes per leg in order to implement network capacity control using the existing CRS. As a consequence, capacity control is executed on CRS booking classes which do no longer represent an actual product, but a mapping of many products to "virtual" one.

Using these "virtual" CRS booking classes for capacity control is called *virtual nesting* and can be described as follows: We are going to use B_i booking classes for leg (resource) $i = 1, \ldots, m$. Because the booking classes on leg i do not reflect actual products they are called *leg buckets*. If product $j = 1, \ldots, n$ uses resource i, it is assigned to one of the B_i leg buckets. This is called clustering or *indexing* of products (we will make some remarks on the problem of indexing below). If $r_{ij} > 0$ let $b_i(j)$ be the bucket of product j on leg i. Note that a certain product j may be in different buckets on different legs. We then consider each of the m legs separately, determine a nesting order of the B_i buckets and nested booking limits β_{ik} for each bucket $k = 1, \ldots, B_i$ on each resource i using an arbitrary optimal or heuristic method suited for single resource problems. Note that optimization techniques to determine nested booking are out of the scope of the virtual nesting method – it is important to stress here that virtual nesting is not about optimization itself, it is a just a "control framework" (Smith and Penn 1988, p. 130).

If a request for product j arrives, we check if one of the booking limits $\beta_{i,b_i(j)}$ for each i with $r_{ij} > 0$ is exceeded. If so, the request is declined, otherwise it is accepted and the booking limits β_{ik} are adjusted in the usual (standard or theft nesting) way. Literally, we accept j if it is accepted "on each leg".

This way of booking limit control was pioneered by American Airlines (Smith and Penn 1988, see also Smith et al. 1992) and United Airlines (Wysong 1988). According to Smith and Penn (1988) the term "'virtual nesting' was chosen to reflect the fact that availability for a market class is never stored in the system; it is determined as necessary from the leg bucket availabilities" (p. 131).

Nowadays, CRS of larger airlines have probably been updated in order to overcome some of the limitations that lead to the development of virtual nesting in the late 80s. However, the idea of virtual nesting has got some remarkable advantages that are still very relevant today:

- Maintaining a CRS is very expensive; and since the CRS is such a crucial part of the sales process it is updated only very cautiously. Smaller airlines and other companies may thus still operate older CRS that suffer from some of the restrictions observed in the 80s. For instance, we are aware that a pretty large German airline's CRS only allows for 26 booking classes per leg because in that CRS a booking class can only be a letter from A to Z.
- The number of products on a network can grow very large. If we e. g. consider a hub-and-spoke network with a single hub and m spokes, we have m local and $m(m-1)/2$ connecting itineraries. If the number of different fares per itinerary is constant on average, the number of products is in the order of m^2, i. e. $O(m^2)$ space is needed to store the booking limits for each and every product. If we use a virtual nesting approach (with a constant number of leg buckets per leg), only $O(m)$ space is necessary. Since m can easily be in the order of hundreds for a larger airline, this saving is certainly relevant.
- Virtual nesting is a method to decompose a network problem with m resources and a huge number of products into m independent single resource problems with a very limited number of products on each resource. This reduction of the problem size can greatly improve the efficiency of RM optimization methods. However, it goes without saying that the decomposition may lead to inferior solutions due to the inherent loss of information.

Virtual nesting controls have received some attention recently, see e. g. Bertsimas and de Boer (2005) and van Ryzin and Vulcano (2005, 2006).

Displacement Adjusted Virtual Nesting

It remains to be shown how the products are indexed to leg buckets – given the loss of information by decomposition of the network problem to a leg-wise problem with a small number of buckets this is obviously a crucial part of the method, see e. g. Talluri and van Ryzin (2004b, p. 105). A classic approach to this problem is using so called *displacement adjusted leg revenues* or *values net of opportunity cost.* The resulting control framework is called *Displacement Adjusted Virtual Nesting*, which is usually attributed to Smith and Penn (1988). The aforementioned authors Bertsimas and de Boer (2005), van Ryzin and Vulcano (2005, 2006) all use DAVN to implement a virtual nesting capacity control. Since the method is only roughly outlined by Smith and Penn (1988), our exposition in Algorithm 2.2 follows Bertsimas and de Boer (2005) using material from Williamson (1992, p. 112-118). Similar descriptions can be found in van Ryzin and Vulcano (2005, 2006).

Algorithm 2.2: Displacement Adjusted Virtual Nesting

1. Solve Model 2.1 (which is an LP) optimally using forecasted values for $d_j, j = 1, \ldots, n$. Let $\mu_i, i = 1, \ldots, m$ be the optimal shadow prices (dual variable values) for the restrictions (2.1).
2. Compute
$$v_{ij} = v_j - \sum_{\substack{k=1 \\ k \neq i}}^{m} r_{kj}\mu_k \qquad \text{for each leg } i = 1, \ldots, m$$
3. For each leg i, index (cluster) all products j with $r_{ij} > 0$ and "similar" v_{ij} into B_i leg buckets. The nesting order among these leg buckets is then such that the bucket with the highest v_{ij} values nests highest.
4. For each leg i, compute (nested) booking limits β_{ik} for each leg bucket $k = 1, \ldots, B_i$ using an arbitrary method suited for single resource problems (recall that issues of optimization are not covered by DAVN).
5. If a request for product j arrives, check if one of the booking limits $\beta_{i,b_i(j)}$ for each i with $r_{ij} > 0$ is exceeded. If so, reject, otherwise accept and update the booking limits β_{ik} according to the standard or theft nesting rules.

The values v_{ij} computed in step 2 are called the displacement adjusted leg revenues (Bertsimas and de Boer 2005) or values net of opportunity cost (Williamson 1992). The shadow prices obtained from

Model 2.1 are used to estimate the opportunity costs of displacing passengers on other legs. Using dual information from deterministic LPs is a standard method to obtain bid prices (opportunity cost estimates) for products, see subsection 2.3.3 for a discussion.

Smith and Penn (1988) propose to index products into leg buckets (step 3) in a way such that demand is evenly distributed among the buckets. Other methods are e. g. discussed by Talluri and van Ryzin (2004b, p. 103-107), Bertsimas and de Boer (2005) and van Ryzin and Vulcano (2005). As mentioned before, a typical indexing scheme will not avoid that the same product j is assigned to different buckets on different legs, i. e. j may be in a very high nesting bucket on leg i_1, but in a lower nesting bucket on leg i_2. As Klein (2005, p. 181) – albeit in another context – points out, this can be a problem, because this may effectively avoid that requests for product j are accepted: If product j is in a very low nesting bucket k on leg i, the booking limit b_{ik} will (especially if theft nesting is used) – run to zero very soon, and further requests for product j will be rejected, although it might be nesting higher in other leg buckets.

Nesting on a Single Resource with Varying Resource Consumption

The concept of nested capacity control is very easy to understand if $m = 1$ and $r_{1j} = c$ or $m \geq 2$ and $r_{ij} \in \{0, c\}$ – then we may assume w. l. o. g. that $c = 1$ and arrive at the airline RM problems which we have just discussed.

The setting gets a little more complex if we consider the single resource-case ($m = 1$) but allow for varying r_{1j}. W. l. o. g. we assume that the production coefficients r_{1j} are positive integers – if some r_{1j} are fractional, we simply multiply r_{1j} and c_1 by the common denominator. We can consequently assume that c_1 is also a positive integer; and since all $r_{1j} \in \mathbb{N}$ the remaining capacity after accepting some requests will always be integer as well.

The varying resource consumption has remarkable consequences for the nesting order. To see this, consider the following small example with $n = 3$ products:

j	r_{1j}	v_j	v_j/r_{1j}
1	2	180	90
2	5	400	80
3	3	255	85

It seems to be natural that the yields v_j/r_{1j} (measured in revenue per unit of capacity) determine the nesting order, i. e. an optimal nesting order is then given by any permutation π such that $\pi(j) > \pi(k) \Rightarrow v_j/r_{1j} \geq v_k/r_{1k}$. However, this is only true if it is possible to fulfill requests – possibly only partly – with continuous amounts of the products. For instance, consider a situation where the remaining capacity is $c_1 = 5$, and a request for product 1 (with the highest yield) arrives. If the aforementioned assumptions hold, we will immediately satisfy this request, because in the future we can at best use the remaining 3 units of capacity to satisfy 1.5 requests for product 1 (at 270), 0.6 requests for product 2 (at 240), or gain 255 by satisfying a single request for product 3. Product 1 is thus indeed nesting highest.

On the other hand, if products can only be sold in discrete amounts, the situation is very different: With $c_1 = 5$, we can at best satisfy two requests for product 1 (at 360), and one request for product 2 and 3 (at 400 and 255, respectively). In this situation, product 2 nests highest. However, this nesting order is not stable: It is easy to see that e. g. for $c_1 = 6$ product 1 nests highest, and for $c_1 = 9$ product 3 nests highest.

Admittedly, the difficulties to define a nesting order diminish if c_1 is large with respect to the r_{1j}. For instance, it is a simple exercise to show that $\pi(1) > \pi(2)$ (i. e. product 1 nests above product 2) if $c_1 \geq 6$, $\pi(1) > \pi(3)$ if $c_1 \geq 16$ and $\pi(3) > \pi(2)$ if $c_1 \geq 21$. The nesting order $\pi(1) = 3, \pi(2) = 1, \pi(3) = 2$ suggested by the yields v_j/r_{1j} is thus optimal and stable for all $c_1 \geq 21$. For a "reasonable" problem instance, a near-optimal (stable) nesting order can thus easily be determined and standard and theft nesting can be applied in the usual way.

Nesting on Multiple Resources with Varying Resource Consumption

We now consider cases with two or more resources and varying production coefficients. As before, we can assume w. l. o. g. that all r_{ij} are non-negative integers and that the available/remaining capacities c_i are integers as well. As a simple example, we use an instance of a RM problem with $m = 2, n = 3$, $c_1 = 250, c_2 = 100$ and the following r_{ij}:

r_{ij}	$j = 1$	$j = 2$	$j = 3$
$i = 1$	4	5	5
$i = 2$	3	1	2

Since the airline network RM problem is a special case of the setting that we discuss here, finding an optimal nesting order is a difficult problem here as well. Suppose, however, that we determined a nesting order heuristically (by a method that is similar to that used in DAVN, say) for our example, and obtained $\pi(j) = j$ for all $j = 1, 2, 3$. Let $c_1 = 250, c_2 = 100$. By the nesting order, $b_{13} = c_1, b_{23} = c_2$. Suppose we wanted to sell at most 30 units of product 1 and 40 units of product 1. This would lead to $b_{11} = 120, b_{12} = 200, b_{21} = 90, b_{22} = 40$. These booking limits are shown in Figure 2.4. Note that the booking limits on resource 1 are according with the nesting order, but on resource 2 they are not (this would require that $b_{21} \leq b_{22} = 40$). Recall that if we use standard nesting, b_{22} will be sooner or later reduced to b_{21}, see (2.7). Theft nesting, however, works, and standard nesting could also be implemented if we refrain from setting b_{ij}^t to a value that is not greater than the booking limit b_{ik}^t of any higher nesting product k.

We are now going to discuss whether a modified standard nesting update rule and the theft nesting update rule as given by (2.8) are a sensible way of capacity control for our small example. Before we begin, it is important to point out that standard and theft nesting work as before if the initial booking limits b_{ij}^0 obey $b_{i,\pi^{-1}(1)}^0 \leq \dots \leq b_{i,\pi^{-1}(n)}^0$. However, as we have seen, this can be – depending on the r_{ij} – quite restrictive.

If the t-th request is for product k and we accept it, we use the following "modified standard nesting" update rule:

$$b_{ij}^t = \begin{cases} \max\left\{0, \min\left\{c_i^t, b_{ij}^{t-1} - r_{ik}\right\}\right\} & \pi(j) \geq \pi(k) \\ \min\left\{c_i^t, b_{ij}^{t-1}\right\} & \pi(j) < \pi(k) \end{cases}$$
$$i = 1, \dots, m, j = 1, \dots, n$$

– since we usually do not update the booking limits of products j with $\pi(j) < \pi(k)$, we have to make sure that all booking limits are non-negative and not greater than the remaining capacity. For theft nesting, however, the update rule (2.8) remains unchanged.

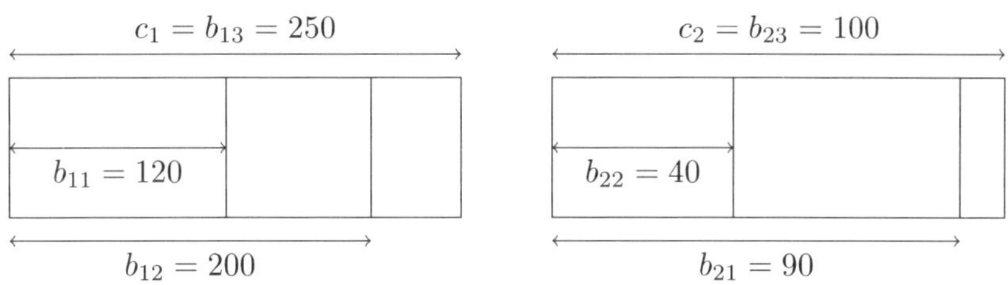

Fig. 2.4: Nesting on Two Resources

Note that for instances with $m \geq 2$ and varying r_{ij} it is absolutely crucial to use the resource specific booking limits b_{ij} instead of the usual product specific booking limits b_j. To see this, note first that a suitable rule for any booking limit to be updated (regardless of the form of nesting to be used) is as follows: Let the t-th request be for product k and accept it. Update b_j (if necessary) by setting:

$$b_j^t = \min_{i=1,\dots,m} \left\{ \frac{b_j^{t-1} r_{ij} - r_{ik}}{r_{ij}} \right\} = \min_{i=1,\dots,m} \left\{ b_j^{t-1} - r_{ik}/r_{ij} \right\}$$

This can lead to booking limits that are systematically to low, as the following example shows: Suppose that at t $(t+1)$ a request for product 2 (1) arrives and is accepted. Since product 3 nests highest, its booking limit is always updated regardless of the form of nesting. Suppose that $b_3^{t-1} = 20$ and equivalently, that $b_{13}^{t-1} = 20 \cdot 5 = 100, b_{23}^{t-1} = 20 \cdot 2 = 40$. We then have for b_3^t, b_3^{t+1} resp. $b_{13}^{t+1}, b_{13}^{t+1}$

$$\begin{aligned} b_3^t &= \min\{20 - 1, 20 - 1/2\} = 19 \\ b_3^{t+1} &= \min\{19 - 4/5, 19 - 3/2\} = 17.5 \\ b_{13}^{t+1} &= 100 - 5 - 4 = 91 \\ b_{23}^{t+1} &= 40 - 1 - 3 = 36 \end{aligned}$$

By the resource specific booking limits, the maximal number of bookings to be accepted for product 3 is $\min\{91/5, 36/2\} = 18$, but the product specific booking limit is already strictly lower (namely 17.5). Formally, this is can be explained by the fact that the min-operation is unnecessarily performed twice:

$$\begin{aligned} b_j^t &= \min_{i=1,\dots,m} \left\{ b_j^{t-1} - r_{i,k_2}/r_{ij} \right\} \\ &= \min_{i=1,\dots,m} \left\{ \min_{h=1,\dots,m} \left\{ b_j^{t-2} - r_{h,k_2}/r_{hj} \right\} - r_{i,k_2}/r_{ij} \right\} \\ &\leq \min_{i=1,\dots,m} \left\{ \frac{b_{ij}^{t-2} - r_{i,k_1} - r_{i,k_2}}{r_{ij}} \right\} \end{aligned}$$

where k_1, k_2 are the first and the second products for which requests are arrive and are accepted.

Thus we are going to use the resource specific booking limits and consider now a stream of 30 requests for product 1. By construction, these requests are all accepted. Since product 1 is nesting lowest, all booking limits are updated, regardless whether standard or theft nesting is used. Clearly $b_{11}^{30} = b_{21}^{30} = 0$ and $c_1^{30} = b_{13}^{30} = 130, c_2^{30} = b_{23}^{30} = 10$. For product 2, we have $b_{12}^{30} = 200 - 3 \cdot 40 = 80$ and $b_{22}^{30} = \max\{0, 40 - 30 \cdot 3\} = 0$. Since $b_{22}^{30} = 0$, we are not going to accept any request for product 2. Obviously, product 1 has used all the capacity that was meant to be used for product 2 – this is certainly not what we wanted when we let product 2 nest above product 1. The result is, however, totally in accordance with the protection levels: As in the initial situation (see Figure 2.4), $b_{12}^{30} = 80$ units of resource 1 are protected for product 2. On resource 2, there was no protection for product 2, though.

These somewhat strange effects are caused by the fact that $r_{ij} > r_{ik}$ for some i and $j \neq k$, but there is also another resource $h \neq i$ such that $r_{hj} < r_{hk}$ – such a case was impossible in the "airline network" setting where $r_{ij} \in \{0, c\}$, because for $j \neq k$ and all $i = 1, \ldots, m$ either $r_{ij} = r_{ik} = c$ or at least one of the production coefficients r_{ij}, r_{ik} is zero. Note that such a case is also impossible in an "airline network with group bookings" setting – where $r_{ij} \in \{0, c_j\}$ and $c_j > 0$ denotes the size of the group –, because if $r_{ij} = c_j \geq r_{ik} = c_k$ for $j \neq k$ and some i, then for all $h = 1, \ldots, m, h \neq i$ either $r_{hj} \geq r_{hk}$ or $r_{hj} = 0$.

We conclude from this small example that standard and theft nesting can be applied to such "non airline" instances in the usual way if the initial booking limits b_{ij}^0 are monotone in accordance with the nesting order, i. e. $b_{i,\pi^{-1}(1)}^0 \leq \cdots \leq b_{i,\pi^{-1}(n)}^0$ holds. Otherwise we have from $r_{ij} > r_{ik}$ and $r_{hj} < r_{hk}$ that the protection level is zero for the higher nesting product on one of the resources, which means that the proper nesting of products is not guaranteed. Table 2.2 summarizes our findings for different types of problems.

It goes without saying that nested booking limits are still advantageous under uncertainty compared to partitioned ones, but it is doubtable whether nested capacity control in the (strict) form as we have discussed it so far is useful for "non airline" RM problems with $m \geq 2$. For such instances, other forms of capacity control that do not exclusively assign capacity to products (thereby capturing positive features of nesting) but are not booking limit controls may be more effective, e. g. the bid prices controls discussed in section 2.3. Another option is to use booking limits without explicitly allocating capacity to products, yet without having to rely on a nesting order of products. This is possible in the context of overbooking, see section 2.4. Figure 2.5 shows how these categories of capacity control methods are related.

Table 2.2: Effectiveness of Nested Booking Limit Controls

	Nesting Order	Standard/Theft Nesting
Airline: Single Leg ($m = 1$, w. l. o. g. $r_{1j} = 1$)	trivial	work
Airline: Network (with Group Bookings) ($m \geq 2, r_{ij} \in \{0, c_j\}$, w. l. o. g. $c_j \in \mathbb{N}$)	Heuristics available	work
Single Resource ($m = 1$, w. l. o. g. $r_{1j} \in \mathbb{N}$)	near-optimal order easy to find	work
Multiple Resource ($m \geq 2$, w. l. o. g. $r_{ij} \in \mathbb{N}$)	Heuristics available	practically limited to monotonic b^0_{ij}

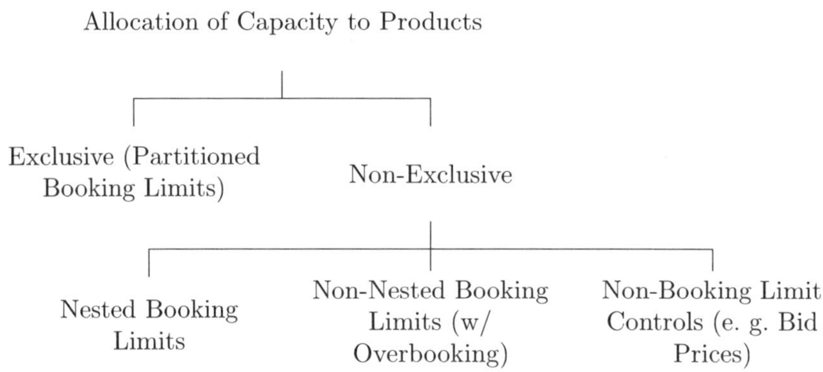

Fig. 2.5: Nested and Non-Nested Capacity Control Strategies

2.2.3 Literature Review

After having explained booking limit controls in great detail we now describe the state of the art. We begin by reviewing the literature on the deterministic demand models. Since partitioned booking limits only make sense in the deterministic setting, and uncertainty is involved in most RM problems in practice, these are at the same time the only models that deal with partitioned booking limits; the remainder of the literature review will thus be devoted to stochastic models to obtain nested booking limits.

It is interesting to note that most authors dealing with overbooking problems use booking limit policies as well. Instead of mentioning those references twice, we defer a discussion of them to section 2.4.

Deterministic Demand

Model 2.1 is a simple LP. If we add the requirement that $b_j \in \mathbb{N}_0$, it becomes fairly general linear integer problem. There is a large body of literature both on LPs and linear integer problems, but there seem to be only quite a few references that explicitly consider a RM context. Glover et al. (1982), for instance, develop a network flow formulation of the airline network RM problem if demand is deterministic (or forecasted values are used). Not every constraint from the airline business can be incorporated into the network flow formulation, though; Glover et al. (1982) thus implement an iterative procedure such that the network flow problem is solved optimally, violated "side constraints" (if any) are added to the problem, the problem is resolved, and the process iterates. Chen (1998) applies the network flow formulation by Glover et al. (1982) to a hotel revenue management problem. Due to the different structure of the RM problem in hotels no side constraints are necessary. To the best of our knowledge, these are the only references that consider deterministic models to obtain booking limits – it goes without saying that many other authors consider deterministic models, however, their aim is usually to obtain bid prices, not (partitioned or nested) booking limits, see subsection 2.3.3.

It should further be noted that if $d_j = 1$ (i. e. $b_j \in \{0, 1\}$) Model 2.1 becomes a so-called *multiconstraint* or *multidimensional knapsack* problem (see e. g. the survey by Fréville 2004). Note that the probabilistic model 2.3 is of this type. If we have $m = 1$ (and $b_j \in \mathbb{N}_0$), the problem is called the bounded knapsack problem (see e. g. Pisinger 2000). Both problems are also discussed in Martello and Toth (1990) and Kellerer et al. (2004).

Littlewood's Rule, Belobaba's EMSR/EMSRb and Related Research

The earliest reference with respect to nested booking limit controls seems to be Littlewood (1972). Littlewood considers a single leg airline RM problem with two fares $v_1 > v_2$. The low fare passengers are assumed to book before the high fare ones; the RM is thus to decide when to stop low fare bookings, i. e. how many seats are to be protected for the high fare passengers. The high fare bookings will then, of course, be accepted until the capacity c_1 is exhausted. We are thus using a single booking limit b_{21}, and if the number of seats allocated to low fare passengers is $a \leq b_{21}$, $c_1 - a$ seats are available for the high fare. The situation is thus identical to the one assumed to derive Algorithm 2.1.

Littlewood (1972) proposed the following formula – which became famous as *Littlewood's Rule* – to compute the protection level $p_{21} = c_1 - b_{21}$. For a consistent presentation, we use the notation and terms of Belobaba (1987b, 1989). Define

$$EMSR_j(p) = v_j \cdot P_j(D_j \geq p) \tag{2.9}$$

where D_j is a random variable denoting demand for product j with distribution $P_j(\cdot)$. $EMSR_j(p)$ is then the additional (marginal) expected revenue if the p-th seat is protected (exclusively!) for product j, or the *expected marginal seat revenue* for short. Littlewood's rule is then: Decrease p_{12} (i. e. accept the low fare passengers) as long as

$$v_2 \geq EMSR_1(p_{12}) \tag{2.10}$$

It is interesting to note that Littlewood's rule (2.10) only depends on the demand distribution of the high fare; the demand distribution of the low fare is completely irrelevant. That seems to be somewhat odd on first sight, but recall that it is assumed that low fare passengers book strictly first. The only decision we thus have to make is when to stop accepting low fare bookings.

Littlewood's rule has got a charming intuitive notion: Accept class 2 requests as long as the certain revenue v_2 is not smaller than the expected revenue if the remaining p_{12} seats are all sold to class 1 passengers – that will happen with probability $P_1(D_1 \geq p_{12})$. Actually, Richter (1982) has shown that if low fare passengers indeed book strictly first, the marginal analysis that is implicitly undertaken to obtain Littlewood's rule is correct, i. e. (2.10) is an optimal decision rule. Furthermore, Titze and Griesshaber (1983) conducted a simulation study and investigated the performance of Littlewood's rule if the "low before high" assumption is relaxed. They found that even if this assumption only holds approximately, the revenue obtained is largely unaffected.

As Brumelle et al. (1990, p. 184) point out, (2.10) has got an interesting, albeit probably unwanted, implication: Transform (2.10) to obtain

$$v_2 \geq v_1 \cdot P_1(D_1 \geq p_{12}) \Leftrightarrow P_1(D_1 \geq p_{12}) \leq v_2/v_1$$

If we assume a continuous demand distribution, we have $P_1(D_1 \geq p_{12}^*) = v_2/v_1$ for the optimal protection level p_{12}^*. If the low fare is, say 40 % of the high fare (i. e. $v_2/v_1 = 0.4$), the optimal protection level will be set in a way such that the probability to turn at least one high yield customer away – i. e. $P(D_1 \geq p_{12})$ – is 0.4 as well. The event of turning down customers is known called spill, and as Brumelle et al. (1990) note, a probability of 0.4 to spill a high yield passenger seems to be "higher than most airline managers would accept" (p. 184). Albeit these observations are certainly correct, three remarks are in order: (1) The argument relies on the fact that there is ample low fare demand such that indeed all $c_1 - p_{12}$ are sold to low fare passengers, and exactly p_{12} seats remain (alas, if low fare demand was low, there was no need for a high fare protection level p_{12} in the first place). (2) Though a spill probability of 40 % might intuitively seem too much, Richter (1982) has proven that Littlewood's rule (2.10) is an *optimal* policy with respect to the *expected* revenue (not with respect to the spill). If the airline managers nevertheless feel that 40 % is too much, they seem to be risk averse, and maximizing the expected revenue (which assumes a risk neutral decision maker) is not the correct objective. It is noteworthy that Brumelle et al. present an approach that assigns penalty costs to high fare passenger spill thereby correcting for risk aversion. Other approaches that consider capacity control under risk aversion are due to Weatherford (2004) and Barz and Waldmann (2006). (3) Even in light of the facts shown by Brumelle et al. (1990), Littlewood's rule shows a sound behavior: If the low fare rises (decreases) relatively to the high fare, the probability to reject a high fare customer rises (decreases), because the opportunity costs of doing so decrease (rise) accordingly.

Belobaba (1987b, 1989) uses the EMSR calculus for problems with three or more fares by applying (2.10) to all pairs of products. Formally, assume that the nesting order is decreasing with the product indexes, i. e. product 1 is nesting highest and product n is nesting lowest. Then, for all $j = 1, \ldots, n$ and all $k = j+1, \ldots, n$ compute the number of seats p_{1j}^k that are protected for k and from j using (2.10), i. e. p_{1j}^k is the smallest number that satisfies

$$v_j \geq EMSR_k\left(p_{1j}^k\right) \tag{2.11}$$

The total protection level for product k is then given by $p_{1k} = \min\left\{\sum_{j=1}^{k-1} p_{1j}^k, c_1\right\}$, and the booking limit is thus $b_k = c_1 - p_{1k}$. Note that Belobaba (1987b, 1989) uses a slightly different terminology: What he calls a "nested protection level" of product k is the difference $b_{1k} - b_{1,k+1}$, i. e. the *additional* number of seats that is protected from $k+1$ for k (and higher nesting products). Since this notion of a protection level is less frequently used, we stay with our definition that p_{ik} is the *total* amount of resource i that is protected from k for all higher nesting products.

As Robinson (1995, p. 257) points out, Belobaba (1987b, 1989) does not take into account that all fare classes $j_1, j_2 < k$ are nested, too. For instance, p_{13}^1 and p_{13}^2 denote separately the number of seats protected from fare class 3 and reserved for 1 and 2, respectively. But fare class 1 has in addition access to p_{12}^1 seats. The optimality condition e. g. of Brumelle and McGill (1993) (this reference is discussed below) takes this into account. Thus, the EMSR method gives (under the assumptions of Littlewood 1972) the optimal protection levels for the first and highest fare class 1, but just heuristic levels for fare classes $2, \ldots, n-1$ (recall that there are no seats protected *for* the lowest class n). Note that this implies that the booking limits for classes 1 and 2 are optimal.

The EMSR-method is in principle presented by Belobaba (1987b, 1989) as a "model free" approach. However, it is implicitly based Littlewood's assumption that the lowest fare class books first, then the second lowest fare class and so forth up to the highest fare class which books last. Such a model of the arrival process of demand is called a *block demand model*; this and other demand models are discussed extensively in section 5.1. Wollmer (1992) and Brumelle and McGill (1993) develop dynamic models for this "low-to-high" booking case – we have already pointed out that the order in which bookings arrive is relevant under nested capacity control and thus a dynamic model is necessary. Roughly speaking, Brumelle and McGill (1993) present a continuous version of Wollmer's model to facilitate the analysis. Robinson (1995) considers a more general case where bookings arrive sequentially by product as well, but that sequence does not have to be monotone with the fares. Note that for all three models – besides the assumption of the sequential booking order – it is of crucial importance that demand is independent, i. e. the random variables D_j are independently distributed of each other, and also independent of the actions of the revenue manager. This assumption may well be violated if closing a lower fare class induces "buy ups", i. e. bookings of higher fare classes by passengers who would have bought a lower one if it was available. We will treat buy ups and other forms of customer behavior influenced by capacity control decisions in chapter 3.

It is interesting to note that Wollmer (1992), Brumelle and McGill (1993) and Robinson (1995) all prove that the optimal policy under block demand is indeed a nested booking limit policy. The similarities of these models and optimality conditions are investigated by Li and

Oum (2002), who show that the models by Wollmer (1992), Brumelle and McGill (1993) and Curry (1990) are analytically equivalent. Lautenbacher and Stidham (1999) present a unified view on the models of Belobaba (1989), Brumelle and McGill (1993), Curry (1990), Littlewood (1972), Robinson (1995), Wollmer (1992) and Lee and Hersh (1993).

Wollmer (1992) found that the EMSR booking limits may be far away from the optimal ones; however, in his study the performance of EMSR with respect to the expected revenue was close to optimal. Brumelle and McGill (1993) agree with both points: They show that EMSR may over- as well as underestimate the optimal protection levels. The revenue performance of EMSR was ca. 0.5 % below the optimum at worst. Robinson (1995) attributes the results of Wollmer (1992) and Brumelle and McGill (1993) to the facts that the number of fare classes used in those studies was small – recall that EMSR gives the optimal booking limits for the two highest fares –, the difference between highest and lowest fare was relatively small and the demand was very high, such that a reasonable RM policy will focus on protecting seats for the higher-valued fare classes (which are treated correctly by EMSR). Robinson (1995) defines a theoretical demand setting in which the EMSR-booking limit of the $n+1$-st fare class approaches zero as $n \to \infty$ while it is a strictly positive constant under the optimal policy. However, it is important to stress that the two aforementioned references (and many others) find that EMSR seems to be a near-optimal policy with excellent revenue performance.

To address the disadvantage of EMSR that nesting is only taken into account between pairs of products, Belobaba (1992) introduced an improved version of this method which he termed EMSRb. The basic idea is to compute the protection level p_{1j} directly, i. e. to set it to the minimum value that satisfies

$$v_j \geq v\left(1, \ldots, j-1\right) P\left(\sum_{k=1}^{j-1} D_j \geq p_{1j}\right)$$

where

$$v\left(1, \ldots, j-1\right) = \frac{\sum_{k=1}^{j-1} E\left[D_k\right] v_k}{\sum_{k=1}^{j-1} E\left[D_k\right]}$$

is the "expected revenue" from fare classes $1, \ldots, j-1$.

The drawback of EMSRb is obviously the need to determine the distribution of $\sum_{k=1}^{j-1} D_k$. However, for certain distributions of the D_j, the distribution of the sum can easily derived. For instance, if the D_j are independently distributed Normal (Poisson) random variables, the sum follows a Normal (Poisson) distribution as well.

A further extensions of the EMSR-concept is due to Belobaba and Weatherford (1996), who incorporate choice behavior (see section 3.2 for an in-depth discussion of choice-based RM). Belobaba and Wilson (1997) test how EMSR-methods perform under competition.

We continue our review by considering references that are similar in structure to Belobaba's work. Brumelle et al. (1990) also consider two fare classes on a single leg and assume that the lower one books strictly first, but they allow for that high- and low fare demand are dependent. They show that Littlewood's rule is still optimal in this case (where the corresponding conditional probabilities are to be used instead of the unconditional ones) if the demand distributions exhibit a certain monotonicity property, called *monotonic association*. This condition may fail to hold if low and high fare demand are negatively correlated. Passenger buy ups – where low fare passengers purchase the high fare because lower fare class bookings are no longer accepted – as a special case of positive demand correlation are examined. The result is the same as given by Belobaba (1987b, eq. 5.53 on p. 140), who proposed it without formal proof.

Bitran and Gilbert (1996) consider the RM problem in hotels where guests with 6pm reservations (i. e. if the customer does not arrive until 6pm, the room may be rented to another guest) arrive first, then walk-ins (i. e. guests without a reservation) and then guests with guaranteed reservations (rooms dedicated to that reservations are not given away at any time). They obtain an optimality condition of similar structure like (2.10).

Van Ryzin and McGill (2000) develop an adaptive approach for a protection level (nested booking limit) policy on a single airline leg where bookings arrive in a "low-to-high" order. Based on the optimality conditions of Brumelle and McGill (1993) they develop a procedure to update the protection levels after demand has been observed. These protection levels are then used to control bookings in the next period, where demand is then observed again, and the process iterates.

Gallego and Phillips (2004) consider the airline RM problem on a single leg with two products and a *flexible* product, i. e. if a customer purchases the flexible product, the airline will decide later whether she will actually receive product 1 or product 2 (see section 3.3 for an in-depth discussion of flexible products). The solution of this problem involves sophisticated usage of EMSRs.

Dynamic Booking Limit Policies

So far we have only considered *static booking limit policies*, i. e. policies that determine booking limits once (at the beginning of the time horizon); and these booking limits remain unchanged over the entire horizon. It goes without saying that all policies which are of static nature can be reoptimized – especially if demand forecasts and other data are updated –, but by a *dynamic booking limit policy* we mean a method that explicitly considers the dynamic nature of the demand process by letting the booking limits b_{ijt} vary with time t. Note that almost all models we have discussed thus fare have (implicitly or explicitly) assumed that requests arrive in a "low-to-high" order. Admittedly, this model of the demand process contains some, albeit very limited form of dynamics[7], and evidently, if a booking limit policy is optimal in the block demand setting it is a static one.

To arrive at a truly dynamic booking limit policy we thus have to consider a more general model of the arrival process. Lee and Hersh (1993) deal with a single leg airline RM problem and propose to divide the time horizon into T periods which are so small (i. e. T is so large) that there is at most one request per period. This is called a micro period model of demand, see section 5.1. Denote the probability that a request for product j arrives in period t by $P_{jt} \geq 0, j = 1, \ldots, n, t = 1, \ldots, T$. Naturally, we require that $\sum_{j=1}^{n} P_{jt} \leq 1$ for all t, and if $\sum_{j=1}^{n} P_{jt} < 1$ there is a positive probability $P_{0t} = 1 - \sum_{j=1}^{n} P_{jt}$ that there is no request in t. Time is counted backwards from T to 0. Denote the maximum expected revenue from period t on with a capacity of c seats remaining by $V_t(c)$. The value function $V_t(c)$ can be defined recursively for all $t = 1, \ldots, T$ and all $c > 0$ by:

$$\begin{aligned} V_t(c) &= P_{0t} V_{t-1}(c) + \sum_{j=1}^{n} P_{jt} \max\left\{V_{t-1}(c), v_j + V_{t-1}(c-1)\right\} \\ &= V_{t-1}(c) + \sum_{j=1}^{n} P_{jt} \max\left\{0, v_j - \Delta V_{t-1}(c)\right\} \end{aligned} \tag{2.12}$$

[7] The "low-to-high" block demand model and other assumptions about the dynamics of demand are thoroughly discussed in section 5.1.

where $\Delta V_{t-1}(c) = V_{t-1}(c) - V_{t-1}(c-1)$ is the marginal cost of capacity, or equivalently the opportunity cost of accepting a request in period t if c seats are remaining. The boundary conditions are $V_0(c) = 0$ for all c and $V_t(0) = 0$ for all t.

We immediately conclude from the definition of $V_t(c)$ that a request for product j in period t given capacity c will be accepted if and only if $v_j \geq \Delta V_{t-1}(c)$, i. e. if the revenue of the request exceeds the opportunity cost of accepting it – a quite intuitive result.

It is important to stress that (2.12) is not a booking limit model per se. Rather an optimal policy would consist of having a table of $\Delta V_{t-1}(c)$ ready for all t and all c, and look the needed value up if a request for product arrives. Note however, since T is in the order of 1,000s or 10,000s methods to reduce the storage space required for such tables, as well as to reduce the computational burden are certainly in order. Fortunately, Lee and Hersh (1993) show that $V_t(c)$ and $\Delta V_t(c)$ are monotone in various respects such that the optimal policy is given by a set of critical booking capacities $p(j,t)$ i. e. a request for product j in period t is accepted if and only if $c \geq p(j,t)$ – in other words $p(j,t)$ is the protection level of product j in period t. Furthermore, these protection levels are non-increasing in t, such that it is sufficient to store the protection levels for those periods t in which $p(j,t+1) > p(j,t)$ holds for the first time. The monotonicity of p also simplifies the computation. To summarize, (2.12) suggests an optimal control based on the opportunity costs $\Delta V_t(c)$, but it turns out that an optimal dynamic protection level control (or equivalently, a dynamic nested booking limit control) exists. Bitran and Mondschein (1995) obtain a similar result for hotel RM if it is assumed that every guests stays for exactly one night. Bitran and Mondschein (1995) also consider dynamic booking limit policies for multiple night stays.

It is interesting to note that Lee and Hersh (1993) also consider group bookings. This is modeled by using the probabilities P_{jkt} that a request for product j in period t is for k tickets. For this case the optimal policy can be characterized by a set of critical decision *periods*, i. e. for each product j, request size k and remaining capacity c there exists a critical period t such that a request for j of size k given c seats remaining is accepted up to t and declined afterwards. Again, this implies a reduction in both computational times and storage space; however, the optimal policy can no longer be formulated using optimal protection levels (or booking limits).

Subramanian et al. (1999) extend Lee and Hersh's model by incorporating *overbooking* (they do not consider group bookings, though).

Remarkably, the optimal policy turns out to be a booking limit policy as well. However, the booking limit of product j does not only depend on the period t, but also on the "state" of the system. The notion of a state depends on the assumptions that govern the cancellation and no-show probabilities. For instance, if these are independent of the product, a one dimensional state variable denoting the total number of requests is sufficient; if more general assumptions are considered, the dimension of the state is unfortunately linear in the number of products, it will thus only be feasible to store the optimal booking limits for each and every state if the number of products is moderate. Furthermore, the booking limits are not necessarily monotone in the remaining time, and for some given state and remaining time, it may be optimal to reject requests of a certain fare class while request for other classes with lower fares are accepted, i. e. the nesting order is not automatically monotone with respect to the fares.

Talluri and van Ryzin (2004a) consider RM problems on a single airline leg without group bookings and overbooking, but they incorporate choice behavior, i. e. they assume that an arriving customer will consider all products that are available at the time of her request and choose one (or none at all) according to a certain choice model. Talluri and van Ryzin (2004a) develop a model that is similar to (2.12). We defer a discussion of choice-base RM and this reference to section 3.2, but take the opportunity to point out that for certain well known choice models a nested booking limit policy turns out to be optimal again.

Zhao and Zheng (2001) consider a single leg airline RM problem with two products (a low and a high fare) and three types of customers: Two types who will only buy the low or the high fare, respectively, and a flexible type, who will buy the low fare if it is available and the high fare otherwise. They assume that demand is generated by a non-homogeneous Poisson process (see chapter 5 for a discussion of such arrival processes). Note that this implies that time is continuous (in contrast to the aforementioned references where time was discrete). A remarkable feature of Zhao and Zheng's model is that the discount fare class cannot be reopened once it has been closed. Using these assumptions it is shown that the optimal policy is a protection level policy, i. e. the discount fare class should be closed if the remaining capacity drops below a certain level. The protection levels depend on the remaining time to departure and are in general not monotone.

Mayer (1976) deals with airline RM and presents booking limit-based models for partitioned capacities (without cancellations and no-shows) and for overbooking. There are two types of passengers (groups and individuals), and the partitioned booking limits depend both on the period t and the available capacity at the beginning of t. Note that Mayer (1976) allows for more than one request per period; his model is thus a macro period model (see section 5.1).

Alstrup et al. (1986) also consider an overbooking problem with macro periods. The booking limits for the two types of reservations (passengers) vary by period.

Nested Booking Limit Controls for Multiple Resources

Thus far we have discussed references which focus on single resource problems. An obvious way to extend those approaches to cases with two or more resources are the virtual nesting controls which we will discuss in the following.

Bertsimas and de Boer (2005) and van Ryzin and Vulcano (2005, 2006) all pursue a simulation optimization approach (see Algorithm 5.1) to a displacement adjusted virtual nesting control (DAVN, see page 48). Bertsimas and de Boer (2005) treat both capacity and demand as discrete measures. Van Ryzin and Vulcano (2005) develop a fluid approximation of Bertsimas and de Boer's model to facilitate the analysis. Van Ryzin and Vulcano (2006) pursue a similar approach in a choice based setting.

Gosavi et al. (2007) also design a simulation optimization method for RM problems on two or more resources including overbooking, but they consider a "pure" booking limit approach where each product j has got its own booking limit and is not mapped into virtual classes like in the virtual nesting approaches mentioned before.

Curry (1990) develops an approach for network RM that has got the flavor of a virtual nesting approach (see page 46 f.): Let N be the set of products. Partition N into subsets such that for every pair of products $j, k \in N_h$ in the h-th subset $r_{ij} = r_{ik}$ holds for every resource $i = 1, \dots, m$. If we consider an airline RM problem, N_h is a set of fare classes that belong to a certain itinerary. Consider each subset N_h separately and cluster similar products into a so called nest. Determine a ranking of products in each of the nests. Higher ranked products can access capacity that is available to lower ranked ones, but capacity is not shared between nests. Note that this especially means that capacity is not nested among different itineraries (in the airline case) or products j, k where $r_{ij} \neq r_{ik}$ for at least one i. The problem is then solved in (roughly) two steps:

1. Allocate capacity exclusively to every nest, i. e. determine partitioned "booking limits" b^g for each nest g.

2. Consider each of the nests separately. For every product in nest g, compute (nested) booking limits given the amount of capacity b^g that has been exclusively assigned to the nest.

Note that the problem is decomposed twice: By partitioning N into subsets of products with the same production coefficients, and by the allocation of all products of a particular subset to the nests. It is important to stress that – in contrast to virtual nesting – the problem to be solved in step 1 is not a single but a multi-resource problem. However, since the products in nest g all have the same production coefficients, the problem in step 2 can be seen as a single resource problem.

2.2.4 Discussion of Booking Limit Controls

Albeit we have seen that it is not obvious how the control policy should actually be implemented if booking limits are nested, booking limit controls are fairly easy to understand. The most important airline computerized reservation systems (CRS) support *only* booking limit controls. Since these CRS are mature information systems of crucial importance to the sales process, changes in the software are typically rare and only minor. Authors who consider to develop capacity control policies that should actually be implemented by major airlines are thus typically forced to focus on booking limit policies, possibly with a very limited number of booking classes per leg such that a virtual nesting approach is in order.

It is interesting to note that booking limit policies do not need to be optimal, i. e. under certain assumptions the optimal capacity control may not be a booking limit policy. As remarked above, Lee and Hersh (1993) have e. g. shown that the optimal policy cannot be expressed by booking limits if group bookings are considered. Subramanian et al. (1999) demonstrated that the optimal booking limits are very difficult to determine and the optimal nesting order may not be given by the fares if overbooking is integrated into the capacity control problem. Furthermore, we have already mentioned that many of the authors who prove that a booking limit policy is optimal rely on that demand for different products is independent. To see that dependent demand can be a problem, consider the following example which is due to Chatwin (1998, example 2 on p. 817): We have a single leg airline RM problem where the capacity of the airline is $c_1 = 1$. There are two fares $v_2 > v_1$; therefore the booking limit for product 2 is obviously $b_{21} = 1$. Demand for the higher valued product is stochastically decreasing in the low-fare demand, i. e. the higher demand for product 1, the lower demand for the other product. Assume that two outcomes for the random variables $D_j, j = 1,2$ are possible: $D_1 = 1, D_2 = 1$, and $D_1 = 2, D_2 = 0$. This implies that there are exactly to requests and the remaining time is naturally divided into two periods (for the first and second request, respectively). Suppose that demand for product 1 arrives strictly before any demand for product 2. Given these assumptions – which are admittedly harsh –, an optimal policy will clearly reject the first request (which can only be a request for the low fare), and accept the second, whatever it is. This means, the booking limit for product 1 would have to be $b_{11} = 1$ (if the second request is a low fare request), and it would have to be $b_{11} = 0$ (if the second request is a high fare request). Note, however, that this problem can be avoided by using a dynamic instead of a static policy, i. e. by letting the booking limits b_{11}, b_{21} vary in the two periods, or (equivalently) by allowing that the booking limits are revised (reoptimized) between the two periods. Chatwin (1998) presents two other examples where the optimal policy cannot be a booking limit policy as well.

2.3 Capacity Control by Bid Prices

2.3.1 Introduction

Capacity control by (nested) booking limits for RM problems with multiple resources is somewhat difficult to implement. Even in the "airline network" case, which is (as we have seen) considerably simpler than the general case with arbitrary r_{ij}, it is not clear what an optimal nesting order is. Furthermore, we have already outlined that an "ideal" capacity control strategy would look very different from a booking limit control (see page 46): The revenue v_j would be compared with the opportunity costs $o_j(t,c)$ of accepting (basically the loss of future revenue by displacing other requests), and we would accept if and only if $v_j \geq o_j(t,c)$.

Note that we have already (implicitly) discussed such an approach; see our remarks with respect to the work of Lee and Hersh (1993, page 61 in this book): As described by (2.12), we will accept a request for j in period t if and only if $v_j \geq \Delta V_{t-1}(c)$ where $\Delta V_{t-1}(c) = o_j(t,c) = V_{t-1}(c) - V_{t-1}(c-1)$. However, Lee and Hersh (1993) have shown that for their micro period model of single leg airline RM (without group bookings) an optimal booking limit policy exists, and Subramanian et al. (1999) and Talluri and van Ryzin (2004a) have extended this result to more general cases. Thus it is not necessary to e. g. store a (presumably large) table of opportunity costs $o_j(t, c)$ to implement capacity control.

On the other hand, the results of Lee and Hersh (1993), Subramanian et al. (1999) and Talluri and van Ryzin (2004a) heavily rely on certain monotonicity properties of the value function $V_t(c)$. We are not going to discuss these properties in detail, but note that already Lee and Hersh (1993) prove that if group bookings are considered, these monotonicity results fail to hold and the optimal capacity control policy is not necessarily a booking limit policy. Subramanian et al. (1999) analogously show that if group bookings are neglected, but overbooking is considered, the optimal policy may no longer be monotone; computing and storing the optimal booking limits is thus impossible for all but the smallest examples. Bertsimas and Popescu (2003) finally provide an example that these monotonicity results do not hold for the multiple resource case ($m \geq 2$); see also Feller (2002) for examples and a discussion.

Let us therefore formulate a recursive value function similar to (2.12) extending the approach by Lee and Hersh (1993) to a problem with $m \geq 2$ resources and group bookings: The time horizon is divided into T discrete periods such that there is at most one request per period. Time is counted backwards. v_j and r_{ij} are (as before) the revenue and production coefficient of product j with respect to resource $i = 1, \ldots, m$, respectively. Define $r_j = (r_{1j}, \ldots, r_{mj})$. Given the initial capacity, the maximal amount of any product that can be demanded by any request is clearly bounded – at most K units of any product can be requested, say. Denote the probability that a request arrives in period $t = 1, \ldots, T$ is for $k = 1, \ldots, K$ units of product $j = 1, \ldots, n$ by $P_{jkt} \geq 0$. We require that $\sum_{j,k} P_{jkt} \leq 1$ holds for all t. The probability of no arrival in t is then $P_{0t} = 1 - \sum_{j,k} P_{jkt} \geq 0$. Denote the maximum expected revenue from period t on with remaining capacity $c = (c_1, \ldots, c_m)$ by $V_t(c)$. The value function $V_t(c)$ can be defined recursively for all $t = 1, \ldots, T$ and all $c \geq 0$ by:

$$\begin{aligned} V_t(c) &= P_{0t} V_{t-1}(c) + \sum_{j=1}^{n} \sum_{k=1}^{K} P_{jkt} \max\left\{V_{t-1}(c), v_j + V_{t-1}(c - r_j)\right\} \\ &= V_{t-1}(c) + \sum_{j=1}^{n} \sum_{k=1}^{K} P_{jkt} \max\left\{0, v_j - \Delta V_{t-1}(c, r_j)\right\} \end{aligned} \tag{2.13}$$

where $\Delta V_{t-1}(c, r_j) = V_{t-1}(c) - V_{t-1}(c - r_j)$ is the marginal cost of r_j units of capacity, or equivalently the opportunity costs $o_j(t, c)$. The boundary conditions are $V_0(c) = 0$ for all $c \geq 0$ and $V_t(c) = -\infty$ for all t and all $c = (c_1, \ldots, c_m)$ such that $c_i < 0$ for at least one i. This value function is investigated intensively by Bertsimas and Popescu (2003), and as mentioned before they present examples showing that the nice monotonicity results of the single leg case do not hold here.

Again, we see that it is optimal to accept a request for j in t given capacity c if and only if $v_j \geq o_j(t, c) = \Delta V_{t-1}(c, r_j)$. Dynamic programming techniques will thus deliver the correct opportunity costs $o_j(\cdot)$, but it is apparent that it will only be possible to compute and store values of $V(\cdot)$ – or equivalently $o_j(\cdot)$ – for very small examples. An obvious alternative of capacity control is to approximate the opportunity costs $o_j(t, c)$ using estimates $o'_j(t, c)$. That is, if a request for j arrives at time t and the vector of remaining capacities is c, we accept if and only if $v_j \geq o'_j(t, c)$. Such an estimate of the opportunity cost is called a *bid price*, and the decision rule is to accept any request that exceeds its bid price.

To lower the storage requirements for the bid prices to a practical level, the values $o'_j(t, c)$ should be given by a function (that can be computed "online" if a request for j arrives given t and c), or a reduced version of an $o'_j(\cdot)$ table should be stored (for some selected values of t and c) such that if a request for j arrives in t and c is the vector of remaining capacities, the required value $o'_j(t, c)$ is interpolated from the stored ones.

2.3.2 Forms of Bid Prices and Their Optimality

The term "bid price" is used in the literature both for resource specific and product specific opportunity cost estimates. For instance, Talluri and van Ryzin (2004b) and Klein (2005) use the term "bid price" for an estimate of the opportunity cost $\omega_i(\cdot)$ of a unit of resource i. A request for product j is then accepted if and only if v_j exceeds (or is equal to) the threshold $\sum_{i=1}^{m} r_{ij}\omega_i(\cdot)$. However, this threshold itself is called the "bid price" e. g. by Bertsimas and Popescu (2003). Actually, they call any threshold $o'_j(\cdot)$ such that a request for product j is accepted if and only if $v_j \geq o'_j(\cdot)$ a (product specific) bid price; and the special cases where $o'_j = \sum_{i=1}^{m} r_{ij}\omega_i(\cdot)$ for some resource specific opportunity cost estimates ω_i – as considered by Talluri and van Ryzin (2004b) and Klein (2005) – are called *additive bid prices*. Bertsimas and Popescu (2003) propose methods to compute non-additive bid prices which will be discussed below.

It is debatable which of the approaches is simpler: In the former case, only m values $\omega_i(t, c)$ are needed (for each t, c), and given these values the product specific bid prices is trivially computed. On the other hand, there is no clue what values of $\omega_i(t,c)$ we should choose, while it is clear that for $o'_j(t,c)$ at most n values have to be considered, namely the values[8] $v_j, j =, 1 \ldots, n$ (this argument is due to Günther et al. 1999). The number of products n may be very large, though.

Bertsimas and Popescu's terminology seems to be reasonable, because if the $o'_j(\cdot)$ are computed in a different, non-additive way, the resulting capacity control policy clearly still belongs to the same class of policies. In this book we will thus differentiate (if necessary) between resource specific bid prices $\omega_i(\cdot)$ and product specific bid prices; however, most of the time "bid price" will mean the latter, i. e. we follow the broader notion used e. g. by Bertsimas and Popescu (2003).

Talluri and van Ryzin (1998) present a very simple example for which any additive bid price policy is suboptimal: We have $m = 2, n = 3, T = 2$ and we assume that any request is at most for $K = 1$ unit of any product, therefore we drop the index k. Demand data, prices, production coefficients and capacities are given by Table 2.3.

Table 2.3: Additive Bid Prices: Counterexample (Talluri and van Ryzin 1998)

r_{ij}	$j=1$	$j=2$	$j=3$	c_i
$i=1$	1	1	0	1
$i=2$	1	0	1	1
v_j	500	250	250	

P_{jt}	$t=2$	$t=1$
$j=1$	0.4	0.8
$j=2$	0.3	0
$j=3$	0.3	0

Obviously an optimal policy would accept the request in period $t = 1$ if it arrives and there is sufficient capacity remaining. Formally:

$$V_1(c) = \begin{cases} 0.8 \cdot 500 = 400 & c = (1,1) \\ 0 & \text{otherwise} \end{cases}$$

The marginal cost of capacity in period $t = 2$ given the initial capacity $c = (1,1)$ is thus $\Delta V_{t-1}(c, r_j) = \Delta V_1((1,1), r_j) = 400$ for all $j = 1,2,3$. An optimal policy would thus accept only the request for

[8] This argument assumes that we do not accept requests if the remaining capacity does not suffice to accommodate it. With overbooking, it might be necessary to explicitly decide that no further request should be accepted (regardless of the product). In this case, an $n+1$-st value (e. g. $\max_{j=1,\ldots,n}\{v_j\}+1$) is necessary.

product 1 (if it arrives) and reject requests for products 2, 3 because $v_1 = 500 > 400 > v_2, v_3$. This yields a total expected revenue of

$$V_2(1,1) = V_1(1,1) + P_{12} \cdot [v_1 - \Delta V_1((1,1), r_1)] = 400 + 0.4 \cdot 100 = 440$$

However, for period $t = 2$ there are certainly no bid prices $\omega_1, \omega_2 > 250$ such that $v_1 = 500 \geq \omega_1 + \omega_2$, i. e. all additive bid price policies are suboptimal.

On the other hand, we have already seen above that for pretty general RM problems an optimal (non-additive) policy using product specific bid prices $\Delta V_t(c, r_j)$ always exists (albeit it is typically computational infeasible). Talluri and van Ryzin (1998, Proposition 1) arrive at a similar conclusion for a much more elaborate dynamic model of the RM problem. They also formally state conditions for the optimality of additive bid prices.

It is interesting to note that a (resource or product specific) bid price can be far away from the true opportunity costs, but the resulting policy can still be optimal (this example is mentioned by Talluri and van Ryzin 1998): Consider an airline single leg RM problem without group bookings, cancellations etc. Suppose that requests arrived in a *high-to-low* order – obviously a "first come first serve" (FCFS) policy is optimal in that case. An FCFS policy can be seen as a bid price policy where all product specific bid prices $o'_j(\cdot) = 0$, or all resource specific bid prices are $\omega_i = 0$ as well. However, for a reasonable instance of an RM problem, the true opportunity costs of allocating product j (like $\Delta V_{t-1}(c, r_j)$ above) of using a unit of resource i will be strictly positive.

The most popular way – and a quite successful approach – to compute additive bid prices is using the shadow prices of linear programs. We will describe this method in detail in the next subsection. We will then discuss the drawbacks of such methods and some more advanced approaches to overcome them.

2.3.3 Additive Bid Prices from Deterministic Linear Programs

Introduction

Model 2.1 is a fairly general LP to describe the capacity control problem, and it elegantly includes cases where we have $m \geq 2$ and/or arbitrary r_{ij}. On the downside, it assumes that demand is a known parameter d_j, and that the amount of product sold is measured on a continuous scale. In most RM applications of interest (airlines, hotels etc.), however, products are sold in discrete units, and demand is a (discrete) random variable D_j. To simplify the problem, set $d_j = E[D_j]$. This is a widely used procedure to replace uncertain quantities with deterministic values in stochastic optimization problems, see e. g. Scholl (2001) for this method as well as for alternatives. Furthermore, we relax the restriction that the amounts of products have to be integer[9] and arrive at our LP, Model 2.1.

If we solve this LP optimally, we obtain partitioned booking limits (with fractional values), but since we are interested in a bid price control we completely ignore these. As a byproduct we get optimal shadow prices (dual variable values) $\mu_i \geq 0$ for the restrictions (2.1). These can be used to compute a bid price for a request of a single unit of product a j as follows:

$$o'_j = \sum_{i=1}^{m} \mu_i r_{ij} \tag{2.14}$$

This is somewhat similar to the computation of the displacement adjusted leg revenues used by DAVN (see Algorithm 2.2). The bid price for a request of $k \geq 0$ units of product j is $k \cdot o'_j$. Observe that (2.14) works fine even for large m and/or arbitrary values of r_{ij}. o'_j is clearly an additive bid price where we estimate the opportunity cost ω_i of a unit of resource i by the shadow prices μ_i.

It is important to stress that o'_j as given by (2.14) depends neither on the remaining capacities c nor on the remaining time t. Since the decision rule is "Accept a request for product j in t given capacities c if and only if $v_j \geq o'_j(t,c)$!", the bid price policy in this case can be expressed by a simple mapping $\nu : \{1,\ldots,n\} \longrightarrow \{0,1\}$ where

$$\nu(j) = \begin{cases} 1 & v_j \geq o'_j \\ 0 & \text{otherwise} \end{cases} \tag{2.15}$$

and we accept any request at any time for all products $j \in N'$ where

$$N' = \{j : \nu(j) = 1\} \tag{2.16}$$

[9] Note that – depending on the r_{ij} – the constraint matrix may be totally unimodular (see e. g. Nemhauser and Wolsey 1988; Schrijver 1986, 2003), implying that an optimal basic solution of the LP will be integer if the input data c_i, d_j is integer as well. Among others this is the case if the LP can be formulated as a network flow problem. A network flow formulation for the airline network RM problem is due to Glover et al. (1982); it can be applied to all airline networks without cycles. This includes e. g. line networks and hub-and-spoke networks with a single hub. See also the discussion by de Boer et al. (2002).

– as long as the remaining capacity suffices to accommodate the request. Williamson (1992, p. 90) formulates: "... inventories are either open to bookings or closed, there are no explicit booking limits for different [products]." In other words, requests for products in N' are controlled in a "first come first serve" (FCFS) fashion. It is interesting to note that this is clearly a form of capacity control with non-exclusive allocation of capacity to products (see Figure 2.5). Bid price controls can easily be implemented in existing CRS that allow for control by nested booking limits only: If the CRS is capable to store a booking limit b_j for each product j we just set

$$b_j = \begin{cases} \min_{\substack{i=1,\dots,m:\\ r_{ij}>0}} \{c_i/r_{ij}\} & j \in N' \\ 0 & \text{otherwise} \end{cases}$$

– or (even simpler), the products $j \in N'$ are not stored at all in the CRS. If the CRS only allows to store a limited number of leg wise booking limits, create a single "leg bucket" (see page 46) for each leg and index all products from N' that use that leg into that bucket. The booking limit of the bucket on any leg i is than simply the capacity c_i.

The concept of bid prices obtained from LP shadow prices has been introduced by Simpson (1989), who proposes to use a network flow formulation (practically identical to the one developed by Glover et al. 1982) to enhance the computational efficiency. The concept was investigated thoroughly e. g. by de Boer et al. (2002), Klein (2005) and Williamson (1992).

Discussion

The method to compute bid prices we just outlined can practically be applied to any industry, as long as the RM problem can be approximated by a deterministic LP – this is usually possible by replacing random variables by certain values and by relaxing integrality constraints. Kimms and Klein (2005), for instance, present a variety of linear models for a broad range of industries.

A bid price policy based on such deterministic LPs is very easy to implement: To compute the shadow prices μ_i basically a forecast of the demand d_j (e. g. $E[D_j]$) is necessary. The resulting LP can be solved efficiently using off-the-shelf software. The storage requirements are low: n bits are practically sufficient (the value of the j-th bit is given by $\nu(j)$). The bid price policy can trivially be expressed as nested, product specific-booking limits b_j (which demands $O(n)$ space) or "leg bucket" booking limits ($O(m)$ space is then necessary for the booking limits). Since the computation of o'_j using (2.14) basically requires to compute a weighted sum; and in practical applications many of the r_{ij} are be zero such that it may even be sufficient just to store the shadow prices μ_i (in $O(m)$ space) and compute o'_j online at each instant where a request for product j arrives. Finally, we can also choose to delete all products $j \notin N'$ and execute a simple FCFS control on the remainder – thereby actually *saving* storage space.

This simplicity with respect to the implementation comes at a cost. The set of products is basically partitioned into two subsets: One set of products for which requests are always rejected, and one set of products that has access to the entire capacity. In the former case, the company has designed and marketed a product of which not a single unit will be sold. Customers will probably be very annoyed if they find that a product that is e. g. heavily advertised by the marketing department is not made available by the revenue managers. On the other hand products with a low yield that belong to the group of "open" products may block capacities that could have been used more profitably later for products of higher value – this was exactly the reason why a capacity control strategy was implemented in the first place. Nested booking limits, in contrast, are a much more precise form of control.

A usual way to tackle the inflexibility of deterministic LP bid prices is to reoptimize the LP on a regular basis using the remaining capacities and updated forecasts of the demand to come. Since capacity is allocated by accepting requests, capacity gets more scarce and thus more valuable. For a typical problem, requests for products with a low yield will arrive earlier, so that high valued demand to come increases relative to lower valued demand, and the opportunity costs of displacing a request increase. Both effects lead to rising shadow prices μ_i, thus products with lower v_j will become closed for sales bit by bit. However, depending on the realization of demand, the number of requests that are actually accepted and the updated forecasts, the shadow prices may also decrease (e. g. if demand between two reoptimizations was unexpectedly low). In this case, a product that has already been closed may become available again – probably an unwanted effect, since it may annoy consumers who purchased products at a high prices before the reoptimization or it may motivate customers to withhold requests in the future in order to await even cheaper offers. If the computational costs of reoptimizations cannot be afforded during the booking process bid price tables can be computed in advance. In either case we approximate bid prices that are varying with t and c. It is interesting to note that there are examples where reoptimization of the LP worsens the performance of the bid price control in revenues terms (see Cooper 2002a,b).

The use of LP shadow prices to estimate opportunity costs is theoretically appealing because the meaning of μ_i is exactly that the objective function value would change by $k \cdot \mu_i$ if the capacity c_i of resource i is increased or decreased by $k \geq 0$ (see e. g. Bertsimas and Tsitsiklis 1997, Winston 1994). However, this statement is actually limited to changes k which are so small that the optimal basis remains unaffected; and the result is limited to LPs, i. e. it does in general not apply to integer problems. If we accept a request for a large and/or integer amount of product j, the opportunity cost estimate o'_j may well be misleading; see Domschke and Klein (2004) for a discussion. Albeit there are some attempts to define the notion of a shadow price for linear integer problem as well – see Domschke and Klein (2004) and the references therein –, none of these methods is actually implemented in solvers that are commercially available, so that using these methods would involve a good deal of programming efforts.

Furthermore, due to an effect that is called *primal degeneracy* the optimal shadow prices may not be unique (this problem is noted by Bertsimas and Popescu 2003 and others). As a consequence, the opportunity costs may not be given correctly by the shadow prices. The aspect of degeneracy is also discussed e. g. by Domschke and Klein (2004) and Talluri and van Ryzin (1999, 1998).

We have already seen that there are very simple examples where any additive bid pricing scheme will be suboptimal. Note however that the additive bid prices (2.14) are asymptotically optimal (Cooper 2002a,b, Talluri and van Ryzin 1998), i. e. if both capacities and demand are scaled by some factor, (2.14) gives optimal bid prices as this factor approaches infinity.

A frequently mentioned issue is that d_j may be a small number. German airline specialists report that $E[D_j]$ may well be smaller than 1. Obviously that would lead to a booking limit $b_j = 0$ for the integer problem; for LP value of b_j may be positive, but then it will be fractional. However, we are not interested in optimal values for b_j (let them be integer or fractional) anyway, we only use the shadow prices.

2.3.4 Advanced Approaches to Compute Additive Bid Prices

We have already mentioned the most important improvement of the bid price method based on deterministic LPs: Frequent reoptimizations help to approximate a variation of the resource specific shadow prices with remaining time t and remaining capacity c. However, this is a rather "ad hoc" method that does not explicitly take the dynamic nature of the demand process into account; and other drawbacks which we have discussed in the previous subsection clearly remain.

One of them is that we use a deterministic model to solve a problem that is of inherently stochastic nature. It is thus natural to use probabilistic models to obtain bid prices. This is not necessarily more complicated than obtaining bid prices from a deterministic LP – consider, for instance, Model 2.3. This model is linear, and if we relax (2.5), we obtain an LP and can derive shadow prices μ_i from the resource restrictions (2.4) as smoothly as before.

Such an approach has been investigated intensively by Williamson (1992) and de Boer et al. (2002) for an airline network without group bookings. Note that Model 2.3 can be simplified considerably for this application. Both find that these *stochastic bid prices* show inferior performance in revenue terms compared with their deterministic counterparts. This is at first surprising, because one would intuitively suspect that an approach that explicitly takes the uncertainty involved into account would perform better. However, as both Williamson and de Boer et al. point out, the deterministic as well as the probabilistic model assumes that capacities are partitioned, while the actual control is nested. As a consequence, the stochastic LP protects more seats for products with high revenues, because the probability that $D_j \geq E[D_j]$ can be quite significant – the deterministic LP simply bounds the booking limit by $E[D_j]$, i. e. the "probability" of more demand is zero. The actual control is a nested one, though and thus the reservation of more seats for higher valued products is not necessary. With the words of Williamson (1992, e. g. on p. 173) the probabilistic model "overprotects" seats. Talluri and van Ryzin (1998) report on further evidence supporting de Boer et al. (2002) and Williamson (1992) and rigorously discuss the reasons on theoretical grounds.

It is important to stress that these results are limited to the simple stochastic model that has been used by Williamson (1992) and de Boer et al. (2002). Higle (2005), for instance, presents much more sophisticated stochastic programs (one of them even explicitly accounts for nesting) and finds that bid prices obtained from these models outperform the classic deterministic ones.

Talluri and van Ryzin (1999) propose another approach to integrate distributional information into the computation of bid prices, yet staying with an easy-to-solve model: If the distributions of $D_j, j = 1, \ldots, n$ are known, we can use a computer simulation to generate realizations

$d_j, j = 1, \ldots, n$ of these random variables (see subsection 5.2.1), use these values as inputs of Model 2.3 and record the shadow prices μ_i. Iterating this procedure N times delivers shadow prices $\mu_i^k, k = 1, \ldots, N$. We then set $\omega_i = \sum_{k=1}^{N} \mu_i^k / N$ and proceed as before. This is not only a very elegant method to include stochastic information in the deterministic LP, but it is also well justifiable on theoretical grounds (see Talluri and van Ryzin 1999). The bid prices obtained by randomized linear programming are thoroughly investigated e. g. by Klein (2005). He finds that the performance of this approach somewhat depend on the context, but he points out that its ratio of (expected) revenue gained to computational time is remarkably good.

Pak and Dekker (2004) and Spengler et al. (2007) pursue a similar approach: Given N simulated realizations of demand, bid prices are computed. The final bid price to be used in actual control is then the average of these bid prices. These references are discussed in some detail in section 6.6.

Klein (2005, 2007) proposes a parametric method to compute resource specific bid prices: Time runs backward from T to 0. Suppose a request arrives at time t. Denote the allocated capacity at t by $\overline{c}_i^t, i = 1, \ldots, m$. Let the random variable D_j be the total demand (over $[T, 0]$) and the random variable D_{jt} be the demand to come from t on (over $[t, 0]$). Define the average capacity demanded of resource i up to time t:

$$u_i^t = \sum_{j=1}^{n} r_{ij} \left(E\left[D_j\right] - E\left[D_{jt}\right] \right)$$

Note that there is a subtle but relevant difference between $\overline{c}_i^t$ and u_i^t: The former is a *constrained* measure of the capacity demand (i. e. after rejecting orders), where the latter is *unconstrained.*

Let $\overline{\omega}_i, \alpha_i, \beta_i \geq 0$ be parameters that guide the computation of the bid price of resource i. Klein (2005, 2007) proposes a time-oriented and resource-oriented way to compute bid prices ω_i^t:

$$\omega_i^t = \overline{\omega}_i + \alpha_i \overline{c}_i^t - \beta_i (T - t) \qquad \text{(time-oriented)}$$
$$\omega_i^t = \overline{\omega}_i + \alpha_i \overline{c}_i^t - \beta_i u_i^t \qquad \text{(resource-oriented)}$$

$\overline{\omega}_i$ is called the base bid price of resource i which is increased or decreased with respect to the allocated capacity and the remaining time t or the unconstrained capacity demand u_i^t.

We certainly have the intuition that bid prices should depend on remaining time and capacity, where bid prices should increase if the remaining time and/or capacity is small. This is modeled in an elegant and efficient way here, making this approach very appealing. Klein uses a linear function with just three parameters per resource to express this, thus $O(m)$ space suffices to store the necessary information and the bid prices can be computed online.

The parameters $\overline{\omega}_i, \alpha_i, \beta_i$ are determined using a simulation optimization approach. Klein (2005, 2007) present results from computational experiments which show that the parametric bid prices perform better in revenue terms than deterministic and randomized linear programming bid prices. On the other hand, the running times of the method are much higher. However, the necessary simulation runs to determine the parameters $\overline{\omega}_i, \alpha_i, \beta_i$ can be undertaken offline before the start of the planning horizon, and albeit reoptimizations are certainly possible, they are – in contrast to other bid prices approaches – not necessary.

2.3.5 Non-Additive Bid Prices and Approximate Dynamic Programming

Resource specific bid prices are appealing from a theoretical point of view, and they are easy to implement. We have just seen that parametric approaches can be used to take the variation of the bid prices with respect to remaining time and capacity into account. The approaches we have discussed in this book allow for an online computation of the product specific bid price (threshold of accepting) o'_j; and they confine themselves to $O(m)$ storage space.

On the other hand, additive bid prices are not able to execute optimal control even for very simple examples like the one depicted in Table 2.3. Talluri and van Ryzin (1998) point out that the failure of additive bid prices are caused by two reasons: The effect of a significant, simultaneous reduction of the capacities of various resources cannot be expected to be equal to the sum of the individual effects in general; and the availability of a product basically depends on the available capacity on the "most constraining" resource – that is, if $r_{ij} > c_i$ for some i, we cannot accept a request for product j even there may be ample capacity left on other resources. This is clearly not a linear relationship between the available capacities and opportunity costs. In fact, in the counterexample, the opportunity costs of accepting a request in period $t = 2$ are independent of the resource consumptions of the products because any acceptance will destroy the possibility to accept a request in period 1.

The RM problem can – in principle – be solved by applying dynamic programming (DP) techniques on the value function (2.13). This leads to optimal bid prices $o_j(t,c) = \Delta V_t(c, r_j)$ and thus to an optimal bid price policy. However, it is not possible to compute $V_t(\cdot)$ for all but the smallest examples – in fact, even if it were possible, the resulting table of $o_j(t,c)$ would be huge and could not feasibly be stored on any computer. We basically have three options to approach this problem. These are obviously not identical, but equivalent with respect to the fact that all try to approximate the optimal policy in a heuristic way:

- Approximate the opportunity costs $o_j(t,c)$ using a function $o'_j(t,c)$ (e. g. a neural network) such that this function depends on a very limited number of parameters (i. e. it can be stored efficiently) and it can be computed online. The capacity control strategy is then to accept a request for product j given t, c if and only if $v_j \geq o'_j(t,c)$.
- Approximate the value function $V_t(c)$ using a function with the same properties as the one discussed for $o'_j(t,c)$. Accept a request for product j given t, c if and only if $v_j \geq V_{t-1}(c) - V_{t-1}(c - r_j)$.
- Denote the optimal action given the state t, c and a request for product j by $a_j(t,c) \in [0,1]$ where $a_j(t,c)$ denotes the probability that the request is accepted[10]. Approximate $a_j(t,c)$ using a function with the same properties as discussed before. If a request arrives for product j given t, c accept/reject according to the approximation $a'_j(t,c)$.

The first two options obviously still constitute bid price policies, while the last is an "indirect" bid price policy in the following sense: Admittedly opportunity cost estimates are no longer explicitly used, but we have seen that the optimal actions – if the true opportunity costs $o_j(t,c)$ were available – would be given by:

$$a_j(t,c) = \begin{cases} 1 & v_j \geq o_j(t,c) \\ 0 & \text{otherwise} \end{cases} \tag{2.17}$$

The third option thus does not estimate the opportunity costs themselves, but tries to mimick the actions of a policy given optimal opportunity costs.

All these options try to approximate exact approaches based on DP. Techniques of approximate DP are usually summarized using the terms Neuro-Dynamic Programming (Bertsekas and Tsitsiklis 1996) or Reinforcement Learning (Sutton and Barto 1998; Spall 2003, chapter 11);

[10] We have seen that the value function (2.13) allows for a deterministic optimal policy such that $a_j(t,c) \in \{0,1\}$, see (2.17. However, a deterministic policy is just a special case of a stochastic one, and it may be useful to allow for non-deterministic heuristics.

see also the edited volumes by Kaelbling (1996) and Si et al. (2004) and the introductory articles and surveys by Kaelbling et al. (1996), Van Roy and Tsitsiklis (1997) and Van Roy (2001). Note that approximate DP techniques are by no means limited to bid price controls; Bertsimas and de Boer (2005), for instance use a simulation optimization approach to approximate a recursive value function using a booking limit control.

Bertsimas and Popescu (2003) present various ideas to approximate the opportunity costs $o_j(t,c)$, and we will briefly summarize some of them here. The first idea is based on the observation that the shadow prices obtained from the deterministic LP can be misleading because the optimal basis may change if the decrease in resource availability is "large". In this case, however, it is possible to reoptimize the LP after having decreased $c_i, i = 1, \ldots, m$ and to compare its optimal revenue with the optimal LP revenue without decreasing the capacity. Formally, suppose that a request for product j arrives in period t given capacity c. Denote the vector of expected demand to come from period t on by d^t. Let $LP(c,d)$ be the optimal objective function value of our deterministic LP (Model 2.1) given capacities $c = (c_1, \ldots, c_m)$ and demands $d = (d_1, \ldots, d_n)$. The opportunity cost estimate of accepting the request is then given by $o_j^{LP}(t,c) = LP\left(c, d^{t-1}\right) - LP\left(c - r_j, d^{t-1}\right)$. A similar idea is used by Pak et al. (2003). Note that this approximation method uses the first of the three options mentioned.

This way of computing opportunity cost estimates controls for changes in the optimal basis, and – as Bertsimas and Popescu (2003) point out – the estimate is unique, regardless of the uniqueness of the dual optimal solutions. On the other hand, the optimal control is still based on a deterministic model, and it is necessary to optimize two LPs "online" whenever a request arrives. However, the second of the LP is only a slightly modified version of the first, and for certain network structures the network flow formulation by Glover et al. (1982) may be used to further enhance the computational efficiency.

To integrate some distributional information into the process Bertsimas and Popescu (2003) pursue a similar approach like Talluri and van Ryzin (1999): If a request for product j arrives given t, c, generate N realizations of the demand vector $d^{t-1,1}, \ldots, d^{t-1,N}$ and compute $o_j^{LP,k}(t,c) = LP\left(c, d^{t-1,k}\right) - LP\left(c - r_j, d^{t-1,k}\right)$ at a time. The opportunity cost estimate is then given by the average: $o_j'(t,c) = \sum_{k=1}^{N} o_j^{LP,k}(t,c)/N$.

A third idea is to use a so-called *rollout policy*. A rollout policy is a standard method for approximate DP, see e. g. Bertsekas and Castanon

(1999), Bertsekas et al. (1997). Its basic idea can be summarized as follows: Let $V(\cdot)$ be any recursive value function that describes the optimal objective function value (maximal expected revenue in our case). If all values of $V(\cdot)$ were given, optimal control would be trivial. Suppose that we confine ourselves to a heuristic policy H, yielding suboptimal values $V^H(\cdot)$. We can then define a new heuristic H' (different from H) that uses the values $V^H(\cdot)$ as if these were the true values $V(\cdot)$, i. e. H' is an "optimal" control given $V^H(\cdot)$ (in contrast to a truly optimal control which would be based on $V(\cdot)$). H' is called a rollout policy (based on H). It is obvious that this process can be iterated, i. e. we can define a rollout policy H'' based on H' and $V^{H'}$ etc.

In our case H could e. g. be the policy using the LP-estimates $o_j^{LP}(\cdot)$ or the randomized policy based outlined above. Denote $V_t^H(c)$ the expected revenue using H from period t on given the remaining capacity c. A rollout policy then uses the estimates $o_j'(t,c) = V_{t-1}^H(c) - V_{t-1}^H(c-r_j)$. It is, however, still computationally infeasible to compute and store all values $V_t^H(c)$; Bertsimas and Popescu (2003) therefore propose to evaluate $V_t^H(c)$ by simulation for only a few values of t, c and interpolate missing values online as needed.

Gosavi et al. (2002, see also Bandla 1998, Gosavi 2004) consider an airline single leg RM problem and apply to it a variant of temporal difference learning (see e. g. Sutton and Barto 1998 for details). Roughly speaking, the algorithm presented by Gosavi et al. (2002) approximates the "reward" that is associated with taking a certain acceptance/rejection decision. In our notation that reward is $v_j - o_j(t,c)$ if a request for product j arrives at time t given capacity c and is accepted.

Cooper and de Mello (2006) consider "hybrid" policies as an approximate DP method. Such policies are based on the observation that an optimal policy (based on exact DP methods) is computationally feasible if the number of periods is small. Therefore a heuristic policy is used until a certain "switching time" after which an optimal policy is used – hence the name "hybrid policy".

2.4 Overbooking

2.4.1 Introduction

The Impact of Overbooking

We have already introduced overbooking in subsection 1.4.1 as the practice of intentionally accepting more requests than can be satisfied using the given (and practically fixed) capacity. For instance, we might accept requests for 110 seats on a given leg despite the fact that the aircraft serving that leg has only got 100 seats. The reasoning behind overbooking is that many customers change their plans (e. g. rebook a flight or depart earlier from a hotel), cancel their request or simply do not show up on time (or not at all) to be serviced. In all cases the company runs the risk to bear opportunity costs due to the loss of potential profit because capacity that was reserved for such requests is not gainfully used. The optimization problem of overbooking is to balance those opportunity costs with the cost of oversales – besides direct costs like fees for customers who voluntarily withdraw from being serviced, penalties, vouchers for drinks, meals, hotels etc. there may be a loss of customer goodwill, especially in the case of downgrades and denied boardings.

The potential of overbooking – at least in the airline industry – is generally considered to be huge: Alstrup et al. (1989) state that the no-show rates are five to twenty percent in Europe and 15 to 30 percent in the US, resulting in an annual revenue loss of around US-$ 50 million for each airline. They estimate that an improved overbooking method could increase the revenue of Scandinavian Airlines by US-$ two million per year. Smith et al. (1992) report that the additional revenue gained by American Airlines due to overbooking is well above US-$ 200 million for each of the years from 1988 to 1990. With overbooking the number of actually empty seats on sold-out flights is now ca. 3 %, while they estimate that it would be around 15 % without. They mention that on average ca. 50 % of all reservations for a flight are cancelled or the reserved passenger does not show up. Klophaus (1998) states that Lufthansa German airlines encountered more than four million no-shows in 1997 (an equivalent of 10,000 empty 747s). Due to overbooking, Lufthansa was able to confirm 630,000 additional requests, yielding ca. DM 250 million extra revenue.

The aforementioned no-show and cancellation rates are easily recorded and thus can be considered to be quite accurate. In this respect there is an obvious potential for overbooking. The revenue gain due to overbooking is somewhat difficult to assess, though. Suzuki (2006, 2002) investigates two aspects of overbooking that may frequently be overlooked in such estimations: Firstly, "bumped" passengers may refrain from traveling with that carrier again, thereby causing future losses in revenue. In an empirical study Suzuki (2002) finds, however, that the current overbooking levels of US carriers yet create gains that outweigh these losses. Secondly, as Suzuki (2006) points out, estimates of the benefits of overbooking are usually based on the assumption that the otherwise empty seats are filled with "new" passengers who e. g. would have purchased tickets of competing airlines, used other modes of transport or not traveled at all if the flight was sold out. He presents a simulation model that also accounts for "flight switchers" who would have bought tickets of the same airline if their requests were declined due to the absence of overbooking. He finds that the true contribution of a passenger accommodated due to overbooking is substantially lower than implied by the assumption of "all new" passengers.

Overbooking alone cannot dissatisfy customers – in fact, overbooking can increase the level of service in at least two ways: By explicitly taking cancellations, no-shows etc. into account, customers whose reservations would have been declined can be serviced, and since successful overbooking policies increase capacity utilization, sales volume and revenues, customers may enjoy lower prices. Even if overbooking leads to oversales, reactions like upgrades may actually raise customer satisfaction. On the other hand, the degree of dissatisfaction can be quite significant, especially if customers are involuntarily denied service. This effect has been investigated empirically by Lindenmeier and Tscheulin (2005, see also Lindenmeier 2004). Wirtz et al. (2003) consider a broader context and present examples for potential conflicts with customers caused by the implementation of capacity control, price differentiation and overbooking. They also report on practical solutions to various of these issues, mentioning e. g. that the efforts of the North American airline industry to actively ask customers to take the next flight (for a compensation, of course) in case of oversales has lead to that 90 % of all passengers denied boarding are now volunteers.

The Relationship of Overbooking and Capacity Control

If there is a capacity control problem to be solved and at the same time overbooking should be implemented, both problems are apparently intimately intertwined. It is though possible that overbooking is practiced without implementing a capacity control policy. * Examples include health care and shared hosting services. In the former case, the capacity control problem is typically avoided by making appointments (the situation thus lacks the necessary condition "operational inflexibility") – except of course for emergencies, where rejecting patients is out of the question. Hence no capacity control problem arises both for emergencies and regular patients. Green et al. (2006), for instance, consider a diagnostic facility at a hospital with three types of patients: outpatients (with scheduled appointments), inpatients (non-emergency cases without appointments) and emergencies. Emergencies have to be treated immediately, but it is allowed to freely choose between in- and outpatients (if one or more patients of each type are waiting for service). Service delays incur a waiting cost, and there is a penalty cost for all patients not treated at the end of the decision period. In principle, however, all patients have to be serviced, i. e. the basic problem is to prioritize waiting patients and to manage the outpatient's appointments.

The capacity control problem is thus indeed absent in most health care facilities like hospitals. Chapman and Carmel (1992), on the other hand, report on a weight control and life-style change center where a mild form of price differentiation was implemented, demanding for a capacity control policy.

In any case, however, patients may cancel their appointments or simply fail to show up on time. We then clearly suffer from some operational inflexibility because existing capacity that was reserved for a particular patient can now has to be used gainfully for others, otherwise it will be wasted. Despite the absence of operational inflexibility (and hence a capacity control problem) under "normal" conditions, overbooking can thus increase the efficiency of the health care provider. This industry is e. g. covered by Kim and Giachetti (2006). Similar observations can be made for shared hosting services, see e. g. Urgaonkar et al. (2002) for an overbooking problem in that business.

A similar reasoning shows that situations with a single product can give rise to overbooking problems while the capacity control problem is trivial: If an airline, say, only sells a single product (i. e. a single itinerary at a single fare) an FCFS strategy is obviously optimal. If there are cancellations and no-shows and overbooking problem nevertheless arises.

2.4.2 Literature Review

In the following we will review the state of the art of overbooking. Since this book focuses on capacity control, we will mainly cover references that deal with overbooking in the context of a RM problem. We will thus concentrate on references stemming from the last 30 years. Surveys of earlier results and reviews of the history of overbooking can be found in Etschmaier and Rothstein (1974) and Rothstein (1971a, 1985). McGill and van Ryzin (1999) survey the literature as well, and very readable introductions to the field of overbooking are given by Phillips (2005, ch. 9) and Talluri and van Ryzin (2004b, ch. 4).

An earlier stream of literature which is nevertheless worth mentioning considers bumping by auctions. Simon (1968) was probably the first to suggest that the selection of passengers to be denied boarding should be solved using an auction. If an airline notices that a particular flight is oversold, it should pass envelopes and bidding forms to passengers, who in turn submit sealed bids denoting the minimum amount of money they are willing to accept as a compensation to wait for the next flight. The lowest bids win, there are as many winning bids as passengers need to be bumped, and the winners are awarded their bids in cash, plus a ticket for the next flight. This proposal has subsequently been discussed by Falkson (1969), Rothstein (1971a), Simon (1970, 1972), Vickrey (1972) and Nagarajan (1979). However, it should be stressed that the procedures discussed in those papers only consider the problem to select those passengers who are denied boarding.

We begin by reviewing the literature dealing with a single product. This case does not give rise to a capacity control problem, but the models and methods for a single product are nevertheless useful to determine the level of overbooking (expressed as *overbooking pads*). Overbooking pads can be seen as a means to solve the overbooking and capacity control problem one after the other. In the next but one section we will then deal with approaches which attempt to solve both problems simultaneously.

Overbooking with a Single Product and Overbooking Pads

An obvious way to deal with both the overbooking and capacity control problem is to determine an *overbooking level* for each and every physical resource, compute the resulting "virtual" capacity, and then choose any of the previously discussed optimization models and methods to solve the capacity control problem using the virtual capacity instead of the physical one. If the overbooking level is 10 %, say, and the physical capacity of a particular resource is 100, capacity control would act as if the actual capacity of that resource was 110. The 10 additional units of resource are called an *overbooking pad*. Determining overbooking pads is sufficient in single product setting (where no capacity control problem is involved), we thus review the literature both on overbooking pads and single product overbooking problems.

Overbooking pads can be determined by setting a lower bound on the service level (i. e. the probability of oversales) or by considering the trade off between the revenue of an (average) product and oversale costs. Such models are e. g. presented by Phillips (2005, ch. 9) and Talluri and van Ryzin (2004b, ch. 4).

Besides the comprehensive treatment in the aforementioned books references dealing with single product overbooking problems or overbooking pads seem to be rare. Rothstein (1971b) considers the overbooking problem of a single product and develops a dynamic model with discrete time, allowing for time varying demand and cancellation probability distributions. This approach is applied to hotels by Rothstein (1974).

Bodily and Pfeifer (1992) deal with the same type of problem and present static decision rules to compute booking limits given various "survival" probability distributions, where "survival" of customers means that they finally show up to be serviced.

Coughlan (1999) roughly describes the overbooking optimization procedures at Aer Lingus. A single leg at a time is considered. Denote the number of products using that leg by n. Let d_j be the historical (mean) demand and s_j be the no-show rate of product j. Compute the overbooking level for the leg: $w = \sum_{j=1}^{n} d_j \left(1 + s_j\right) / \sum_{j=1}^{n} d_j$. The expected revenues and costs using that overbooking levels are then estimated and w is updated until convergence is reached. The resulting "padded" capacity is then used as a basis to compute nested booking limits using the EMSR method.

Recently, the overbooking problem for cargo airlines has received some attention. We have already mentioned that cargo RM has got some unique features in contrast to passenger RM (see page 9). In particular, cargo does not mind taking another route or waiting for hours in inconvenient places for a connecting flight (as long as the final destination is reached on time). With respect to overbooking, this implies that cargo does not care about being denied "boarding" either – cargo can simply be *offloaded* in the case of oversales, and stored somewhere to wait for another flight (possibly on a different route). However, offloading and storing cargo is connected with costs, and the carrier certainly has to take care that all orders are finally satisfied on time. Luo et al. (2005) develop models and corresponding methods that minimize the sum of expected *spoilage cost* (if the overbooking level was to low) and the expected *offloading cost*. They consider a single aircraft and (at most) two dimensions of the cargo (volume and weight). Demand (in the sense of requests before no-shows are revealed) is an aggregate measure, i. e. there are random variables B_v, B_w denoting the total demanded volume and weight, respectively. Remarkably, this implies that there is no capacity control problem to be solved, because the possibility varying values of requests is intentionally not taken into account.

An aggregate formulation like the one by Luo et al. (2005) is examined (and rationalized) by Moussawi and Çakanyıldırım (2005). They argue that usually so many orders are loaded into an aircraft that the size of a typical shipment is negligible compared to the aircraft's capacity and it is justified to assume that cargo is divisible. Furthermore, showing up, loaded and offloaded cargo have the same density (weight per volume) in practice. Both arguments together imply that it is not necessary to distinguish between individual shipments. Moussawi and Çakanyıldırım (2005) consider a profit maximizing approach (where profit is revenues minus offloading costs) and show that the aggregate model is a useful approximation for what they call the "detailed formulation". However, since the revenue of an order of volume v and weight w is effectively given by $a \cdot \max\{v, w\}$ – where v has to be scaled appropriately –, and a similar relation holds for the offloading cost, given the "same density" and "divisible cargo" assumption a capacity control problem does not arise here as well.

Simultaneous Approaches to Capacity Control and Overbooking

Capacity control and overbooking are obviously interdependent: The decision whether or not requests should be accepted beyond the availability of capacity has certainly got implications for capacity control. The capacity control policy, on the other hand, decides which requests are accepted or rejected and thus determines to a great degree the probability of oversales and oversale costs. It is thus reasonable to solve both problems simultaneously.

Booking limit policies are naturally suited for capacity control if overbooking is implemented at the same time – compared with the non-overbooking case, the booking limits will simply be higher. The formulas we presented in subsection 2.2.2 which describe standard and theft nesting can then be applied without any change; it is however interesting to note that these somewhat complicated "bookkeeping" procedures are not necessary with overbooking: Suppose we are given booking limits $b_1, \ldots, b_n$ for n products and simply accept requests as long as the number a_j of confirmed units of product j is not greater than b_j. a_j is possibly altered every now and then by cancellations, rebookings etc. In some point in time, no-shows are revealed and $s_j \leq a_j$ requests for product j have to be satisfied. Note that up to now not a single unit of capacity was assigned to any product, and we thus have a capacity control policy with booking limits, non-exclusive allocation of capacities, but there is no explicit nesting order (see Figure 2.5).

To determine now which requests (if any) are though declined, a bumping procedure is implemented. This procedure at the same time assigns resource capacity to all non-bumped requests. It is important to stress that this step is also necessary if the booking limits are updated in the usual standard or theft nesting way. Like for nested booking limit controls without overbooking we thus need a dynamic model with at least two periods: One *reservation period* in which requests arrive and one *service period*[11], where we decide which requests are finally satisfied.

To summarize, if overbooking is implemented using booking limits, it is not necessary (but possible) to distinguish standard and theft nesting, because capacity will only be assigned to requests after no-shows have been revealed and no further requests arrive. Due to this bumping procedure, a capacity control strategy based on booking limits thus always implicitly belongs to the class of policies that do not assign capacities exclusively to products. Note that a nesting order is not necessary. Many of the problems that we outlined in Table 2.2 are therefore avoided.

It is also possible to implement overbooking by bid prices: Let $o'_j(t, c)$ be the estimated opportunity costs of accepting a request at time t given the vector of remaining capacities $c = (c_1, \ldots, c_m)$. With overbooking, some c_i may be negative. The overbooking level can then be controlled by setting $o'_j(t, c) > v_j$ if some c_i have dropped below certain (non-positive) values. A bid price approach taking overbooking into account is due to Bertsimas and Popescu (2003). To the best of our knowledge, however, this is the only bid price approach so far, and the references we mention in the following are all booking limit approaches to simultaneously solve the capacity control and overbooking problem.

Chatwin (1998) investigates the overbooking problem on a single leg. Models for problems with a single ("stationary") fare and with time-varying ("nonstationary") fares are presented. The latter case includes a capacity control problem, while the former obviously does not. Chatwin (1998) focuses on conditions implying that a booking limit policy is optimal[12]. He presents settings for which optimal booking limits can be derived by dynamic programming and studies the monotonicity properties of the recursive value functions used. Chatwin (1999) ex-

[11] The terms service and reservation period are due to Karaesmen and van Ryzin (2004b). We will discuss this reference in some detail below.

[12] We have already presented an example due to Chatwin (1998) for the non-optimality of booking limit policies on page 65. In this example the use of overbooking was unnecessary, though.

tends this work by allowing for time-dependent cancellation refunds as well, i. e. there is still only a single type of service, but a request (cancellation) at time t will be related with a revenue (cancellation refund) of $f(t)$ resp. $c(t)$ where both $f(t)$ and $c(t)$ are known, piecewise constant functions of time. Chatwin (1999) proves that for this setting an booking limit policy exists such that the booking limit is a piecewise constant function of time as well.

Liberman and Yechiali (1978) examine the overbooking problem at a hotel where they focus on a single type of room sold for a particular night (i. e. they deal with a single resource problem). The room is basically sold for a single fixed price per night (a single product problem in that respect), but Liberman and Yechiali (1978) allow for two remarkable actions on the part of the hotel's management: If bookings are relatively low, rooms are marketed more intensively by increased advertising efforts, introducing a discount etc., leading to additional acquisition costs which actually decrease the contribution margin of the product. If bookings are relatively high (and oversales are likely), management can cancel confirmed reservations (at a penalty cost).

Alstrup et al. (1986) consider a single leg overbooking problem with two types of passengers and apply a stochastic dynamic programming approach. A remarkable feature of their model is that though the aircraft is divided into cabins (one in the front part for the higher class, a second in the rear part for the lower class), the high class cabin in the front can be split between low and high class passengers using a cabin divider. Low fare passengers seated in the front part will thus enjoy a slightly higher level of service due to an increased legroom, but nevertheless they will receive the same meals like the passengers seated in the rear part of the aircraft. A similar problem is studied by Ringbom and Shy (2002). Pak et al. (2003) consider a comparable setting for a network problem. Alstrup et al. (1989) report on a study conducted at SAS and estimate that the improved overbooking method described by Alstrup et al. (1986) could increase the revenue of Scandinavian Airlines by US-$ two million per year.

Koide and Ishii (2005) deal with capacity control and overbooking at hotels. They cover reservations of a specific room type for a single night, i. e. the scope of the paper is a RM problem with a single resource. That particular room type is rented at two different rates. Reservations and cancellations follows a "low to high"-like pattern.

Zhao and Zheng (2001) study a single leg airline RM problem with two products (a low and a high fare) and three types of customers: Two types who will only buy the low or the high fare, respectively, and a flexible type, who will buy the low fare if it is available and the high fare otherwise. An extension of their model takes no-shows and overbooking into account.

Belobaba (1987b, 1989) presents an extension of his EMSR heuristic (see page 55 ff.) to incorporate overbooking levels ("overbooking factors"). These overbooking levels are assumed to be given and a method to determine them is not presented.

Subramanian et al. (1999) consider the single leg airline RM problem with an arbitrary number of products. They show that the optimal policy is a booking limit policy, where the optimal booking limits depend in general on the remaining time and the number of accepted requests (see our discussion on page 62). Furthermore, they show that the optimal policy is in general not monotone and the optimal nesting order is not necessarily given by the fares.

Brumelle and Walczak (2003) extend the approach due to Subramanian et al. (1999) by considering group bookings ("batch arrivals") in addition. They also show that in general the value function (and hence the optimal policy) is not monotone.

The absence of monotonicity implies that it will be impossible to compute or store the optimal policy for all but the smallest examples. Gosavi et al. (2002, see also Bandla 1998, Gosavi 2004) thus pursue a heuristic approach for the overbooking problem on a single leg based on an approximate dynamic programming technique called temporal difference learning (see subsection 2.3.5 for an overview of capacity control by approximate dynamic programming). The aim of temporal difference learning is to approximate the acceptance/rejection decisions of the optimal policy. In this sense the approach by Gosavi et al. (2002) is not a booking limit policy, and the authors intentionally make no attempt to examine the structure (or type) of an optimal policy.

Amaruchkul et al. (2006) consider a cargo RM problem on a single leg where demand can be categorized into a finite number of types. The volume V_{il} and weight W_{il} of the l-th request of type i are random variables. A revenue function r_i is associated with each type i, thus in contrast to the previously mentioned references on cargo overbooking (see page 85) a capacity control problem has to be solved. The model allows for that the (random) volume and weight showing up at departure differs from the volume and weight announced at the time of request, i. e. the carrier faces the problem of "partial show-ups" (and, as an extreme case, no-shows). Consequently, overbooking is simultaneously taken into account.

Shlifer and Vardi (1975) present optimality conditions for one and two types of passengers booking on a single flight leg, and for a network consisting of two consecutive legs. In the latter case, there is only one type of passengers for each of the three itineraries. El-Haber and El-Taha (2004) also consider two-leg networks and pursue an approach similar to Subramanian et al. (1999). They also outline an extension to networks of three or more consecutive legs (line networks).

Karaesmen and van Ryzin (2004b, see also Karaesmen 2001) consider an overbooking problem with an arbitrary number of "reservation classes" (products). Their approach can roughly be described as follows: Bookings arrive during a *reservation period*. A request for reservation class $i = 1, \ldots, n$ is accepted if and only if the number of accepted reservations x_i is not greater than the "overbooking level" (booking limit) u_i. In the following *service period*, the number of no-shows is revealed and surviving requests are assigned to "inventory classes" $j = 1, \ldots, m$ with finite capacities c_j. If a reservation class i request is assigned to inventory class j a profit a_{ij} (or cost if $a_{ij} \leq 0$) results – a request for a rental car may for instance be satisfied by a larger or smaller car, resulting in an increase or decrease of customer satisfaction reflected by the a_{ij}. Survivors are assigned to inventory classes such that the sum of the a_{ij} is maximized (this is a transportation problem which can be solved easily). One of the inventory classes is a "virtual" one with practically unlimited capacity such that service is in fact denied to requests which are assigned to that particular class.

The setting considered by Karaesmen and van Ryzin (2004b) can be seen as a capacity control/overbooking problem on a single group of substitutable resources. Karaesmen and van Ryzin (2004a, see also Karaesmen 2001), on the other hand, jointly solve the capacity control and overbooking problem on a network (with two or more resources). Substitution of capacities is not taken into account, though.

Gosavi et al. (2007) develop a simulation optimization approach for airline RM problems with two or more legs and an arbitrary number of products. Their approach is "model free" and thus allows for a variety of demand and cancellation processes.

3

Recent Advances in Revenue Management

3.1 Introduction

3.1.1 Problems with Substitution and/or Multimodal Products

Thus far we have discussed models and methods of capacity control and overbooking that are already well established RM tools. However, almost every approach which we have discussed up to now was implicitly based on the following two assumptions:

- The mode of production is fixed and known to the customer before the time of purchase. For instance, if a customer buys a ticket for a single seat from Dresden to San Francisco we have assumed that the itinerary and the travel times are explicitly known to both the passenger and the airline at the time the ticket is bought. Speaking more generally, for each product $j = 1, \ldots, n$ and each resource $i = 1, \ldots, m$ a known constant $r_{ij} \geq 0$ was given denoting the amount of resource i that is necessary to deliver a unit of product j.
- Because the mode of production was fixed, there were no decisions to be made for the supplier (except of course whether to accept or reject an arriving request). Similarly, customers did not make choices either – we have assumed that an arriving customer has got a preference for a certain designated product j and if j should not be available she just exits the market.

In this chapter we will relax one or both of these assumptions. We begin with so called *choice-based RM* problems which arise in situations where customers make choices, all else being like in the previous chapter. More precisely, the attributes of all products are fixed before purchase, customers observe the set of available products (the so called *offer set*) as they arrive to make a request and choose a product from the offer set (or decide not to purchase at all and exit). In retailing or similar industries where customers arrive and choose from inventory on hand – such situations are frequently considered for pricing approaches – we speak of *substitutable demand*. Under these circumstances availability of products is typically not driven by a capacity control policy but rather by influencing demand (e. g. by dynamic pricing) such that inventories are depleted in an organized way; see our discussion on page 20.

If the mode of production is not defined before purchase (i. e. multiple modes of production are possible and either the customer or the supplier chooses a mode of production later) we speak of *multimodal products* (Petrick and Klein 2005) – in contrast to *unimodal products* where the mode of production is fixed before purchase. Gallego and Phillips (2004) use the term *specific product* for unimodal products. In this book, we will use both expressions interchangeably.

If a customer purchases a multimodal product one option is that she chooses which resources are used and when (i. e. the mode of production is defined by the consumers). An example (which we have already mentioned on page 9) is German Railways (Deutsche Bahn, DB), where a regular ticket does not oblige to take a particular train at a designated time but the passengers may (more or less freely) choose the actual departure time. To the best of our knowledge RM problems with this way of customer behavior have not yet been discussed in the literature, but we propose the term *flexible customers* for such situations (DB speaks of "uncontrolled traffic"). It is interesting to note that DB's RM department accounts for uncontrolled traffic by simply subtracting the expected number of flexible passengers from the number of available seats in a particular train. Then, "conventional" RM methods are applied to control the remaining capacity (Köhler 2005).

Both choice-based RM/substitutable demand and flexible customers are subsumed under the term *customer-driven substitution*. It is important to stress that this term refers to the fact that some final choices are made by customers. It goes without saying that their choices are limited (but not precisely "driven") by previous decisions of the supplier, in particular those to offer or not to offer certain products.

If we reverse the situation and assume that the supplier makes choices – besides the decisions connected with capacity control and overbooking as we have discussed them in the previous chapter – we speak of *supplier-driven substitution*. Based on the first assumption we can distinguish situations with uni- and multimodal products.

In the latter case, the decision to define the mode of production is explicitly reserved for the supplier. For instance, the aforementioned trip from Dresden (DRS) to San Francisco (SFO) involves connecting either in Munich (MUC) or in Frankfurt/Main (FRA). Thus far we have assumed that a passenger chooses one of the itineraries. Now we also allow that the customer agrees to that the carrier defines the exact route after purchase. If the supplier commits to a particular mode of production (a route in this case) and notifies the customer immediately after purchase, this is called *routing control* (in reference to the airline industry). If the supplier reserves some flexibility and notifies the customers well after purchase (e. g. shortly before production begins and uncertain demand has mostly been revealed) we speak of *flexible products*.

It is important to stress the distinction between flexible products and e. g. upgrades in car rental companies: In the former case, the customer demands a compact car and the supplier agrees to deliver exactly this type of vehicle at the designated date and location. If the supplier is not able to deliver a compact car due to oversales or the inherent uncertainty of capacity in the car rental business (see page 12) and provides a midsize car, this is simply an upgrade. Oversales and other circumstances leading to (unplanned) upgrades are typically considered to be nasty events associated with excessive costs and roughly speaking (but somewhat simplifying) our goal was to keep the probability of such incidents very low. We might say that if the mode of production has to be changed after purchase because of oversales or the like, this is a (usually negative) surprise for the seller and/or the customer.

The possibility of such upgrades is of course a very relevant aspect which has to be taken into account for capacity control and overbooking methods, but it is fundamentally distinctive from a situation where customers are indifferent between two or more options and agree with the supplier that their requests can be satisfied e. g. either by a compact or a midsize car. In the such a case, for instance, the supplier will have to pay a certain premium for the additional flexibility, i. e. the indifferent customer will enjoy a lower price. This implies that flexible products have to be designed and priced very carefully to avoid cannibalization of customers who would have bought the existing specific products (at a higher price) if the multimodal products had not been available. In the case of upgrades it is finally uncertain whether an upgrade will become necessary or not, hence it is uncertain whether the supplier has to bear the costs associated with it – in contrast to the certain price premium the supplier has to pay for the additional degrees of freedom associated with flexible products.

If the actual mode of production is fixed before purchase and there can still be some opportunities for the supplier to make decisions: Analogously to the substitutable demand case where customers e. g. decide which goods to pick from a retailer's shelf we can think of *substitutable inventories* where suppliers decide which type of product is used to satisfy a certain request given the amounts in stock. In this case the production already has taken place, thus its mode is trivially fixed before purchase. A typical setting of such a problem will assume that inventories are allocated to requests after demand has been revealed and a fundamental part of the problem is to decide about the amount of initial inventory.

It is necessary to emphasize some distinctive characteristics between substitutable inventories and flexible products: In the former case we are typically dealing with a given amount of finished products (i. e. physical goods). Then, uncertain demand is revealed fully or in part and we have to allocate the given inventories to demands according to certain rules (e. g. demand for a 1.8 GHz processor may be satisfied using a 2 GHz processor but not vice versa), where it may be allowed to leave some demand unsatisfied (at a cost, e. g. holding costs) to save some inventories for subsequent periods. Typically there is a one-to-one correspondence between units of the substitutable products, i. e. exactly one unit of product j is necessary to satisfy a demand for one unit of product $i \neq j$. An important part of the problem is to determine the initial inventory of each and every product.

Problems with flexible products, on the other hand, do not feature substitutable products but substitutable *resources*. In principle, demand for a unit of a certain product (e. g. a flight from Dresden to San Francisco) is – in the absence of overbooking – satisfied with a unit of that exact product, but the supplier decides which resources are actually used to provide the product (i. e. the DRS-MUC/MUC-SFO legs or the DRS-FRA/FRA-SFO legs). Finally, the amount of resources available is assumed to be given, i. e. the capacity investment decisions have already taken place and are out of scope of the problem at hand.

Table 3.1 summarizes the various kinds of problems we have outlined so far based on the distinction between customer and supplier-driven substitution on the one hand and the time to define the mode of production on the other hand.

Table 3.1: Categorizing Problems with Substitution and/or Multimodal Products

	Before purchase, the mode of production is	
	fixed (unimodal products)	*open (multimodal products)*
Customer-driven substitution	Choice-based RM, Substitutable Demand	Flexible Customers
Supplier-driven substitution	Substitutable Inventory	Routing Control, Flexible Products

It is important to stress that Table 3.1 only shows how problems can be categorized based on the two dimensions. It is however possible to consider mixtures of those "pure" problems – Gallego et al. (2004a), for instance, deal with a problem with flexible products and take as well into account that passengers observe the offer set and choose between flexible and specific products.

3.1.2 Relationship to the Field of RM

A typical problem with substitutable demand or inventory involves stocks of finished goods; the operational flexibility is thus not very limited – some authors even allow for backlogging of demand. As mentioned before, the situation is typically considered as a "newsvendor-like" problem where the fundamental decision is to determine the initial amount of capacity or inventory and – in the case of substitutable inventory – to allocate the given capacity to realized demand. Such problems are certainly related to the field of RM (namely choice-based RM) – in particular, some problems may appear as subproblems in typical RM settings. Consider, for instance, a car rental company: Capacity is uncertain, so after capacity control decisions have been made a rental station may decide to get cars from other stations which expect a relatively low demand. After both the uncertain demand and the uncertain capacity are revealed, capacity is assigned to orders. We thus basically have a substitutable inventory problem: Capacity is purchased in an investment phase (with random yields in this case) and subsequently allocated to demand. This example is e. g. mentioned by Netessine et al. (2002).

However, problems where inventory decisions are to be made are somewhat out of scope of RM in the strict sense as it is considered in this book (see our discussion on page 20). The reader interested in substitutable inventory is thus referred to Bassok et al. (1999), Bitran and

Dasu (1992), Hsu and Bassok (1999), Netessine et al. (2002), Shumsky and Zhang (2004) and Van Mieghem and Rudi (2002), where transshipments of stocks are also allowed, as well as Bish and Wang (2004), who also include pricing decisions in their model. Noteworthy in this context is the overbooking approach of Karaesmen and van Ryzin (2004b) where it is similarly assumed that demands are allocated to capacity after no-shows have been revealed and it is obvious whether oversales have occurred or not (see page 90).

Substitutable demand problems at retailers etc. where customers choose among the available products and the fundamental problem is as well to determine the initial stock levels are e. g. covered by Agrawal and Smith (2003), Anupindi et al. (1998), Bell (2001), Mahajan and van Ryzin (2001b), Netessine and Rudi (2003) and Smith and Agrawal (2000). Parlar (1988) considers a game theoretic approach for a problem with two competing firms which offer a substitutable product and customers choose between firms. Mahajan and van Ryzin (2001a) extended this approach to multiple competitors.

Since there are no references dealing with flexible customers the sequel of the chapter will be devoted to choice-based RM and flexible products. In section 3.2 we deal with the former and present models and methods which take into account that customers make choices depending on the set of products which is available at the time of their request. As a consequence our decisions to open or close products for sale influence the demand process – an issue that we have neglected so far. Our exposition complements the work of Kimms and Müller-Bungart (2006), who present a very readable introduction to the field of choice-based RM. In section 3.3 we consider routing control and flexible products.

3.1.3 Further Recent Advances of the Field

There are yet other novel aspects about RM that have only recently attracted attention from researchers. These include RM problems with cooperating firms, giving rise to so called *alliance RM* problems; see e. g. Belobaba and Darot (2001), Boyd (1998), Domschke et al. (2005) and Vinod (2005). Another new area of RM research includes RM in competitive environments. An earlier simulation study is due to Belobaba and Wilson (1997); however, RM under competition has not attracted much interest until the work of Chen (2000), Dasci (2003), Netessine and Rudi (2003), Netessine and Shumsky (2005) and Froeb and Tschantz (2003), who consider a pricing problem with two competing firms in the context of the Princess-Carnival cruise line merger (see page 11).

Gallego (2004) and Gallego et al. (2004b) have proposed another innovative approach which they term RM of *callable products*. If a customer purchases one of the callable products the supplier reserves the right to later "rebuy" the product to use the regained capacity for other, higher yielding products. Of course, the supplier will have to pay the customer a "recall price" (which has to be higher than the original purchase price); and callable products will have to be deeply discounted (compared to non-callable products) because customers will expect a premium for their potential loss of utility.

While both alliance RM, RM under competition and callable products are very interesting and new developments, there are not many references to discuss yet and we thus refrain from covering them in this book in more detail.

3.2 Choice-based RM

3.2.1 Introduction

A typical assumption for capacity control models is that our decisions to accept or reject requests for certain products do not influence demand. In other words we assume that each of our clients is interested in only one particular product and if the request is rejected the prospective consumer just exits the market. This model of customer behavior is called *independent demand* (ID) because the demand process is independent of our decisions (see section 5.1 for this and other ways to categorize demand models).

The ID assumption seems to be a bit simplifying because customers may obviously react in many different ways if their requests are rejected:

- Rejected customers may be willing to buy a product at a higher price (e. g. a flight from Dresden to Frankfurt at € 200 if tickets for € 109 are not available). This is called a vertical shift (Belobaba 1987b, 1989), an upgrade (Brumelle et al. 1990), diversion (Belobaba and Weatherford 1996, Zhao and Zheng 2001) or a buy up (Andersson 1998).
- Consumers frequently purchase a slightly different product from the same company if the exact product which they demanded in the first place is not available. Passengers, for instance, may choose to travel at twelve o'clock if no tickets (at prices which they find acceptable)

are available for the eight o'clock flight. This is called a horizontal shift (Belobaba 1987b, 1989) or recapture (Andersson 1998).

- Some customers will acquire a similar competitive product (e. g. a flight with carrier B instead of A). This is called deviation (Andersson 1998) or overflow (Netessine and Shumsky 2005).
- Finally customers may buy a substitute good (e. g. they travel by rail instead of by air), or they completely give up their plans and exit the market.

Despite this abundance of customer reactions the ID assumption is underlying almost all models and methods which we have discussed in the previous chapter. Assuming ID is quite convenient because it allows to model the demand for product j as a simple exogenous random variable D_j (or analogously a as stochastic process with fixed and known properties, e. g. in the case of micro period models). If we explicitly consider buy up behavior or the like, demand for a certain product can no longer be described by parameters with known values but are a result of our decisions.

ID can be somewhat justified by fencing (see page 5), i. e. the efforts of the seller to avoid that customers with a high willingness to pay can purchase products with a low price (e. g. Saturday night stay over restrictions for discounted airline tickets). This should prevent buy ups because ideally a customer will demand a certain product if and only if the price matches her willingness to pay, i. e. she does not qualify for similar product which is available at a lower price and is not willing to buy up to a product which is offered at a higher price.

However, we cannot expect that the means of fencing are always implemented so perfectly that buy up behavior can be neglected; and fencing certainly does not preclude horizontal shifts or deviation. Furthermore, buy ups reduce the positive effect of overbooking (Suzuki 2006) – in some cases it may be useful to overbook less and close fare classes earlier to encourage buy ups and thus increased revenues without the risk of oversales. Finally, neglecting choice behavior can lead to very undesirable results in the long run, as a thorough analysis by Cooper et al. (2006) shows: They consider a single leg airline RM problem with just two fares. It is reasonable to assume that some customers who purchase the low fare (if it is available) are willing to buy up to the high fare as well. As a consequence, the observed (constrained or unconstrained) demand for the low fare will be higher than the "pure" low fare demand, i. e. the demand by passengers who are only willing or able to buy the low fare. If more low fare bookings are accepted (e. g. because the protection level of the high class is lowered), more low fare tickets will be sold at the expense of the high fare. Since most RM models assume independent demand, the forecasted high yield demand will decrease, the high fare protection level will thus be decreased even more, and the process iterates. The result is a down spiral with ever decreasing protection levels for the high class and consequently decreasing high yield sales and revenues.

In the remainder of this section we will discuss various approaches to incorporate customer choice behavior. We will disregard deviation to competitive or substitute products. Our exposition will begin with airline single leg problems – in this case the only relevant aspects of behavior are buy ups. A simple means of accounting for this kind of action are buy up probabilities. We discuss two types of policies with such probabilities, namely booking limit policies and so called offer set policies – the latter type of policy is new in comparison to the previous chapter because under ID it was not necessary to explicitly consider the impact of the set of products which are (not) offered.

As mentioned in section 1.5, this book focuses on capacity control. However, we are only aware of two references that deal with choice-based pricing anyway: Zhang and Cooper (2005b), whose approach will be discussed on page 110, and Bitran et al. (2006). The latter consider a pricing problem of a retailer. Inventories of substitutable products are already given, consumers observe the set of available products (i. e. those which have not already stocked out) and choose among them according to a choice model based on the price set by the retailer. A remarkable feature of this approach is that two types of customer-driven substitution are taken into account: Inventory-driven substitution – stock outs force customers to choose other products (or to leave the store) – and price-driven substitution – consumers may decide to purchase a different product because they find their first choice to expensive.

3.2.2 Airline Single Leg Problems

Booking Limit Policies for Single Leg Problems with Buy Up Probabilities

Belobaba (1987b, 1989) extended his EMSR-heuristic to incorporate vertical shifts using buy up probabilities. Recall the basic formulas (2.9), (2.11) of the EMSR method without buy ups: The expected marginal revenue of the p-th seat for product j is defined as

$$EMSR_j\left(p\right) = v_j \cdot P_j\left(D_j \geq p\right)$$

where v_j and D_j are the revenue and random demand of product j, respectively. Product 1 is nesting highest and n is lowest. Then set the number of seats p_{1j}^k that are protected for product $k = j+1, \ldots, n$ and from j to the smallest number satisfying

$$v_j \geq EMSR_k \left(p_{1j}^k\right)$$

Now denote the probability that a customer whose request for fare $j > 1$ has been rejected buys up to $j - 1$ by u_j (Belobaba 1987b, 1989 only considers buy ups to the next higher fare class). It is assumed that u_j is known and constant. If $u_j > 0$ we will want to protect an additional number of q_j seats for $j-1$ from j to encourage buy ups. The value of protecting the q_j-th seat can then be computed as follows: This seat can be used for a customer buying up to $j - 1$, yielding v_{j-1} with probability u_j. If there is no buy up – this happens with probability $1 - u_j$ – the seat can employed to a class $j - 1$ customer in the usual way. We thus set q_j to the smallest number satisfying

$$v_j \geq u_j v_{j-1} + (1 - u_j) \, EMSR_{j-1} \left(p_{1j}^{j-1} + q_j\right) \tag{3.1}$$

As Hopperstad (2000) points out (albeit in an other context) this and other models with buy up probabilities have got a "self-fulfilling prophecy feature": If the buy up probability u_j gets larger so does the additional protection q_j. The lower fares will thus close earlier and the fraction of buy ups may indeed be (somewhat) higher. However, it goes without saying that this effect decays in practice if the protection level q_j is set to a very high value.

Brumelle et al. (1990) prove that the decision rule (3.1) is optimal for $n = 2$ (recall that EMSR delivers the optimal booking limits for the two highest products as well for the case without buy ups). As they note on p. 190, Pfeifer (1989) basically derives the same result.

Bodily and Weatherford (1995) extend the methods by Pfeifer (1989) and Brumelle et al. (1990) to obtain a heuristic decision rule for problems with three or more fare classes. Belobaba and Weatherford (1996) subsequently outperformed this method by incorporating buy up probabilities in the EMSRb (Belobaba 1992, see page 59 in this book).

Botimer and Belobaba (1999) propose a modeling framework where the burden of a customer to accept the additional restrictions imposed on fare classes with lower prices is given by a cost function. Demand is a deterministic function of the prices and these costs. Booking limits are used to encourage buy ups.

Zhao and Zheng (2001) consider a problem with two fares and three types of customers: Two "rigid" types (who will only demand either the lower or the higher fare) and a "flexible" type, who prefers the lower fare but will buy up if the low fare class is closed. A remarkable feature of Zhao and Zheng's model is that the discount fare class cannot be reopened once it has been closed. Under these assumptions the optimal policy is a protection level policy, i. e. the discount fare class should be closed if the remaining capacity drops below a certain level. The protection levels depend on the remaining time to departure and are in general not monotone. An extension of the model accounts for no-shows and cancellations by overbooking.

Offer Set Policies for Single Leg Problems

buy ups to class j may occur if we close a lower fare class $i > j$. Speaking more generally demand for a product j depends on the subset S of products that is offered, the so called *offer set*. It is thus natural to consider the offer set S as a decision variable.

There is a noteworthy link between offer sets and bid prices policies: We have demonstrated that bid prices policies partition the set of all products $\{1,\ldots,n\}$ into the set N' of products which are offered (and has access to the entire available capacity) and the complement $\{1,\ldots,n\}\setminus N'$ which is not at all available – see (2.15), (2.16). However, the "offer set" N' of bid price policies was the result of the decision rule that a product j is available if and only if $v_j \geq o'_j$ where o'_j is the bid price (opportunity cost estimate) of product j. With choice-based RM the offer set is explicitly made a decision variable.

In the following we discuss two models for single leg airline RM problems using offer sets as decision variables. Both are extensions of the micro period model by Lee and Hersh (1993).

You's (2001) Model

Recall the assumptions used by Lee and Hersh (1993, see page 61 in this book): The time horizon is partitioned into T micro periods, i. e. T is so large that there is at most one request per period. Time runs backwards from T to 0. $P_{jt} \geq 0, j = 1,\ldots,n, t = 1,\ldots,T$ is the probability that a request for product j arrives in period t. Denote the maximum expected revenue from period t on with a capacity of c seats remaining by $V_t(c)$. As before 1 is the index of the most expensive product and n denotes the lowest fare.

Similar to the references we have discussed in the previous paragraphs You (2001) uses buy up probabilities to account for vertical shifts: Let $u_{ij} \geq 0$ be the probability that a passenger denied fare class $i = 2, \dots, n$ buys up to $j = 1, \dots, i-1$. Naturally we require that $\sum_{j=1}^{i-1} u_{ij} \leq 1$; and if this inequality is strict there is a positive probability that a customer exits if class i is not available. Note that u_{ij} is constant, implying that if class i and j are both unavailable an arrival demanding class i is lost with probability u_{ij} – in particular the fraction of customers u_{ij} that buy up from i to j will not "further buy up" to one of the classes $1, \dots, j-1$. This greatly simplifies the analysis of the model.

Let $U_t^i(c)$ be the maximum expected revenue from period t on with a capacity of c seats remaining if product $i = 1, \dots, n$ is not available. Define the *complete sets*[1] $A_j = \{1, \dots, j\}$ for all $j = 1, \dots, n$. For the convenience of notation let $A_0 = \emptyset$. $U_t^i(c)$ is then given for all $t = 1, \dots, T$, $i = 1, \dots, n$ and $c \geq 1$ by

$$\begin{aligned} U_t^i(c) &= \max_{S \subseteq A_{i-1}} \left\{ \sum_{j \in S} u_{ij} \left(v_j + V_{t-1}(c-1) \right) + \left(1 - \sum_{j \in S} u_{ij} \right) V_{t-1}(c) \right\} \\ &= V_{t-1}(c) + \max_{S \subseteq A_{i-1}} \left\{ \sum_{j \in S} u_{ij} \left[v_j - \Delta V_{t-1}(c) \right] \right\} \end{aligned} \tag{3.2}$$

where $\Delta V_{t-1}(c) = V_{t-1}(c) - V_{t-1}(c-1)$ is (as before) the marginal cost of capacity. For all i the boundary conditions are $U_0^i(c) = 0$ for all c and $U_t^i(0) = 0$ for all t. We thus conclude that $U_t^i(c) \geq 0$ for all i, t and c.

It is important to stress that determining the maximizer $S \subseteq A_{i-1}$ is trivial if the value $\Delta V_{t-1}(c)$ is readily available because u_{ij} is a constant not depending on S. An optimal offer set is therefore given by $S = \{j \in A_{i-1} : u_{ij} [v_j - \Delta V_{t-1}(c)] \geq 0\}$. Because $v_1 > \dots > v_n$ and $\Delta V_{t-1}(c)$ is a constant independent of S and i we have:

$$\begin{aligned} j \in S \Rightarrow v_j \geq \Delta V_{t-1}(c) &\Rightarrow v_k \geq \Delta V_{t-1}(c), k = 1, \dots, j-1 \\ &\Rightarrow k \in S, k = 1, \dots, j-1 \end{aligned}$$

As a consequence, the maximizing offer set S is always a complete set $A_j \subseteq A_{i-1}$ where $j = j_t^i(c)$ is the cheapest fare class we offer given a request for $i = 2, \dots, n$ in t given capacity c:

[1] This term is used by Talluri and van Ryzin (2004a), a reference which we will discuss next.

$$j_t^i(c) = \max\{k \in A_{i-1} : v_k \geq \Delta V_{t-1}(c)\}$$

To simplify the notation in the following define $j_t^1(c) = 0$ for all t and c.

Given a request for product j it is obviously optimal to accept if and only if $v_j + V_{t-1}(c-1) \geq U_t^j(c)$. $V_t(c)$ is thus recursively defined as follows for all $t = 1, \ldots, T$ and $c \geq 1$:

$$V_t(c) = \left(1 - \sum_{i=1}^{n} P_{it}\right) V_{t-1}(c) + \sum_{i=1}^{n} P_{it} \max\left\{U_t^i(c), v_i + V_{t-1}(c-1)\right\}$$

$$= V_{t-1}(c) + \sum_{i=1}^{n} P_{it} \cdot \max\left\{\max_{S \subseteq A_{i-1}} \left\{\sum_{j \in S} u_{ij}\left[v_j - \Delta V_{t-1}(c)\right]\right\}, v_i - \Delta V_{t-1}(c)\right\}$$

$$= V_{t-1}(c) + \sum_{i=1}^{n} P_{it} \max\left\{\sum_{j=1}^{j_t^i(c)} u_{ij}\left[v_j - \Delta V_{t-1}(c)\right], v_j - \Delta V_{t-1}(c)\right\}$$

As before the boundary conditions are $V_0(c) = 0$ for all c and $V_t(0) = 0$ for all t. We see from the last formula that the optimal offer set if a request for product i arrives in t given capacity c is basically determined by accepting the request or choosing the cheapest available fare class $j_t^i(c) < i$.

You (2001) thoroughly investigates the monotonicity properties of the value function and the structure of the optimal policy. The results can be formulated as follows: For each period t and each product i there exists a critical capacity $c_t(i)$ such that a request in t for i with c seats remaining is accepted if and only if $c \geq c_t(i)$, i. e. $c_t(i)$ is a time dependent protection level. If a request is rejected, the cheapest product $j_t^i(c) < i$ determining the offer set can analogously be found: If $c < c_t(i)$ the request is rejected and there exists critical capacities $\gamma_t(i,j)$ such that $j^i(t) = j$ if and only if $\gamma_t(i, j-1) < c \leq \gamma_t(i,j)$. Again, $\gamma_t(i,j)$ is something like a "protection level".

Note that these results are somewhat natural extensions of those due to Lee and Hersh (1993). You (2001) subsequently also considers group bookings and again obtains results analogous to those of Lee and Hersh (1993): Critical booking capacities do not longer exist, but the optimal policy can be formulated as a set of critical decision periods.

Talluri and van Ryzin's (2004a) Model

You's model is still based on a rough approximation of choice behavior: If product i is not available a fraction u_{ij} of passengers buy up to j. If this is also not available, they exit. Modeling choices made by customers in a more subtle way would assume that the customers observe the offer set $S \subseteq \{1, \ldots, n\}$ and choose among the available products. The choice process would be described by a choice model, e. g. based on utility maximization assumptions.

It is important to stress that such a way of modeling customer choice has got implications which may seem counterintuitive and are novel in comparison to the ID models as well as the models with buy up probabilities we have discussed so far (including You 2001). For instance, the following holds for policies derived from those "classic" models: If a request for fare class j is accepted all more expensive products should be available as well. This is the basic idea behind nested booking limits; and it was easy to see that the assumptions of You (2001) also implied that all optimal offer sets are complete sets $A_i = \{1, \ldots, i\}$ (recall that product 1 is nesting highest and n nests lowest). However, if we assume that customers always observe the offer set and then make a choice we can easily see that this is not necessarily the case. Consider, for instance, an example with $n = 3$. It can be optimal to offer the incomplete set $\{1, 3\}$ if enough customers who buy the most expensive product 1 under these circumstances would buy the cheaper product 2 if it was available and/or customers who now purchase the cheapest product 3 would not buy 2 anyway even if it was available (i. e. there are no buy ups from 3 to 2). We will soon demonstrate this more formally.

Talluri and van Ryzin (2004a) develop a choice-based model for the airline single leg case allowing for complex choice behavior. It is a micro period model as well, similar to Lee and Hersh (1993) and You (2001), i. e. T is the number of periods, there is at most one arrival per period and time runs backward to 0. Let $N = \{1, \ldots, n\}$ be the set of products. Let λ be the (time independent) probability of an arrival in any period. Denote the probability that an arriving customer buys product $j \in S$

if $S \subseteq N$ is the offer set by $P_j(S)$. We will see below that this way of modeling includes ID as a special case.

The value function is given by:

$$\begin{aligned} V_t(c) =& \max_{S \subseteq N} \left\{ \sum_{j \in S} \lambda P_j(S) \left(v_j + V_{t-1}(c-1)\right) \right. \\ & \left. + \left(1 - \sum_{j \in S} \lambda P_j(S)\right) V_{t-1}(c) \right\} \\ =& V_{t-1}(c) + \max_{S \subseteq N} \left\{ \sum_{j \in S} \lambda P_j(S) \left(v_j - \Delta V_{t-1}(c)\right) \right\} \end{aligned} \tag{3.3}$$

where $\Delta V_{t-1}(c) = V_{t-1}(c) - V_{t-1}(c-1)$ is (as before) the marginal cost of capacity; and we have the usual boundary conditions $V_t(0) = 0$ for all t and $V(0, c) = 0$ for all c.

In contrast to (3.2) it is not easy to determine the maximizer S in (3.3). The important difference between those formulas is that in the former u_{ij} was a constant (independent of S) while the analogous probability $P_j(S)$ in the latter depends on S. As a consequence, the inclusion of a product j in an offer set S being a maximizer in (3.3) is in general independent of its margin $m_j(t-1, c) = v_j - \Delta V_{t-1}(c)$ – in the ID case and in You's model mainly the sign of m_j is relevant. To demonstrate the difference we consider the situation for a given period t and capacity c and drop the arguments of m_j to improve readability. Note that $\Delta V_{t-1}(c)$ is a constant independent of the product for given t and c. The following (somewhat surprising) situations may arise:

- It may be optimal to turn down demand for products j with a positive margin $m_j > 0$. This will be the case if enough customers who purchased j if it was available buy up to the more expensive product i (which has an even higher margin $m_i = m_j + v_i - v_j$). This is the case which we have describe verbally in the above example: It was optimal to offer $\{1, 3\}$ because there were enough buy ups from $j = 2$ to $i = 1$.
- It may be optimal to turn down demand for products i with high margins m_i, even though products j with lower margins $m_j < m_i$ are available. Natural examples for this case arise if fencing is imperfect. Let i, j be products such that $v_j < v_i$ and suppose for the ease of simplicity that no effective fencing measure are implemented, i. e. no customer buys i if j is available. Assume further that the probability

of purchase of other products than i, j is not affected by whether i, j, or both are available or not; and likewise, the probability of purchase of i or j depends only on the inclusion of i or j into the offer set. As noted before the marginal costs of capacity of i and j are identical, implying and $m_i > m_j$. Assume that $m_j > 0$. In the independent demand case, an optimal policy will accept both i and j. In the choice based case this is certainly possible, but if we offer j customers willing to buy i will purchase j instead. So we will offer either i or j; and offering both is effectively equivalent to offering j only. In the former case we loose all customers willing to buy the cheaper product j only; in the latter, all high-yield customers will divert to the cheaper product j. If the "low yield only" demand is high, it may be advantageous to offer j, but not i, because the additional demand will overcompensate the loss due to the "buy downs" of high yield customers.

- It may be optimal to accept demand for a product j with a negative margin $m_j < 0$. Of course, this can be optimal if and only if the inclusion of j to the offer set will stimulate enough demand for some other products i with a positive margin $m_i > 0$, i. e. the inclusion of j into S will increase the probability $P_i(S)$. It seems to be hard to imagine a realistic situation that gives rise such a behavior of $P_i(S)$, but a possible explanation could be a so called *extremeness aversion* of consumers: Customers seem to be reluctant to choose alternatives with extreme values of certain attributes (e. g. the most expensive product). Simonson and Tversky (1992), for instance, report on an experiment where respondents were asked to choose between two cameras, one of which was somewhat better but also more expensive. The preference for the second (more expensive) alternative increased significantly after a third (even more expensive) camera was added. The same paper gives an account of a similar experiment with microwave ovens yielding practically the same result. Speaking more generally, adding products to the offer set can change the "frame of reference" (Smith and Nagle 1995) of customers thereby increasing the probability of sale of other products.

We can summarize the differences between the optimal policies in the ID case and the choice-based case as modeled by Talluri and van Ryzin (2004a) as follows: In the independent demand case, the optimal policy can easily be determined if a table of ΔV is available – a product is available at time t given remaining capacity c if and only if $v_j \geq \Delta V_{t-1}(c)$. In the choice base case, even if a table of ΔV is available, finding the maximizer $S \subseteq N$ of

$$\sum_{j \in S} \lambda P_j(S)(v_j - \Delta V_{t-1}(c))$$

is (in general) not trivial. If the probabilities $P_j(S)$ lack a convenient structure there may be no better way than searching exhaustively over all subsets of N. However, the number of subsets is exponential in n.

Talluri and van Ryzin (2004a) nevertheless are able to prove important monotonicity properties of ΔV. They furthermore show that in general only *efficient sets* can be maximizers in (3.3), i. e. an optimal policy only offers efficient sets. To characterize efficient sets define the probability of purchase $Q(S)$ and the expected (immediate) revenue $R(S)$ for each offer set $S \subseteq N$:

$$Q(S) = \sum_{j \in S} P_j(S) \tag{3.4}$$

$$R(S) = \sum_{j \in S} P_j(S)\, v_j \tag{3.5}$$

A set $T \subseteq N$ is inefficient if there exist probabilities $\alpha(S) \geq 0$, $\sum_{S \subseteq N} \alpha(S) = 1$, such that

$$\sum_{S \subseteq N} \alpha(S) R(S) > R(T) \qquad \text{and} \tag{3.6}$$

$$\sum_{S \subseteq N} \alpha(S) Q(S) \leq Q(T) \tag{3.7}$$

Otherwise, T is efficient. Note that obviously a deterministic optimal policy always exists so that it is in principle not necessary to allow for random policies as used in the definition of efficient sets. However, this minor technical change greatly simplifies the analysis.

This notion of efficiency is quite intuitive: If there exists a randomization of offer sets with a strictly greater revenue, but with a lower or equal probability of purchase (i. e. a lower or equal probability to consume scarce capacity), T seems to be a poor choice for an offer set.

Denote the number of efficient sets by $m \leq 2^n$. Let the collection of efficient sets be indexed such that $Q(S_1) \leq Q(S_2) \leq \ldots \leq Q(S_m)$. Then $R(S_1) \leq R(S_2) \leq \ldots \leq R(S_m)$ as well – if $S_i \neq S_j$ were efficient sets such that $Q(S_i) \leq Q(S_j)$ but $R(S_i) > R(S_j)$, S_j would not be efficient.

We use that fact to simplify our notation a little further: Define $Q_k = Q(S_k), R_k = R(S_k)$, $k = 1, \ldots, m$ where Q_k, R_k are indexed such that both are increasing with k. The Bellman optimality equation (3.3) becomes:

$$V(t,c) = V(t-1,c) + \max_{k=1,\ldots,m} \{\lambda (R_k - Q_k \Delta V(t-1,c))\} \qquad (3.8)$$

Talluri and van Ryzin (2004a) then prove that an optimal policy is monotone in the following sense: An optimal policy selects an offer set from the ordered collection of efficient sets, i. e. an index k^* that is a maximizer in (3.8). k^* is decreasing in remaining capacity and increasing in remaining time. Note that this result is totally independent of the actual structure of the choice model, i. e. of the $P_j(S)$.

The efficient sets can in general (for arbitrary $P_j(S)$) only be determined by complete enumeration. Talluri and van Ryzin (2004a) try to derive necessary and sufficient conditions for that the optimal policy is nested by fares, i. e. all efficient sets are complete sets $A_i = \{1,\ldots,i\}$ and the order of those sets is exactly $A_1,\ldots,A_n$. When we discussed an example with $n = 3$ products above we have already mentioned conditions under which it is optimal not to offer the "middle" product 2 but both the most expensive and cheapest products $1,3$. In this case an optimal policy would not be nested by fares. Talluri and van Ryzin (2004a) present a numerical example illustrating such a situation.

Since the example shows that the optimal policy is not nested by fares for arbitrary choices of $P_j(S)$ Talluri and van Ryzin (2004a) focus on special choice models and are able to show that for certain structures of $P_j(S)$ a nested by fares policy is optimal for the ID case (this is exactly the result of Lee and Hersh 1993), a choice model where customers purchase the lowest open fare and the multinomial logit model of choice. We will briefly describe these models in turn, i. e. we will show how they are defined in terms of the $P_j(S)$.

In the ID model of "choice", customers will either buy a specific product (if it is available) or not at all:

$$P_j(S) = \begin{cases} q_j & j \in S \\ 0 & j \notin S \end{cases}$$

where $q_j \geq 0$ is the probability that an arriving customer chooses product j (if it is available). We require that $\sum_{j=1}^{n} q_j \leq 1$.

If customers purchase the lowest open fare the choice probabilities can be stated formally as follows:

$$P_j(S) = \begin{cases} q_j & j = \max S \\ 0 & \text{otherwise} \end{cases} \qquad j = 1,\ldots,n,\ S \subseteq N$$

Again, $q_j \in [0, 1]$ is the probability that an arriving customer purchases product j (if it is the cheapest product available). Note that it is not necessary that $\sum_{j=1}^{n} q_j \leq 1$ holds.

A necessary condition for the optimality of a "nested by fares" policy is that $Q(S)$ is increasing in S. Note that $Q(S) = q_{\max S}$. Let $S \subset T \subseteq N$ and compare $Q(S)$ and $Q(T)$. Let $j_T = \max T \backslash S$. If $j_T < \max S$, we have $Q(T) = Q(S)$. If $j_T > \max S$, we have $Q(T) = q_{j_T}$. So to satisfy this condition we have to require that $q_1 \leq q_2 \leq \ldots \leq q_n$. This does not seem restrictive, though: It is natural to assume that fewer customers purchase (i. e. q_j drops) if the prices raise (i. e. $\max S$ drops).

In a multinomial logit model (MNL) of choice each alternative $j \in N$ is assigned a utility u_j. We denote the utility of the no-purchase option by u_0. Since utility is ordinal w. l. o. g. $u_0 = 0$. The choice probabilities under a MNL can be formally defined as follows: Define $w_j = e^{u_j} > 0$ and note that $w_0 = 1$. Then the choice probabilities are given by

$$P_j(S) = \frac{w_j}{w_0 + \sum_{j \in S} w_j} = \frac{w_j}{1 + \sum_{j \in S} w_j} \qquad j \in S \cup \{0\}$$

and zero otherwise.

The MNL is a choice model with rather convenient analytical properties. This and other models of choice are studied extensively by e. g. Ben-Akiva and Lerman (1985), Maier and Weiss (1990), Ortúzar and Willumsen (1994) and Train (2003). The MNL has got some drawbacks (see e. g. Bhat 2000, Koppelman and Sethi 2000, Müller-Bungart 2002 for a discussion and alternatives), but it is nevertheless widely used in the airline industry. A typical application of the MNL and related choice models is forecasting of market shares – in this case the utility u_j of a product is expressed by a function depending on attributes like departure time, flight duration etc. The probability $P_j(S)$ is then interpreted as forecast of the market share of product j if S is the set of available products. Coldren et al. (2003), for instance, use a MNL model for this purpose; the pitfalls of MNL in this area of application as well as improvements are e. g. discussed by Grammig et al. (2005), Müller-Bungart (2002) and Scheidler (2003).

3.2.3 Network Problems

If we extend our focus from single legs to networks we not only have to take buy ups but also recaptures into account. In light of our discussion in the previous subsection an obvious approach is to use both buy up and recapture probabilities to describe both kinds of behavior. Jiang and Miglionico (2006), for instance, extend the model of You (2001) with buy up probabilities to the network case.

Andersson (1998, see also Algers et al. 1993) reports on at project at Scandinavian Airlines Systems (SAS). Survey and actual booking data are used to calibrate a logit model of choice (see Algers and Beser 2001 for details). If the parameters of the logit model are estimated with the choice set S and once again with the set $S \backslash \{i\}$ for a product i the fraction of passengers u_{ij} that buy product $j \in S \backslash \{i\}$ if product i is not available can be computed (Algers and Beser 2001, S. 42).

The u_{ij} can be interpreted as buy up (if i and j share the same itinerary) or recapture probabilities. These values are used as parameters in a deterministic LP to determine nested booking limits (under a given nesting order).

Tontsch and Hoehl (2005) report on a similar effort at German Railways: buy up and recapture probabilities are estimated based on survey and booking data. The estimation problem is complicated by the fact that customers who buy up to regular full-fare tickets are free to choose their travel times (see page 9).

Zhang and Cooper (2005a) do not consider a full network of flights but a single pair of cities (one origin and one destination) and a set of (two or more) non-stop flights connecting them. The demand process is a mixture of ID and a choice model: On the one hand each passenger is willing to pay a certain designated price only, i. e. there are no buy ups or downs. However, each passenger will choose between all flights for which the chosen fare is still available. Zhang and Cooper (2005b) consider a pricing problem on a network of the same structure (i. e. a set of n parallel substitutable flights between one origin and one destination). At any time there is only one price for v_j for flight $j = 1, \ldots, n$. Arriving customers will choose among the flights (or do not purchase at all) where the probability to choose flight j (or to exit) depends on the vector of prices.

Van Ryzin and Vulcano (2006) consider a virtual nesting booking limit control (see page 46) for a multi-resource problem. Customers are assumed to behave as follows: Every customer can rank the n products according to preference. An example of such a ranking for $n = 5$ would be $(2, 1, 5, 0, 0)$, i. e. the customer strictly prefers 2; if 2 should not be available 1 would be chosen, and then 5. 3 and 4 will never be chosen regardless of the availability of 2, 1 and 5. Demand of each customer is a continuous random variable Q. This demand is satisfied in continuous amounts from the available supply according to the ranking (note that the available amounts of the products are consequences of the decisions

– protection levels or booking limits – of the seller). For instance, if $Q = 4$ in our example and 3.5, 2 and 0.5 units of products 2, 1 and 5 are respectively made available, the customer will receive 3.5 units of product 2 and 0.5 units of product 1. These assumptions – especially the fact that demanded and satisfied amounts are continuous quantities – simplify the analysis.

If we assume that customers observe the offer set and make a choice it is natural to extend the recursive value function (3.3) to the network case: Let m be the number of resources and $c = (c_1, \ldots, c_m)$ be the vector of remaining capacities. Let $r_{ij} \geq 0$ be the amount of resource $i = 1, \ldots, m$ needed to produce a single unit of product $j = 1, \ldots, n$. Let $r_j = (r_{1j}, \ldots, r_{mj})$ be the vector of production coefficients of product j. Note that this way of modeling not only covers network problems (with $m \geq 2$) but also problems with group bookings. For instance, if product j represents a booking of a group of four using legs two, three and five out of five we would have $r_j = (0, 4, 4, 0, 4)$.

For the ease of notation define $N(c) = \{j \in N | \, r_j \leq c\}$, the set of sellable products (without overbooking) given remaining capacities c. The value function is then given by:

$$\begin{aligned} V_t(c) = & \max_{S \subseteq N(c)} \left\{ \sum_{j \in S} \lambda P_j(S) \left[v_j + V_{t-1}(c - r_j) \right] \right. \\ & \left. + \left(1 - \sum_{j \in S} \lambda P_j(S) \right) V_{t-1}(c) \right\} \\ = & V_{t-1}(c) + \max_{S \subseteq N(c)} \left\{ \sum_{j \in S} \lambda P_j(S) \left(v_j - \Delta V_{t-1}(c, r_j) \right) \right\} \\ = & V_{t-1}(c) + \max_{S \subseteq N(c)} \left\{ \sum_{j \in S} \lambda P_j(S) \, m_j(t-1, c) \right\} \end{aligned}$$

where $\Delta V(t-1, c, a) = V(t-1, c) - V(t-1, c-a)$ denotes the marginal cost of the capacity a and $m_j(t-1, c) = v_j - \Delta V(t-1, c, r_j)$ denotes the margin of product j given remaining capacity c and time t. Due to the use of $N(c)$ only the boundary condition $V_0(c) = 0$ for all c is necessary.

Similar formulations are e. g. presented by Gallego et al. (2004a) and van Ryzin and Liu (2004). Gallego et al. (2004a) also incorporate flexible products, consequently we defer a discussion of their approach to the next section. Van Ryzin and Liu (2004) draw upon ideas and results of Gallego et al. (2004a) and approximate the stochastic dynamic value function by a static deterministic LP. This LP can be derived as follows: As with the single leg case – see (3.5) – define $R(S) = \sum_{j \in S} P_j(S) v_j$ and assume that $R(S)$ is the deterministic revenue associated with the decision to offer the set $S \subseteq N$ of products. Analogously to (3.4) define $Q_i(S) = \sum_{j \in S} P_j(S) r_{ij}$ and assume that this is a deterministic amount of resource i used by any request. Finally, assume that λ is a deterministic rate of arrival. Our decision is now how long a certain offer set S should be made available, i. e. we have to decide on the number of micro periods $t(S)$ in which $S \subseteq N$ is the offer set. Note that it is not necessary to decide on precisely *when* to offer a particular set of products because all parameters – especially λ and $P_j(S)$ – are deterministic and independent of the periods t. Originally $t(S)$ has to be integer, but we consider a continuous relaxation. The result is an LP, see Model 3.1.

Model 3.1: LP to Approximate Choice-based Network RM (Gallego et al. 2004a, van Ryzin and Liu 2004)

$$\max \sum_{S \subseteq N} \lambda R(S)\, t(S)$$

s. t.

$$\sum_{S \subseteq N} \lambda Q_i(S)\, t(S) \leq c_i \qquad i = 1, \ldots, m$$

$$\sum_{S \subseteq N} t(S) \leq T$$

$$t(S) \geq 0 \qquad S \subseteq N$$

Model 3.1 has got two drawbacks: The number of variables $t(S)$ is exponential in the number of products, thus a column generation approach is in order. We cannot expect that the subproblem of such an approach (i. e. the problem to find a new column with negative reduced costs – or to prove the no such column exists) can be solved efficiently for an arbitrary choice of the $P_j(S)$, but Gallego et al. (2004a) show that the MNL model of choice provides a tractable subproblem. Van Ryzin and Liu (2004) present an alternative proof. Furthermore, an optimal solution of Model 3.1 only specifies how long certain products should be offered – in which periods they should be offered is irrelevant in the deterministic time homogeneous setting, but under stochastic settings the offer set should depend on remaining time (and remaining capacity). Van Ryzin and Liu (2004) thus develop a heuristic based on a DAVN-like decomposition of the network problem into single leg problems (see Algorithm 2.2).

Van Ryzin and Liu (2004) show that the optimal objective function value of the deterministic LP and a reformulation of the stochastic problem are asymptotically identical where "asymptotic" refers to the fact that both the number of periods T and the vector of capacities c (i. e. the right hand sides of the LP) are scaled by a common factor θ and the limit for $\theta \to \infty$ is considered. An analogous result holds for the deterministic LP of network RM with independent demand (see page 74).

For the single leg case Talluri and van Ryzin (2004a) have shown that an optimal policy only offers efficient sets $S \subseteq N$. The definition of efficient sets – see (3.6), (3.7) – carries over to the network case if we define $Q(S) = (Q_1(S), \ldots, Q_m(S))$. Van Ryzin and Liu (2004) mention that in the network case inefficient sets cannot be eliminated from consideration in general. However, it can be shown that an optimal solution of Model 3.1 only uses efficient sets.

3.3 Routing Control and Flexible Products

The discussion in the previous section was devoted to choice-based RM with unimodal products. In this section, we consider multimodal products (namely routing control and flexible products), but we disregard choice behavior first. At the very end of the chapter, however, we will discuss an approach by Gallego et al. (2004a) which incorporates both flexible products and customer choice behavior.

3.3.1 Introduction

Supplier-driven substitution means that the actual mode of production can be defined by the provider of a good or service and not by the customer. If this choice is made immediately after purchase – e. g. an airline tells a customer the definite itinerary right after booking – we speak of *routing control*. If the supplier reserves the right to commit to a certain mode of production well after purchase, we speak of *flexible products*. With a little abuse of the terminology we apply the term "multimodal product" in this section to both routing controlled and flexible products to increase readability.

We have already mentioned that multimodal products are the use in some industries because the customer simply does not care about the mode of production. In cargo transport (see page 9), for instance, the customer will typically be indifferent with respect to the route taken by the goods as long as they arrive on time. In the broadcasting industry, where the RM problem arises because customers want advertisements to be placed in commercial breaks of limited length, it is not completely irrelevant when a particular spot will be broadcast, but the airtimes will only be roughly defined by the customer in a typical contract and flexible products are thus prevalent in this industry. Broadcasting companies are discussed extensively in chapter 6.

In other industries, however, flexible products are quite novel. Aida Cruises, for instance, recently started to offer holidays where the customer only chooses the length of the trip, type of cabin and date of travel and the company will then choose the actual ship and cabin such that the customer's preferences are satisfied (Petrick and Klein 2005).

Whether routing controlled/flexible products are added to an existing portfolio of specific products or the bulk of products is multimodal is irrelevant for an obvious advantage: Demand can be allocated to capacity after uncertainty has (mostly) been revealed (acceptance/rejection decisions, however, still have to be made under uncertainty). This reduces the operational inflexibility (which is a defining prerequisite for RM problems; see our discussion on page 4) and allows to better balance capacity supply and demand. Gallego and Phillips (2004) use the term "risk pooling" to summarize this advantage. risk pooling is especially relevant if demand is volatile and demand forecasts are very unreliable. This effect has been investigated by Petrick and Klein (2005) in a small simulation study. They considered a situation with three single leg flights departing within a time window of two hours. There were three fares for each flight, where the third fare was either a specific product (priced € 150) or a flexible product (at € 120). The former "unimodal" setting yielded a better revenue if the forecast error was five percent or less – the multimodal setting strongly suffered from cannibalization in those scenarios –, but if the forecast error was ten percent or higher the multimodal setting outperformed the unimodal one, where the effect of risk pooling (and hence the revenue advantage) increased with the forecast error.

For a further discussion of advantages and disadvantages of flexible products it is important to distinguish between cases where the majority of products is unimodal, i. e. the supplier commits to a precise mode of production before purchase (e. g. airlines, cruises) and cases where it is common that the customers do not know which resources are used to satisfy their orders (e. g. cargo, broadcasting). For instance, for the cargo or broadcasting industry (where flexible products are prevalent) the relationship of prices of uni- and multimodal products or the design of the latter in comparison to the former is not an issue because specific products are virtually inexistent. The differentiation is similar to our discussion on page 5: In the one case the product range is standardized, in the other a product is defined as a bundle of standardized subservices.

If the bulk of products is unimodal, a routing controlled/flexible product which is added to the existing portfolio of specific products is typically a "menu of (existing unimodal) products". For instance, an airline that offers trips from DRS to SFO via FRA or MUC will certainly sell two specific products (the DRS-FRA-SFO and DRS-MUC-SFO itineraries). A multimodal product "DRS-SFO" where the airline chooses if the DRS-FRA/FRA-SFO or DRS-MUC/MUC-SFO legs are respectively used is closely related to both unimodal products – namely, the price of the multimodal product will have to be lower, i. e. the airline will have to pay a premium for the gain in flexibility; or conversely, the customers expect a premium for their loss of utility. However, since the multimodal product will be considered inferior to the existing unimodal ones, it is possible to demand a lower price for a product that is very similar to existing ones without cannibalizing much existing demand. We can hope that the bulk of requests for the new multimodal product stems from "new" customers who are not able or not willing to buy one of the unimodal products (this is what Gallego and Phillips 2004 call "demand induction"). An interesting dilemma arises here, though: If new multimodal products are too "cheap" (compared with their specific counterparts), the probability of demand induction is high, but so is the probability of cannibalization because customers will "buy down" from the specific products. If they are too "expensive", cannibalization due to buy downs will be negligible, but not much additional demand will be created either. An analogous situation arises if a deeply discounted (specific) product is added to an existing portfolio with very similar products (i. e. flights that traverse the same itinerary) at much higher prices. As before, we thus have to implement a careful capacity control strategy to limit access to both deeply discounted and multimodal products in order to avoid blocking of revenues and cannibalization.

Petrick and Klein (2005) add that not only pricing but also the design of multimodal products may be an issue – for instance, if an airline reserves the right to assign the customer a departing flight within a time window of twelve hours, this can be considered “unfair” by prospective passengers and this multimodal product will not be bought even if the price is very low.

3.3.2 Literature Review

We have mentioned some references dealing with cargo RM on page 10. However, most of the references deal with single leg problems (where routing is trivially not an issue), Bartodziej and Derigs (2004) and Pak and Dekker (2004) being the only exception. Pak and Dekker (2004), however, intentionally disregard the possibility of routing cargo and assume that all products are unimodal. Bartodziej and Derigs (2004) use forecasted values of future demands in a deterministic model where the problem of routing cargo through the network is solved under the objective of maximizing the yield per kilogram. In this model, cargo is treated as a “fluid” though, i. e. it is possible to route arbitrary fractions of kilograms along paths.

The broadcasting industry is discussed extensively in chapter 6, so we postpone a discussion of the relevant literature. In section 6.6 we highlight the relationship between the broadcasting and cargo RM problems.

We begin our review of literature related to routing control and flexible products with the former: Talluri (2001) considers an airline network RM problem. For every origin-destination pair there is a fraction of passengers who are indifferent between various routes as long as the departure and arrival times do not vary much. Talluri (2001) assumes independent demand, i. e. there are some passengers who are interested in a single specific product and exit if it is not available, while some passengers are only willing to buy a single multimodal product (i. e. a single origin-destination pair). In particular, the latter group of passengers will not “buy up” to one of the specific products (because these are more expensive, for instance). Talluri (2001) presents model and a bid price method for this problem. The bid price method works as follows: Let v_j be the revenue of the multimodal product and M_j be the set of routes – or more generally, the set of modes of production. Let r_{ij}^p be the amount of resource i consumed if mode $p \in M_j$ is used to provide j. Let ω_i denote a resource-specific bid price which Talluri (2001) obtains from deterministic or probabilistic linear programs. Define the bid price of product j if mode p is used: $o_j^p = \sum_{i=1}^m \omega_i r_{ij}^p$. Let $p^* = \arg\min_{p \in M_j} \left\{ o_j^p \right\}$. Determining this minimum is – in the airline case – a shortest path problem; in the general case it can be done through complete enumeration if the number of modes $|M_j|$ is not too large. If $v_j \geq o_j^{p^*}$ accept and use mode p^* (a route in Talluri's case) for j, otherwise reject. Since the mode of production (route) p^* is never changed in the future, the supplier commits immediately to a mode of production, i. e. we have an example for multimodal products in the form of routing control.

Chen et al. (2003) consider the same problem and propose bid prices approaches based on deterministic and stochastic programs as well as approximate dynamic programming. They argue that the standard way to compute bid prices (as carried out by Talluri 2001) may be misleading because the demand constraint is no longer a simple upper bound on a decision variable (see inequality (2.2) in Model 2.1). They propose an improved bid price method which requires to solve an LP, obtain shadow prices from the optimal solutions, find the K shortest paths based on those shadow prices and iterate until convergence is reached.

Gallego and Phillips (2004) consider a problem with two flights A and B, each with a single fare. As a third product the carrier offers flexible product flexible product AB where the carrier will assign passengers to one of both flights well after purchase. Independent demand for all three products is assumed. The decision horizon is divided into two periods. In the first period all products are available, in the second period passengers can only book the specific products.

The authors are able to prove some very appealing results for the second period problem: Let a_A, a_B be the number of accepted bookings during the first period for the specific products A and B, respectively. Let c_A^1, c_B^1 be the initial capacities and define $c_j^2 = c_j^1 - a_j$ for $j = A, B$. Let a be the number of accepted bookings for the flexible product. If overbooking is not allowed in the second period and b_A^2, b_B^2 are the booking limits to be used $b_A^2 + b_B^2 = c_A^2 + c_B^2 - a$ holds and it is optimal to assign $c_j^2 - b_j^2$ seats on flight $j = A, B$ to the flexible product at the *beginning* of period 2.

Gallego and Phillips (2004) show that – in the absence of overbooking – the optimal booking limits b_A^2, b_B^2 can be determined by selecting the $c_A^2 + c_B^2 - a$ highest EMSR values of both flights. This solution can be used as a basis to determine optimal booking limits with overbooking by successively increasing either of the booking limits. Gallego and Phillips (2004) finally propose a heuristic for the first period problem (where both the two specific and the flexible product are available).

Gallego et al. (2004a) consider a problem with flexible products on $m \geq 2$ resources. The company offers a set P of specific products and a set F of flexible products where each flexible product $j \in F$ is associated with a subset $P_j \subseteq P$ of specific products such that a request for product j can be satisfied by any product in P_j. We require that $F \cap P = \emptyset$. Demand for product j follows a homogeneous Poisson process with rate λ_j (see chapter 5 for details on this and other forms of arrival processes). The assignment of specific products to flexible product requests takes place at the very end of the decision period. Gallego et al. (2004a) present a dynamic programming formulation whose basic ideas can be summarized as follows: Let $c = (c_1, \ldots, c_m)$ be the vector of remaining capacities and $f = \left(f_1, \ldots, f_{|F|}\right)$ be a vector such that f_j is the number requests accepted for the j-th flexible product. The expected revenue from period t on given c and f is denoted by $V_t(c, f)$. If we accept a request for a specific product c is decreased accordingly; if a request for the j-th flexible product is accepted we increase f_j. Time runs forward and the end of the decision period is T. The boundary conditions are then given by:

$$V_T(c, f) = \begin{cases} -\infty & \text{if it is impossible to satisfy the } f \text{ requests for} \\ & \text{flexible products with the remaining capacity } c \\ 0 & \text{otherwise} \end{cases}$$

Gallego et al. (2004a) then study a deterministic approximation of the stochastic problem. If stochastic demand is replaced by deterministic quantities, the resulting problem is basically to determine partitioned booking limits for the specific and the flexible products. Define $N = P \cup F$ and let d_j, v_j, b_j be the given demand, revenue and booking limit of product $j \in N$, respectively. A suitable model formulation has to make sure that it is always possible to accommodate all requests for flexible products. We therefore define the decision variable z_{jk} to denote the number of specific products $k \in P_j$ to satisfy demand for product $j \in F$. For each $k \in P$ define the set F_k of flexible products j such that $k \in P_j$. Model 3.2 then describes the deterministic control problem.

Gallego et al. (2004a) consider the LP-relaxation of that model and prove that it provides an asymptotically optimal policy (i. e. if both the length of the decision period T and the available capacities are scaled by a common factor θ and the limit for $\theta \to \infty$ is considered).

Model 3.2: LP to Approximate Network RM with Flexible Products (Gallego et al. 2004a)

$$\max \sum_{j \in N} v_j b_j$$

s. t.

$$\sum_{k \in P} r_{ik} \left(b_k + \sum_{j \in F_k} z_{jk} \right) \leq c_i \qquad i = 1, \ldots, m$$

$$\sum_{k \in P_j} z_{jk} = b_j \qquad j \in F$$

$$z_{jk} \in \mathbb{N}_0 \qquad j \in F, k \in P_j$$

$$b_j \in \mathbb{N}_0 \qquad j \in N$$

Furthermore, they use the LP to derive resource-specific bid prices. Like Talluri (2001, see above), they propose to accept a request for a flexible product j if its revenue v_j exceeds the minimum bid price of the products in P_j.

Finally, the authors extend their approach by incorporating choice behavior. To do this, they let the rate of the arrival process $\lambda_j(S)$ depend on the offer set S. The resulting stochastic problem is again approximated by a deterministic LP, which is basically a mixture of Models 3.1 and 3.2. The number of variables in this LP is exponential in $|N|$, but it can be solved efficiently by column generation for certain “attraction models” of choice, namely the MNL model. As before, the LP provides an asymptotically optimal solution to the stochastic problem.

4

Evaluating Revenue Management Techniques: Instance Generation

After having described a wealth of RM techniques we are now ready to develop instance generation methods suitable to evaluate their performance. To the best of our knowledge we are the first to address this question in detail. This chapter introduces the problem of generating instances and highlights several related issues. We will see that the most important module of an instance generator is a simulator for stochastic demand data streams. This aspect will be extensively covered in the following chapter.

4.1 Introduction

Different methods for optimization problems vary in many ways. In the end, both researchers and practitioners are interested in those methods which "perform best", where performance is measured in running time, quality of the solution (i. e. objective function value) and memory usage. Various approaches exist to evaluate optimization methods (or other algorithms) with respect to those measures. Two prominent examples are worst case analysis and computational studies. The latter requires to implement the method, run it on a test bed of systematically generated instances and record the desired quantities (e. g. running time in wall clock seconds, average deviation of the objective function value from a bound, number of Branch and Bound nodes).

If authors develop new procedures and want to publish results with respect to their performance it would be desirable to have an established standard test bed available for at least two reasons: A common set of agreed-upon instances obviously facilitates the comparison of different methods for the same problem. Furthermore, authors save the time of developing an instance generator – a quite formidable task, as we will see in this and the subsequent chapter.

While a standard test bed would thus be beneficial for all researchers in a given field, to the best of our knowledge no such test bed for RM problems is publicly available to date. In this chapter, we thus make a first attempt to outline relevant aspects of RM instance generation. We categorize these aspects into static (or deterministic), stochastic (or dynamic) and statistical ones. The static/deterministic aspects are highly application specific, so we only cover them very briefly. Subsection 6.5.1, which contains a description of our instance generator for the broadcasting RM problem, can serve as an example here: The exposition of the instance generating method is mostly devoted to features which are specialties of the broadcasting industry. Stochastic/dynamic aspects are introduced in section 4.3 and extensively discussed in the next chapter. When generating instances, we should also keep some statistical issues in mind. These are outlined in section 4.4, and we will make some remarks on selected issues from that area (namely parameter estimation) in section 5.4 as well.

Because we focus on capacity control as being the core problem of RM in this book, the features of the capacity control problem will act as a guideline for our exposition. However, since the aim of this chapter is to introduce and overview instance generation, our findings should be fairly general and apply to e. g. dynamic pricing problems as well. The same holds for large parts of the next chapter.

4.2 Deterministic/Static Aspects

Deterministic aspects are known before the evaluation of methods begins. A typical example for objects whose properties are revealed in advance are products and resources, while e. g. demand is stochastic. As a consequence, the latter may vary between subsequent replications while resources and products are static.

As mentioned in the introduction of this chapter, a reasonable method to generate those static objects (e. g. products and resources) highly depends on the considered application. In an airline RM problem, for instance, the resources will be described by a network of nonstop flights (legs). Each leg i will be associated with a capacity c_i denoting the number of seats on the aircraft. If there are multiple cabins (e. g. economy, business and first class) on the aircraft and the RM problem at hand allows for up- or downgrades of passengers (e. g. in the case of oversales), c_i will be a vector of capacities denoting the number of seats in each cabin. The dimension of c_i may depend on i if aircrafts serving different legs may have a different number of cabins.

A typical way to define an airline network is to consider a particular structure, e. g. single leg, line or hub-and-spoke networks (see e. g. Klein 2005). If we confine ourselves to a certain type of network, an actual instance can typically be described with just a few parameters, e. g. the number of line segments or the number of hubs and inbound and outbound spokes. The capacities are then usually set to a realistic number of seats (100 to 400, say), taking the structure of the network into account – for instance, it is reasonable to assume that the number of seats on in- and outbound spokes are identical, while the capacity on inter-hub links is somewhat larger. However, as we will see in the next section, the absolute amount of capacity is not too relevant; much more important is the relationship of demand to available capacity.

In many applications the number of products is connected in a natural way with the number of resources and their relationship (e. g. legs which are linked to network of flights). For instance, if we consider the a hub-and-spoke network with m^i inbound and m^o outbound spokes, there will be $m^i + m^o$ local and $m^i \cdot m^o$ connecting itineraries. It is reasonable to assume that the number of fares for each itinerary is a constant f, yielding $f \cdot \left(m^i + m^o + m^i \cdot m^o\right)$ products.

Defining the characteristics of the products can be somewhat more difficult, though. In our airline example we have e. g. to define the fares in a reasonable way. If the fares are decision variables (e. g. in a dynamic pricing problem), we have to define a finite or infinite set of feasible prices and to describe how demand reacts on price. Setting prices gets even more difficult if group bookings are taken into account. However, if we decide to consider groups of sizes up to four persons, the resource consumption of product j is trivially defined – $r_{ij} = g_j$ (where $g_j \in \{1, 2, 3, 4\}$ is the group size) if the itinerary corresponding to j uses leg i, otherwise $r_{ij} = 0$.

If flexible products should be added to the problem and each flexible product should be defined as a "menu" of specific products those menus have to be properly defined. The situation gets more difficult if specific products are virtually inexistent; for instance, when we developed our instance generator for the broadcasting industry (see subsection 6.5.1) a large amount of details had to be taken into account. Another example is the cargo industry – in this application, each order's weight and volume (and maybe even the price) is unique. In this case, products are no longer deterministic objects and the characteristics of any order are to be generated along with the stochastic and dynamic demand process. This aspect will be discussed next; and we return to the cargo example after having described some more general features.

4.3 Stochastic/Dynamic Aspects

In RM problems we frequently have to deal with a random demand process. Not only the total number of requests and the times when they arrive are unknown, but there are also related issues like cancellations, no-shows and other uncertain events associated with the demand process, e. g. early departures at hotels or rental cars which are returned too late or at other stations than expected. Further random events which are possibly of relevance are e. g. varying yields of a production process or machine breakdowns. However, the latter issues are typically disregarded in RM problems; in the following we will thus focus on demand as the primary source of randomness. It is to be understood that the term "demand" subsumes in this chapter not only the arrival process of requests, but also cancellations, no-shows etc.

While there are many examples of unpredictable events in typical RM problems, it may be well justified to study settings where demand and other parameters are deterministic quantities, e. g. if the degree of uncertainty is very low in the application at hand. For instance, our investigation of the broadcasting industry revealed that there are very good reasons to use a deterministic model (section 6.2); see also subsection 5.1.2 for a more general assessment of the utility of deterministic models and references on RM problems under certainty. Deterministic models for RM problems will frequently be a static ones similar to Model 2.1, possibly extended to incorporate multiple periods (such a model is e. g. presented by Kimms and Müller-Bungart 2003) or special features of a particular industry (Kimms and Klein 2005, for instance, develop models for various industries). In these cases, demand for product j is basically given by a parameter d_j, and it is sufficient to draw these parameters from a suitably defined random distribution to generate multiple instances. However, if flexible products are prevalent and a typical request is for a bundle of those demand data generation can be a very complicated process even in the deterministic setting; see e. g. our discussion for the broadcasting industry in subsection 6.5.1.

Let us now consider the problem of generating demand data if demand is stochastic. Since a defining characteristic of an RM problem is the necessity to integrate external factors (see section 1.2), products have to be booked in advance, because customers have to be encouraged to provide those factors at the time of production well before it begins.

It is thus typically not sufficient to draw the total demand from a random distribution, because the exact times at which requests occur are relevant. Consequently, it is necessary to simulate a stochastic process creating arriving booking or cancellation requests. We will extensively deal with such processes in the subsequent chapter, so we refrain from a more detailed discussion at this point.

For other aspects of demand it may be sufficient to use (static) random variables with suitably defined distributions. The number of customers who have purchased product j but do not show up at the time of production may e. g. be denoted by a random variable N_j. In this case, instance generation – very roughly – means choosing a distribution of N_j (e. g. Normal), generating parameters (e. g. mean and standard deviation) by drawing from a random distribution (e. g. uniform over some interval) and drawing a realization n_j^i of N_j for each replication i. However, while the number of no-shows (and similar aspects) may reasonably described by static distributions, they are certainly related to the stochastic demand process. For instance, when generating a realization of n_j^i of N_j, we have to make sure that $n_j^i \leq d_j^i$ where d_j^i is the realized (and accepted) demand for product j in the i-th replication. Albeit N_j describes a static event, the distribution of N_j thus has to depend on the stochastic demand process in a suitably defined way.

An arriving request may have properties which are random as well. In the previous section we have mentioned the example of the cargo industry, where each incoming order practically has got unique volume, weight and probably even price. The arrival process thus has got the flavor of so called compound processes (see e. g. Ross 2003). In our example, each arrival is associated with realizations of three (possibly dependent) random variables, namely weight W, volume V and price R. In contrast to the number of no-shows N_j there is not necessarily a relationship between the stochastic arrival process and the random variables V, W and R, but it is easy to imagine that e. g. the price R depends on the arrival time – if an order is submitted shortly before the transportation should begin, this may well be an urgent express delivery which is priced higher.

Regardless of demand being stochastic or deterministic, the data describing the static and the dynamic dimensions of a RM problem have to be related in a meaningful way: For instance, consider a capacity control problem with n products and a single resource of capacity c. To produce a single unit of any product, we need r units of the resource. Since r does not vary across the products we can assume w. l. o. g. that

$r = 1$. Demand is stochastic and arrives from n independent processes where arrivals from process j will demand product j and exit if it is not available (i. e. we assume independent demand). Cancellations, no-shows etc. are neglected. Let the random variable D represent the total demand and note that by construction D is as well the amount of the resource that is required to satisfy each and every request. If $P(D > c)$ is now very low, a “first come first serve” (FCFS) policy will be close to optimal, and it is probably not useful to test other methods of capacity control on such an instance. To obtain meaningful results in this setting, the parameter c and the parameters defining the n stochastic demand processes (which determine the distribution of D) cannot be generated independent of each other. A useful requirement, for instance, could be that $E[D]/c$ is larger than, say, 0.9. A similar argument obviously holds if demand is deterministic and D is a known constant.

The relationship $E[D]/c$ (or D/c in the deterministic setting) is called the *nominal load factor*. It seems to be useful to define various demand scenarios for a given c by starting with a ratio $E[D]/c$ of e. g. 0.9 and to subsequently increase it until it is well above 1. The need for capacity control (and the effectiveness of sophisticated capacity control policies compared to FCFS) should ceteris paribus increase with $E[D]/c$.

Related with the stochastic demand process are e. g. decisions concerning customer choice models. We might define, for instance, that customers choose according to utility maximization principles (e. g. they behave according to multinomial logit model of choice), and utility of a product j is given as a linear function of price and restrictions associated with it.

4.4 Statistical Aspects

Revenue Management is an application-oriented area of research. To test RM models and methods it is thus desirable to use actual problem data from practice (e. g. a historical demand data stream of an airline). Analogously, if we have chosen, say, a particular stochastic demand process, we will want to assess whether this process fits demand processes observed in practice. Many aspects of practical RM instances can easily be observed, namely the static and deterministic ones (e. g. how many seats are in a typical aircraft’s economy class cabin, what types or cars are in use in most rental companies etc.). To capture the dynamic and stochastic nature of demand of RM problems in practice, demand data samples are necessary. It is typically a formidable task to obtain a sample of demand data in practical applications, though, because typically only *sales data* is recorded, i. e. we have only information about the fraction of requests that have been accepted, and demand that has been rejected by an RM policy or simply because the available capacity was exhausted is not covered. Almost any "demand data" in practice is thus – at best – a record of the so-called *constrained demand*, and *unconstraining* is necessary to gainfully use this data for estimation and forecasting, see e. g. Talluri and van Ryzin (2004b). Furthermore, the primary purpose of information systems used to record sales data is usually not data collection, but the processing and/or support of the sales process. Relevant information may thus be missing, and facts found in the database may be erroneous or implausible, see e. g. Müller-Bungart (2002) who reports on typical flaws in airline reservation systems data.

The situation gets worse if we are dealing with choice-based RM problems: Since we assume that an arriving customers observes the offer set and selects a product (or decides to exit) according to some choice model, it would be necessary to record the set of products which was available at the time of any arriving request in order to be able to analyze customers' choice behavior. This information is however almost never been stored in the sales database in practice, but it can be possibly retrieved from the optimization systems in the RM department.

It is thus difficult (but not impossible) to extract the necessary demand data from information systems which are used in practice. Furthermore, if RM models are enriched e. g. by incorporating choice behavior and revenue improvements are estimated to be significant, it will pay off to modify sales databases and related software such that relevant data is recorded more precisely and additional aspects (e. g. about available offer sets) are captured. Thus suppose that an accurate sample of a demand data stream is given. Two questions are now relevant with respect to instance generation: Does our chosen model of the stochastic arrival process fit such a typical data stream? Our arrival process will depend on some parameters which allow for a very broad range of arrival patterns. What values of parameters have to be used to create an instance which closely resembles situations encountered in practice? Knowing the answer to that question allows us to not only use a few given demand data streams, but also to create many different streams as they could have occurred in practice.

To answer both questions it is necessary to *estimate* the parameters of the chosen arrival process from the given demand data samples. When choosing a stochastic process for demand data, we should thus always keep in mind that the parameter estimation problem does not get too difficult. In the following chapter, we will cover issues related to stochastic arrival processes in great detail. We make some brief remarks on parameter estimation in section 5.4.

5

Simulation of Stochastic Demand Data Streams

The previous chapter contained a comprehensive overview on the instance generation problem. It turned out that the deterministic aspects of an RM problem are highly application specific. In addition, we have seen that some statistical issues, e. g. cleaning and unconstraining demand data obtained are also relevant. While the former again strongly depends on the actual degree of errors or omissions in the data, standard methods for the latter are available. In this chapter we thus focus on the dynamic and stochastic aspects of instance generation: the simulation of stochastic demand data streams.

To simulate stochastic arrival processes it is necessary to implement a random instance generator which produces demand data streams as an output. Doing this is quite a formidable task to do, because of at least two reasons. Firstly, the demand data must fit to the resource structure and the capacity limits in a meaningful way (see our discussion in section 4.3). And secondly, the details of implementing portable demand data generators, i. e. generators which output the same reproducible, stochastic data stream even when run on different computers involve a huge amount of technical details. Our impression is that up to today, the research community does not use a common, established method in this area. The creation and simulation of test demand data is usually described very roughly and it seems to be very hard if not impossible to use precisely the same data that other authors used before. To the best of our knowledge, no demand data generator (let alone a complete instance generator) is available to the public.

In this chapter, we will give an in-depth description of how to implement a portable generator for stochastic demand data streams. One of the results of our efforts is an executable program for Microsoft Windows platforms.

We begin by reviewing the literature with respect to demand models and demand data generation. We continue by giving an in-depth description how a single demand data stream can be generated (section 5.2), then we show how to combine multiple data streams in a meaningful way (section 5.3) under independent demand, choice-based RM and for RM problems with flexible products. We make some brief remarks on parameter estimation, i. e. on how to compute the necessary inputs for our demand data generator given records of actual, historic demand in section 5.4. Section 5.5 summarizes our findings and points out what has to be done further to develop a fully-fledged instance generator.

A preliminary version of sections 5.2 and 5.3 can be found in Kimms and Müller-Bungart (2007b).

5.1 Literature Review

Lee (1990) describes a censored Poisson process to model the booking process at airlines. He assumes that reservations arrive according to a non-homogeneous Poisson process (NHPP). He focuses on estimation and forecasting, especially in light of censoring due to limited aircraft capacities and booking limits. Albeit Lee (1990) does not explicitly treat the simulation of data streams, his work can be seen as "a starting point for developing simulations of the airline booking process" (Lee 1990, p. 13).

Weatherford et al. (1993) present a model of the demand process in some detail. Like Lee (1990) they use a NHPP with a specified rate function. A slightly varied version of their approach is used by de Boer et al. (2002), who conduct an in-depth simulation study on airline network RM methods, and Bertsimas and de Boer (2005), who develop a simulation optimization approach to airline network RM with nested booking limits. Klein (2005) gives a quite detailed description of the methods he used to simulate stochastic demand data.

We will discuss the arrival process introduced by Weatherford et al. (1993) and the variant used by de Boer et al. (2002) and Bertsimas and de Boer (2005) in great detail in subsection 5.2.3. We will show that their approach has got some advantages in comparison to Klein (2005). But to the best of our knowledge, these are the only references explicitly covering at least some aspects of demand data generation. To analyze whether these approaches provide a useful starting point for a RM demand data generator we will review references presenting RM models or methods in the following. We will focus on two aspects related to demand data generation: What generation procedures are used in classic references, and what models of demand are used in the first place to develop RM models and methods – i. e. we are dealing with both the issues of simulating and modeling demand. The latter aspect is relevant because the demand simulator has to fit the demand model. Our review will emphasize demand models, because if authors conduct a simulation study to test their methods, this seems to be done frequently in a rather "ad hoc" manner and details of the simulated demand process are rarely given. Obviously we cannot cover each and every reference in the field of RM, so that we will attempt to give a representative overview by reviewing demand models and simulation methods from some of the more influential papers. We also consider literature that deals with overbooking and dynamic pricing. We begin with categorizing demand models. We will then take a closer look at different methods to model the dynamics of the arrival process.

5.1.1 Categorizing Demand Models

Demand models in the literature can be characterized along the following two dimensions:

- The degree of interaction of customers and the environment
- The dynamics of the arrival process

With respect to the degree of interaction in the current literature basically two types of demand models have appeared so far: *Independent demand* and choice models (see section 3.2). In the former case demand is independent of the environment. In particular, it is assumed that the RM policy – especially the decision of the company (not) to offer a certain product – does not influence the customer's behavior. As an example, if a prospective airline passenger desires to book a ticket from A to B on a certain itinerary at fare X, and she finds that this particular product is not offered at the time of her request, she just exists the market and refrains from buying anything. In particular, she will not pay a higher or lower price, she will not travel half an hour later or sooner, or choose a different itinerary. So in an independent demand model, there is hardly any interaction at all between the customers and the environment. Under a *choice model of demand*, on the other hand, an arriving customer will take the set of available products (the offer set) into account and choose among these products (or decide not to buy at all), e. g. based on a utility maximization scheme.

As van Ryzin (2005) points out, the choice model may be augmented and broadened by taking other possible forms of customer behavior into account. For instance, a customer may not only choose from the offer set, but also strategically decide about when to demand a product. As an example, consider a retailing company that follows a markdown pricing scheme. Customers being flexible with respect to the time of purchase will probably learn to wait until prices have been lowered. Other examples include markdown pricing of package holidays; see page 12 for a discussion and references. Besides this strategic "demand timing" behavior, customers will also consider offers of competing companies, where the notion of competition can be very broad: With respect to travel, for example, airlines and railroads may be competitors.

The independent demand model seems to be a simplifying approximation of customer behavior only. On the other hand, Müller-Bungart (2002) found empirical evidence for that a large part of airline passengers in the North American market is indeed "loyal" to a certain product (i. e. a combination of origin, destination, time of travel etc.). This evidence is, however, based on sales and check in data (i. e. constrained demand after rejecting customers, overbooking, no-shows etc.), and some factors that are likely to be important for the traveler (namely the fare) were missing in the data.

5.1.2 Modeling the Dynamics of Demand

With respect to the *dynamics of demand* the models used in the literature so far can roughly be classified as depicted in Figure 5.1. In this subsection, we will review the literature along these categories of demand models, mentioning the methods of simulation (if simulation experiments have been conducted) at a time. We will then discuss some references that deal with simulation optimization approaches which are independent of a particular demand model.

Deterministic Demand

At the first level of Figure 5.1, we can differentiate between deterministic and stochastic demand. Deterministic demand seems to be somewhat less appropriate for RM problems because a large part of the problem's complexity arises from the uncertainty. There are nevertheless a number of good reasons to consider deterministic demand:

- Even if the number of incoming requests and their properties are known with certainty, given the scarce resource capacity knapsack-like problems typically arise. In all but the simplest cases these problems are NP-hard and thus challenging research problems in their own right.

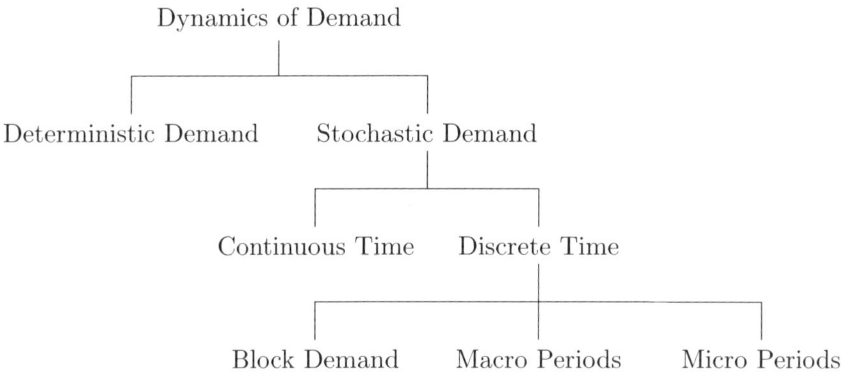

Fig. 5.1: Modeling the Dynamics of Demand

- The degree of uncertainty may in some settings be very low so that a deterministic approach is justified (see e. g. the discussion in section 6.2 for the broadcasting industry) or forecasted values may safely be used for the unknown quantities. Glover et al. (1982), for instance, present a deterministic model for airline network RM based on forecasted demands.
- Solutions obtained from deterministic models can be used to approach the problem under uncertainty heuristically. A classic example are bid price methods. Bertsimas and Popescu (2003), Pak et al. (2003) and Talluri and van Ryzin (1999), for instance, develop rather sophisticated methods to compute such bid prices from deterministic models; see also Pak and Dekker (2004) and Spengler et al. (2007) who also deal with bid prices but describe the RM decision problem using a micro period model (see below). All of these references contain computational studies, where homogeneous and non-homogeneous Poisson processes are used to simulate the arrival process of demand.
- In some RM problems under uncertainty their NP-hard deterministic counterparts may actually appear as subproblems. In the broadcasting industry, for example, it may not be trivial to decide if an incoming request (with then known properties) can feasibly be accepted. An analogous problem arises if bid price controls should be used, because it is not trivial to estimate an order's opportunity cost as well. Both aspects are investigated in detail in section 6.6.

Stochastic Demand, Continuous Time

Continuous Time models of stochastic demand are frequently used in dynamic pricing papers, see e. g. Gallego and van Ryzin (1994, 1997) and Feng and Gallego (2000, 1995). The models in these papers assume that demand is generated by a "controlled" Poisson process, where the term "controlled" refers to the fact the intensity of demand (i. e. the rate of the Poisson process) depends on price in the dynamic pricing context.

Gallego et al. (2004a) consider RM problems with flexible products (see section 3.3). They assume a choice model of demand where arrivals are generated by a Poisson process. The rate of the process $\lambda(S)$ depends on the offer set S. This dependency is formalized by an "attraction model", e. g. the Multinomial Logit model of discrete choice. Virtamo and Aalto (1991) consider a number of servers accepting reservations arriving from a non-homogeneous Poisson Process (NHPP). Zhao and Zheng (2001) deal with a single leg airline RM problem with two fares and three types of customers: Two "rigid" types (who will only demand either the lower or the higher fare) and a "flexible" type, who prefers the lower fare, but will buy the other product if the low fare class is closed. The arrivals of the customer types are created by NHPPs.

All of the mentioned references except Feng and Gallego (1995) and Gallego and van Ryzin (1994) contain simulation studies where the respective variant of Poisson processes is used to generate arrivals.

Block Demand

A classic example for *block demand* is the "lower fare classes book first" assumption. In this model, n products are sold at distinct prices. If we order the products non-decreasingly by price (i. e. product 1 is the cheapest and n is most expensive), it is assumed that all requests for product i arrive strictly before any request for products $i+1, \dots, n$, so that if the first request for product i arrives no further requests for products $1, \dots, i-1$ will ever appear. The assumption that lower fare classes book strictly before higher ones is – of course – a simplification, albeit a useful one, because if high value customers arrived early, the opportunity costs of displacing later arriving customers decreases or even vanishes. Clearly, the RM problem is more severe if customers with a low valuation arrive earlier and possibly displace customers with substantially higher valuations.

Speaking more generally, in a block demand model it is assumed that requests can be partitioned into a finite number of groups such that requests from each group arrive in homogeneous "blocks". The time horizon is naturally divided into discrete periods by these blocks. Typically, references presenting a block demand model assume independent demand as well, but from a theoretical point of view a block demand does not necessary imply independent demand. We may, for instance, use block demand in a choice based RM setting by defining the two blocks "leisure travelers" and "business travelers" (where the former strictly arrive before the latter), and customers from each group will behave according to a different choice model (the leisure travelers may e. g. put great weight on the price, but be flexible with respect to travel time, while it is the other way round for business travelers). Van Ryzin and Vulcano (2006), for instance, use a block demand-like model in their simulation experiments on an RM problem with choice behavior.

Littlewood (1972) introduced his famous "marginal seat revenue" rule based on the assumption that two types of passengers (low- and high fare passengers) book on a single flight leg, and that the low fare passengers book first. Richter (1982) has shown by marginal analysis that (under these assumptions) Littlewood's rule is an optimal policy. Brumelle et al. (1990) also consider two fares booking on a single leg where demand for the high fare depends on the booking limit for the low fare (i. e. some denied low fare passengers may decide to "buy up"), and low and high fare demand do not need to be stochastically independent.

Belobaba (1987b, 1989) formalizes Littlewood's rule in a systematic way and develops the "Expected Marginal Seat Revenue" (EMSR) method that is applicable to three or more fares. Belobaba (1992) presents an improved version of this method which he terms EMSRb. Belobaba and Weatherford (1996) incorporate choice behavior, and Belobaba and Wilson (1997) test how EMSR-methods perform under competition. Note, however, that despite its close connection to the block demand model of Littlewood, the EMSR-method is presented as a "model free" approach, i. e. it is not based on a particular demand model. Thus it is just a heuristic (albeit a very successful one with widespread use in practice). Curry (1990), Wollmer (1992) and Brumelle and McGill (1993), on the other hand, present exact approaches to the "lower fare classes book first" demand model with three or more fares. Li and Oum (2002) prove that the optimality conditions of all three models are equivalent. Robinson (1995) extends the "lower fare classes book first" setting and considers a block demand model where different fare classes book sequentially, albeit the sequence is not necessarily monotone with respect to the fares. Lautenbacher and Stidham (1999) present a unified view on the contributions of Belobaba (1989), Brumelle and McGill (1993), Curry (1990), Littlewood (1972), Robinson (1995), Wollmer (1992) and Lee and Hersh (1993), where the latter is a micro period model (see below).

Other references with block demand models include Bitran and Gilbert (1996), Coughlan (1999), Gallego and Phillips (2004) and van Ryzin and McGill (2000).

To implement methods based on block demand models it is clearly sufficient to know the distribution of the total demand D_j in block j. Belobaba and Weatherford (1996) and Bitran and Gilbert (1996), for instance, use Poisson distributions, Belobaba (1987b) uses Normal distributions, Brumelle and McGill (1993) and Wollmer (1992) assume that D_j is approximately Normal. Brumelle et al. (1990) consider dependent demands and thus assume a bivariate Normal distribution. Belobaba (1987b, 1989) and Coughlan (1999) also test their methods on real airline data.

Macro Periods

A straight-forward way to relax the strict assumptions of block demand models is to partition the booking period into T discrete periods such that the demand mix in two periods is not related. If these periods are very small (i. e. T is very large) we can safely assume that at most one request appears in any period t and arrive at what we call a demand model with *micro periods* (micro period model for short). If the periods are larger, so that many requests for different products can show up during any period t we obtain a model with *macro periods*. In both cases the aim is typically to describe the RM problem at hand in terms of a recursive value function $V_t(\cdot)$ that gives the maximal expected revenue from period t on. The problem can then be solved exactly by dynamic programming techniques (at least for smaller examples).

In a macro period model, it is assumed that the distribution of demand D_{jt} in period t is given, where the index j could denote the product (in an independent demand model) or a certain group of customers with a certain type of choice behavior (in a choice model of demand). The exact order of requests in period t is not modeled, so that the situation is practically equivalent to collecting all requests over period t and record the totals D_{jt} at the end of the period. Like in a block demand model, knowing the distribution of the "aggregate" D_{jt} is absolutely sufficient. The resulting arrival process has got the flavor of a compound counting process, but its actual mathematical properties depend crucially on the distributions of D_{jt} and the periods' lengths. Note that – from a very technical point of view – a block demand model is a special case of a model with macro periods where T is the number of blocks and $P(D_{jt} = 0) = 1$ for all $j, t = 1, \ldots, T, j \neq t$.

Macro period models are certainly appropriate if immediate acceptance/rejection is not necessary and requests can be "batched" over a longer period of time. This is e. g. the case in broadcasting companies, see chapter 6 and in particular section 6.6. However, the macro period assumption seems to be a bit unrealistic for many classical RM applications (the airline industry, for instance) where immediate response to any request is necessary. In such cases, macro period models seem to be only appropriate if rather simple RM policies are used, e. g. partitioned booking limits. Under a partitioned booking limit control customers can always be notified immediately (just check if the booking limit is already exceeded), and the dynamics of the arrival process are simply irrelevant (one "macro period" covering the entire planning horizon is sufficient). Macro periods are nevertheless useful if booking limit policies are used in connection with overbooking, because in that setting it is not necessary to immediately allocate capacity to a request (that can be done shortly before the service commences, at the same time when it is decided which customers are rejected). Therefore, immediate notification of customers is possible (again, just check the booking limits), but some form of nesting capacities among products is also implicitly involved. Karaesmen and van Ryzin (2004b), for instance, develop an overbooking model with just two periods (see page 90). The first period is the reservation period (where requests arrive), and the second period is the service period (where the number of no-shows is revealed). Incoming requests in the first period are accepted according to a booking limit policy. Capacity is not allocated to requests until the service period, where it is decided which customers have to be rejected after all (if not all requests can be accommodated due to the overbooking). Karaesmen and van Ryzin (2004b) use Poisson demand in a computational study.

The first RM model with macro periods is due to Laux (1971). He considers order acceptance/rejection in a make-to-order environment. Mayer (1976) deals with airline RM and presents booking limit-based models for partitioned capacities (without cancellations and no-shows) and for overbooking. Alstrup et al. (1986) also consider an overbooking problem where all macro periods are days. They use data from Scandinavian Airlines Systems and assume that the number of requests in period t follow a Poisson distribution with time-dependent intensity $\lambda(t)$. The number of cancellations is assumed to follow a Binomial distribution. Chan et al. (2006) consider a pricing problem in manufacturing. They assume that demand D_t in macro period t is a (general) stochastic function of price. They use the *coefficient of variation* (defined as Standard deviation $(D_t)/\text{Mean}(D_t))$ to measure what they call "demand uncertainty". Williamson (1992) reviews and tests various methods for RM problems in airline networks. In her simulation experiments a macro period approach is pursued: The booking horizon is divided into periods by so called "revision points" at which the RM policies are reviewed and reoptimized. Independent demand is assumed, and the distribution of demand to come D_{jt} for product j in each of the future periods t is assumed to be given. The author uses Poisson, Normal, and Gamma distributions in her simulations.

Micro Periods

Macro period RM models are rare, because classic RM applications require immediate acceptance/rejection of orders. Micro period models are therefore more common: They allow for notifying customers and allocating capacity at the moment the request arrives, because in every period t there is at most one request. The periods will have to be small for that purpose, so that the resulting arrival process has got the flavor of a non-homogeneous Poisson process (NHPP) where the probability of two or more events in any time interval is likewise negligible if that interval is small (see e. g. Ross 2003). Typically, the demand process is described by probabilities $P_{jt} \geq 0$ where the index j could denote again the product or a group of customers with a distinct type of choice behavior. Of course $\sum_j P_{jt} \leq 1$ has to hold for every t, and if $\sum_j P_{jt} < 1$ there is a positive probability that there is no arrival in period t. Note that micro period models imply nested capacity control, because it is assumed that the company decides on each request one at a time, so that there is no exclusive allocation of capacities to demand classes.

Lee and Hersh (1993, see page 61 in this book) develop a micro period model for airline RM on a single leg without overbooking and independent demand. In a second model they also take group bookings (i. e. requests for more than one seat) into account. The arrival process in this case is described by the probabilities P_{jmt} that an arrival in period t requests $m \in \{1, \ldots, M\}$ seats at fare j where M is an upper bound for the number of seats demanded in a single request (e. g.

$M = C$, where C is the number of seats on the aircraft, but M can be set to much smaller values for practical purposes). They show how to determine the number of micro periods T and the probabilities P_{jt} based on the assumption that demand for product j follows a NHPP with piecewise constant rate (as was mentioned earlier, the Poisson process seems to be closely connected in spirit to micro period models of demand). They also compute the necessary number of periods T for somc examples. Interestingly, Lautenbacher and Stidham (1999) present a Markov decision process unifying Lee and Hersh's micro period model and the block demand models of Belobaba (1989), Brumelle and McGill (1993), Curry (1990), Littlewood (1972), Robinson (1995) and Wollmer (1992).

Subramanian et al. (1999) extend Lee and Hersh's first model by including overbooking (they do not consider group bookings, though). In their demand model, in each period there is either demand for a single seat at a single fare, or a cancellation of a single seat at a single fare, or no request at all. They present two approaches to estimate the needed probabilities from the parameters of a NHPP (one is identical to the method proposed by Lee and Hersh 1993).

Both Lee and Hersh (1993) and Subramanian et al. (1999) conduct computational experiments on some small examples. Tables of the probabilities P_{jt} used in the experiments are given. Two other references where a micro period model is developed and tested in a simulation study where the probabilities are given by tables are You (1999) and van Ryzin and Liu (2004).

Since the micro period model is so closely related to a NHPP, Bertsimas and Popescu (2003), Bitran and Mondschein (1995), Pak and Dekker (2004), Spengler et al. (2007) and Talluri and van Ryzin (2004a) use Poisson processes in their simulation studies of their micro period models.

Simulation Optimization Methods

Numerous authors have recently developed simulation optimization methods for RM problems. These methods are typically independent of a demand model, hence we review them separately in this section. A simulation optimization approach is roughly outlined as Algorithm 5.1.

Bertsimas and de Boer (2005) use a slight variant of the NHPP defined by Weatherford et al. (1993) in their simulation optimization approach to airline network RM with a nested booking limit control. Van Ryzin and Vulcano (2005) present a continuous version of Bertsimas and de Boer's approach. In their experiments, they assume a "low

Algorithm 5.1: Simulation Optimization

1. Choose a particular control method, e. g. a booking limit control or a bid price control. Denote the control variables by $x_1, \ldots, x_n$.
2. Choose an initial control $x_1^0, \ldots, x_n^0$, e. g. by using a heuristic, or by choosing the values x_i^0 at random from a suitable domain.
3. Simulate stochastic demand data streams and execute the current control. Record relevant data (e. g. revenue, load factor) for each replication.
4. Update the control in light of the simulation results and iterate until convergence (or another stopping criterion) has been reached.

to high fare" block demand arrival process, where the total demand for each fare follows a truncated Normal distribution. The same authors pursue a similar approach (both with respect to the methods and the computer experiments) in a choice based setting (van Ryzin and Vulcano 2006). Like Bertsimas and de Boer (2005) and van Ryzin and Vulcano (2005), Gosavi et al. (2007) also consider booking limit controls on a network with independent demand, but they also incorporate overbooking. Klein (2005, 2007) implements a simulation optimization approach for a bid price control on a network with independent demand and without overbooking (see page 76). Both Gosavi et al. (2007) and Klein (2005, 2007) use NHPPs in their simulations.

Van Ryzin and Vulcano (2005, 2006) assume that demand is sufficiently "smooth" to prove local convergence of their approach, but they apply it to discrete demand cases in their computational studies as well. The other references practically allow for any demand process (however, their methods do not converge or no rigorous proof for convergence is given). Hence we can indeed claim that simulation optimization approaches that have recently appeared are independent of the demand model. At the same time, we note that the bulk of authors use NHPPs in their simulations, van Ryzin and Vulcano (2005) – who use a block demand model for that purpose – being the only exception.

Summary

We categorized the RM literature based on the underlying model of the dynamics of demand. Figure 5.1 shows the relationships of the different categories. In addition, there are approaches – namely those based on simulation optimization – that do not rely (or at least not much) on a particular model of demand.

During the course of our literature review, we found that continuous time models are explicitly based on Poisson processes. In dynamic pricing or choice-based RM situations the intensity of these processes is "controlled" by the prices or the offer set. Not surprisingly in computational experiments on continuous time models such Poisson processes are used for simulation as well. For the purely deterministic models and especially the micro period models and simulation optimization approaches the NHPP seems to be the state of the art, so we focus on the NHPP in the following.

For block demand and macro period models, only the aggregate distribution of demand (per block or per period, respectively) is relevant. Our literature review has revealed that most of the references with block demand models have appeared in the 80s and early 90s. Macro period models are rare because they are only of limited scope with respect to potential RM applications. We thus do not explicitly consider simulating demand for block demand and macro periods further. Note, however, that the methods to simulate a NHPP we are going to describe can nevertheless be used to generate stochastic demand data streams to evaluate the performance of such methods if the rather strict assumptions on the demand process are relaxed.

Most references implement a NHPP with a piecewise constant rate (with a very limited number of steps), and the choice of a particular rate function is almost never explained. A notable exception is Klein (2005, 2007), who uses a triangular rate (see Figure 5.2): There is no arrival before t^b. At this point, the intensity grows linearly until a maximum λ^* at time t^*, and then decays to 0 such that there are no arrivals after t^e. This approach is fairly general (since the four parameters can be chosen arbitrarily), the resulting arrival process seems to be realistic from an intuitive point of view, and – as Klein (2005) shows – the resulting NHPP is very easy to simulate. However, there seems to be no empirical evidence supporting Klein's process. In the following section, we will give an in depth description of the arrival process introduced Weatherford et al. (1993) and the variant used by de Boer et al. (2002) and Bertsimas and de Boer (2005). As we will see, this process has got a number of advantages compared to Klein's approach.

5.2 Simulating a Single Demand Data Stream

We begin by describing how to simulate a single demand data stream. If we assume independent demand and have n productsk, we can (in principle) use n such streams to generate demand data for all products.

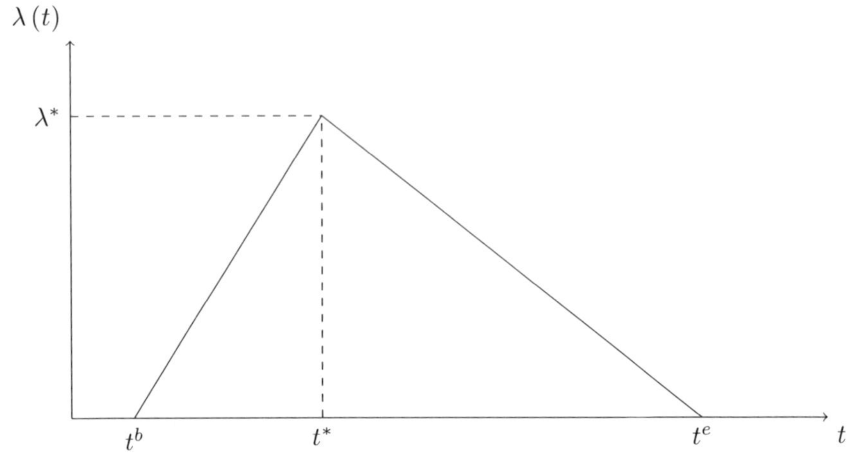

Fig. 5.2: triangular Arrival Rate as Used by Klein (2005, 2007)

Since the purpose of demand data simulation is to test RM models and methods, the n data streams have to relate to each other in a meaningful way. We will address this question in section 5.3.

In choice-based RM problems, a single demand data stream may already be enough – it creates a single stream of customer arrivals who then choose among the available products. If it is desired to differentiate between, say, n different classes of customers (e. g. business and leisure travelers in the airline case) and customers of different types arrive according to different demand processes, we can analogously use n data streams to generate arrivals of n types of customers.

Our exposition here (and in the following sections) will be completely independent of the area of application. This is to say that the methods are not limited to the airline case (or any other industry). We will confine ourselves to arrival processes of a certain mathematical structure. This structure – which is backed by some limited empirical evidence from the airline industry – covers a broad range of arrival patterns and should thus be suitable for many industries and applications.

Simulating a stochastic data stream requires to generate random numbers with computers. We therefore start by making some brief remarks on random number generation. We then describe how such random numbers can be used to simulate NHPPs. We continue by defining a special structure for the rate function of the NHPP and show how a simulation of NHPPs with that particular rate function can be implemented. We then review its properties and demonstrate its advantages in comparison to previous approaches.

5.2.1 Random Number Generation

A computer is a deterministic machine, thus it is not capable to produce streams of "truly random" outputs. The best we can expect is that if a computer simulates tosses of a fair coin, say, the output will appear as if it was constructed by tossing a real fair coin. Therefore random number-generating methods are often called *pseudorandom number generators*. Actually all pseudorandom number generators of interest are of the form $x_{n+1} = f(x_n)$ where x_n, x_{n+1} are the n-th and $n+1$-st random numbers, respectively, and f is a deterministic function. As a consequence, anybody that knows f and x_n can predict the following random numbers $x_{n+1}, x_{n+2}, \ldots$ with absolute accuracy. This seems to be odd, but it is – in fact – a desirable property, because researchers conducting simulation studies can supply f (in form of a C++-program, for instance) and the so called *seeds* x_0 to their fellows, who will then be able to reproduce the complete stream of random numbers. A random number generator with that property is called *portable*. Note that it is somewhat difficult to port random number generators between operating systems or even different machine types, because some implementation details (libraries, processor word length etc.) are different.

Developing a pseudorandom number generator which indeed outputs streams that appear to be truly random is a formidable task and numerous authors point out that the implementations of random number generators shipped with programming languages and operating systems may not be very good (Bratley et al. 1987, p. 192, Knuth 1998, p. 193, Law and Kelton 2000, p. 406). We use L'Ecuyer's portable pseudorandom number generator MRG32K3A that has been thoroughly tested. A C-implementation is given in L'Ecuyer (1999), packages for other programming languages are available for download (L'Ecuyer et al. 2002).

Like almost all pseudorandom number generators MRG32K3A generates uniformly distributed random numbers from the real interval $[0, 1]$. Random numbers following other, uni- or multivariate distributions have to be obtained from these uniform random numbers by transformations. There is a large body of literature on such transformations, e. g. Bratley et al. (1987), Devroye (1986), Knuth (1998), Law and Kelton (2000) and Niederreiter (1992).

5.2.2 Simulating NHPPs (with Arbitrary Rate Functions)

We are now going to show how a non-homogeneous Poisson process (NHPP) can be simulated. A NHPP is characterized by its *rate function* $\lambda_j(t)$ such that the higher $\lambda_j(t)$ for any point in time t, the more arrivals from this process are to be expected. If $\lambda_j(t) = c$ for all t and a constant c, the intensity of arrivals does not vary over time, and the resulting process is called a homogeneous (or stationary) Poisson process (HPP). A detailed introduction into HPPs and NHPPs is e. g. given by Ross (2003).

We are given a random number generator which is able to produce uniformly distributed random numbers from the real interval $[0, 1]$. In the following, we denote such random variables by $U \sim U(0, 1)$. As usual, capital letters indicate random variables, and the corresponding lower-case letters indicate realizations, e. g. u is a realization of U. We use superscripts to denote a sequence of independent random variables or their realizations, e. g. $U^1, U^2, \ldots, U^N$ or $u^1, u^2, \ldots, u^N$.

Using the realizations $u^1, u^2, \ldots$ we want to simulate the j-th stream of demand, i. e. a NHPP with rate $\lambda_j(t)$. "Simulating" precisely means to generate an ordered list $t^1, t^2, \ldots$ such that t^i is the time of the i-th arrival. Denote the time horizon by $[0, T]$ where 0 is the beginning and T is the end of the horizon.

If $\lambda_j(t) = \lambda$ for all $t \in [0, T]$ and a constant λ, we actually have a homogeneous Poisson process (HPP). This process is not particularly realistic, but very easy to simulate: It is a well known fact (see e. g. Ross 2003) that the interarrival times of a HPP are exponentially distributed with rate λ. To generate random numbers $X \sim \exp(\lambda)$, we can use the so called *Inverse Transformation method* (see Bratley et al. 1987, Law and Kelton 2000, for instance): If u is a realization of a random variable $U \sim U(0, 1)$ then $x = -\ln u/\lambda$ has got the desired distribution. To simulate the HPP, we generate a stream $x^1, x^2, \ldots, x^N$ of N realizations of $X \sim \exp(\lambda)$ such that $\sum_{i=1}^{N} x^i > T$ and $\sum_{i=1}^{N-1} x^i \leq T$. Then the counting process having arrival times $\sum_{j=1}^{i} x^j, i = 1, \ldots, N-1$ is a realization of the desired HPP.

The situation is a little bit more complicated for a true non-homogeneous Poisson process with a non-constant rate, because the interarrival times can no longer be computed in such a simple way. Lewis and Shedler (1979) have developed an elegant method to simulate a NHPP, which is called *Thinning*, based on the following idea: Assume that $\lambda_j(t) < \infty$ for all $t \in [0, T]$ (a very reasonable assumption, especially when we have the purpose of generating demand data in mind). It follows that for each $t \in [0, T]$ a finite real number $\overline{\lambda}_j(t)$

exists such that $\tau \in [t,T] \Rightarrow \overline{\lambda}_j(t) \geq \lambda_j(\tau)$. Suppose that arrival times for the interval $[0,t]$ have already been generated. Simulate a HPP (as described before) with a rate of $\overline{\lambda}_j(t)$. Literally speaking, this HPP has got "too many" arrivals, so reject an arrival at time τ with probability $\lambda(\tau)/\overline{\lambda}_j(t)$, thereby "thinning out" the stream of arrivals (hence the name of the method).

The complete simulation technique can then be formally describe as follows: Given the values $\overline{\lambda}_j(t)$, we generate a sequence of independent random variables X^1, U^1, X^2, U^2, ... where X^i is a random variable with exponential distribution with rate $\overline{\lambda}_j(t_i)$ and $t_i = \sum_{j=1}^{i-1} x^j$. We stop as soon as we have reached a sequence of length N such that $\sum_{i=1}^{N} x^i > T$ and $\sum_{i=1}^{N-1} x^i \leq T$. Consider now the set of indices

$$I = \left\{ i \in \{1,\ldots,N-1\} : u^i \leq \frac{\lambda_j\left(\sum_{j=1}^{i} x^j\right)}{\overline{\lambda}_j(t_i)} \right\}$$

The counting process having arrival times $\sum_{j=1}^{i} x^j, i \in I$ constitutes the desired NHPP with rate $\lambda_j(t)$.

Since the Thinning method is obviously most efficient if $\overline{\lambda}_j(t)$ is as small as possible, we simply set

$$\overline{\lambda}_j(t) = \max_{\tau \in [t,T]} \lambda_j(\tau) \tag{5.1}$$

This maximum can be computed by a closed formula for our rate functions $\lambda_j(t)$ (see below).

5.2.3 The Beta-Gamma Arrival Process

The Thinning method is completely independent of the rate function $\lambda_j(t)$ and works for all NHPPs with finite intensities. We are now going to specify the details of the rate function as we have implemented it.

Properties of a General NHPP

We start by pointing out some key properties of a NHPP (see e. g. Ross 2003) with rate $\lambda_j(t)$: Denote the number of arrivals up to time t by the random variable $N_j(t)$. The expected number of arrivals is $E[N_j(t)] = \Lambda_j(t)$ where $\Lambda_j(t) = \int_0^t \lambda_j(u)\,du$. The number of arrivals in the interval $(t, t+d]$ is then distributed Poisson with rate $\Lambda_j(t+d) - \Lambda_j(t)$, i. e. we have:

$$P\left(N_j\left(t+d\right)-N_j\left(t\right)=x\right)=e^{-\left(\Lambda_j\left(t+d\right)-\Lambda_j\left(t\right)\right)}\frac{\left(\Lambda_j\left(t+d\right)-\Lambda_j\left(t\right)\right)^x}{x!} \tag{5.2}$$

In particular, for the number of arrivals in the interval $(0, T]$ (i. e. the total demand) we have:

$$P\left(N_j\left(T\right)=x\right)=e^{-\Lambda_j\left(T\right)}\frac{\Lambda_j\left(T\right)^x}{x!}$$

The total demand is thus a random variable that follows a Poisson distribution with parameter λ_j where the constant λ_j is defined by $\lambda_j = \Lambda_j\left(T\right)$; and an analogous statement holds for the demand in any interval $(t, t+d] \subset [0, T]$, see (5.2).

The following aspect is also interesting: Suppose, we have recorded exactly n arrivals up to time $u \geq 0$. The probability to have exactly x arrivals in the interval $(t, T]$ is then

$$P\left(N_j\left(T\right)-N_j\left(t\right)=x\middle|\, N_j\left(u\right)=n\right)=P\left(N_j\left(T\right)-N_j\left(t\right)=x\right)$$

This equality follows from the "independent increments" property of the NHPP, which is also known under name "memoryless property".

In words, a NHPP has got the following features:

- Demand in any subinterval as well as total demand follows a Poisson distribution.
- Observed demand does not convey information about demand to come.

The first property implies the following: Since demand is Poisson, the distribution of demand depends only on the single parameter λ_j of the Poisson distribution, where the mean demand is $\mu_j = \lambda_j$, the standard deviation is $\sigma_j = \sqrt{\lambda_j}$, and the coefficient of variation is $\sigma_j/\mu_j = 1/\sqrt{\lambda_j}$. As e. g. Williamson (1992, p. 146) points out, this is certainly a loss of flexibility compared to distributions like the Normal or the Gamma, where the standard deviation and the coefficient of variation can be defined independently of the mean.

The second property seems to be somewhat odd as well. Note that both properties are totally independent of the actual form of $\lambda_j\left(t\right)$, as long as $\Lambda_j\left(t\right)$ is a constant for all $t \in [0, T]$. Actually, $\lambda_j\left(t\right)$ can be an arbitrary complicated deterministic function – as long as it is integrable, the integral $\Lambda_j\left(T\right) = \int_0^T \lambda_j\left(u\right) du$ evaluates to a constant, and the above stated properties provably hold. This is the case for almost any rate function used in the literature so far, namely the popular (piecewise) constant and (piecewise) linear rates, e. g. the one used by Klein (2005, 2007, see Figure 5.2).

Description of the Beta-Gamma-Rate Function

To overcome the disadvantages we just noted, we propose to use the following rate function, which was introduced by de Boer et al. (2002) and Bertsimas and de Boer (2005) based on ideas of Weatherford et al. (1993):

$$\lambda_j(t) = D_j \cdot \beta(t) \tag{5.3}$$

where D_j is a random variable that follows a Gamma distribution with parameters γ_j, δ_j and $\beta(t)$ is the density function of the Beta distribution standardized on the interval $[0, T]$.

The density function of the Gamma distribution is defined as

$$f(d_j) = \frac{\delta_j^{-\gamma_j}}{\Gamma(\gamma_j)} e^{-d_j/\delta_j} d_j^{\gamma_j - 1} \qquad \text{with} \qquad \Gamma(\gamma_j) = \int_0^\infty e^{-x} x^{\gamma_j - 1} dx \, .$$

A few examples of this function are plotted in Figure 5.3. Expectation and standard deviation of the Gamma distribution are given by the following formulas:

$$E[D_j] = \gamma_j \delta_j \qquad \sigma(D_j) = \sqrt{\gamma_j}\delta_j \tag{5.4}$$

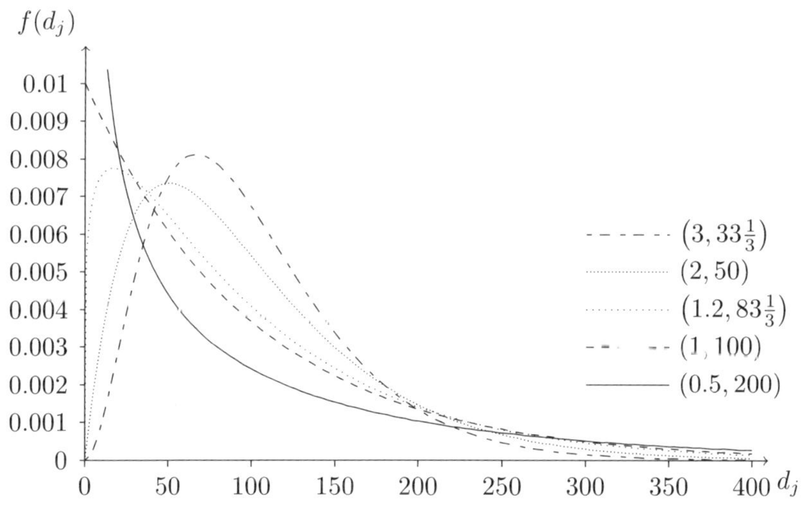

Fig. 5.3: Examples of Gamma Density Functions with Parameters (γ_j, δ_j)

We have implemented a method described by Marsaglia and Tsang (2000) to generate Gamma random variables with parameters γ_j and δ_j. For this procedure, a random variable with standard Normal distribution is required. Marsaglia and Tsang (2000) provide an algorithm for generating standard Normal random numbers as well, but we have implemented a simpler textbook routine named Polar method that is described, for instance, by Knuth (1998) and Law and Kelton (2000).

The density function of the Beta distribution over the interval $[0, T]$ is defined as

$$\beta(t) = \frac{1}{T \cdot B(\alpha_j, \beta_j)} \left(\frac{t}{T}\right)^{\alpha_j - 1} \left(1 - \frac{t}{T}\right)^{\beta_j - 1}$$

where $B(\alpha_j, \beta_j)$ is the *Beta function*

$$B(\alpha_j, \beta_j) = \int_0^1 t^{\alpha_j - 1}(1-t)^{\beta_j - 1} dt = \frac{\Gamma(\alpha_j)\Gamma(\beta_j)}{\Gamma(\alpha_j + \beta_j)} \tag{5.5}$$

See Figure 5.4 for an illustration of the density function of the Beta distribution.

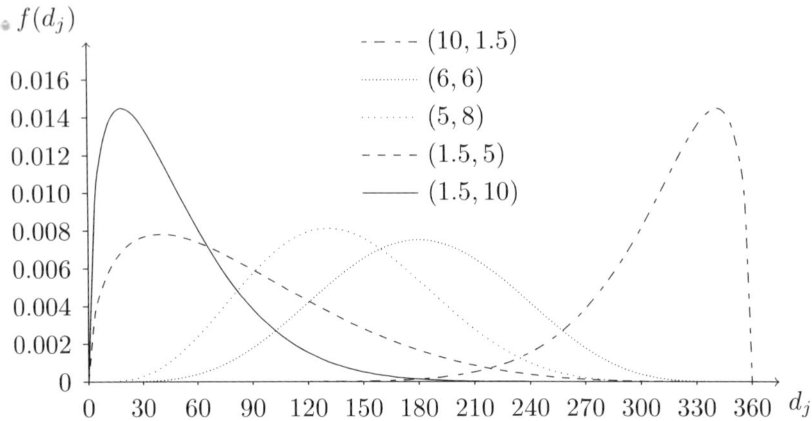

Fig. 5.4: Examples of Beta Density Functions with Parameters (α_j, β_j) and $T = 360$

Note that $\lim_{t\to 0} \beta(t) = \infty$ if $\alpha_j < 1$, and $\lim_{t\to T} \beta(t) = \infty$ if $\beta_j < 1$, so we should always choose $\alpha_j \geq 1$ as well as $\beta_j \geq 1$ to generate demand data. It should be remarked that for $\alpha_j > 1$ and $\beta_j > 1$ the Beta density function has a unique peak at

$$\frac{\alpha_j - 1}{\alpha_j + \beta_j - 2} T \tag{5.6}$$

Three special cases are worth to be mentioned:

(1) If we choose $\alpha_j = 1$ as well as $\beta_j = 1$, we get $\lambda_j(t) = \frac{D_j}{T}$ – a constant rate.

(2) If we choose $\alpha_j = 1$ and $\beta_j = 2$, we get $\lambda_j(t) = \frac{2D_j}{T} - \frac{2D_j}{T^2}t$ – a linear rate with $\lambda_j(T) = 0$.

(3) If we choose $\alpha_j = 2$ and $\beta_j = 1$, we get $\lambda_j(t) = \frac{2D_j}{T^2}t$ – a linear rate with $\lambda_j(0) = 0$.

If we want to compute the Beta density function, the basic problem is to evaluate the Beta function $B(\alpha_j, \beta_j)$ which means that we need to evaluate the Gamma function $\Gamma(x)$. Unfortunately, the integral that defines $\Gamma(x)$ has no closed-form solution in general, therefore we have to approximate the value of $\Gamma(x)$ numerically. Note that $\Gamma(x) = (x-1)\,\Gamma(x-1)$ holds for $x > 1$ and

$$x \in \mathbb{N} \Rightarrow \Gamma(x) = (x-1)!$$

The values of Γ thus grow very fast, so that it became common practice to approximate $\ln \Gamma$ (see e. g. Press et al. 1992). We have implemented the approximation along the lines of Pugh (2004). $B(\alpha_j, \beta_j)$ can then be computed using

$$B(\alpha_j, \beta_j) = e^{\ln \Gamma(\alpha_j) + \ln \Gamma(\beta_j) - \ln \Gamma(\alpha_j + \beta_j)}$$

Properties of the Beta-Gamma-NHPP

Since the rate of the Beta-Gamma-NHPP depends on the random variable D_j, it is a special case of a so called *doubly stochastic Poisson process*, which is sometimes called a *mixed Poisson process* (Cox and Isham 1980, p. 10-11, 70-75) or a *Cox Process* – this term is based on the seminal paper by Cox (1955). These special kind of point processes are covered in some more advanced textbooks, see e. g. Kingman (1993, chapter 6), Reiss (1993, p. 59-61), Daley and Vere-Jones (2003, p. 169-175). A comprehensive treatment can be found in Grandell (1976, 1997).

This process is to be simulated as follows: For each replication, generate a realization d_j of D_j. (5.3) then becomes a deterministic function, and we can use the Thinning method to generate the arrival times. This again clarifies the term conditional Poisson process: The realization of the process is conditioned on the realization of D_j.

Since $\beta(t)$ is a density function over $[0,T]$, we have $\int_0^T \beta(t)\,dt = 1$, and the expected demand $E[N(T)|D_j = d_j]$ is:

$$E[N_j(T)|D_j = d_j] = \Lambda_j(T|D_j = d_j) = \int_0^T d_j\beta(t)\,dt = d_j$$

– in other words, the total demand (which is a random variable, D_j) is spread over the interval $[0,T]$ by the density function $\beta(j)$. Interestingly, similar approaches are used to model arrivals to call centers, see e. g. Avramidis et al. (2004) and Jongbloed and Koole (2001).

It is worth to be highlighted that there is empirical evidence to use a Gamma distributed random variable for modeling the expected total demand of a product. For instance, Beckmann and Bobkoski (1958) report that a Gamma distribution is reasonable for the total demand in the airline case. Similarly, de Boer et al. (2002) report that in de Boer's master's thesis it turned out that the sales process of tickets in an airline case fits (5.3).

In addition to the empirical relevance, there are also good theoretical reasons for using a Gamma distributed random variable. One reason is that the marginal distribution of the NHPP turns out to be a negative Binomial distribution. We thus do not only avoid the potential pitfalls of Poisson demand, but we can also compute the probability that the total demand equals a certain value d_j with a closed formula (see e. g. Stuart and Ord 1987). Furthermore, the parameter estimation problem is simplified (see section 5.4). Another reason is that the posterior distribution of the events of the NHPP turns out to be a Gamma distribution as well[1] (see e. g. DeGroot 1970). Both properties are certainly not relevant for the simulation of demand data streams alone, but they are of course extremely important for any RM optimization technique.

Note that these advantageous features are unique compared to any other demand process that has been used in the literature so far.

The variant used by Weatherford et al. (1993)

It is interesting to note that Weatherford et al. (1993) assume a slightly different rate, namely:

$$\lambda_j(t) = D \cdot p_j \cdot \beta(t)$$

where D is a single Gamma random variable (which does not depend on j) and p_j is the probability that an arrival is of type j (where type can,

[1] For the convenience of the reader, both results are presented in Appendix A, along with some additional remarks.

again, be a product, a customer group with a specific choice behavior etc.). This approach seems to be considerably less flexible, because for fixed p_j, means and variances can only be varied simultaneously and not individually for a particular j. Using our approach we can, for instance, keep the average number of arrivals of type j constant and only increase or decrease the variance. Therefore, we have chosen to implement the variant of de Boer et al. (2002) and Bertsimas and de Boer (2005).

Defining the Parameters

So far we have intensively discussed the structure of the rate function to be used in our simulations, as well as the properties of the resulting NHPP and the demand. It remains to be described how the parameters α_j, β_j of the Beta density function and the parameters γ_j, δ_j of the Gamma distribution should be chosen. The former define solely the intensity of arrivals over time, and the latter solely determine the total demand to come, thus we can decide about α_j, β_j and γ_j, δ_j in isolation.

For the former, we assume that it is intuitive for the user to specify the value of the mode

$$\frac{\alpha_j - 1}{\alpha_j + \beta_j - 2} T$$

(i. e. where the peak intensity is) as input. In addition, the user of our simulator has to specify the value of the variance of the beta distribution

$$\frac{\alpha_j \beta_j}{(\alpha_j + \beta_j)^2 (\alpha_j + \beta_j + 1)}$$

as input as well. In our setting, this is not the variance af a random variable but it defines the shape of the peak: If the variance is low, the peak is very sharp and off-peak demand is negligible. If the variance is high, the peak "flattens" and there is also considerable demand before and after the peak. Figure 5.5 illustrates several Beta distribution functions with the same mode for different values α_j and β_j (and the corresponding variance). Given mode and variance, the parameters α_j and β_j can be derived uniquely.

The parameters γ_j, δ_j can easily be specified by defining the mean and standard deviation of D_j using formulas (5.4), that is, the conditional expectation of the total demand is defined. Since we know that the marginal distribution of the total demand is a negative Binomial, we can also specify mean and standard deviation of the total demand directly, and then derive the parameters γ_j, δ_j defining the distribution of D_j. However, since the choice of γ_j, δ_j influences total demand,

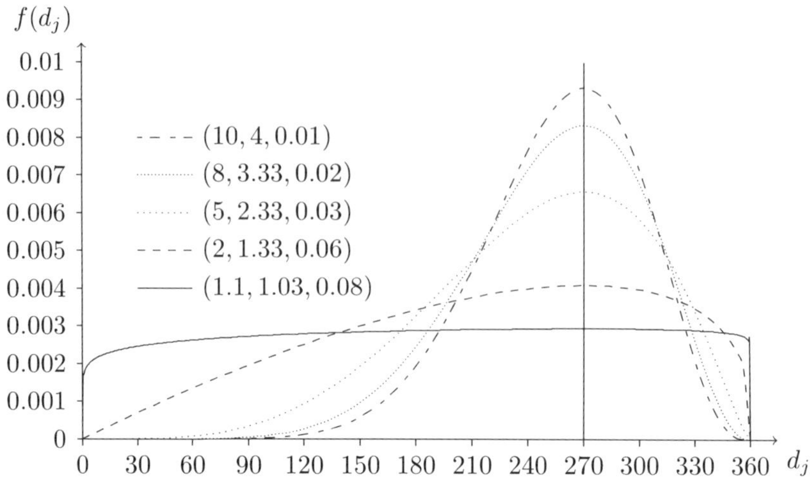

Fig. 5.5: Several Beta Distribution Functions with Parameters (α_j, β_j) and $T = 360$ such that the Variance Lies within 0.01 to 0.08 and the Mode Equals 270

in the following section we argue that the parameters γ_j, δ_j should be determined jointly in a systematic way for all j.

5.3 Simulating Multiple Demand Data Streams

To determine the parameters which influence the total volume of demand, we propose to base the choice on the expected capacity utilization: If demand is high, capacity utilization will also be high, and the RM problem gets more difficult. So if we want to be able to generate instances with predefined characteristics, capacity utilization is certainly a relevant measure. The expected capacity utilization is sometimes called "nominal load factor", because it specifies the "load" on the available resources as a percentage of the resource availability. This load is only "nominal", because in a reasonable RM setting, this load factor will be close to or higher than 1 – if expected demand was considerably lower than the available resources, there would be no need for RM techniques in the first place, and a simple FCFS policy would be optimal. The "actual" load factor will of course be at most 1.

Determining the expected capacity utilization does not only depend on the resource capacities and the dynamics of demand (namely our parameters γ_j, δ_j), but also on the degree of interaction of customers and the environment. We will thus differentiate in the following between independent demand and choice models of demand. In our software, we have implemented the former, because – as we will see – taking the nominal load factor into account when generating demand for RM problem with choice behavior depends heavily on the choice model to be used. In subsection 5.3.3, we demonstrate how our methods can be used to cover RM problems with flexible products, both with independent demand and choice models of demand.

5.3.1 Expected Capacity Utilization Under Independent Demand

Let E be the set of resources and N be the set of products. We are going to use $|N|$ independent data streams to generate demands for each of the products. $c_e > 0$ denotes the capacity of resource $e \in E$. For each resource $e \in E$ and each product $j \in N$, let $r_{je} \geq 0$ be the capacity on resource e that is needed for one unit of product j. In the airline case, for example, r_{je} is the number of seats that are occupied on leg e if one ticket of type j is sold. Thus for single-person tickets, it holds that $r_{je} \in \{0, 1\}$ and a value $r_{je} = 0$ indicates that the flight for which ticket j is sold does not use leg e. Note, however, that the following procedure is by no means limited to the airline case without group bookings – since we do not make any further assumptions about the relationship of resources and E, the capacities c_e and the coefficients r_{je}, any application can be covered by our method.

The expected capacity utilization $\mathcal{U}_e$ on resource e is then

$$\mathcal{U}_e = \frac{\sum_{j=1}^{n} r_{je} E\left[D_j\right]}{c_e}$$

As indicated before, $\mathcal{U}_e$ is an input used by our software to derive the parameters γ_j, δ_j. We assume that the load factor on each resource is identical, i. e. that $\mathcal{U}_e = \mathcal{U}$ holds for all $e \in E$. An instance is easier to define this way, and much less parameters are needed to describe it. This facilitates the comparison of computational results. Furthermore, the additional flexibility of allowing $\mathcal{U}$ to vary with e does not seem to add much to an instance generation scheme. If we consider, for instance, a hub-and-spoke network with two hubs, it may well be that the load factor on the inter-hub link is considerably higher. The RM problem will then be driven by the bottleneck, and the load factor on the spoke legs will not be very important. It would thus be no harm to increase the load factor on the spoke legs as well. However, using resource specific capacity utilizations $\mathcal{U}_e$ in the following would not at all be a problem.

Given $\mathcal{U}$ we define the parameters γ_j, δ_j for all $j \in N$ using Algorithm 5.2. An important prerequisite for that algorithm is that for each resource $e \in E$ there exists at least one product such that the product only uses this resource, i. e. there has to exist a product j such that $r_{je} > 0$ and $r_{jf} = 0, f \in E \backslash \{e\}$. We believe that this assumption is not restrictive in most applications. For the airline case, for instance, it seems to be reasonable to assume that tickets are available for each single non-stop flight.

Algorithm 5.2: Defining γ_j, δ_j using $\mathcal{U}$ under Independent Demand

1. Set $P = \emptyset$ where P denotes the set of all products for which demand data has already been generated.
2. Given $\mathcal{U}$, the "available" capacity c'_e on resource e is computed to be $c'_e = \mathcal{U} \cdot c_e$ for all resources $e \in E$.
3. Determine the set E' of resources with $c'_e > 0$. If $E' = \emptyset$ then stop.
4. Choose an resource e^* such that $c'_{e^*} \leq c'_e$ for all $e \in E'$.
5. Consider the set $P_{e^*} \subseteq \{1, \ldots, n\}$ of all products j with $r_{je^*} > 0$ which are not in P already (i. e. $j \notin P$).
6. For each product $j \in P_{e^*}$ the user is requested to specify a proportion $\pi_j > 0$ as input to define what amount of the capacity is expected to be demanded by product j. These proportions must be set such that $\sum_{j \in P_{e^*}} \pi_j = 1$ holds. To ease the usage of our software, our code automatically chooses $\pi_j = \frac{1}{|P_{e^*}|}$ so that no further user input is needed.
7. For each product $j \in P_{e^*}$ determine γ_j, δ_j such that
$$\gamma_j \delta_j = \frac{\pi_j c'_{e^*}}{r_{je^*}}$$
holds. To do this, we request the user to specify the value of the coefficient of variation
$$\frac{\sigma(D_j)}{E[D_j]} = \frac{1}{\sqrt{\gamma_j}}$$
for each product $j \in \{1, \ldots, n\}$ as input which yields γ_j and from which δ_j can then be derived.
8. Update $P = P \cup P_{e^*}$.
9. For each product $j \in P_{e^*}$ consider all resources $e \in E'$ with $r_{je} > 0$ and update $c'_e = c'_e - r_{je} E[D_j]$.
10. Goto 3.

5.3.2 Expected Capacity Utilization Under a Choice Model of Demand

Let E, N, c_e, r_{je} be as before. Under a choice model of demand, we do not have a one-to-one correspondence between products and demand data streams – in fact, the number of streams can be chosen arbitrarily. For the ease of exposition, we will consider the case with a single demand data stream first, i. e. the problem is to define parameters γ, δ in a meaningful, systematic way based on an (expected) nominal load factor $\mathcal{U}$.

A choice model of demand specifies a choice probability $P_j(S)$ that product $j \in S$ is chosen if $S \subseteq N$ is the offer set. In a reasonable choice model, we have $P_j(S) \geq 0$, $j \notin S \Rightarrow P_j(S) = 0$ and $\sum_{j \in S} P_j(S) \leq 1$ – it is allowed that $\sum_{j \in S} P_j(S) < 1$, i. e. there may be a positive probability that no product is chosen if set S is offered.

For given values γ, δ and a fixed offer set $S \subseteq N$, the expected utilization of resource $e \in E$ is then:

$$\mathcal{U}_e(S) = \gamma\delta \frac{\sum_{j \in S} P_j(S)\, r_{je}}{c_e} \tag{5.7}$$

In this formula, $P_j(S)$ is the probability that r_{je} units of resource e are consumed. The expected capacity consumption for any request is then $\sum_{j \in S} P_j(S)\, r_{je}$, and $\gamma\delta$ is the expected number of requests. The offer set S is though unknown at the time of instance generation because it depends on the RM policy, and our instance generation scheme should clearly be independent of the method to be tested. Note that this problem did not occur in the independent demand case because we assumed that customers will choose a single, known product. If their desired product is not available they will exit the market. While the actual load factor thus depends on the RM policy indeed, the "nominal" load factor does not.

For the choice setting, it seems natural to use the offer set N in (5.7), i. e. we consider the case the choice of product is not restricted by the RM policy. This is (in some sense) analogous to the independent demand case where we define the nominal load factor to be the fraction of capacity of each resource demanded under the assumption that choice is in the first place not restricted by the RM policy as well. Note that even if all products N are offered this does not guarantee that any request is granted under all circumstances, because we may run out of capacity for some of the products in the offer set. For given values γ, δ we therefore define the expected utilization of resource $e \in E$ to be

$\mathcal{U}_e(N)$. However, it would be absolutely no problem to replace N with any non-empty offer set $S \subseteq N$ in the following.

It is obviously impossible to choose γ, δ such that $\mathcal{U}_e(N) = \mathcal{U}$ holds for some given $\mathcal{U}$ and all $e \in E$ like in the independent demand setting. We therefore require that $\mathcal{U}$ is the *average* nominal load factor:

$$\mathcal{U} = \frac{\sum_{e\in E} \mathcal{U}_e(N)}{|E|} = \frac{\gamma\delta}{|E|} \sum_{e\in E} \sum_{j\in N} P_j(N) \, r_{je}/c_e \tag{5.8}$$

In addition, the coefficient of variation should be specified. Like in Algorithm 5.2, this yields γ, and δ can then be derived from (5.8).

If we use $m \geq 2$ demand data streams where demand of type $i = 1, \ldots, m$ follows choice model $P_{ij}(S)$, we have:

$$\mathcal{U}_e(S) = \sum_{i=1}^{m} \gamma_i \delta_i \frac{\sum_{j\in S} P_{ij}(S) \, r_{je}}{c_e}$$

As for the independent demand case, we then need values $0 < \pi_i < 1$, denoting the fraction of total demand arriving from stream i. Let $\mathcal{U}$ be again the average nominal load factor. We have:

$$\pi_i \mathcal{U} = \frac{\gamma_i \delta_i}{|E|} \sum_{e\in E} \sum_{j\in N} P_{ij}(N) \, r_{je}/c_e \tag{5.9}$$

If the coefficient of variation with respect to stream i is specified as well, it can be used together with (5.9) to derive γ_i, δ_i.

5.3.3 Expected Capacity Utilization with Flexible Products

Under a choice model of demand, defining the expected capacity utilization becomes a little bit tricky because the choice behavior of customers introduces uncertainty about the resource consumption induced by arrivals. With flexible products, the situation is somewhat similar, because which resources are actually consumed by a request is determined by the supplier in that case.

For the ease of exposition, we assume independent demand first. Let N be again the set of products – some of which may be flexible –, and we have demand arriving from $|N|$ stochastic data streams such that customers from stream j will try to buy product j and exit the market if it is not available.

Let E and c_e be defined as before. The problem is now to specify the resource consumption coefficients r_{je} for a flexible product j. For instance, let j be a flexible product that is either produced on resource $e \in E$ or on resource $f \neq e$. We model this situation by using the coefficients r'_{je}, r'_{jf}, where r'_{je} denotes the amount of resource e that is consumed by product j *if* j *is actually scheduled to use* e. Let us assume that we have an estimate $\pi_{je} \geq 0$ of the probability that product j will be scheduled on resource e. We require that $\pi_{je} = 0 \Leftrightarrow r'_{je} = 0$. We can then define the expected resource consumption coefficients $r_{je} = \pi_{je} r'_{je}$ and proceed by using Algorithm 5.2.

It remains to be defined how sensible estimates π_{je} can be obtained – these probabilities obviously depend heavily on the realized demand process, the acceptance/rejection policy and the method used to schedule the flexible products. However, since flexible products will be scheduled in a way to fill up capacity that would otherwise not be used, an estimate can be obtained as follows: Let j be a flexible product that can either use resource e or resource f. Then it is reasonable to assume that the probabilities to consume resource e or f are given by

$$\pi_{je} = \frac{\mathcal{U}_e}{\mathcal{U}_e + \mathcal{U}_f} \text{ and } \pi_{jf} = \frac{\mathcal{U}_f}{\mathcal{U}_e + \mathcal{U}_f}, \text{ respectively.}$$

Since we want to generate an instance where the nominal loads $\mathcal{U}_e$ are identical for each resource $e \in E$, these probabilities are exactly 1/2. To formalize this finding, let $E'_j(e) \subseteq E$ be the set of resources that can be used instead of $e \in E$ for the production of j. As a convention, let $e \in E'_j(e)$, such that we have $E'_j(e) = \{e\}$ for all non-flexible products j. The desired probabilities are then given by $\pi_{je} = 1/|E'(e)|$.

If we desire to generate demand data for a RM problem with flexible products under a choice model of demand, we simply define $r_{je} = \pi_{je} r'_{je} = r'_{je}/|E'(e)|$ as for the independent demand case and proceed using the ideas presented in subsection 5.3.2.

5.4 Some Remarks on Parameter Estimation

If real-world demand data is given, it is certainly interesting to estimate the parameters $\alpha_j, \beta_j, \gamma_j, \delta_j$ so that "real" demand data (that is, demand data generated using actual parameter values) can be simulated. This is also a crucial part needed to assess if our model of arrivals (5.3) fits demand data from practice. In this section, we will make some brief remarks on how to estimate $\alpha_j, \beta_j, \gamma_j, \delta_j$ given a sample of the j-th demand data stream. We have already mentioned in section 4.4 that it may be difficult to obtain such a sample in practice for various reasons;

in the following we will however assume that the recorded sales data has already been cleaned and unconstrained properly.

Since we know that total demand follows a negative Binomial distribution, γ_j, δ_j can easily be estimated given a sample of the observed total demand, see Avramidis et al. (2004) and Jongbloed and Koole (2001) for a description that is directly related to negative Binomial demand created by a NHPP with a rate function governed by a Gamma random variable.

Many authors describe non-parametric methods to estimate the rate function $\lambda_j(t)$ of a NHPP; see e. g. the seminal paper by Leemis (1991) who describes how a piecewise linear approximation of the rate can be obtained. However, such methods are not suitable for our purposes, because we actually want to estimate the parameters α_j and β_j from a given sample and use these estimates as inputs for our simulator.

Estimating α_j, β_j poses some difficulties, because the Beta function can only be evaluated numerically. We will roughly outline a weighted least squares estimator and a maximum likelihood estimator along the lines of Massey et al. (1996), who consider the (already non-trivial) problem to estimate the parameters a, b for a NHPP with a linear rate, i. e. $\lambda(t) = a + bt, t \in [0, T]$. Since the demand data streams are independent, we will omit the index j in the following to improve readability.

In principle, a realization of a NHPP is the number n of total arrivals observed in $[0, T]$ and an ordered list of event times $t_1 < \ldots < t_n$. These event times can be used directly for estimation, see e. g. Johnson et al. (1994) and Kuhl et al. (1997). However, like Massey et al. (1996), we assume that the $[0, T]$ has been divided into N subintervals. Let t_k be the beginning of the k-th interval, $k = 1, \ldots, N$. We require that $t_1 = 0$ and for ease of notation we define $t_{N+1} = T$. Denote the total demand, i. e. the observed number of arrivals by d. It is important to emphasize that given the sample of the realized process d is no longer a random variable but a known constant. Denote the number of arrivals in the k-th interval by Y_k – a random variable (depending on α, β) following a Poisson distribution with parameter λ_k where

$$\begin{aligned}
\lambda_k &= \int_{t_k}^{t_{k+1}} \lambda_j(t)\, dt = \int_{t_k}^{t_{k+1}} d \cdot \beta(t)\, dt \\
&= d \int_{t_k}^{t_{k+1}} \frac{1}{T \cdot B(\alpha, \beta)} \left(\frac{t}{T}\right)^{\alpha-1} \left(1 - \frac{t}{T}\right)^{\beta-1} dt
\end{aligned}$$

Upon substituting $z = g(t) = t/T \Rightarrow dt = dz/g'(x) = T dz$ we obtain:

$$\lambda_k = d \cdot \frac{1}{B(\alpha,\beta)} \int_{t_k/T}^{t_{k+1}/T} z^{\alpha-1}(1-z)^{\beta-1}\,dz$$
$$= d\left[I_{t_{k+1}/T}(\alpha,\beta) - I_{t_k/T}(\alpha,\beta)\right]$$

where

$$I_t(\alpha,\beta) = \frac{1}{B(\alpha,\beta)} \int_0^t z^{\alpha-1}(1-z)^{\beta-1}\,dz \qquad \text{for all } t \in [0,1] \quad (5.10)$$

is the *incomplete Beta function*[2]. Comparing (5.10) with (5.5) we see that $I_1(\alpha,\beta) = 1$.

For the weighted least squares estimator, we assume that $Y_k = \lambda_k + \varepsilon_k$, where ε_k is a random variable with mean 0. As usual, let y_k be the realization of Y_k and denote the weight of the k-th observation by w_k. To obtain weighted least squares estimates α^w, β^w for the unknown parameters α, β we have to solve the following optimization problem:

$$\min_{\alpha^w,\beta^w} \sum_{k=1}^{N} w_k (y_k - \lambda_k)^2$$
$$= \min_{\alpha^w,\beta^w} \sum_{k=1}^{N} w_k \left(y_k - d\left[I_{t_{k+1}/T}(\alpha^w,\beta^w) - I_{t_k/T}(\alpha^w,\beta^w)\right]\right)^2 \quad (5.11)$$

For the derivatives of the objective function with respect to α^w, β^w the derivative of the incomplete Beta function is necessary. Like the Beta function, the incomplete beta function and its derivatives have no closed form and numerical approximation is necessary – see e. g. Boik and Robison-Cox (1998), who present a suitable method as well as Fortran 77, Matlab and S-Plus source codes.

For the maximum likelihood estimator, recall that $Y_k \sim Po(\lambda_k)$, thus

$$P(Y_k = y) = e^{-\lambda_k} \frac{\lambda_k{}^y}{y!}$$

Since a NHPP has independent increments (the "memoryless property"), $Y_1, \ldots, Y_N$ are independent random variables, and the likelihood of the sample $y_1, \ldots, y_n$ is given by

[2] Note that some references also use the term incomplete beta function for the integral $\int_0^t z^{\alpha-1}(1-z)^{\beta-1}\,dz$. (5.10) is then called "regularized (incomplete) Beta function" or "incomplete Beta function ratio".

$$L(y_1,\ldots,y_n\,|\alpha,\beta) = \prod_{k=1}^{N} e^{-\lambda_k}\frac{{\lambda_k}^{y_k}}{y_k!}$$

$$\Rightarrow \ln L(y_1,\ldots,y_n\,|\alpha,\beta) = \sum_{k=1}^{N} \ln e^{-\lambda_k}\frac{{\lambda_k}^{y_k}}{y_k!}$$

$$= -\sum_{k=1}^{N}\lambda_k + \sum_{k=1}^{N} y_k \ln\lambda_k - \sum_{k=1}^{N}\ln(Y_k!)$$

Since

$$\sum_{k=1}^{N}\lambda_k = d\sum_{k=1}^{N} I_{t_{k+1}/T}(\alpha,\beta) - I_{t_k/T}(\alpha,\beta) = d$$

and
$$\ln\lambda_k = \ln d + \ln\left[I_{t_{k+1}/T}(\alpha,\beta) - I_{t_k/T}(\alpha,\beta)\right]$$

the optimization problem to be solved is

$$\max_{\alpha^m,\beta^m}\sum_{k=1}^{N}\ln\left[I_{t_{k+1}/T}(\alpha^m,\beta^m) - I_{t_k/T}(\alpha^m,\beta^m)\right]$$

Again, numerical methods are necessary to evaluate the derivative of $I_t(\alpha,\beta)$.

5.5 Summary and Future Research Opportunities

In this section we have shown how to simulate stochastic demand data streams to test RM methods. Based on an extensive study of the existing literature, we have selected an approach that has got a number of advantages over existing methods. The approach is totally independent of the area of application and it is suitable for independent demand, choice-based RM and RM problems with flexible products.

In light of the typical "ad hoc" nature of demand data generation in current research practice, we have made an important step towards the creation of systematic test-bed for RM problems.

Future work should develop these core algorithms further to yield a fully fledged instance generator for RM problems. Then a standard test-bed should be established and be used by researchers working in this field in order to ease the comparison of different RM approaches. In more detail, the following steps are necessary:

1. Identify what characteristics of resources, products, capacities etc. make RM problems hard or easy to solve.

2. Develop an instance generator that creates instances (i. e. resources, products, capacities etc.) with given characteristics, especially a given degree of "difficulty".
3. Generate a systematical set of test-instances in the spirit of, for example, Barr et al. (1995) to establish a standard test-bed for future work.

Another interesting project is to assess the fit of the model of arrivals (5.3) to real-world data of various industries. As mentioned, there exists (albeit somewhat limited) supporting evidence for the airline industry. Assessing the fit of the model requires estimating the parameters $\alpha_j, \beta_j, \gamma_j, \delta_j$ for a given stream of demand data. In section 5.4 we have outlined the estimation problem very briefly. We haven seen that the estimation problem provides a fruitful area of challenging research problems as well.

6

Revenue Management in Broadcasting Companies

Advertising is the predominant source of revenues for most broadcasting companies like TV or radio stations. Much like a seat in an airplane (which cannot be sold after departure) ten seconds of time in a TV or radio program cannot be sold to an advertiser once this time frame has passed. Given the inflexibility of adjusting the "capacity" (i.e. advertising time slots) with a varying demand, broadcasting companies are strongly motivated to differentiate prices, thereby exploiting customer heterogeneity, attracting more customers (= advertisers) and increasing demand. Faced with operational inflexibility on the one hand and different values of demand on the other hand, RM problems arise.

Based on a detailed description of the RM problem in broadcasting companies (section 6.1), we derive a mathematical decision model in section 6.2. Section 6.3 deals with feasible, 6.4 with optimal solutions of the problem. The methods proposed in these sections are evaluated on a test bed of 18,000 instances. The instance generation procedure and the test results are described in section 6.5. 6.6 provides an outlook on stochastic and dynamic aspects of the problem. 6.7 contains some concluding remarks.

An earlier version of sections 6.1 and 6.2 can be found in Belloch Egea, Kimms, and Müller-Bungart (2007). Kimms and Müller-Bungart (2007a) present preliminary results on the heuristics (section 6.3).

6.1 Introduction

6.1.1 Case Study: Broadcasting in Spanish Television

To obtain a realistic impression of the advertising business in broadcasting, we conducted an in-depth research of Spanish television corporations. In particular, the following description is based on two broadcasting networks, RTVE and RTVV.

RTVE (Radio Television Espanola) is a public company, but the main source of its revenues is advertising: In 2003, the overall revenue was € 877.2 million, of which € 697.2 million (79.5 %) came from advertising and sponsoring, only € 83.9 million (9.6 %) were funded by public authorities. RTVE runs two national TV channels ("La Primera" and "La Dos"), on which the following description will focus. "La Primera" and "La Dos" gained a market share of 23.4 and 7.2 %, respectively, in 2003, where the largest competitors, "Tele 5" and "Antena 2", obtained 21.5 and 19.5 %. In addition, RTVE runs a multitude of regional TV channels and four national, 17 regional and 46 local radio stations.

RTVV is a regional broadcasting company based in the area of Valencia, which covers Valencia, Castellon and Alicante. It runs the TV channel "Canal 9" and some radio stations. The market share of "Canal 9" (with respect to its limited regional coverage) was 18.2 % in the first quarter of 2005. Canal 9 is the market leader for regional newscasts with a market share of 23.8 %, ahead of its competitors Telecino (22.4 %), Antena 3 (20.7 %) and TVE1 (19.7 %). RTVV was publicly owned until October 1st, 2003, when it was transferred into private ownership. Two thirds of its funds are still supplied by its owners and public sources. Advertising revenues where ˜40 million in 2003.

In the remainder of this section, we describe how orders are placed, prices are determined and spots are scheduled in these two companies. However, the situation in other broadcasting companies is very similar – see e. g. Bollapragada et al. (2002) who describe the situation at NBC, a US broadcasting company[1]. The reader should especially keep in mind that – although we will mostly speak about TV – the problem analogously arises in radio stations.

6.1.2 The Process of Ordering and Scheduling TV Ads

The process of ordering and scheduling TV ads can roughly be described as follows: An advertiser (synonym: customer, client) sends an order to a broadcasting company. The advertiser may be the company whose products are described in the ads, or an intermediary, such as an advertising agency. The order defines the number of spots to be broadcast, and when these spots should be aired. It is very common that the advertiser does not precisely define the airtimes of its spots, but only some rather general rules. For example, the advertiser may

[1] This reference is discussed in some detail in section 6.1.6.

request that all spots should be aired within the next 30 days, where 20 percent of which should be aired on weekdays in the morning, and 80 percent should be aired on weekends in the afternoon. Thus, we are dealing with multimodal (or flexible) products, where the actual mode of "production" is not precisely defined by the customer's order, but can be decided on by the broadcasting company. The price the advertiser has to pay for the order, however, is fixed and known to both parties before the spots are actually scheduled by the TV network.

Advertisers may cancel scheduled spots according to certain rules. The broadcaster may or may not charge a cancellation fee (penalty), and the advertisers may be fully, in part, or not at all refunded, in case they have already paid. Naturally, there are no "no-shows" in this application: Cancellations close to the planned airtime (48 hours in advance, say) are not allowed, because it is impossible to modify the planned schedule for technical reasons, i. e. if the advertiser has not canceled until that time, the full price will be charged and the spot will be aired.

In the following subsection we describe how prices are determined for a single spot. Usually, however, an order consists of a many spots, and special price setting rules apply. These are described in the next but one subsection.

6.1.3 Determining Prices for Single Spots

The price to be paid by an advertiser for a single spot is basically determined by the following aspects:

- Context of its airing
- Duration
- Scheduling Flexibility

Context

Advertisements (typically consisting of a couple of spots) may interrupt a running show or be aired between two consecutive parts of the TV program. A group of spots which is consecutively aired is called a commercial break (or simply a break for short). The parts of the program which surround a break are called its context. The context determines how many viewers and what target groups will (probably) be reached by the spots in a particular break. It goes without saying that the price for a spot in peak-demand contexts is much higher. To determine a basic fee for a spot, the broadcasting companies partition the weekdays in time windows ("hour strips"). Table 6.1 shows a simplified example of prices for a 20 second-spot – this is the standard length in Spanish television – with respect to its context, defined by the weekday, the hour strip and the show. Note that the price for a second ranges from € 27.50 to € 510.

Table 6.1: Spot Price with Respect to Context

<table>
<tr><th></th><th>Monday to Friday</th><th>Saturday</th><th>Sunday</th></tr>
<tr><td>07:00</td><td rowspan="2">Telediario[a]
Matinal € 550</td><td colspan="2" rowspan="3">Infantil[b] € 1,505</td></tr>
<tr><td>08:00</td></tr>
<tr><td>09:00</td><td>Los Desayunos de
TVE € 640</td></tr>
<tr><td>10:00</td><td>Saber Vivir € 640</td><td>Infantil[b] € 1,505</td><td>Infantil[b] € 2,405</td></tr>
<tr><td>11:00</td><td>Por la Mañana € 870</td><td rowspan="3">Música Uno € 1,600</td><td rowspan="3">Redifusión € 2,700</td></tr>
<tr><td>12:00</td><td>Así con las cosas
€ 1,050</td></tr>
<tr><td>13:00</td><td>Así con las cosas
€ 4,500</td></tr>
<tr><td>14:00</td><td>Corazón de Otoño
€ 7,300</td><td>Cartelera TVE
€ 2,900</td><td>Cartelera TVE
€ 3,350</td></tr>
<tr><td>15:00</td><td colspan="3">Telediario [a] € 10,200</td></tr>
<tr><td>16:00</td><td rowspan="2">Telenovela[c]
€ 6,700</td><td colspan="2" rowspan="2">Sesión de
tarde € 6,900</td></tr>
<tr><td>17:00</td></tr>
<tr><td>...</td><td>...</td><td>...</td><td>...</td></tr>
</table>

[a] Newscast
[b] Program for children
[c] Soap opera

Duration

Given a price table like Table 6.1, the price of a second in a particular break is basically determined and the price of a spot of given length can easily be computed. For spots which are longer than 45 or shorter than 15 seconds a surcharge on the basic fee is applied, i. e. very short or very long spots are penalized. The minimum length of spot is typically defined by the terms and conditions of the broadcasting company or even regulated by law. RTVE and RTVV do not accept spots that are shorter than five seconds, and very short spots are only accepted if they are closely related to other, longer spots of the same advertiser in the same break.

Scheduling Flexibility

As mentioned before, orders sent to broadcasting companies represent multimodal products. The price tables published by the broadcasting companies (like Table 6.1) are only a rough representation of the actual TV program. If a customer chooses an hour strip for a spot, the broadcasters are usually free to schedule a spot in any break in the desired time window. The companies will typically notify the client of the planned airtime, however, they are usually not obliged to pay a compensation if the actual airtime should be different. In addition, a typical contract allows the broadcaster to schedule the spot without compensation in the hour strip immediately before or after the booked one, as long as the difference is not greater than half an hour and the same spot is not aired twice in the same break.

On the other hand, the advertiser may define the actual break where a spot is to be aired, or even the actual position in break for a surcharge. Because it is assumed that the viewer's attention is maximal at the very beginning and end of a commercial break, these positions are most expensive. Some advertisers may like to define other positions than the first or the last as well, e. g. if two spots that advertise the same product should be aired with a fixed time lag.

6.1.4 Determining Prices for a Bundle of Spots

So far we have described how prices for a single spot are determined. In addition, there are certain rules that may apply if an order consists of more than one spot. First of all, most broadcasting companies offer a kind of volume discount: If the overall value of an order exceeds a certain amount, the price is discounted by some percentage. Special scales of discounts apply to special programs. Table 6.2 shows the scale of discount for spots that are placed in the context of football matches, depending on when the spot should be aired and how many matches are covered by the order.

Broadcasting companies also offer bundles of hour strips and contexts as so called modules. Typically, these modules are derived from the viewing habits of certain target groups. Table 6.3 exemplarily shows a "family module", which is meant to cover the preferred viewing times of families. If advertisers book this module, they receive a discount of 55 % on the basic fees as defined by the broadcaster's price table (see e. g. Table 6.1). The value of the order placed by the customer must be no less then € 14,000 (after discount). 10 % of this value has to be used to place spots in the time window Monday to Sunday, 14:00 - 15:30.

Table 6.2: Special Scale of Discount for Football Matches

Airtime	*Number of Matches* Single Match	Complete Round (19 Matches)	Complete Season (38 Matches)
Before Match	0 %	15 %	35 %
Half-Time	0 %	15 %	35 %
After Match	0 %	15 %	35 %
Before+Half-Time	5 %	20 %	40 %
Before+Half-Time+After	20 %	35 %	55 %

Broadcasting companies use modules to acquire high-valued orders. Another major advantage is that a module forces customers to place spots in hour strips of relatively low demand (between 24:30 and 03:00 in the module depicted in Table 6.3, for example). The customers, on the other hand, profit from the very high discounts. Furthermore, they can use modules to easily address certain target groups (families in our example).

6.1.5 The Revenue Management Problem in Broadcasting Companies

Having clarified how orders are placed and prices for orders are determined we proceed by summing up the preconditions for the RM problem in broadcasting companies:

Table 6.3: Family Module

Day	*Time Window*	*Necessary Quota*
Monday to Sunday	14:00 - 15:30	10 %
Monday to Friday	21:00 - 24:00	15 %
Saturday and Sunday	20:30 - 24:00	
Monday to Friday	16:00 - 20:30	45 %
Saturday and Sunday	16:00 - 20:00	
Monday to Friday	09:30 - 12:30	10 %
Monday to Sunday	24:30 - 03:00	20 %

Discount: 55 % on the basic fees
Minimal Order Value: € 14,000 (after discount)

Customer Integration

For the production of the "spot broadcasting" service it is evidently necessary that the customer sends an order to the broadcasting company in which the number of spots, their lengths, the desired hour strips etc. are defined – the situation here is very similar to "manufacture-to-order" production systems. In later stages of the production process, the material to be broadcast has to be supplied (i. e. taped TV spots or the like).

Limited Resource Flexibility

The essential resources involved in the production process are time slots, i. e. potential commercial breaks interrupting the program for advertisements. The number and length of these commercial breaks is clearly limited in two ways: The audience will not tolerate an arbitrarily high number of spots – after a certain quantity of advertising is exceeded, the viewer's attention will deteriorate. Plus, the amount of time used for advertisements is limited by law in many countries, e. g. in the European Union (Council of the European Communities 1989). On the other hand, the number of commercial breaks cannot be arbitrarily reduced, because broadcasting advertisements is a major (if not the predominant) source of income for many companies.

Furthermore, once the broadcasters have decided about the TV program (most likely including approximate numbers and lengths for commercial breaks in every hour strip) and published a price table like Table 6.1, they are bound to follow that scheme, because potential advertisers (and possibly the audience as well) expects this schedule to be stable for some time. The situation here is very similar to airlines which cannot arbitrarily change their flight schedules once they have been published as well.

Heterogeneous Customer Behavior

It goes without saying that given the variety of products which can be advertised on TV or radio, different advertisers will address different target groups. In addition, the advertiser's valuation of TV spots will strongly depend on product and target group characteristics – for some products TV advertising will be more effective than for others. As a consequence, different customers will prefer different hour strips, the amount of spots to be broadcast will strongly depend on the clients, and their willingness to pay will certainly vary.

Product Range

Price tables like Table 6.1 essentially represent a standardized product range. Special scales of discount or modules (see Table 6.2 and Table 6.3 for examples) allow customers to combine these "basic products" into an individual product tailored to their specific needs. This can be compared to an airline, where customers can combine multiple non-stop flights to an individual itinerary.

Like a flight schedule, a TV program will stay stable for a longer period of time. Slight modifications – like postponing a certain show for a quarter of an hour or replacing the comedy series A with comedy series B – are possible, but the context of an hour strip will only be marginally affected. In addition, the viewing habits can be expected to be very stable over time. For instance, the audience might expect that there is a newscast on weekday mornings, a soap opera in the late afternoon and a program for children on weekends.

In summary, all four conditions are satisfied, and opportunities to gainfully use RM techniques in broadcasting companies exist. Although the broadcaster's ability to match demand for advertising time slots and available capacity is limited, a typically order does only roughly specify time windows where spots should be aired. So the companies still have some flexibility in substituting capacities to satisfy their customers needs – broadcasting companies can be seen as a typical example for multimodal products.

Do TV and radio stations currently make use of RM? Our research of Spanish companies revealed that both RTVE and RTVV will indeed reject orders, at least if not all spots of a given order can be scheduled according to the client's preferences. If an order is rejected, RTVE and RTVV will respond with a counteroffer, in which they propose different airtimes for the spots. However, these counteroffers only seem to occur if an order cannot be accommodated, i. e. feasibly scheduling the given spots is impossible. But this mechanism of offers and counteroffers could easily be augmented by RM techniques, such that an order is voluntarily rejected because the broadcaster chooses to protect remaining time slots for orders to come with higher revenues. This idea is rarely treated in current research, though, as the following review of the relevant literature shows.

6.1.6 Literature Review

The only publicly available reference with respect to RM in broadcasting companies seems to be Bollapragada et al. (2002). The authors picture the sales process at NBC, a US television network. The situation they describe is very similar to the one we found at RTVE and RTVV: Potential customers send orders to NBC. A typical order only loosely specifies the time windows when spots should be aired. NBC will try to meet the customer's specifications. However, due to the limited "airtime inventory" (Bollapragada et al. 2002) available for advertising it may be infeasible to fully match the customer's preferences. In this case NBC prepares a schedule that follows the original order as closely as possible. The proposed schedule is sent back to the customer, who may reject it. In this case, negotiations take place. If they fail, the deal is lost.

The vast majority of the entire airtime inventory (60 to 80 percent) is sold during two or three weeks, shortly after the new programming schedule has been published. This is called the up-front market; the remaining market is called the scatter-market.

Bollapragada et al. (2002) do not consider to reject orders: All orders are – in principle – accepted (possibly after a modification by NBC and/or the client), hence all spots have to be scheduled according to the rules defined by the customers' orders. The resulting schedule is called a sales plan by NBC. Since the revenue that can be obtained is fixed, NBC applies a cost-minimizing approach. The cost of a sales plan consists of two major components:

- The airtime inventory is limited, and highly-demanded airtime (which Bollapragada et al. 2002 call premium inventory) is more valuable than others. It is desirable to use as little premium inventory as possible in a given sales plan because this airtime can probably be sold later at premium prices. Thus, Bollapragada et al. attach a "cost per second" factor to each time slot in the planning horizon, reflecting opportunity cost of blocking airtime that can be profitably used to accommodate subsequent orders.
- Since all orders are accepted, it is typically impossible to completely satisfy all specifications as defined by the customers' orders. The failure to meet a customer's guidelines is reflected in penalty costs.

In contrast to this work, the approach we pursue here will be a capacity control scheme where orders are rejected if we expect to be able to allocate the scarce inventory to more valuable orders later. Like done by Bollapragada et al. (2002), this will mean to take the different opportunity costs of airtime inventory into account. Furthermore, we will not allow for a violation of the customer's specifications, not even at a penalty cost.

Also closely connected to our work is Köcher (2002, 2000, 2004), who discusses a controlling scheme for ad sponsored companies. Köcher (2002, chap. 10) describes on a conceptual level how a system of accepting and rejecting orders to maximize revenues could be designed. Though Köcher does not develop models or methods for this RM problem, her work stresses the relevance of our approach.

To the best of our knowledge, other references dealing with RM problems in broadcasting companies are not publicly available. Loosely related RM-problems can be found in the cargo industry and in make-to-order environments. We will briefly summarize these references in section 6.6. Here we proceed by reviewing the literature on closely related, but not identical topics.

Scheduling a given set of TV spots (which is a crucial part of the RM problem we will cover) has been dealt with in only quite a few papers. Brown (1969) describes the situation at the TV channel "Thames Television" and demonstrates various difficulties of scheduling spots manually. He outlines an algorithm for the systematic exchange of spots of different lengths between breaks to gain room for additional spots. Balachandra (1977) presents a simulation study concerned with the impact of spots depending on the advertising schedule. Hägele et al. (2000) prove that the problem as defined by Brown (1969) is NP-complete. Bollapragada et al. (2004) refer to the problem at NBC and develop an algorithm to schedule spots which should be aired more than once such that all transmissions of the spot are distributed as uniformly over time as possible. Bollapragada and Garbiras (2004) again refer to NBC and describe the scheduling problem using some of the restrictions we will also use here. In that respect the work of Bollapragada and Garbiras (2004), which deals with the problem of scheduling but not with order acceptance/rejection, is very similar to a major part of our problem. An important distinction between both approaches is, though, that Bollapragada and Garbiras (2004) allow for the violation of some constraints (at a penalty cost), where our approach strictly enforces all constraints (to be described later). This requirement makes finding a feasible schedule for a given set of orders much more thorny in our problem.

Quite a large body of the literature deals with designing TV timetables that attract many viewers, e.g. Cancian et al. (1995), Horen (1980), Reddy et al. (1998), Rust and Eechambadi (1989). Webster (1985) models audience behaviors and analyzes whether a spectator watching a certain show will also watch the following program. Although we assume throughout the chapter that the TV timetable has already been defined, this research is relevant because the timetable determines the attractiveness of the program for viewers, and hence influences the decision of advertisers to place orders and choose time windows for spots.

The scheduling of advertisements on web pages is related to the problem at hand, albeit not identical. Frequently discussed problems in this area are how so called advertising banners of varying sizes should be placed on the screen, and how the banners should change over time (e.g. Adler et al. 2002, Aggarwal et al. 1998, Dawande et al. 2003, 2005, Dean and Goemans 2003, Freund and Naor 2004). Other areas of research related to Internet advertising include how the impact of online commercials can be evaluated (e.g. Cao 1999), how banners on web pages can be inserted depending on the actual, individual visitor (e.g. Yager 1997), or how individualized advertisings by email (not spam) can be designed (e.g. Ansari and Mela 2003). Messages tailored to individual customers (or groups of customers) are also discussed in the area of mobile telephony (e.g. Barwise and Strong 2002, de Reyck and Degraeve 2003) and digital television (e.g. Lekakos et al. 2001, Thomas 2000).

General information and statistics on TV advertising are regularly published, for Germany for example by the German Association of the Advertising Industry (Zentralverband der deutschen Werbewirtschaft 2004). Text books on media economics also cover television, of course, see e.g. Heinrich (1999) or Altmeppen and Karmasin (2004).

A comprehensive overview on the radio business is presented by Czygan (2003), for instance. Numerous authors investigate the impact of radio advertising. Geer and Geer (2003), for example, analyze the effect of political ads in election campaigns, Verhoef et al. (2000) focus on radio commercials intended to provoke an immediate reaction of the listener (e.g. a telephone call), and Verhoef and Donkers (2005) compare advertisements by mail, Internet, radio and TV. To the best of our knowledge, research directly related to the scheduling of radio spots is rare, Lambert (1983) and Marx and Bouvard (1990) seem to be the only exceptions.

Summing up, a review of the literature reveals that research dealing with accepting orders and scheduling of ads at the same time does not yet exist. We therefore describe an approach to these interdependent problems, aiming at solving them simultaneously. We continue by developing a concise mathematical model for the simultaneous solution of order acceptance and spot scheduling.

6.2 Mathematical Model

This section (and the remainder of the chapter) will mainly deal with the RM problem in broadcasting companies under certainty, i. e. we will assume that all orders, their values, the spots to be scheduled and their properties are completely known. We will give an outlook on how to take uncertainty into account in section 6.6.

We have chosen to focus on the problem under certainty for the following reasons:

- As reported by Bollapragada et al. (2002), the vast majority of airtime in the US market is sold in a short period of time (the up-front market). That means that quite a large body of all orders can be collected and whether to accept or reject a particular order can be decided upon given a batch of other orders, whose properties are known with certainty. The situation at NBC is further simplified by the fact that there are only 250 customers, where 20 % of the customers account for 80 % of the revenues and the variation of each customer's buying behavior is low, so that this year's demand can easily be predicted using last year's demand. Consequently, Bollapragada et al. (2002) have chosen a deterministic approach as well. Although we are not aware of the transaction volumes in the up-front and the scatter markets or the customer distribution in Spanish television, we know that it is not necessary to immediately notify advertisers about whether their orders have been accepted or not, so at least some "batching" of orders is certainly also possible in that market.
- Under uncertainty, if an order arrives, the following questions have to be answered:
  - Is it possible to accommodate the order, given the remaining resource capacity and taking possible reschedules of already accepted orders into account?
  - If so, it is profitable to accommodate the order? Note that this strongly depends on the resources to which the order is assigned.

  In a standard airline RM problem (without overbooking), it is trivial to see whether the remaining resource capacity suffices to accommodate a given order, largely because rescheduling passengers to other planes is (not yet) an option. In the problem at hand with multimodal products, however, answering the first question is equivalent to finding a feasible schedule for all orders that have already been accepted, plus the order that has just arrived. In addition, we will have to decide to which resources we (at least temporarily) assign the new order (this is also trivial in the standard airline case). Thus, under uncertainty, we also need decision models and methods to deal with these subproblems. Since these problems also arise in the deterministic setting, the models and methods we are going to present will also form a crucial part of any method that deals with the problem under uncertainty. We will take a closer look on that aspect in section 6.6.

- In the broadcasting industry, practically all products are flexible, and while most Spanish broadcasting companies will notify customers shortly after their orders have been accepted about the actual airtimes of the spots, these may be changed without incurring penalties later. The final scheduling of spots thus takes place in a deterministic setting, after uncertainty of demand has been fully revealed. Since we deal with the simultaneous problems of accepting orders and scheduling spots this problem can be solved easily by the models methods we will subsequently discuss – only the decision variables representing the acceptance/rejection decisions have to be fixed.
- We will also see in section 6.6 that developing an exact model for the problem under uncertainty is cumbersome. Namely, it seems to be impossible to define the stochastic process creating incoming orders in a useful way. Plus, like for many other RM problems, any exact model will mainly consist of a recursive value function that could (in principle) be computed by dynamic programming. However, the "curse of dimensionality" (i. e. the exponential growth of the state space with the size of the problem) will render an exact approach based on that model impracticable anyway. Successful heuristic approaches in such cases often depend on deterministic models (like those we are going to present here), where unknown quantities are replaced by "typical" values. Bid prices computed from an LP where the uncertain demand is replaced by its expected value are a prominent example. In the context of dynamic programming such approaches are called certainty equivalent control (CEC, cf. Bertsekas 2000, section 6.1). A CEC-scheme has been successfully applied to RM problems by Bertsimas and Popescu (2003), for instance.

Thus, in the remainder of the section, we develop a deterministic, linear mixed-integer program for the problem at hand after introducing some notation.

6.2.1 Formalizing the Supply Side

The timetable (TV program) which has been published by the TV network is the base for all advertising contracts. This timetable remains fixed over the planning horizon. The timetable defines a number of time slots for commercial breaks of a determined length. Denote the set of all breaks in the planning horizon by B. For each $b \in B$, let $0 \leq d_b^{\min} \leq d_b^{\max}$ be the minimum and maximum duration, respectively, of break b. We chose to model the length of a commercial break like this, because it seems unrealistic that the length of b is known and fixed before the actual schedule of spots is determined. However, if this should be the case for some break b, we can easily represent this by letting $d_b^{\min} = d_b^{\max}$. Furthermore, if a commercial break is optional, we can set $d_b^{\min} = 0$.

6.2.2 Formalizing the Demand Side

Let O be the set of orders sent to the TV network by advertisers. With each order $o \in O$, there is associated a price (revenue, profit, ...) of $v_o > 0$. An order $o \in O$ consists of a non-empty set of spots S_o. For the convenience of notation, we assume that the total number of spots is S and that the set of all spots is $\{1, \ldots, S\}$, so that $S_o \subseteq \{1, \ldots, S\}, o \in O$. Naturally, we require $\bigcup_{o \in O} S_o = \{1, \ldots, S\}$ and $S_o \cap S_p = \emptyset$ for all $o, p \in O, o \neq p$. An order $o \in O$ must either be accepted in its entirety (i. e. all spots $s \in S_o$ have to be feasibly scheduled), or fully rejected.

For each spot $s = 1, \ldots, S$ a set of breaks $\emptyset \neq B_s \subseteq B$ where s could be scheduled is given. Note that the advertiser may precisely define the commercial break where s will be aired by letting $|B_s| = 1$. The length of $s = 1, \ldots, S$ is denoted by $0 < l_s \leq \min_{b \in B_s} \{d_b^{\max}\}$. Bundles of spots that should be scheduled in the same break in any event (i. e. a short one following a longer one to "remind" the audience and increase the advertising effect) can formally be treated as a single spot of appropriate length. Denote the set of all spots (regardless of the order to which they belong) that can be scheduled in break $b \in B$ by $S(b) \subseteq \{1, \ldots, S\}$. $S(b)$ can be formally defined as follows:

$$S(b) = \{s = 1, \ldots, S \mid b \in B_s\}$$

We require $\sum_{s \in S(b)} l_s \geq d_b^{\min}, b \in B$ without loss of generality.

It is common to assure that ads for two competing products (e. g. BMW and Chrysler cars) are not aired in the same break. We model these conflicts as follows: Let $\mathcal{C} \subseteq 2^{\{1, \ldots, S\}}$. $C \in \mathcal{C}$ implies that all spots $s \in C$ are in conflict and cannot be scheduled in the same break.

In addition to specifying a set of breaks where a spot s can be scheduled, the advertiser may define that s should be the first spot or the last spot in a break. Of course, we have to make sure that there is at most one spot in the first and last position, respectively, in each break. We model this fact as follows: For each break, add two conflict sets to $\mathcal{C}$, say $C_b^{first}, C_b^{last} \subseteq S(b)$. If $s \in C_b^{first}$, s should be scheduled in the first position; C_b^{last} is analogously defined[4].

6.2.3 A Linear, Mixed-Integer Model

We will now derive a linear, mixed-integer model from our formal description. We use the following decision variables:

$$y_o = \begin{cases} 1 & \text{if order } o \text{ is accepted} \\ 0 & \text{otherwise} \end{cases} \qquad o \in O$$

$$x_{sb} = \begin{cases} 1 & \text{if spot } s \text{ is scheduled in break } b \\ 0 & \text{otherwise} \end{cases} \qquad s = 1, \ldots, S, b \in B_s$$

Note that the binary decision variable x_{sb} is absolutely sufficient to represent a feasible schedule, although the position of s in b is not precisely determined: The exact order of spots that have been scheduled in break b is irrelevant in our setting.

For notational convenience, define

$$BC := \{(b, C) \in B \times \mathcal{C} \mid |S(b) \cap C| \geq 2\}$$

The objective is to maximize revenues obtained from accepted orders. The complete model is given as Model 6.1. By (6.2), revenue v_o can be obtained if and only if all spots of order o are scheduled. (6.3) restricts the length of all breaks $b \in B$ to the given minimal and maximal lengths. By (6.4), no conflicting spots are scheduled in the same break.

[4] Some TV networks, e. g. RTVV, allow the advertiser to specify the exact position of a spot in a break (the fifth, the tenth, ...). Our modeling approach here restricting the advertisers' choice of position to the first and the last is accordance with Bollapragada and Garbiras (2004). However, additional positions can easily be added to our model: Add corresponding sets $C_b^5, C_b^{10}, \ldots$ to $\mathcal{C}$; plus additional restrictions to ensure that exactly three spots are scheduled between the first and the fifth, for example. Note that it may then be difficult to determine a feasible schedule, though: The TV network cannot guarantee an advertiser that his spot will be aired as, say, the fifteenth spot in a break b, because the number of spots in b is result of the scheduling process, and this number may be smaller than or equal to 15.

Since $C_b^{first}, C_b^{last} \in \mathcal{C}$, this restriction ensures as well that each break $b \in B$ has got at most one first and last spot, respectively. Restrictions (6.5) define the decision variables x_{sb} as stated verbally before. Finally, it's sufficient to require $y_o \in [0, 1]$ in (6.6): Since the x_{sb} are binary, y_o will be integer by (6.2).

Model 6.1: Broadcasting Model

$$\max \sum_{o \in O} v_o y_o \tag{6.1}$$

s. t.

$$\sum_{b \in B_s} x_{sb} = y_o \qquad o \in O, s \in S_o \tag{6.2}$$

$$d_b^{\min} \leq \sum_{s \in S(b)} l_s x_{sb} \leq d_b^{\max} \qquad b \in B \tag{6.3}$$

$$\sum_{s \in C \cap S(b)} x_{sb} \leq 1 \qquad (b, C) \in BC \tag{6.4}$$

$$x_{sb} \in \{0, 1\} \qquad s \in \{1, \ldots, S\}, b \in B_s \tag{6.5}$$

$$0 \leq y_o \leq 1 \qquad o \in O \tag{6.6}$$

The problem at hand is NP-hard in the strong sense, because it contains the Multiple Knapsack problem as a special case (cf. Martello and Toth 1990, p. 8 for a proof). Therefore, we have to develop enumerative methods to solve it optimally. To enhance the efficiency of enumerative methods, lower bounds are needed. We deal with this issue in the next section, where we develop heuristics so that lower bounds can be derived from feasible solutions.

6.3 Heuristics

6.3.1 Assessing the Difficulty of Finding Feasible Solutions

If $d_b^{\min} = 0, b \in B$, accepting no orders and scheduling no spots (i. e. setting $y_o = 0, o \in O$, $x_{sb} = 0, s \in \{1, \ldots, S\}, b \in B_s$) is trivially feasible. Unfortunately, if $d_b^{\min} > 0$ for some break b, finding a feasible solution is difficult:

Theorem 6.1 *If $d_b^{\min} > 0$ for some $b \in B$, finding a feasible solution to Model 6.1 is NP-complete.*

Proof. Clearly, the problem is in NP. We proof NP-hardness by restriction (Garey and Johnson 1979, p. 63-64). Consider an instance of Model 6.1 with a single break, i. e. $B = \{1\}$ and $0 < d_1^{\min} \leq d_1^{\max}$. As a further simplification, let there be no conflicts ($\mathcal{C} = \emptyset$), and $|S_o| = 1, o \in O$, so that we can decide about each spot in isolation. Therefore, the problem to find a feasible solution can be stated as follows: Is there a subset of spots $T \subseteq S(1)$ such that $\sum_{s \in T} l_s \leq d_1^{\max}$ and $\sum_{s \in T} l_s \geq d_1^{\min}$?

This is a Knapsack problem where $S(1)$ is the set of items, l_s is both profit and weight of item $s \in S(1)$, $d_1^{\max}$ is the Knapsack's capacity and $d_1^{\min}$ is the "value goal" (profit threshold). Since Knapsack is NP-hard, the problem of finding a feasible solution to Model 6.1 is indeed NP-complete.

Therefore, if $d_b^{\min} > 0$ for some $b \in B$, finding a feasible problem is – roughly speaking – as difficult as finding the optimal solution. As a consequence, we will mainly consider the case $d_b^{\min} = 0, b \in B$ in the following development of heuristics, i. e. we will allow our heuristic methods to fail if $d_b^{\min} > 0$ for some $b \in B$, though a feasible solution might exist. The reader should also note here that the minimum duration constraints are less restrictive in practice, since breaks can always be filled by trailers of the broadcasting company promoting the TV program. Plus, since revenue tends to increase with the number of scheduled spots, we can hope that solutions with relative high objective function values will tend to "fill up" the breaks and therefore automatically satisfy $d_b^{\min}$. Finally, if the broadcasting company has notorious problems to fill many of the breaks with spots, demand seems to be to low for being able to reject orders, and thus there would be no need for capacity control techniques in that particular company.

Before we begin to develop heuristics, it is also noteworthy that we obtain a difficult feasibility problem if an assignment of values to the variables $y_o, o \in O$ is given, even though $d_b^{\min} = 0, b \in B$ holds. For the trivial assignment $y_o = 0, o \in O$, there exists of course a feasible schedule, so we restrict ourselves to nontrivial assignments (where $\sum_{o \in O} y_o \geq 1$) in the following. For a given assignment, denote the set of accepted spots (that have to be scheduled) by $S^a = \bigcup_{o \in O: y_o = 1} S_o$. Analogously, define $S^a(b) = S^a \cap S(b)$. If $|B_s| = 1, s \in S^a$, it is trivial to verify whether a feasible schedule exists or not. If more than one break is possible for some spots, the problem gets difficult:

Theorem 6.2 *Let a non-trivial assignment be given. If $|B_s| > 1$ for some spots $s \in S^a$, deciding whether a feasible schedule exists or not is NP-complete, even if there are no conflicts.*

Proof. Clearly, the problem is in NP. We then restrict ourselves to instances with just two breaks, i. e. $B = \{1, 2\}$, where $d^{\max} := d_1^{\max} = d_2^{\max} > 0$ (recall that we assume $d_1^{\min} = d_2^{\min} = 0$). Spots s where $B_s = \{1\}$ or $B_s = \{2\}$ could be scheduled trivially, so w.l.o.g. let $B_s = B, s \in S^a$. Therefore, deciding whether a feasible schedule exists or not requires to answer the following question: Is there an assignment $f : S^a \longrightarrow \{1, 2\}$ such that

$$\sum_{s \in S^a : f(s) = b} l_s \leq d^{\max} \qquad b \in \{1, 2\}$$

holds. This is the Bin Packing Problem, which is NP-hard in the strong sense (Garey and Johnson 1979, p. 124). Deciding whether a feasible schedule exists is thus NP-complete.

Finally, for a non-trivial assignment of values to the variables $y_o, o \in O$, taking the conflicts into account is again difficult, even if the number of breaks for some spots is not greater than 3, and the break length restrictions are not restrictive:

Theorem 6.3 *Let a non-trivial assignment be given. If $|B_s| \geq 2$ for all spots $s \in S^a$ and $|B_s| \geq 3$ for some spots $s \in S^a$, deciding whether a feasible schedule exists or not, is Π_2^p-complete, even if the break length constraints are not restrictive (i. e. $d_b^{\max}$ is sufficiently large, e. g. $\sum_{s \in S_b^a} l_s \leq d_b^{\max}, b \in B$ holds).*

Proof. We show that our problem is equivalent to a graph coloring problem: Let $G = (V, E)$ be the conflict graph where $V = S^a$ and we add an edge $\{s_1, s_2\}$ to E if the spots s_1 and s_2 can be scheduled in the same break and are in conflict, i. e. $\{s_1, s_2\} \subseteq S^a(b)$ for some $b \in B$ and $\{s_1, s_2\} \subseteq C$ for some $C \in \mathcal{C}$. To each node $s \in S^a$ we assign a list of colors B_s. The problem is now to decide whether there exists a list coloring of the conflict graph, i. e. an assignment $g : s \in V \longrightarrow B_s$ such that $g(s_1) \neq g(s_2)$ for all $\{s_1, s_2\} \in E$. This problem is Π_2^p-complete (cf. Erdös, Rubin, and Taylor 1979, where the result is attributed to A. L. Rubin).

As mentioned before, we will focus on the case $d_b^{\min} = 0, b \in B$. Using AMPL and CPLEX 8, we implemented two general MIP-based heuristics, *Dive-and-Fix* and *Relax-and-Fix* along the lines of Wolsey (1998, p. 214-216), two heuristics based on the LP Relaxation of the model and a Greedy heuristic.

6.3.2 MIP-Based Heuristics

The idea of the *Dive-and-Fix* heuristic is to solve the LP relaxation, fix some variables that are "almost binary" (but have fractional values) to 0 or 1 and resolve the resulting LP. It consists of the steps described as Algorithm 6.1.

Algorithm 6.1: Dive-and-Fix Heuristic

1. Solve the LP-Relaxation of the problem.
2. Let $x^*_{sb}, s \in \{1, \ldots, S\}, b \in B_s$ be the optimal values of the x-variables. Let $F = \{(s,b) : x^*_{sb} \notin \{0,1\}\}$ be the set of x-variables that are fractional.
3. If $F = \emptyset$, a feasible solution has been found, so STOP. Otherwise let
$$F^* = \left\{(s,b) \in F \,\middle|\, \min\{x^*_{sb}, 1 - x^*_{sb}\} = \min_{(s',b') \in F} \{\min\{x^*_{s'b'}, 1 - x^*_{s'b'}\}\}\right\}$$
be the indices of the variables closest to integer (but fractional).
4. For all $(s^*, b^*) \in F^*$: If $x_{s^*b^*} < 0.5$, fix $x_{s^*b^*} = 0$, otherwise fix $x_{s^*b^*} = 1$.
5. Resolve the resulting LP. If it is infeasible, the heuristic has failed, so STOP. Otherwise goto 2.

The *Relax-and-Fix* heuristic processes the orders sequentially in a greedy fashion. If order o is processed, the integrality restriction (6.5) is enforced for all $s \in S_o, b \in B_s$ and relaxed for all other variables. If a feasible solution is found, the values of $x_{sb}, s \in S_o, b \in B_s$ are fixed, and the next order is processed. A detailed description is given as Algorithm 6.2.

In contrast to Dive-and-Fix, Relax-and-Fix will always return a feasible solution, because we can always fix variables to 0 in step 3 to ensure feasibility.

6.3.3 LP-Based Heuristics

While Dive-and-Fix and Relax-and-Fix solve LPs (or MIPs, respectively) in an iterative fashion, the heuristics to be described in this section have a simpler structure: Only one LP is solved, and after that a single IP is solved. Therefore, we can expect these heuristics to be much faster. In the first heuristic, called *ForceOnes*, we solve the LP relaxation of the problem, fix all variables y_o, x_{sb} with an optimal LP-value of 1 to that value and try to find an optimal (or at least feasible) solution for the remaining IP in five seconds using CPLEX. *ForceZeroes*

Algorithm 6.2: Relax-and-Fix Heuristic

1. For the ease of exposition, let the orders be indexed such that $v_1 \geq \ldots \geq v_{|O|}$. Let $o^* = 1$.
2. Consider the relaxed problem:

$$\max \sum_{o \in O} v_o y_o$$

s.t. (6.2), (6.3), (6.4), (6.6) and

$$\begin{aligned} x_{sb} &\in \{0,1\} & s &\in S_{o^*}, b \in B_s \\ 0 \leq x_{sb} &\leq 1 & s &\in \{1,\ldots,S\} \setminus S_{o^*}, b \in B_s \end{aligned}$$

Try to find an optimal solution to that problem using CPLEX while imposing a time limit of two seconds (wall clock time) on the computation.
3. If an optimal (or at least a feasible) solution was found, fix y_{o^*} and $x_{sb}, s \in S_{o^*}, b \in B_s$ to the values returned by CPLEX. Otherwise, fix y_{o^*} and $x_{sb}, s \in S_{o^*}, b \in B_s$ to 0.
4. Let $o^* = o^* + 1$. If $o^* \leq |O|$ goto 2.

works analogously: Variables with an optimal LP-value of 0 are fixed to that value, and the remaining IP is solved using CPLEX, again with a time limit of five seconds. Note that ForceZeroes will always return a feasible solution, where ForceOnes may fail to find one, though the (integer) feasible region of the original problem is non-empty by assumption.

6.3.4 Greedy Heuristic

Like Relax-and-Fix, *Greedy* processes the orders sequentially according to their prices. If order o is processed, we try to find a feasible solution such that $y_o = 1$. If that succeeds, the values of y_o and $x_{sb}, s \in S_o, b \in B_s$ are fixed, and the next order is processed. Otherwise we fix y_o and $x_{sb}, s \in S_o, b \in B_s$ to 0. The Greedy heuristic is summarized as Algorithm 6.3. Since we fix variables to 0 in step 4 if no feasible schedule for an order was found, Greedy always generates a feasible solution in our instances.

Note that Greedy will, in general, not produce the same solution as Relax-and-Fix: For some $o \in O$, the latter may find that $y_o = 0$ is an optimal solution to the relaxed problem in step 2. Thus, y_o is fixed to 0. Greedy, on the other hand, may find that a feasible solution with $y_o = 1$ exists, so y_o is fixed to 1.

Algorithm 6.3: Greedy Heuristic

1. For the ease of exposition, let the orders again be indexed such that $v_1 \geq \ldots \geq v_{|O|}$. Let $o^* = 1$.
2. Solve the LP relaxation of the problem. If $y_{o^*} = 1$ and $x_{sb} \in \{0,1\}, s \in S_{o^*}, b \in B_s$, an integer feasible schedule for o^* has been found, so fix these variables and goto 5.
3. Otherwise consider the modified problem:

$$\max \sum_{o \in O} v_o y_o$$

s.t. (6.2), (6.3), (6.4), (6.6) and

$$\begin{aligned} x_{sb} &\in \{0,1\} && s \in S_{o^*}, b \in B_s \\ 0 \leq x_{sb} &\leq 1 && s \in \{1,\ldots,S\} \setminus S_{o^*}, b \in B_s \\ y_{o^*} &= 1 \end{aligned}$$

Try to find an optimal solution to that problem using CPLEX, imposing a time limit of two seconds on the computation.
4. If an optimal (or at least a feasible) solution was found, fix $y_{o^*} = 1$ and $x_{sb}, s \in S_{o^*}, b \in B_s$ to the values returned by CPLEX. Otherwise, fix y_{o^*} and $x_{sb}, s \in S_{o^*}, b \in B_s$ to 0.
5. Let $o^* = o^* + 1$. If $o^* \leq |O|$ goto 2.

6.4 Optimal Solutions: Branch and Cut

As mentioned before, the problem at hand is NP-hard, so we have to resort to enumerative methods of exponential worst-case complexity. For linear models like Model 6.1, two fundamental techniques have proven to be very effective: Branch and Bound (B&B) and cutting plane methods. Introductory discussions of both techniques can be found in Winston (1994, chapter 9) and Bertsimas and Tsitsiklis (1997, chapter 11), for instance.

To find provably optimal solutions for the problem at hand, we use a combination of both methods that is called Branch and Cut. After outlining cutting plane methods, we will introduce some basic concepts of polyhedral theory. Then, we will describe how to separate and lift cover cuts in great detail.

6.4.1 General Outline of Cutting Plane Methods

Consider the LP-relaxation of an integer problem (IP). This LP can be solved efficiently, but an optimal solution will almost certainly have fractional variables, i. e. it will not be a feasible solution for the original problem (if so, an optimal solution to the original IP has been found as well and we can stop here). This situation is depicted in Figure 6.1, where a graphical representation of a very simple LP with two variables (x_1 and x_2) and two restrictions (drawn as solid lines) is shown[5]. The two linear restrictions, together with the non-negativity constraints given by both axes form the feasible region of the LP (shaded area). Since the cutting planning method is totally independent of the objective function anyway, we have intentionally omitted it for the sake of clarity. Nevertheless, assume that the extremal point $(2.4, 2.2)$ is an optimal solution to the LP.

Let us now enforce integrality restrictions on both decision variables, i. e. $x_1, x_2 \in \mathbb{N}_0$ should hold. The integer feasible points form a two-dimensional point grid which is also shown in the figure. As a consequence, the new integer problem has only got 14 feasible solutions, namely the dots that happen to fall in the shaded area. As we can clearly see from the figure, the LP optimum is not integer feasible. We now add a so called *cutting plane* (or a cut for short) to the problem. A cutting plane is a linear inequality with the following two properties:

- The inequality is a *valid inequality*, i. e. every integer feasible point satisfies it.
- The valid inequality is *violated* by the current LP-optimum, i. e. it is being "cut off" from the feasible region by the cutting plane.

The reader can easily verify that the cutting plane shown as a dashed line in the figure satisfies both properties.

As a simple example, consider the feasible region of a small knapsack problem:

$$40x_1 + 50x_2 + 60x_3 \leq 100 \qquad x_1, x_2, x_3 \in \{0, 1\} \tag{6.7}$$

Since at most two items can be packed into the knapsack, $x_1 + x_2 + x_3 \leq 2$ is a valid inequality, i. e. it is satisfied by any binary feasible point. If we consider the LP-feasible point $x_1 = x_2 = 1, x_3 = 1/6$, we immediately see that this valid inequality acts as a cutting plane, cutting of this point from the feasible region.

The fundamental idea of a cutting plane method is now to add cutting planes to the LP-relaxation of a (thorny) problem with integer valued variables until the optimal LP-solution satisfies "by chance" all integer constraints, and – because of the fact that no cutting plane

[5] A similar picture appears in many references on cutting plane methods, see e. g. the cover of Schrijver's (1986) book and Winston (1994, Figure 30 on p. 541).

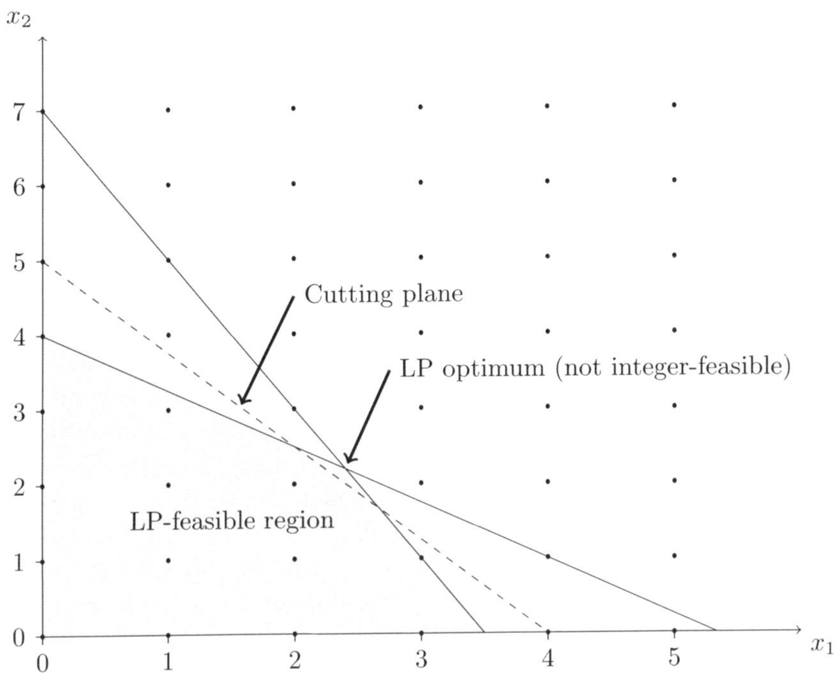

Fig. 6.1: LP- and Integer-feasible Region for a Simple Linear Model

cuts off an integer feasible point – an optimal integer solution has been found. This approach is outlined in Algorithm 6.4.

Algorithm 6.4: Outline of a General Cutting Plane Method

1. Consider the LP-relaxation of a linear integer problem.
2. Optimally solve the LP. If the optimal solution satisfies all integrality constraints, it is an optimal solution to the binary problem as well: STOP.
3. Otherwise, add one (or more) cutting plane(s) to the problem and goto step 2.

A crucial part of the algorithm is obviously finding a cutting plane in step 2. This is called the *separation problem*, because we try to find a valid inequality that separates the current LP optimum from the feasible region. Typically, we will not try to find an arbitrary violated linear inequality but restrict ourselves to certain types, i. e. inequalities of a certain mathematical structure. Before we address the separation problem for specific types of inequalities in detail, we discuss an important question with respect to Algorithm 6.4: Does this algorithm terminate in a finite number of iterations for any linear integer problem? Interestingly, the answer is yes. In his seminal work, Gomory (1960a, 1958, 1963, 1960b) defined general cutting planes suitable for *any* linear integer problem, i. e. given an integer-infeasible solution in step 2, a so called "Gomory cut" that is violated by it can (quite easily, in fact) be derived from the optimal Simplex tableau. It can be shown that adding Gomory cuts in each iteration leads to an optimal solution (given that one exists) in a finite number of steps under some minor technical conditions, see e. g. Schrijver (1986, section 23.8) for a proof.

Gomory's method is easy to understand and can be applied to all problems where all variables (including slack/excess variables) are integer. However, it has not been very successful in practice (Bertsimas and Tsitsiklis 1997, p. 482-484). In addition, it requires the optimal simplex tableau and detailed information about which variables are (non-)basic, so it is somewhat difficult to implement with standard LP-solvers.

Note that like in an LP-based Branch and Bound-scheme, we add a linear inequality in step 3 that is violated by the current fractional solution. But in contrast to B&B-methods, this inequality does not "cut off" any integer solutions, so the feasible region is not divided in two (or more) parts, and branching is not required. This constitutes the major advantage of this method: Although we need some extra memory for additional inequalities added to the problem, storing a (potentially huge) B&B-tree is not necessary. Another nice feature (that was already mentioned) is that a cutting plane approach is totally independent of the objective function, where it is a crucial part for B&B, at least for the bounding part. So if we decide to change the objective function of our problem – maximizing the sheer number of scheduled spots, minimizing costs like Bollapragada et al. (2002), subtracting penalty costs from the revenue function (6.1), or the like – our approach remains unchanged. Finally, adding cutting planes (= new restrictions) to a problem can only decrease the LP upper bound. So if a good feasible solution is available, we may prove its optimality without iterating over and over until Algorithm 6.4 delivers a feasible solution.

The disadvantages, on the other hand, of a pure cutting plane method are:

- An exponential number of cutting planes (i. e. an exponential number of iterations) might be necessary.
- Solving the separation problem in step 2 of the algorithm can be (depending on the type of valid inequality we are using) an NP-hard problem.

- For some problems, only a limited number of types of valid inequalities are known, so that it may technically be impossible to solve the problem to optimality only using the narrow range of available cutting planes.
- It was mentioned that adding cutting planes may help to decrease the LP upper bound. However, practical experience suggests that this (theoretically positive) effect usually has got a rather limited impact, because after a few iterations the bound will no longer improve significantly. This behavior is called "tailing off".

Since we are trying to solve an NP-hard problem, the first disadvantage is inherent (unless $P = NP$), but of course for certain problems other enumerative methods may exist that have a better average performance than a pure cutting plane approach.

Given all these disadvantages, it may be (practically) impossible or inefficient to optimally solve the problem using cutting planes alone. Instead, we are using a combination of cutting planes and B&B, which is called *Branch and Cut* (B&C): If we can no longer (efficiently) find violated inequalities, we make a branching step, hoping to bring some progress into the process.

6.4.2 Effectiveness of Cutting Planes

We have already pointed out that although Gomory cuts represent a general approach to any linear integer problem, they do not seem to be very effective in practice. So a few remarks about the potential effectiveness of valid inequalities are in order. We start by repeating some concepts from Wolsey (1998, p. 15):

Definition 6.1 *Let $X \subseteq \mathbb{R}^n$. Then*

$$conv\,(X) = \left\{ x : x = \sum_{i=1}^{t} \lambda_i x^i, \right.$$
$$\left. \sum_{i=1}^{t} \lambda_i = 1, i = 1, \ldots, t \text{ where } t < \infty, \{x^1, \ldots, x^t\} \subseteq X \right\} \tag{6.8}$$

is called the convex hull *of X. $conv\,(X)$ is the set of all points that can be expressed as a convex combination of a finite set of points from X.*

Proposition 6.1 *$conv\,(X)$ possesses the following properties:*

1. *$conv\,(X)$ is a polyhedron.*
2. *The extreme points of $conv\,(X)$ all lie in X.*

As a consequence, an optimization problem with a linear objective function on the *arbitrarily defined* feasible set X can be replaced by an LP, whose feasible region is *conv* (X). This impressing result is of limited use, though, because for many problems of interest an exact description of the polyhedron *conv* (X) is unknown or of exponential size.

Algorithm 6.4 utilizes Proposition 6.1 as follows: Starting with a description of X given by the linear restrictions plus the integrality constraints, it relaxes the integrality constraints to obtain a (first) polyhedron and augments the resulting constraint matrix with cutting planes until a "sufficient" approximation of *conv* (X) has been reached. By sufficient we mean that it is possible to identify an extremal point of *conv* (X) that is found to be an optimal solution for the original problem. Thus, at its core, a cutting plane methods tries to find an approximation of the polyhedron *conv* (X) using linear inequalities. Of course, we will restrict ourselves to valid inequalities; a concept which has already been introduced informally. It can be defined formally as follows:

Definition 6.2 *Let* $X \subseteq \mathbb{R}^n, \pi \in \mathbb{R}^n, \pi_o \in \mathbb{R}$. *The linear restriction* $\pi x \leq \pi_0$ *is called a* valid inequality *if* $x \in X \Rightarrow \pi x \leq \pi_0$.

For efficiency, we will certainly want to add only valid inequalities that are "absolutely necessary" to approximate *conv* (X). Before we formally define what "necessary" means, Figure 6.2 (which is a slightly modified version of Figure 6.1) demonstrates the geometric notion of this concept. The shaded area is still the LP-feasible region, where the straight lines representing the linear restrictions have been shortened for the sake of clarity. The lower dashed line is the original cutting plane from Figure 6.1. It is clearly superior to the upper dashed line, which is not even necessary do define the shaded LP-polyhedron. However, although the original cutting plane cuts a bit of the LP-feasible region, it is clearly inferior to the valid inequalities depicted by dotted lines. These two dotted lines (together with the axes, i. e. the non-negativity constraints) are what Wolsey (1998, p. 14-15) calls an "ideal" representation, because no integer feasible point is cut off, and every extremal point of the resulting polyhedron is integer.

How can we find such beautiful inequalities that are necessary to describe *conv* (X) (or any other polyhedron)? An important result for our further efforts is that a valid inequality is necessary for the description of a polyhedron if and only if it is a so-called *facet*. Since we are not concerned about the technical details – the interested reader is re-

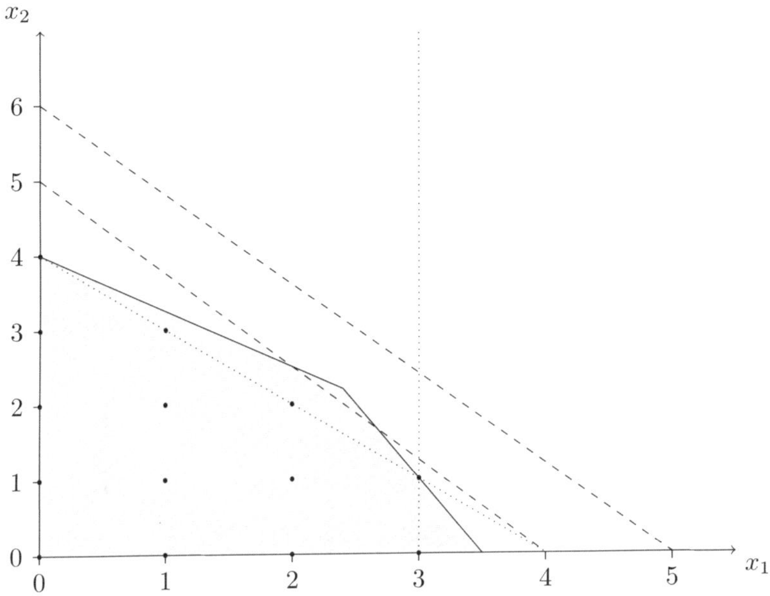

Fig. 6.2: Visualization of the Necessity of Various Cuts

ferred to Wolsey (1998, p. 142-147) and Neumann and Morlock (1993, p. 530-535) –, we just summarize the important results here:

Definition 6.3 *Let P be a polyhedron and $\pi x \leq \pi_0$ be a valid inequality for P.*
$\pi x \leq \pi_0$ is called a supporting inequality *of P if $\{x \in P : \pi x \leq \pi_0\}$ is not empty.*
The set $F = \{x \in P : \pi x = \pi_0\}$ is called a face *of P. We say that the valid inequality $\pi x \leq \pi_0$* represents *or* defines *F. F is called* proper *if $\emptyset \neq F \neq P$ holds.*
A proper face F is called a facet *of P if F is maximal, i. e. no other face of P contains F as a proper subset.*

Proposition 6.2 *Under certain technical conditions, a valid inequality is necessary for the description of a polyhedron if and only if it is facet (cf. Wolsey 1998, p. 142).*

We will demonstrate the use of Proposition 6.2 by means of an example on page 198.

Thus, we will try to only use cutting planes that are facets of the convex hull of the integer feasible region.

6.4.3 Cutting Planes for Knapsack Restrictions: Cover Cuts

We will only use restrictions of the knapsack type to generate cutting planes, i. e. constraints of the form:

$$\sum_{j \in J} a_j x_j \leq a \qquad x_j \in \{0,1\}, j \in J \tag{6.9}$$

W.l.o.g. we assume that a_j and a are integers and that $0 < a_j \leq a, j \in J$ (cf. Glover 1965, p. 890 and Martello and Toth 1990, p. 14).

We are interested in the *knapsack polyhedron* P_K, defined as the convex hull of all binary points that satisfy (6.9):

$$P_K = conv \left\{ x_j \in \{0,1\}, j \in J : \sum_{j \in J} a_j x_j \leq a \right\}$$

A subset of items $C \subseteq J$ is called a *cover* if $\sum_{j \in C} a_j > a$. Since a_j, a are integers, this is equivalent to $\sum_{j \in C} a_j \geq a + 1$. If C is a cover, the following inequality is obviously valid for P_K:

$$\sum_{j \in C} x_j \leq |C| - 1 \tag{6.10}$$

(6.10) is called a *cover inequality* or *cover cut* for P_K. The valid inequality $x_1+x_2+x_3 \leq 2$ for the knapsack restriction $40x_1+50x_2+60x_3 \leq 100$ – see (6.7) – was a cover cut, since $40 + 50 + 60 > 100$.

A cover C is *minimal* if any subset $C' \subset C$ is not a cover. If C is a minimal cover, (6.10) defines a facet of the restricted polyhedron:

$$conv \left\{ x_j \in \{0,1\}, j \in C : \sum_{j \in C} a_j x_j \leq a \right\} \tag{6.11}$$

– this polyhedron is restricted in the sense that all variables $x_j, j \in J \backslash C$ are forced to 0.

Our focus on constraints of the knapsack type (6.9) with positive integers a, a_j is not restrictive, since Model 6.1 only contains binary variables anyway, and any constraint in a model containing only binary variables can be transformed into one or two knapsack constraints. To see this, consider the equality restriction (6.2) for some fixed $o \in O, s \in S_o$ as an example:

$$\sum_{b \in B_s} x_{sb} = y_o \Leftrightarrow \sum_{b \in B_s} x_{sb} \geq y_o \text{ and } \sum_{b \in B_s} x_{sb} \leq y_o$$

We proceed with the $\geq$-constraint (the method works in exactly the same way for the $\leq$ constraint):

$$\sum_{b \in B_s} x_{sb} \geq y_o \Leftrightarrow y_o - \sum_{b \in B_s} x_{sb} \leq 0$$

Substituting x_{sb} with its complement $\overline{x}_{sb} = 1 - x_{sb}$ as described by Glover (1965) and Martello and Toth (1990) yields the desired form:

$$y_o - \sum_{b \in B_s} x_{sb} \leq 0 \Leftrightarrow y_o - \sum_{b \in B_s} (1 - \overline{x}_{sb}) \leq 0 \Leftrightarrow y_o + \sum_{b \in B_s} \overline{x}_{sb} \leq |B_s|$$

Analogous transformations for the other inequalities (if necessary) lead to the following set of knapsack constraints with positive coefficients:

$$y_o + \sum_{b \in B_s} \overline{x}_{sb} \leq |B_s| \qquad o \in O, s \in S_o \qquad (6.12)$$

$$\overline{y}_o + \sum_{b \in B_s} x_{sb} \leq 1 \qquad o \in O, s \in S_o \qquad (6.13)$$

$$\sum_{s \in S(b)} l_s x_{sb} \leq d_b^{\max} \qquad b \in B \qquad (6.14)$$

$$\sum_{s \in S(b)} l_s \overline{x}_{sb} \leq -d_b^{\min} + \sum_{s \in S(b)} l_s \qquad b \in B \qquad (6.15)$$

$$\sum_{s \in C \cap S(b)} x_{sb} \leq 1 \qquad (b, C) \in BC \qquad (6.16)$$

However, many of these knapsack constraints cannot be used to derive a *violated* cover cut. For instance, consider (6.12) for some fixed $o \in O, s \in S_o$. We have $|B_s| + 1$ items of weight 1 and a knapsack of capacity $|B_s|$. The only subset of items that has got a total weight greater than $|B_s|$ is thus the set of all $|B_s|+1$ items, yielding the cover cut:

$$y_o + \sum_{b \in B_s} \overline{x}_{sb} \leq (|B_s| + 1) - 1 = |B_s|$$

– this cover cut is identical to (6.12). The knapsack constraints (6.13) and (6.16) explicitly state that at most one item can be packed into the knapsack, thus any cover will contain at least two items, and lead to a cover cut with a right hand side of at least $2 - 1 = 1$, i. e. it will never be stronger than the original inequality. Since we typically deal with instances where $d_b^{\min} = 0, b \in B$, we focus our exposition in the following on the constraints:

$$\sum_{s \in S(b)} l_s x_{sb} \leq d_b^{\max} \qquad b \in B \tag{6.17}$$

– however, the methods we are going to describe can be applied to the transformed minimum break length restrictions (6.15) without any change.

So if $C \subseteq S(b)$ is a minimal cover of the break length constraint of break $b \in B$, the resulting cover inequality defines obviously a facet of the restricted polyhedron

$$P_C = conv\left\{x_{sb} \in \{0,1\}, s \in C : \sum_{s \in C} l_s x_{sb} \leq d_b^{\max}\right\} \tag{6.18}$$

In the remainder of this subsection we will address the separation problem, i. e. the question of how to find violated cover cuts for a given break length constraint (6.17). The covers we will find will usually not be minimal, so we are going to minimize them. As mentioned before, a minimal cover defines a facet of the restricted polyhedron (6.11). So we will finally show how to obtain a facet for the original polyhedron P_K by a procedure called *lifting*. We will describe two methods that deal with the necessary steps of separation, minimization, and lifting:

1. A "classic" method, that closely follows standard references on the separation problem and the lifting procedure.
2. A method along the lines of Gu et al. (1998).

"Classic" Method

Separation

The problem to separate a violated cover cut for the break length constraint of some break $b \in B$ can be stated as follows: We are given an optimal LP-solution $x_{sb}^* \in [0,1], s \in S(b)$ such that at least one of the variables has a fractional value. We have to find a subset $C \subseteq S(b)$ (if one exists) such that:

$$\sum_{s \in C} l_s \geq d_b^{\max} + 1 \tag{6.19}$$

$$\sum_{s \in C} x_{sb}^* > |C| - 1 \Leftrightarrow |C| - \sum_{s \in C} x_{sb}^* = \sum_{s \in C} (1 - x_{sb}^*) < 1 \tag{6.20}$$

(6.19) states that C is a cover. By (6.20) the solution at hand violates the cover inequality defined by C.

We approach the separation problem by defining the following binary decision variables:

$$z_s = \begin{cases} 1 & \text{if } s \in C \\ 0 & \text{otherwise} \end{cases} \qquad s \in S(b)$$

Using these decision variables, the separation problem for cover cuts can be stated as the following auxiliary knapsack problem:

$$\zeta = \min_{z_s \in \{0,1\}, s \in S(b)} \left\{ \sum_{s \in S(b)} (1 - x^*_{sb})\, z_s : \sum_{s \in S(b)} l_s z_s \geq d_b^{\max} + 1 \right\} \qquad (6.21)$$

Let $z^*_s, s \in S(b)$ be an optimal solution and $C = \{s \in S(b) : z^*_s = 1\}$ be the corresponding cover. By (6.20), the corresponding cover cut $\sum_{s \in C} x^*_{sb} > |C| - 1$ will be violated by x^*_{sb} if $\zeta < 1$. If it is indeed violated, it is at the same time the "most violated" cover, i. e. the difference $\sum_{s \in C} x^*_{sb} - (|C| - 1)$ is maximal. In other words, ζ measures the "degree of violation" of the cover inequality, where $\zeta \geq 1$ signifies no violation; and if $\zeta < 1$, the violation gets greater if ζ gets smaller. We can exploit this fact in our Branch and Cut procedure as follows: If $\zeta = 0.99$, say, we have clearly found a violated cover; but it is not "very violated", and the LP-solution will probably not improve much if we add the cover inequality and re-solve the resulting LP. So we may well decide to save the effort if $\zeta \geq \zeta'$ where ζ' is a threshold of 0.95 (say).

It remains to be shown how we intend to solve the knapsack problem (6.21), which is obviously NP-hard itself. However, the problem can usually be enormously reduced by removing quite a large number of spots from $S(b)$, thereby reducing the mere size of the knapsack problem to be solved. These simplifications are given by Crowder et al. (1983, p. 813, eq. (2.13)), and for the convenience of the reader we briefly summarize them here:

1. We can remove all s from $S(b)$ where $x^*_{sb} = 0$, because they can never be in a violated cover. Intuitively, these spots cannot "contribute to the violation" of the cover inequality, because adding them to C just increases $|C| - 1$, but does not increase $\sum_{s \in C} x^*_{sb}$. To formally prove this observation, suppose that C is a cover violated by x^*_{sb} and that $\exists t \in C : x^*_{tb} = 0$. Then $\sum_{s \in C} (1 - x^*_{sb}) \geq 1 - x^*_{tb} = 1$, contradicting (6.20).
2. We can remove all s from $S(b)$ where $x^*_{sb} = 1$, because if a violated cover exists, there exists a violated cover such that all these spots

are in it. To see this, we give the knapsack problem to be solved (6.21) a closer look: If $x^*_{sb} = 1$ for some s, its objective function coefficient is 0, so that the objective function does not increase if $z_s = 1$. On the other hand, since $l_s > 0$ it became easier to satisfy the knapsack restriction. Thus, if an optimal solution to (6.21) exists, we can always find an optimal solution z^*_s such that $x^*_{sb} = 1 \Rightarrow z^*_s = 1$.

We therefore basically have to deal with the following two subsets of spots:

$$C_2 = \{s \in S(b) : x^*_{sb} = 1\} \tag{6.22}$$

$$K_1 = \{s \in S(b) : 0 < x^*_{sb} < 1\} \tag{6.23}$$

C_2 is the subset of spots that we can put into the cover without further consideration. K_1 is the subset of spots on which we effectively have to make a decision. Define $d := d_b^{\max} - \sum_{s\in C_2} l_s$, the remaining time that has to be "covered" by the spots in K_1. Note that $d \geq 0$, i. e. the spots in C_2 alone do not suffice to cover $d_b^{\max}$, because x^*_{sb} satisfies the break length restriction of break b and therefore:

$$d_b^{\max} \geq \sum_{s\in S(b)} l_s x^*_{sb} \geq \sum_{s\in C_2} l_s x^*_{sb} = \sum_{s\in C_2} l_s$$

Obviously, if $\sum_{s\in K_1} l_s < d+1$, no cover exists and we can stop here (this is especially the case if $K_1 = \emptyset$). Otherwise, we finally remove some spots from K_1 because of their lengths l_s as follows: In a classical knapsack problem with a max-objective and a $\leq$-constraint – see (6.9) – we can rule out all "big" items j with $a_j > a$: These items cannot feasibly be put into the knapsack. Our separation problem is a min-problem with a $\geq$-constraint, but we can analogously identify some "big" spots in K_1 that have to be in the cover, thus further reducing the problem. To see what signifies a big spot, we consider the transformation to a $\leq$-knapsack constraint (see Appendix B for a transformation of the entire knapsack problem):

$$\sum_{s\in K_1} l_s z_s \geq d+1 \Leftrightarrow -\sum_{s\in K_1} l_s\left(1-\overline{z}_s\right) \leq -d-1$$

$$\Leftrightarrow \sum_{s\in K_1} l_s \overline{z}_s \leq \sum_{s\in K_1} l_s - d - 1$$

where $\overline{z}_s = 1 - z_s$ as before. The set of big spots is thus defined as $big = \left\{s \in K_1 : l_s > \sum_{s\in K_1} l_s - d - 1\right\}$. Let $small = K_1 \backslash big$. Note that every spot $s \in big$ has to be in the cover indeed, i. e. we have

$$t \in big \Rightarrow \sum_{s \in small} l_s + \sum_{s \in big \setminus \{t\}} l_s < d + 1$$

To see this, just insert the definition of a "big" spot into that formula:

$$\sum_{s \in small} l_s + \sum_{s \in big \setminus \{t\}} l_s = \sum_{s \in K_1} l_s - l_t < \sum_{s \in K_1} l_s - \left(\sum_{s \in K_1} l_s - d - 1 \right) = d + 1$$

Thus, a very small knapsack problem remains: Only the spots in *small* are relevant. We solve this knapsack problem using the COMBO algorithm by Martello, Pisinger, and Toth (1999). A C-implementation of this algorithm can be downloaded from Pisinger's website (`http://www.diku.dk/~pisinger/codes.html`). Appendix B shows how we dealt with some minor technical issues of using this implementation gainfully in our context.

COMBO is very fast, and the remaining knapsack problems are typically very small, so this exact approach to the separation problem has proven to be effective. The whole procedure of cover cut separation is summarized as Algorithm 6.5.

Minimization

Let C be a cover separated by Algorithm 6.5. Obviously, C is not necessarily minimal, but deriving a minimal cover from C is particularly easy: Just remove spots from C until C is a minimal cover. In the following paragraphs we make some brief remarks on how to choose spots to be removed.

As before, let z_s^* be an optimal solution to the knapsack problem (6.21), i. e. $z_s^* = 1$ if $s \in S(b)$ is part of the cover (and 0 otherwise). By construction, Algorithm 6.5 sets $z_s^* = 1$ for all $s \in C_2$, thus C consists of two distinct parts, namely all spots in C_2 and possibly some spots from K_1: $C = C_2 \cup \{s \in K_1 : z_s^* = 1\}$.

As a starting point, we show that only spots $s \in C_2$ can be removed from C to obtain a minimal cover. To prove this, suppose $C \setminus \{t\}$ with $t \in K_1$ was also a cover, i. e. $C \setminus \{t\}$ is also a feasible solution of (6.21). The objective function value of C in (6.21) was:

$$\sum_{s \in C} (1 - x_{sb}^*) = \sum_{s \in C_2} (1 - x_{sb}^*) + \sum_{s \in K_1} (1 - x_{sb}^*)\, z_s^*$$

On the other hand, the objective function value of $C \setminus \{t\}$ is:

Algorithm 6.5: Separation of Cover Cuts

Input: A break $b \in B$, the relevant data of this break: $d_b^{\max}, S(b)$, l_s for all $s \in S(b)$, a fractional solution x_{sb}^* for all $s \in S(b)$ and a threshold $\zeta' \leq 1$.
Output: A "most violated" cover $\emptyset \neq C \subseteq S(b)$ and its degree of violation $\zeta < \zeta'$, or the information that no violated cover with a degree of violation below the threshold exists.

1. Identify the set C_2 of spots that are trivially in the cover, and the set K_1 of "interesting" spots:
$$C_2 = \{s \in S(b) : x_{sb}^* = 1\} \qquad K_1 = \{s \in S(b) : 0 < x_{sb}^* < 1\}$$
2. Let $d \leftarrow d_b^{\max} - \sum_{s \in C_2} l_s$. If $\sum_{s \in K_1} l_s < d+1$: STOP – no violated cover exists.
3. If $|K_1| = 1$ let $\zeta \leftarrow \sum_{s \in K_1} (1 - x_{sb}^*)$. If $\zeta < \zeta'$ return $C = C_2 \cup K_1$ and ζ. Otherwise STOP – no violated cover with a degree of violation below the threshold exists.
4. Partition K_1 in big and small items:
$$big = \left\{ s \in K_1 : l_s > \sum_{t \in K_1} l_t - d - 1 \right\} \qquad small = K_1 \backslash big$$
5. Let $\zeta \leftarrow \sum_{s \in big} (1 - x_{sb}^*)$. If $\zeta \geq \zeta'$: STOP – no violated cover with a degree of violation below the threshold exists.
6. Let $d \leftarrow d - \sum_{s \in big} l_s$. If $d + 1 \leq 0$ return $C = C_2 \cup big$ and ζ.
7. Note that $\sum_{s \in small} l_s \geq d + 1$ (see step 2). Therefore the following knapsack problem is feasible; solve it using COMBO:
$$z = \min \left\{ \sum_{s \in small} (1 - x_{sb}^*) z_s : \sum_{s \in small} l_s z_s \geq d+1, z_s \in \{0,1\}, s \in small \right\}$$
8. Let $\zeta \leftarrow \zeta + z$.
If $\zeta < \zeta'$ return $C = C_2 \cup big \cup \{s \in small : z_s = 1\}$ and ζ.
Otherwise STOP – no violated cover with a degree of violation below the threshold exists.

$$\sum_{s \in C \backslash \{t\}} (1 - x_{sb}^*) = \sum_{s \in C_2} (1 - x_{sb}^*) + \sum_{s \in K_1 \backslash \{t\}} (1 - x_{sb}^*) z_s^*$$

Since $t \in K_1 \Rightarrow 0 < x_{tb}^* < 1 \Rightarrow 1 - x_{tb}^* > 0$ the latter is strictly smaller, contradicting the optimality of C.

Furthermore, if we only remove spots $s \in C_2$ from C, the "degree of violation" ζ will not change:

$$\zeta = \sum_{s \in C} (1 - x^*_{sb}) = \sum_{s \in C_2} (1 - x^*_{sb}) + \sum_{s \in K_1} (1 - x^*_{sb})\, z^*_s = \sum_{s \in K_1} (1 - x^*_{sb})\, z^*_s$$

This implies:

- If the cover inequality was not violated before minimization (i. e. $\zeta \geq 1$), it will neither be afterwards.
- If the cover inequality was violated before (i. e. $\zeta < 1$), it will also be afterwards.
- In either case, the difference between left hand side and right hand side of the cover inequality will remain unchanged, and it will still be the "most violated" one.

So with respect to (6.20), we could safely remove C_2 completely from C; but of course we will also have to keep in mind that the resulting subset of C should also be a cover, i. e. it should satisfy (6.19). So we iteratively remove spots from C_2 as long as

$$\sum_{s \in C} l_s \geq d_b^{\max} + 1 \Leftrightarrow \sum_{s \in C_2} l_s \geq d_b^{\max} + 1 - \sum_{s \in C \setminus C_2} l_s$$

There seems to be no agreed-upon method in the literature how to select the "victims" to leave the cover. But given the fact the we obtain a facet of the restricted polyhedron (6.18), it seems to be desirable to keep C as large as possible. Finding the largest subset $C' \subseteq C$ still satisfying (6.19) such that no proper subset of C' satisfies (6.19) is again a knapsack-like problem. We simply use Dantzig's (1957) procedure to heuristically solve it and remove spots from C_2 with decreasing lengths l_s to obtain a minimal cover. If we denote the cover found in this way by C', we have obtained a facet of the restricted polyhedron $P_{C'}$.

Lifting

Since we consider only a single break length restriction at a time, the best we can expect is to find a facet for the polyhedron $P_{S(b)}$, but up to now, we only have a facet of a restricted version of it. This facet induces of course a valid inequality for $P_{S(b)}$, but typically this cut will not be very strong. To see this, consider a slightly modified version of the knapsack constraint (6.7):

$$40x_1 + 50x_2 + 60x_3 + 30x_4 \leq 100 \qquad x_1, x_2, x_3, x_4 \in \{0, 1\} \tag{6.24}$$

Clearly, the inequality

$$x_1 + x_2 + x_3 \leq 2 \tag{6.25}$$

is still valid (because $\{1, 2, 3\}$ is still a cover). However,

$$x_1 + x_2 + x_3 + x_4 \leq 2 \tag{6.26}$$

is also valid, and this inequality is stronger, because some feasible solutions (e. g. $x_1 = x_4 = 1, x_2 = 0, x_3 = 0.5$) satisfy the former, but not the latter. Using Proposition 6.2, we can give a theoretical argument why this is the case: Let

$$X = \{x_1, x_2, x_3, x_4 \in \{0,1\} : 40x_1 + 50x_2 + 60x_3 + 30x_4 \leq 100\}$$

and consider the (unrestricted) polyhedron *conv* (X). Let F_1, F_2 be the faces of *conv* (X) defined by (6.25) and (6.26), respectively. F_1 is clearly a proper subset of F_2, so (6.25) does not define a facet of *conv* (X).

Literally speaking, our cutting plane will be stronger if more variables appear in it with a non-zero coefficient. Fortunately, variables that are missing in a given valid inequality can be added using a procedure called *lifting*. To introduce this concept formally, consider the knapsack polyhedron P_K. Let

$$\sum_{j=1}^{n} \pi_j x_j \leq \pi_0 \tag{6.27}$$

be a valid inequality for P_K. Let $U = \{j \in \{1, \ldots, n\} : \pi_j = 0\}$ be the set of variable indexes that appear with a zero coefficient in this inequality. As we have seen, If $U \neq \emptyset$, (6.27) will frequently not be a facet of the P_K, because if some $k \in U$ and some $\pi'_k \neq 0$ exist such that

$$\sum_{\substack{j=1 \\ j \neq k}}^{n} \pi_j x_j + \pi'_k x_j \leq \pi_0 \tag{6.28}$$

is also a valid inequality for P_K, then the face defined by (6.27) is clearly a proper subset of the face defined by (6.28). So lifting is basically a method of trying to find such non-zero coefficients π'_j for all $j \in U$. We will demonstrate this method using our example: Consider the knapsack polyhedron for the restriction (6.24) and the valid inequality (6.25). We are searching for a so called *lifting coefficient* $\pi_4 \geq 0$ such that

$$x_1 + x_2 + x_3 + \pi_4 x_4 \leq 2 \tag{6.29}$$

is also valid. If $x_4 = 0$, we can choose an arbitrary value for π_4. If $x_4 = 1$, (6.29) is valid if and only if $x_1 + x_2 + x_3 + \pi_4 \leq 2$ is valid for all $x_1, x_2, x_3 \in \{0, 1\}$ satisfying $40x_1 + 50x_2 +$

$60x_3 \leq 100 - 30 = 70$. (6.29) is particularly hard to satisfy if $x_1 + x_2 + x_3$ is maximal, i. e. $\pi_4 \leq 2 - \eta$ has to hold where $\eta = \max\{x_1 + x_2 + x_3 : 40x_1 + 50x_2 + 60x_3 \leq 70, x_1, x_2, x_3 \in \{0,1\}\}$. In our example, $\eta = 1$ and we have $\pi_4 \leq 2 - 1 = 1$. Certainly, we obtain the strongest inequality for the maximum value of π_4, namely $\pi_4 = 1$. The resulting inequality happens to be (6.26).

The procedure we have just shown using our tiny examples can be generalized to larger problems. Using that procedure, which is due to Padberg (1975), variables are lifted one by one by solving a sequence of Knapsack problems, hence this method is called *sequential (up-)lifting*. Algorithm 6.6 summarizes the details of the general procedure.

With respect to the quality of the resulting cuts, we have the following result (Padberg 1975, p. 835):

Theorem 6.4 *If the valid inequality $\sum_{j \in C} \pi_j x_j \leq \pi_0$ used as in input for Algorithm 6.6 is actually a facet of the restricted polyhedron*

Algorithm 6.6: Sequential Up-Lifting (Padberg 1975)

Input: A knapsack restriction $\sum_{j \in J} a_j x_j \leq a$, valid inequality $\sum_{j \in C} \pi_j x_j \leq \pi_0$ such that $C \subset J$.

Output: Lifting coefficients $\pi_j, j \in J \backslash C$ such that $\sum_{j \in J} \pi_j x_j \leq \pi_0$ is also a valid inequality.

1. Let $U = J - C$. Order the elements in U arbitrarily, i. e. let $U = \{j_1, \ldots, j_t\}$ where $t = |U|$. We are going to lift the elements in U using the order $j_q, q = 1, \ldots, t$. For the ease of notation define the sets:

$$U_q = \begin{cases} \emptyset & q = 0 \\ \{j_1, \ldots, j_q\} & q = 1, \ldots, t \end{cases}$$

2. Let $q = 1$.
3. Solve the following knapsack problem:

$$z_q = \max \sum_{j \in C} \pi_j x_j + \sum_{j \in U_{q-1}} \pi_j x_j$$

s. t.

$$\sum_{j \in C} a_j x_j + \sum_{j \in U_{q-1}} a_j x_j \leq a - a_{j_q}$$

$$x_j \in \{0,1\} \qquad\qquad j \in C \cup U_{q-1}$$

4. Set $\pi_{j_q} = \pi_0 - z_q$ and increment q. If $q \leq t$ goto 3.

$$conv\left\{x_j \in \{0,1\}, j \in C : \sum_{j \in C} a_j x_j \leq a\right\}$$

the output of this algorithm be will actually be a facet of P_k.

The theorem states in words: If we start with a "strong" inequality for the restricted polyhedron, we obtain a strong inequality for the unrestricted polyhedron as well.

It is interesting to note that lifting may turn a non-violated valid inequality into a violated one. To see this, consider the knapsack restriction (6.24) and the LP-feasible point $x_1 = x_4 = 1, x_2 = 0, x_3 = 1/2$. This point does not violate the valid inequality (6.25) but its lifted version (6.26). As a second example, consider the minimal cover $\{1,2,4\}$ for (6.24), inducing the valid inequality $x_1 + x_2 + x_4$, which – in contrast to (6.25) – defines a facet of a restricted polyhedron. By lifting we obtain the facet $x_1 + x_2 + x_3 + x_4 \leq 2$. The LP-feasible point $x_1 = 1/4, x_2 = 0, x_3 = x_4 = 1$ violates the latter, but not the former.

Since the solution of knapsack problems is involved, sequential lifting is typically an NP-hard task as well. Note, however, that an upper bound $\overline{z_q} \geq z_q$ is absolutely sufficient to define the lifting coefficient π_{j_q} in step 4 of the algorithm – precisely, we can safely set

$$\pi_{j_q} = \max\{0, \pi_0 - \overline{z_q}\}$$

and still obtain a valid inequality (albeit the resulting inequality may no longer be facet defining). It is also evident, however, that using an upper bound $\overline{z_q}$ will result in smaller lifting coefficients π_{j_q}, i. e. the resulting inequality will be stronger if we use stronger bounds $\overline{z_q}$ (or, at best, the true optimum z_q).

For cover cuts – i. e. valid inequalities such that $\pi_j = 1, j \in C$ –, the use of upper bounds $\overline{z_q}$ is not necessary, because Zemel (1989) has developed an efficient implementation of Padberg's procedure based on dynamic programming. It is summarized as Algorithm 6.7. One key point of Zemel's algorithm is that we can readily compute numbers $\beta_s, \gamma_s, s \in S(b) \backslash C$ such that $\beta_s \leq \alpha_s \leq \gamma_s$, where β_s and γ_s are integers with a difference of at most one, i. e. either $\beta_s = \gamma_s$ or $\beta_s + 1 = \gamma_s$. $\beta_s = \gamma_s \Rightarrow \alpha_s = \beta_s = \gamma_s$ immediately, and the rest of the spots can be efficiently treated by dynamic programming techniques.

Algorithm 6.8 summarizes the complete "classic" method of cover cut separation, minimization, and lifting in a nutshell. Note that we have deliberately chosen not to lift a non-violated cover inequality – despite the fact that a violated inequality may be obtained from a

Algorithm 6.7: Efficient Lifting Procedure for Cover Cuts (Zemel 1989)

Input: A cover C, the set $S(b)$ and the spot lengths $l_s, s \in S(b)$.
Output: Lifting coefficients α_s for each $s \in S(b) \setminus C$.

1. Let $U \leftarrow S(b) \setminus C$. Compute:

$$\begin{aligned}
m_k &\leftarrow \text{Sum of the } k \text{ smallest } l_s, s \in C && k = 0, \ldots, |C| \\
b_k &\leftarrow \text{Sum of the } k \text{ greatest } l_s, s \in C && k = 0, \ldots, |C| \\
\beta_s &\leftarrow \text{Largest integer } k, \text{ such that } b_k \leq l_s && s \in U \\
\gamma_s &\leftarrow \text{Smallest integer } k, \text{ such that } m_{|C|-1-k} \leq b - l_s && s \in U
\end{aligned}$$

2. Determine the set I of "trivial" and the set J of "non-trivial" spots:

$$I \leftarrow \{s \in U : \beta_s = \gamma_s\} \qquad J \leftarrow \{s \in U : \beta_s + 1 = \gamma_s\}$$

   Let $\alpha_s \leftarrow \beta_s, s \in I$.
3. Order the elements in J arbitrarily, i. e. $J = \{s_1, \ldots, s_{|J|}\}$ and compute the lifting coefficients for each $s \in J$ by dynamic programming:
   a) Let $A_{s_1}(z) \leftarrow m_z, z = 0, \ldots, |C| - 1$.
   b) For all $k = 1, \ldots, |J|$:
      i. Let $z_{s_k} \leftarrow \max\{z : A_{s_k}(z) \leq d_b^{max} - l_{s_k}\}$.
      ii. Let $\alpha_{s_k} \leftarrow |C| - 1 - z_{s_k}$.
      iii. If $\alpha_{s_k} = 0$ or $z < \alpha_{s_k}$, let $A_{s_{k+1}}(z) \leftarrow A_{s_k}(z)$ for all $z = 0, \ldots, |C| - 1$.
      Otherwise we let $A_{s_{k+1}}(z) \leftarrow \min\{A_{s_k}(z), \alpha_{s_k} + A_{s_k}(z - \alpha_{s_k})\}$ for all $z = 0, \ldots, |C| - 1$.

non-violated one by lifting. This was done because preliminary computational experience suggested that the additional lifting effort rarely pays off by increasing the efficiency of the entire Branch and Cut-scheme. This observation can intuitively explained as follows: Let $x_{sb}^* \in [0, 1]$ be the LP-optimal solution and C be the minimal cover obtained in step 2 of Algorithm 6.8. After lifting, we obtain the facet $\sum_{s \in C} x_{sb} + \sum_{S(b) \setminus C} \pi_s x_{sb} \leq |C| - 1$. By construction, only variables with $x_{sb}^* < 1$ and a relatively small value of l_s are not in C and have been lifted (see steps 1 and 4 to 7 of Algorithm 6.5). The latter property implies that $\beta_s = 0$ will frequently hold in Algorithm 6.7 such that $\pi_s \in \{0, 1\}$. So we can expect $\pi_s x_{sb}^*$ to be very small, and adding $\sum_{S(b) \setminus C} \pi_s x_{sb}^*$ to the left hand side of the cover cut will not change the degree of violation much. Thus, if we lift a non-violated inequality in step 3, the result will frequently be not violated as well, and if violated it will rarely be strong.

The Method by Gu et al. (1998)

Gu et al. (1998) point that it may not be worth the effort to separate the most violated cover inequality if we are finally interested in a violated *lifted* inequality, because (as we have already seen) lifting may turn a non-violated inequality into a violated one. They therefore propose a separation scheme that is very strongly driven by the optimal LP-values x^*_{sb}, see Algorithm 6.9.

Note that step 1 of Algorithm 6.9 is identical to the first step of Algorithm 6.5. Also note that adding the variables with the largest x^*_{sb} to the cover – see steps 2 and 3 of Algorithm 6.9 – is a simple greedy approach to solving the knapsack problem (6.21) of the "classic" method by selecting the items with the smallest objective function coefficient $1 - x^*_{sb}$. Because this step is almost completely independent of the co-

Algorithm 6.8: Classic Method of Cover Cut Separation, Minimization, and Lifting

For each $b \in B$:

1. Try to separate a cover cut for b by Algorithm 6.5 using a threshold of $\zeta' = 0.95$. If no cover cut can be found with the desired degree of violation: STOP.
2. Minimize the given cover by successively removing elements from C_2 until any further removal will lead to a violation of the cover property. As argued before, this will not change the degree of violation.
3. Lift all variables that are not in the cover using Algorithm 6.7.

Algorithm 6.9: Cover Cut Separation as Proposed by Gu et al. (1998)

1. Identify the set C_2 of spots that are trivially in the cover, and the set K_1 of "interesting" spots:

$$C_2 = \{s \in S(b) : x^*_{sb} = 1\} \qquad K_1 = \{s \in S(b) : 0 < x^*_{sb} < 1\}$$

   Set $C \leftarrow C_2$.
2. Sort the elements in K_1 in order of non-increasing x^*_{sb}.
3. While $\sum_{s \in C} l_s \leq d_b^{\max}$, add elements from K_1 to C according to the sorting order.
4. If $\sum_{s \in C} l_s \leq d_b^{\max}$: STOP, no violated cover exists. Otherwise return C.

efficients l_s, Gu et al. (1998) call their approach *coefficient independent cover generation.*

To minimize a cover C returned by Algorithm 6.9, Gu et al. (1998) define $C_1 = C \backslash C_2$ and remove elements from C_1 until C_1 is empty or no element from C_1 can be removed without violating the cover property. It is easy to see, though, that the resulting cover is not necessarily minimal. Consider the following example: Let $d_b^{\max} = 70$ and $C_2 = \{1,2\}, C_1 = \{3\}$ where $l_1 = 30, l_2 = 20, l_3 = 45$. We cannot remove spot 3 from C_1, because $30+20 \leq 70$. Spot 2, however, can be removed from C_2 to obtain the minimal cover $\{1,3\}$. So we have decided to also remove spots from C_2 (again starting with spots of greater length) if the resulting cover is not minimal after removing spots from C_1.

To strengthen the cover inequality by lifting the variables that are not in the cover Gu et al. (1998) do not only use the up-lifting procedure we just described, but also a concept that is called *down-lifting.* The difference is that up-lifting starts with a valid inequality of a restricted polyhedron where a subset of variables – call it U – is fixed to 0 and systematically modifies the coefficients of variables from U to obtain a valid inequality for the unrestricted polyhedron – literally speaking, the variables in U are "lifted up" from their fixed value of 0 to a value of 1. If variable s is "lifted up" to 1, we obtain its lifting coefficient π_s by Algorithm 6.6 – recall that π_s can be chosen arbitrarily if $x_{sb} = 0$. The lifted inequality is valid regardless of the value of x_{sb}. Analogously, down-lifting starts with a valid inequality of a restricted polyhedron where a subset of variables U is fixed to 1 and obtains a valid inequality for the unrestricted polyhedron by "lifting down" the fixed variables to a value of 0.

Formally, down-lifting means starting with a valid inequality (or even a facet) of

$$conv \left\{ x_j \in \{0,1\}, j \in J : \sum_{j \in J} a_j x_j \leq a; x_j = 1, j \in J \backslash C \right\} \tag{6.30}$$

– note the restriction $x_j = 1$ – and (sequentially) considering the case $x_j = 0, j \in J \backslash C$ to obtain a valid inequality (or facet) of the unrestricted polyhedron.

Finding a facet of (6.30) is cumbersome, though. As a first approach to the problem, select an arbitrary subset C of J such that $1 \leq |C| < |J|$ to avoid trivial cases. Setting $x_j = 1, j \in J \backslash C$ implies the modified knapsack constraint:

$$\sum_{j\in C} a_j x_j \leq a - \sum_{j\in J\backslash C} a_j$$

Let $C' \subseteq C$ be a minimal cover for this constraint. It induces a facet of

$$conv \left\{ x_j \in \{0,1\}, j \in J : \right.$$
$$\left. \sum\nolimits_{j\in J} a_j x_j \leq a; x_j = 1, j \in J\backslash C; x_j = 0, j \in C\backslash C' \right\}$$

– this polyhedron is only a restricted version of (6.30) unless $C = C'$, which is unlikely to hold since C' is minimal. So we restrict ourselves to the less ambitious task to start with a facet of

$$P = conv \left\{ x_j \in \{0,1\}, j \in J : \right.$$
$$\left. \sum\nolimits_{j\in J} a_j x_j \leq a; x_j = 1, j \in C_2; x_j = 0, j \in J\backslash (C_1 \cup C_2) \right\}$$

where $C_1, C_2 \subseteq J, C_1 \cap C_2 = \emptyset$ and $|C_1| \geq 2$. Such a facet is easy to find: Let C be a minimal cover of the knapsack constraint. Then partition C arbitrarily into two disjoint subsets C_1, C_2. C induces the valid inequality

$$\sum_{j\in C_1} x_j + \sum_{j\in C_2} x_j \leq |C_1| + |C_2| - 1$$

Clearly,

$$\sum_{j\in C_1} x_j \leq |C_1| - 1 \tag{6.31}$$

is valid for and defines a facet of P, because the definition of P assumes that $x_j = 1, j \in C_2$. These restrictions are typically crucial for the validity of (6.31). To see this, let $C_1 = \{1,2\}, C_2 = \{3\}, a_1 = a_2 = 1, a_3 = 1000, a = 1001$. Since the weights of the items in C_1 is very small, they are not able to cover the whole capacity a without the very large item in C_2, such that (6.31) – which becomes $x_1 + x_2 \leq 1$ in this example – is indeed valid only if $x_3 = 1$.

As we see from this example, the right hand side of (6.31) has to be increased if $x_j = 0$ for some $j \in C_2$. Formally, we have to find *down lifting coefficients* $\pi_j \geq 0, j \in C_2$ such that

$$\sum_{j\in C_1} x_j + \sum_{s\in C_2} \pi_j x_j \leq |C_1| - 1 + \sum_{s\in C_2} \pi_j$$

is a valid inequality.

Continuing our small example, we have to find $\pi_3 \geq 0$ such that $x_1 + x_2 + \pi_3 x_3 \leq 1 + \pi_3$ is a valid inequality. Obviously, it is valid for any π_3 if $x_3 = 1$. If $x_3 = 0$, we clearly want π_3 to be as small as possible. It is easy to see that $\pi_3 = 1$ is the minimal feasible value, and we obtain the valid inequality $x_1 + x_2 + x_3 \leq 2$ – which is (by chance) the original cover inequality for our initial cover $C = C_1 \cup C_2 = \{1, 2, 3\}$.

The generalization of this procedure is straightforward and leads to Algorithm 6.10, which is a direct analogue of Algorithm 6.6. Note that this algorithm does not assume that $C_1 \cup C_2 = J$, i. e. there may be some variables remaining in $J \setminus (C_1 \cup C_2)$ that can be up-lifted afterwards.

Again, we have to solve a sequence of NP-hard knapsack problems in step 3 of the algorithm, and again, it is clearly sufficient to use an upper bound $\overline{z_q}$, where smaller bounds will deliver stronger inequalities. Since Gu et al. (1998, p. 433) report that Martello and Toth's (1977) procedure to compute an upper bound for the knapsack problem performs as good as an exact approach based on dynamic programming, we have thus chosen to implement the former.

After separating and minimizing a cover, Gu et al. (1998) partition the remaining variables into various subsets and up- or down-lift them in a particular order. Algorithm 6.11 summarizes the details of the entire approach as we have implemented it. Note that in steps 4a), b) and c) we process the variables in the given order that results from the previous steps of separation and minimization, i. e. F (which is basically the remainder of K_1 from Algorithm 6.9) is sorted non-increasingly by x^*_{sb}, C_2 is sorted non-increasingly by l_s and R is in no particular order. Gu et al. discuss different possibilities for this "second level ordering" of variables to be lifted, but they mention that the second level ordering is not important (p. 433).

6.4.4 Heuristics Applied During the Branching Process

After having described how we have implemented the Cutting Plane-part of our Branch and Cut-method, we now deal with some of the questions with respect to the Branch and Bound-part. As argued before, adding cutting planes can only decrease the LP-upper bound, so we have chosen not to implement any other methods to compute upper bounds. The forthcoming subsection describes how we branch into subproblems and how the next node to be processed is selected from the tree of unprocessed nodes. Here we will describe how we try to find feasible solutions to derive lower bounds. The heuristics we have described in section 6.3 provide a first lower bound, but this bound can

Algorithm 6.10: Sequential Down-Lifting

Input: A knapsack restriction $\sum_{j \in J} a_j x_j \leq a$, two disjoint subsets $C_1, C_2 \subseteq J$, an inequality $\sum_{j \in C_1} \pi_j x_j \leq \pi_0$ that is valid if $x_j = 1, j \in C_2$.
Output: Down-lifting coefficients $\pi_j, j \in C_2$ such that $\sum_{j \in C_1 \cup C_2} \pi_j x_j \leq \pi_0$ is a valid inequality regardless of the value of any variable in $C_1 \cup C_2$.

1. Let $U = C_2$. Order the elements in U arbitrarily, i. e. let $U = \{j_1, \ldots, j_t\}$ where $t = |U|$. We are going to lift the elements in U using the order $j_q, q = 1, \ldots, t$. For the ease of notation define the sets:
$$U_q = \begin{cases} \emptyset & q = 0 \\ \{j_1, \ldots, j_q\} & q = 1, \ldots, t \end{cases}$$
2. Let $q = 1$.
3. Solve the following knapsack problem:
$$z_q = \max \underbrace{\sum_{s \in C} \pi_s x_s + \sum_{s \in U_{q-1}} \pi_s x_s}_{\substack{\text{LHS of the} \\ \text{current valid inequality}}}$$
s. t.
$$\underbrace{\sum_{s \in C} a_s x_s + \sum_{s \in U_{q-1}} a_s x_s}_{\substack{a_{j_q} \text{ does not appear here,} \\ \text{because } x_{j_q} \text{ is fixed to } 0}} \leq b - \underbrace{\sum_{U \setminus U_q} a_s}_{\substack{\text{These variables are} \\ \text{still fixed to } 1}}$$
$$x_s \in \{0, 1\} \qquad s \in C \cup U_{q-1}$$
4. Set $\pi_{j_q} = z_q - \underbrace{\left(\pi_0 + \sum_{j \in U_{q-1}} \pi_j \right)}_{\substack{\text{RHS of the} \\ \text{current valid inequality}}}$ and increment q by 1. If $q \leq t$ goto 3.

be considerably improved after a few branching steps where some of the variables have been fixed to binary values. The basic idea of the two heuristics we are going to describe is to use the current LP values $y_o^*, o \in O$ and $x_{sb}^*, s \in \{1, \ldots, S\}, b \in B_s$ to find a feasible solution. As before, we assume that $d_b^{\min} = 0, b \in B$. Since the two heuristics only differ in how they select the next spot to be scheduled – one uses a deterministic, the other a randomized selection rule –, both are summarized as Algorithm 6.12. Note that we use both heuristics on every

Algorithm 6.11: Cover Cut, Separation, Minimization, and Lifting Along the Lines of Gu et al. (1998)

For each break $b \in B$:

1. Separate a cover using Algorithm 6.9.
2. Consider the elements in C_1 with non-decreasing values of x^*_{sb}. Remove spot t if $\sum_{s \in C_1 \cup C_2 \backslash \{t\}} l_s \geq d_b^{\max} + 1$.
3. Consider the elements in C_2 with non-decreasing values of l_s. Remove spot t if $\sum_{s \in C_1 \cup C_2 \backslash \{t\}} l_s \geq d_b^{\max} + 1$.
4. Let C be the resulting minimal cover. Define $\overline{C} = S(b) \backslash C$, $F = \{j \in \overline{C} : x^*_j > 0\}$, $R = \overline{C} \backslash F$. Lift the variables in the following order using the following methods:
   a) Up-lift the variables in F using Algorithm 6.7.
   b) Down-lift the variables in C_2 using Algorithm 6.10 where z_q is replaced as described by the Martello/Toth bound $\overline{z_q}$ to save time.
   c) Up-lift the variables in R. Since the valid inequality we have obtained so far is no longer a cover cut, we cannot use Algorithm 6.7. Instead, we directly implemented Algorithm 6.6 where z_q is replaced by the Martello/Toth bound $\overline{z_q}$ to save time.

node where the LP was feasible but the LP-solution is not integer. If the deterministic heuristic finds a spot that is "nasty" to schedule, it is saved in s_{branch} proposed for branching (see Branching Rule 2 below).

6.4.5 Branching Rules and Node Selection

Our method uses four branching rules in total. It is to be understood that the branching rules are processed in the order given, i. e. if the first branching rule fails to branch the given node, we use the second etc. The fourth branching rule is constructed in a way that it will always be able to branch the given node.

For the description of the branching rules, let $y^*_o, o \in O$ and $x^*_{sb}, s \in \{1, \ldots, S\}, b \in B_s$ be the given LP solution.

Branching Rule 1

If not all y^*_o are binary, choose an y^*_o that is closest to 0.5 (using v_o to break ties) and create to children using the restrictions $y_o = 0$ and $y_o = 1$, respectively. This branching rule has got three major advantages: The upper bound will almost certainly decrease. It is virtually impossible that both children will lead to an optimal solution. Fixing $y_o = 0$ in the down branch will force all $x_{sb}, s \in S_o, b \in B_s$ variables to zero. These

Algorithm 6.12: Heuristics Applied At Each Node

1. Let $y_o^*, o \in O$ and $x_{sb}^*, s \in \{1, \ldots, S\}, b \in B_s$ be the optimal LP-solution at the current node. Start with an empty plan and schedule all spots s where all $x_{sb}^*, b \in B_s$ are binary. If a spot s is scheduled in this way, the corresponding order is considered to be "fixed".
2. Let $o(s)$ be the order to which spot s belongs. Sort the remaining spots by $y_{o(s)}^*$. Break ties using $v_{o(s)}, l_s$ and $\max_{b \in B_s} x_{sb}^*$ (in that order), where higher values are preferred, respectively. The result is the ordered list P. Set $s_{branch} = 0$.
3. If P is empty: STOP. Otherwise schedule the first spot s from P using a
   deterministic rule: Try to schedule s in each $b \in B_s$ with decreasing x_{sb}^*. If that fails, try to remove an already scheduled spot that belongs to an order of lower revenue. If such a spot exists, remove it from the plan, add it to the back of P, and schedule s. In either case, if $s_{branch} = 0$, set $s_{branch} = s$.
   stochastic rule: Select one $b \in B_s$ at random, where the distribution is given by the x_{sb}^* and try to schedule s in b. Note that if $\sum_{b \in B_s} x_{sb}^* < 1$, there is a positive probability that no b is selected and scheduling s is not even tried.
4. If s has not been scheduled remove all spots belonging to the same order from the plan and from P.
5. Goto 3.

variables can be removed from the problem, so that the LP to be solved in the down branch will often be considerably smaller.

Branching Rule 2

If the deterministic heuristic (see the previous subsection) has proposed a spot s for branching and not all x_{sb}^* are binary, consider restriction (6.2): $\sum_{b \in B_s} x_{sb} = y_o$. Since all y_o^* are binary at this point by the first branching rule, the fact that some x_{sb}^* is fractional implies $y_o^* = 1$ and $|B_s| \geq 2$, so that (6.2) has got the form of an special ordered set (SOS) constraint for the current LP-values. Therefore, we will perform a branching step that is similar to an SOS-branching, where the basic idea is to partition B_s into two subsets B_s^1 and $B \backslash B_s^1$ such that $\sum_{b \in B_s^1} x_{sb}^*$ is as close to 0.5 as possible, and then to branch into two children using the restrictions $\sum_{b \in B_s^1} x_{sb}^* = 0$ and $\sum_{b \in B \backslash B_s^1} x_{sb}^* = 0$, respectively. Note that none of the branches explicitly or implicitly fixes y_o.

Finding a subset $B_s^1 \subseteq B_s$ such that $\sum_{b \in B_s^1} x_{sb}^*$ is as close to 0.5 as possible, however, is a knapsack problem. The problem is trivial if $\max_{b \in B_s} x_{sb}^* \geq 0.5$. Otherwise, a simple heuristic approach is to sort all non-zero $x^*_{sb}, b \in B_s$ and add all b to B^1_s (a) with increasing x^*_{sb}, (b) with decreasing x^*_{sb}, or (c) alternating (i. e. adding the largest, then the smallest, then the second largest etc.) until $\sum_{b \in B^1_s} x^*_{sb} > 0.5$. Table 6.4 shows various examples and the results obtained by the three heuristic rules. As we can see, all rules can fail badly, so we have chosen to implement all three and chose the best solution.

Since s was proposed by the heuristic for branching, we hope that this branching rule helps to find a better feasible solution with an improved lower bound.

Branching Rule 3

Use the conflict restriction (6.4) to branch in the following way: For some fixed $(b, C) \in BC$, let $C \cap S(b) = \{1, \ldots, n\}$. (6.4) implies that either spot 1, or spot 2, or ..., or spot n, or none of these is scheduled in break b. Using this observation, we create $n + 1$ children.

We select a particular conflict restriction to branch on as follows: Consider the conflict restrictions first where the inequality is tight, i. e. $\sum_{s \in C \cap S(b)} x^*_{sb} = 1$ holds. Find a conflict restriction such that at least one fractional variable appears in it and $\sum_{s \in C \cap S(b)} l_{sb}$ is maximal. Break ties using the relative frequency of fractional variables in the restriction. If no such conflict restriction is found, consider the remaining conflict restrictions where the inequality is strict (i. e. $\sum_{s \in C \cap S(b)} x^*_{sb} < 1$ holds) in exactly the same manner.

Branching Rule 4

If none of these rules produced a branching yet, search for a spot with a fractional x^*_{sb} of greatest length l_s (breaking ties using the revenue v_o of the corresponding order if necessary). At this point we may also choose the spot such that x^*_{sb} is closest to 0.5, but since the x_{sb} variables do not influence the objective function, many LP-solutions with the same

Table 6.4: SOS-Branching: Examples

x^*_{sb}	$\sum_{b \in B^1_s} x^*_{sb}$ increasing	decreasing	alternating
$\{0.25 - \varepsilon, 0.25, 0.25, 0.25 + \varepsilon\}$	$0.75 - \varepsilon$	$0.5 + \varepsilon$	0.75
$\{2\varepsilon, 0.5 - \varepsilon, 0.5 - \varepsilon\}$	$0.5 + \varepsilon$	$1 - 2\varepsilon$	$0.5 + \varepsilon$
$\{0.25 + \varepsilon/2, 0.25 + \varepsilon/2, 0.5 - \varepsilon\}$	$0.5 + \varepsilon$	$0.75 - \varepsilon/2$	$0.75 - \varepsilon/2$
$\{0.125, 0.25, 0.25, 0.375\}$	0.625	0.625	0.5

($\varepsilon > 0$ is a small number.)

objective function value do probably exist, so the fact that some x^*_{sb} is close to 0.5 conveys almost no information. Since we have already dealt with the conflict restrictions in the previous branching rule (and found nothing), we focus on spots of great length, because they have the greatest impact on the remaining constraints, namely the break length restrictions.

Having chosen a spot s, we perform an SOS-branching on s as described in Branching Rule 2.

Node Selection

As long as the gap between global upper bound UB and best lower bound LB (defined as $(UB - LB)/LB$) is greater than a parameter g, we use a "depth first" approach, because feasible solutions that can help to improve the lower bound are found deeper in the tree. Among nodes of the same depth, we prefer nodes with a larger upper bound. If the gap is smaller than or equal to g, we switch to a "best first" approach, processing nodes with larger upper bounds first. Ties (if any) are broken by depth (where greater depth is preferred).

6.4.6 Additional Implementation Details

Reduced Cost Variable Fixing

Reduced cost information from the optimal LP solution can be used to fix variables if a lower bound for the optimal objective function value is given. This method is e. g. described by Nemhauser and Wolsey (1988, p. 389), see also Wolsey (1998, p. 109-110). It is based on a variant of the simplex method for bounded variables, which allows variables to be nonbasic if they attain their lower or upper bound even though these bounds may be non-zero (see e. g. Winston 1994, p. 587-591). The basic result follows, stated for max-problems:

Theorem 6.5 (Reduced Cost Variable Fixing) *Let $x_j \in \mathbb{R}, j = 1, \ldots, n$ be the optimal solution to an LP relaxation of an IP. Denote the reduced costs of x_j by c_j where*

$$c_j \leq 0 \textit{ if } x_j \textit{ is nonbasic at its } \text{lower} \textit{ bound}$$
$$c_j \geq 0 \textit{ if } x_j \textit{ is nonbasic at its } \text{upper} \textit{ bound}$$

Let z_{LP} be the optimal objective function value of the LP relaxation. Let $\underline{z}$ be a lower bound.

If x_j is nonbasic at its lower bound in the optimal LP solution and $z_{LP} + c_j \leq \underline{z}$, then x_j can be fixed to its lower bound.

Analogously, if x_j is nonbasic at its upper bound in the optimal LP solution and $z_{LP} - c_j \leq \underline{z}$, then x_j can be fixed to its upper bound.

Reduced cost fixing has turned out to be crucial for the effectiveness of our method.

Fixing variables, Removing Columns and Rows

To find more variables that can be fixed we consider each row of the LP at hand one by one. If the row contains only non-negative coefficients and its sense is $=$ or $\leq$ we update the upper bounds of all variables in that row. Since all our variables are binary, this frequently means that a variable can be fixed to 0 (namely if its upper bound drops below 1).

Because smaller LPs are easier to solve, we remove columns from the problem whenever variables are fixed, let it be by branching, updating bounds or reduced cost fixing. Due to the removal of columns, rows will get empty or contain only a single element. In the former case, we check if the problem became infeasible; if not, the row is simply removed. In the latter case, we update the upper or lower bound (if the row has got a $\leq$ or $\geq$ sense, respectively) or fix the variable (if the row has got a $=$ sense) and remove the row.

Cut Pool Management

Cut Pool Management serves two purposes: The first is to control LP size by removing cuts that are no longer effective, the second is to reuse cuts that have proven to be effective. The former issue is dealt with a *local cut pool*, for the latter we use a *global cut pool*. A very readable overview on cut pool management (and other issues related to implementing a Branch and Cut scheme) is given by Ralphs et al. (2001).

Though we remove some rows (and columns) using the routines described above, adding cutting planes (see step 3 of Algorithm 6.4) means adding rows to the LP at hand, which thus tends to grow larger and larger. But the larger an LP is, the longer it takes to solve it. Therefore we keep track of the cuts we added to the LP in a local cut pool: For each cut in each LP, we record the so-called age of a cut. If a cut is slack in an iteration, the age is increased, otherwise the age is reset to 0. If a cut gets older than a certain age (this is a parameter of our implementation), it is removed from the LP. When branching, the local cut pool information is transferred to the children.

A global cut pool improves the efficiency of a B&C-scheme as follows: If we separate a (violated) cut in a certain node, and we know that it is globally valid (i. e. the valid inequality is also valid in any other node, regardless of the previous branching/cutting steps), we store it in a global cut pool. At any given node, before we try to separate a violated inequality – typically an operation of high computational cost –, we iterate over the cuts in the global cut pool and add any cut that is presently violated to the LP (and to the local cut pool). Note that all the cuts we discussed so far are globally valid, so in our implementation we can add any cut that we just separated to the global cut pool. To control the size of the global cut pool, we record an "age" of any cut in it. Analogously to the local cut pools, this age is reset to 0 if a cut is restored into any LP, and it is increased every time it is not found violated. Cuts older than a certain age (a parameter) are removed.

6.5 Test Bed

We have implemented the B&C approach in C++ using the CPLEX 8 Callable Library to solve the LPs. We used a Pentium 4 computer at 3.06 GHz with 1 GB of RAM for all computational experiments. In this section we present results on the performance of our heuristics (see section 6.3) and our B&C-scheme based on a carefully defined test bed of 18,000 instances. We start by describing our instance generation procedure.

6.5.1 Instance Generation Procedure

To the best of our knowledge, no systematic test-bed for this problem (or a similar one) is available from the literature. Bollapragada and Garbiras (2004, p. 343-344) briefly summarize the data of their example, a practical instance from NBC: It contained 4500 spots and 900 breaks. They also mention that their instance had 662 conflicts. However, only 516 conflicts can feasibly be resolved. Note that Bollapragada and Garbiras (2004) assume that all spots have to be scheduled. Unresolved conflicts incur a penalty cost. In contrast, our model does not allow for any conflicts, but not all spots have to be scheduled.

Our test-bed is based on strong practical evidence from Spanish television (see subsection 6.1.1). Bollapragada and Garbiras (2004) describe a similar situation for NBC, so we do strongly believe that the setting we describe in the following is representative for many broadcasting companies.

Preliminary Considerations: Length of Breaks and Spots

In all of our instances, we let $d_b^{\min} = 0$. In this case, a trivial feasible solution exists ($y_o = x_{sb} = 0$).

It seems reasonable that all breaks have the same length, so we set $d_b^{\max} = 360$ (6 minutes) for all $b \in B$. In Spanish television, for instance, the standard length of a spot is 20 seconds, so we should have 18 spots in a break on average. The minimum length of a (regular) spot is 10 seconds, and the length of a spot hardly exceeds 120 seconds. Therefore, we choose l_s at random, where the distribution p_l is given by the following table:

l	p_l	$l \cdot p_l$
10	0.395	3.95
20	0.450	9.00
30	0.070	2.10
45	0.050	2.25
60	0.020	1.20
90	0.010	0.90
120	0.005	0.60
$\sum$	1	20

Size of the Instances and Prices

It remains to be defined how we determine the number of breaks (i.e. the set B), the overall number of spots (S), the number of orders (O), the distribution of spots among orders (S_o) and breaks (B_s) and the conflicts ($\mathcal{C}$).

We let the number of breaks be $|B| \in \{10, 15, 20, 50, 100\}$. Given $|B|$, we let $S = NLF \cdot |B|$, where $NLF \in \{15, 18, 20, 25, 30, 35\}$. The reasoning behind this is as follows: In RM problems, it is common to define the relation between demand and available resource capacity (see Kimms and Müller-Bungart (2007b) and section 4.3 for a discussion). This relation is called the nominal load factor. In all our instances, we can schedule on average 18 spots per break. So if $NLF \leq 18$, the number of spots that we can schedule is mostly limited by the conflicts, hence it should be possible to accept (almost) all orders. As the nominal load factor grows, the RM problem becomes c. p. more important since more and more orders will have to be rejected.

We assume that the spots are evenly distributed among the breaks – a reasonable assumption, otherwise it won't make sense to have breaks of (roughly) the same length in practice – so for each $s \in \{1, \ldots, S\}$ we let $|B_s| = \lfloor \alpha |B| \rfloor$, where $\alpha \in \{0.1, 0.2\}$. Then, we uniformly choose $|B_s|$ breaks from B for each $s = 1, \ldots, S$.

To determine the number of orders $|O|$ and the distribution of spots to orders (i.e. the sets S_o), we use the following procedure: Let $q \in \{1, 5, 10, 20, 50, 100\}$ and then define $|O|$ and S_o as follows: Let $|O| = \lfloor S/q \rfloor$. If S/q is integer, we assign the first q spots to S_1, the second q spots to S_2 and so forth, i.e. $|S_o| = q, o \in O$. Otherwise, we raise q by redefining $q = \lfloor S/|O| \rfloor$. If $S/|O|$ is integer, we assign the first q spots to S_1, the second q spots to S_2 and so forth, i.e. $|S_o| = q, o \in O$. Otherwise, the sets $S_o, o = 1, \ldots, S - q \cdot |O|$ are assigned $q + 1$ spots each, and the rest of all orders are assigned q spots each.

Given the B_s, we can compute the sets $S(b)$. We will use these sets to define conflicts as follows: Denote the number of conflicts per break by $c \in \{0, 1, 5\}$. Each $C \in \mathcal{C}$ has the same size $|C| \in \{2, 3\}$. So for each break $b \in B$ we create c conflicts by selecting $|C|$ spots at random from $S(b)$ each time.

For the prices v_o, we compute the total length of all spots in o by $l_o := \sum_{s \in S_o} l_s$. Then, we let $v_o = l_o \cdot u_o$, where $u_o \sim U(25, 500)$. This means that a second costs between € 25 and 500; that is the usual price charged in Spanish television.

Summary

Summing up, we have varied the parameters as follows:

$$
\begin{aligned}
|B| &\in \{10, 15, 20, 50, 100\} \\
NLF &\in \{15, 18, 20, 25, 30, 35\} \\
\alpha &\in \{0.1, 0.2\} \\
q &\in \{1, 5, 10, 20, 50, 100\} \\
c &\in \{0, 1, 5\} \\
|C| &\in \{2, 3\} \qquad\qquad (\text{if } c > 0)
\end{aligned}
$$

Therefore, we had $5 \cdot 6 \cdot 2 \cdot 6 = 360$ combinations of $|B|, NLF, \alpha, q$. So there were 360 parameter combinations with no conflicts, and $360 \cdot 2 \cdot 2 = 1,440$ instances with conflicts, that's 1,800 combinations altogether. For each combination we generated 10 instances, totaling up to 18,000 instances. For $|B| \geq 15$ we just generated 10 instances for each combination and used them as they were. For $|B| = 10$ we generated instances for each combination until we could optimally solve them with AMPL/CPLEX 8 on a Pentium 4 computer at 3.06 GHz within 60 seconds[6] to assess the performance of our heuristics in comparison to optimal solutions. In all cases CPLEX was started on the solution obtained by the Greedy heuristic supplying an initial lower bound.

On average, an optimal solution for an instance with 10 breaks could be obtained in 3.35 seconds (with a standard deviation of 9.55 seconds). Table 6.5 reveals that almost 80 % of all instances could be solved in a second or less. On the other hand, 138 instances took more than 30 seconds.

Table 6.5: Optimal Solution Times

Time	*Instances (abs.)*	*Instances (%)*
up to 1 second	2873	79,8 %
1 to 5 sec.	243	6,8 %
5 to 10 sec.	115	3,2 %
10 to 30 sec.	231	6,4 %
30 to 60 sec.	138	3,8 %

Not surprisingly, the average computational time increases with NLF and α and decreases with q. The effect of the number of conflicts per break and the number of conflicting spots, c and $|C|$ is less clear, though (see Table 6.6): On the one hand, the computational times are higher for $c = 5$. On the other hand, if there are more conflicts, the feasible region gets smaller, and a Branch and Bound procedure may converge faster, so instances with $c = 1$ have been solved faster (on average) than instances with $c = 0$.

[6] Recall that all computational times reported on in this book are wall clock times.

Table 6.6: Effect of Conflicts on Computational Times

c	$\|C\|$	*Instances*	*Avg. Time*
0	-	720	3.23
1	2	720	2.87
1	3	720	3.03
5	2	720	3.58
5	3	720	4.05

6.5.2 Heuristics

Heuristic Performance on Instances with 10 Breaks

We are now going to evaluate the performance of our heuristics. We start with the instances with $|B| = 10$, where we can compare the heuristic LBs with the known optimal revenues. We begin with reviewing the computational times and the number of feasible solutions found for each heuristic in Table 6.7. Relax-and-Fix, Greedy and ForceZeroes were guaranteed to find feasible solutions for all 3,600 instances. ForceOnes and Dive-and-Fix found feasible solutions in approx. 80 % of all cases.

Before we summarize the computational times, note that the average and maximal times given in Table 6.7 refer to all 3,600 instances, i.e. the cases where ForceOnes and Dive-and-Fix have not found a feasible solution are included.

For the small instances here (with $|B| = 10$), ForceOnes and ForceZeroes were very fast and never reached their time limit of 5 seconds. Dive-and-Fix and Relax-and-Fix performed well on average. The Greedy heuristic was a bit slower. Also note that the time limit of 2 seconds for each order used by Relax-and-Fix and Greedy was (on average) not restrictive.

Table 6.7: Feasible Solutions and Computational Times

Heuristic	*feasible solution*				*Time*	
	found		*not found*		*Avg.*	*Max.*
Dive-and-Fix	2,991	83.1 %	609	16.9 %	0.84	9.00
Relax-and-Fix	3,600	100.0 %	0	0.0 %	0.67	9.00
ForceOnes	2,764	76.8 %	836	23.2 %	0.05	0.61
ForceZeroes	3,600	100.0 %	0	0.0 %	0.05	0.14
Greedy	3,600	100.0 %	0	0.0 %	2.15	29.00

425 instances had an optimal revenue of 0, and all heuristics found this optimal solution in all cases. Table 6.8 assesses the quality of the lower bounds for the remaining 3,175 instances using the percentage gap between lower bound and optimum, which is defined as follows:

$$\text{Gap} = \frac{\text{Optimal Revenue} - \text{Lower Bound}}{\text{Optimal Revenue}} \in [0, 1]$$

The very bad performance of Dive-and-Fix is due to the fact that it produced a lower bound of 0 in 2210 of the 2566 instances (ca. 86 %), though the optimal revenue was non-zero. These instances have a gap of 100 %. The average gap for the remaining 356 instances is only 6.4 %, with a standard deviation of 8.8 % and a maximum of 71.9 %. Nevertheless, the performance of Dive-and-Fix is unsatisfactory.

ForceOnes produced the best gaps. On the other hand, it failed to produce a lower bound at all for over 25 % of all instances with non-zero optimal revenue. This also largely explains why the number of optimal solutions found is relatively small: ForceOnes indeed found optimal solutions in only 35 % of the 3,175 instances, but in over 48 % of the instances where it found a feasible solution.

Relax-and-Fix is outperformed by ForceOnes with respect to gaps. On the other hand, Relax-and-Fix is guaranteed to find a feasible solution (in our instances), where ForceOnes is not, and it finds the most optimal solutions. Its gaps are better than ForceZeroes' (which will also find a feasible solution for sure), but the latter is faster. Greedy performs slightly worse than ForceZeroes on average, but the deviation of the gaps is smaller.

Table 6.8: Heuristic Gaps

Heuristic	*Feasible solutions*		*Gap* *Avg.*	*Std.-Dev.*	*Max.*	*Optimum found*	
Dive-and-Fix	2566	80.8 %	87.0 %	32.5 %	100.0 %	1	0.03 %
Relax-and-Fix	3175	100.0 %	2.9 %	9.9 %	100.0 %	1444	45.48 %
ForceOnes	2339	73.7 %	1.4 %	2.9 %	36.4 %	1138	35.84 %
ForceZeroes	3175	100.0 %	4.0 %	13.1 %	100.0 %	1312	41.32 %
Greedy	3175	100.0 %	4.8 %	7.6 %	61.3 %	1262	39.75 %

Instances with a Large Number of Breaks

For the larger instances with $|B| \in \{15, 20, 50, 100\}$ we could not obtain optimal solutions within satisfactory computational times, so in this section we will compare the heuristics among each other. Table 6.9 shows that it got clearly more difficult for Dive-and-Fix and ForceOnes to find feasible solutions for medium-sized instances with $|B| \in \{15, 20\}$. For instances with 50 and 100 breaks we had to impose an overall time limit of 60 seconds on Dive-and-Fix, Relax-and-Fix and Greedy to finish the computational study within a reasonable amount of time. Thus, Relax-and-Fix and Greedy may now fail to find a feasible solution due to the time limit. Table 6.9 shows that indeed for the majority of instances with 100 breaks, both did not finish within 60 seconds.

Except for Dive-and-Fix, the relationship of computational times given by Table 6.10 is similar to the small instances with $|B| = 10$: ForceOnes and ForceZeroes were very fast. Both have reached their time limits of five seconds now (marked by "*" in the table). However, their typical performance is clearly not affected by the time limit. To obtain a meaningful average time for Dive-and-Fix, Relax-and-Fix and Greedy, we have excluded the instances where the time limit of 60 seconds (marked by "***" in the table) has been reached. Relax-and-Fix and Greedy performs satisfactory on a typical instance. Both do in general not seem to be restricted by the maximum processing time of two seconds per order. The computational time of Dive-and-Fix is less favorable, though.

For $|B| = 15$, there were 283 instances where the best lower bound found was 0. All these instances were feasibly solved by all heuristics. The remaining 14,117 instances were again compared using a percent-

Table 6.9: Feasible Solutions for $|B| \in \{15, 20, 50, 100\}$

Heuristic	*15 Breaks: feasible solution*				*20 Breaks: feasible solution*			
	found		*not found*		*found*		*not found*	
Dive & Fix	2298	63.8 %	1302	36.2 %	1022	28.4 %	2578	71.6 %
ForceOnes	2585	71.8 %	1015	28.2 %	1358	37.7 %	2242	62.3 %

Heuristic	*50 Breaks: feasible solution*				*100 Breaks: feasible solution*			
	found		*not found*		*found*		*not found*	
Dive & Fix	571	15.9 %	3029	84.1%	155	4.3 %	3445	95.7 %
Relax & Fix	3047	84.6 %	553	15.4 %	1022	28.4 %	2578	71.6 %
ForceOnes	1127	31.3 %	2473	68.7 %	1087	30.2 %	2513	69.8 %
Greedy	2903	80.6 %	697	19.4 %	1203	33.4 %	2397	66.6 %

Table 6.10: Wall Clock Times in Seconds

("*" and "***" indicate that the time limit of 5 resp. 60 seconds was reached)

Heuristic	*15 Breaks*		*20 Breaks*		*50 Breaks*		*100 Breaks*	
	Avg.	Max.	Avg.	Max.	Avg.	Max	Avg.	Max.
Dive & Fix	3.75	25.00	9.60	41.00	26.85	***	43.46	***
Relax & Fix	1.10	11.00	2.52	21.00	16.62	***	30.86	***
ForceOnes	0.07	*	0.13	*	0.63	*	1.23	*
ForceZeroes	0.07	1.28	0.13	0.73	0.84	*	3.57	*
Greedy	3.65	52.00	5.94	76.00	14.79	***	28.93	***

age gap defined as follows:

$$\text{Gap} = \frac{\text{Best Lower Bound} - \text{Lower Bound}}{\text{Best Lower Bound}} \in [0, 1] \tag{6.32}$$

For $|B| \in \{15, 20\}$, Dive-and-Fix suffers again from the fact that it delivers a lower bound of 0, though the best bound is strictly greater. However, the effect is smaller: Only 755 (37.5 %) and 19 (1.9 %) instances (out of all instances where Dive-and-Fix found a feasible solution) are affected, respectively.

Table 6.11 summarizes the statistics on the gaps as defined by (6.32). For $|B| = 15$, the results are pretty similar to the previous case: ForceOnes is best, but fails to find a bound on many instances. Relax-and-Fix is (slightly) better than ForceZeroes on average. The former finds the best bound more often, but the latter is much faster. Greedy performs slightly worse than both, but is very robust in the sense that the deviation of the gaps is small.

For $|B| = 20$, the performance of Dive-and-Fix was again unsatisfactory. ForceZeroes retained its position. Relax-and-Fix was clearly best, but Greedy competed well, showing again a very small deviation of the gaps. Surprisingly, ForceOnes was outperformed by both Relax-and-Fix and Greedy. For the very large instances with $|B| \in \{50, 100\}$, all heuristics have a similar performance with respect to the gaps, only ForceZeroes is slightly behind. However, ForceZeroes is very successful in delivering the best bound for $|B| = 100$, albeit this observation can largely be attributed to the fact that all other heuristics fail to produce a bound at all on more than two thirds of the instances.

6.5.3 Branch and Cut

In this subsection we present computational results on our B&C-scheme. We compare our method with AMPL/CPLEX 8. Furthermore, we investigate the effectiveness of the heuristics applied during the B&C-process and the effectiveness of our cutting planes. Before we begin, we have a closer look at the performance of our five heuristics with respect to optimal solutions.

Instances That Have Already Been Solved by the Heuristics

Since we intend to supply the best known lower bound to both CPLEX and our B&C-method, it is reasonable to check which of the instances have already been solved optimally by the heuristics. A rather simple

Table 6.11: Gaps for Instances with $|B| \in \{15, 20, 50, 100\}$

	Heuristic	*Feasible solutions*		*Gap* Avg.	Std.-Dev.	Max.	*Best Bound*	
$\|B\| = 15$	Dive & Fix	2015	60.7 %	43.0 %	45.8 %	100.0 %	432	13.0 %
	Relax & Fix	3317	100.0 %	3.3 %	12.4 %	100.0 %	2195	66.2 %
	ForceOnes	2302	69.4 %	0.9 %	2.0 %	22.7 %	1241	37.4 %
	ForceZeroes	3317	100.0 %	3.6 %	9.0 %	100.0 %	1424	42.9 %
	Greedy	3317	100.0 %	4.6 %	7.4 %	61.7 %	1438	43.4 %
$\|B\| = 20$	Dive & Fix	1022	28.4 %	8.2 %	19.4 %	100.0 %	468	13.0 %
	Relax & Fix	3600	100.0 %	0.5 %	2.0 %	33.0 %	2918	81.1 %
	ForceOnes	1358	37.7 %	1.6 %	1.9 %	12.5 %	416	11.6 %
	ForceZeroes	3600	100.0 %	4.5 %	7.1 %	35.6 %	361	10.0 %
	Greedy	3600	100.0 %	1.9 %	2.9 %	13.3 %	1877	52.1 %
$\|B\| = 50$	Dive & Fix	571	15.9 %	0.0 %	0.0 %	0.5 %	561	15.6 %
	Relax & Fix	3047	84.6 %	0.3 %	1.1 %	13.1 %	2338	64.9 %
	ForceOnes	1127	31.3 %	0.7 %	1.0 %	5.6 %	557	15.5 %
	ForceZeroes	3600	100.0%	4.1 %	4.0 %	20.7 %	453	12.6 %
	Greedy	2903	80.6 %	1.0 %	1.7 %	13.1 %	1601	44.5 %
$\|B\| = 100$	Dive & Fix	155	4.3 %	0.0 %	0.1 %	0.6 %	153	4.3 %
	Relax & Fix	1022	28.4 %	0.2 %	0.8 %	6.3 %	802	22.3 %
	ForceOnes	1087	30.2 %	0.4 %	0.7 %	3.8 %	633	17.6 %
	ForceZeroes	3600	100.0 %	1.9 %	3.3 %	15.1 %	2286	63.5 %
	Greedy	1203	33.4 %	0.2 %	0.8 %	6.4 %	1063	29.5 %

indicator is the LP-bound: Let LB be the best lower bound found by any of the five heuristics. Let UB be the simple LP-upper bound that is obtained by simply solving the LP-relaxation of Model 6.1 without adding any cutting planes. An optimal solution obviously has been found if $LB = UB$ holds.

Define Gap $= \frac{UB-LB}{LB}$ for $LB > 0$. Table 6.12 shows aggregated values for that gap, as well as how many instances have already been solved to optimality by the heuristics. If we subtract this number from 3,600 – this is the number of instances for each $|B| \in \{10, 15, 20, 50, 100\}$ –, we get the remaining number of instances that have to be solved by CPLEX and our own B&C implementation.

If we compare Table 6.12 with Table 6.8 we see that the LP bound is indeed a bad indicator of optimality: For $|B| = 10$, only 471 instances have been provably solved to optimality by the heuristics, while the true value is (at least) more than twice as high. We also see, however, that large instances seem to be solved quite satisfactorily by the heuristics. This is somewhat surprising, but can be attributed to the

Table 6.12: Heuristic Lower Bounds vs. LP Upper Bounds

Breaks	*Instances*					*Gap*		
	Best LB > 0		*optimal*		*Remaining*	*Avg.*	*Std.-Dev.*	*Max.*
10	3,175	88.2 %	471	14.8 %	3,129	15.3 %	33.0 %	360.0 %
15	3,317	92.1 %	485	14.6 %	3,115	15.0 %	38.2 %	529.1 %
20	3,600	100.0 %	817	22.7 %	2,783	4.4 %	7.7 %	170.0 %
50	3,600	100.0 %	758	21.1 %	2,842	2.1 %	2.4 %	14.5 %
100	3,600	100.0 %	651	18.1 %	2,949	4.2 %	4.0 %	19.0 %

fact that we have varied the parameter q (which determines the number of spots per order) between 1 and 100, while the overall number of spots increases with the number of breaks. We have selected ForceZeros (which delivered feasible solutions for all 18,000 instances) to demonstrate this effect in Table 6.13: Clearly, the smaller q is, the smaller the number of spots per order and the LP bound gets better, because the impact of orders which are only "partly" scheduled gets smaller. On the other hand, for fixed q the LP bound's quality increases with $|B|$, due to the fact that for fixed NLF, an instance with 10 breaks will have $10 \cdot NLF$ spots (i. e. approximately $10 \cdot NLF/q$ spots per order), where an instance with 100 breaks will have $100 \cdot NLF$ spots, i. e. ten times the number of spots per order. Again, the impact of fractional orders decreases in the latter case. However, it seems to be reasonable that the number of spots per order q is independent of the overall number of spots S, so we have intentionally chosen not to modify our instance generator.

Parameter Settings

Like most B&C-schemes our program allows for a fairly large number of parameters to be varied. In the following we outline some of the most influencing choices we can make:

- We can add cuts in the root node only or in other nodes as well. If we decide to add cuts in non-root nodes, too, there are yet more options:
  - We can add cuts in each and every node.
  - We can refrain from adding cuts if at least one y_o is fractional. In that case the next branching step will branch on one of the fractional y_o variables anyway, and this may change the LP solution dramatically (see subsection 6.4.5). It is thus questionable if it is worth the effort to add cuts based on the current LP solution.

Table 6.13: ForceZero's Bounds vs. LP Upper Bounds

Breaks	q	*Instances* w/ $LB > 0$	*Gap* *Avg.*	*Std.-Dev.*	*Max.*
10	1	600	0.7 %	0.5 %	2.6 %
10	5	600	2.8 %	2.1 %	24.7 %
10	10	600	9.0 %	13.3 %	99.5 %
10	20	592	29.3 %	51.2 %	360.0 %
10	50	477	38.9 %	39.5 %	267.6 %
10	100	257	49.7 %	22.8 %	94.3 %
15	1	600	0.7 %	0.5 %	2.9 %
15	5	600	2.5 %	1.4 %	15.7 %
15	10	600	7.5 %	11.4 %	129.4 %
15	20	599	27.2 %	54.1 %	529.1 %
15	50	521	45.3 %	57.9 %	336.2 %
15	100	396	53.0 %	35.0 %	130.9 %
20	1	600	0.9 %	0.5 %	3.0 %
20	5	600	2.6 %	0.9 %	5.3 %
20	10	600	4.3 %	1.3 %	8.4 %
20	20	600	7.0 %	1.9 %	13.1 %
20	50	600	15.2 %	4.8 %	31.5 %
20	100	600	30.4 %	16.6 %	170.0 %
50	1	600	0.8 %	0.5 %	1.8 %
50	5	600	2.6 %	0.7 %	4.3 %
50	10	600	4.0 %	1.0 %	6.7 %
50	20	600	5.9 %	1.3 %	9.5 %
50	50	600	10.2 %	2.4 %	16.1 %
50	100	600	16.6 %	4.6 %	26.9 %
100	1	600	0.9 %	0.5 %	1.9 %
100	5	600	2.8 %	0.8 %	4.6 %
100	10	600	4.4 %	1.2 %	7.1 %
100	20	600	6.5 %	1.6 %	10.2 %
100	50	600	9.6 %	2.0 %	14.6 %
100	100	600	13.5 %	2.5 %	19.0 %

- We may choose not to add cuts if all y_o variables are already fixed to binary values, because in this case the objective function value (which depends on y_o only) is also fixed, therefore adding cuts can no longer improve the bound. On the other hand, it is uncertain whether the remaining feasibility problem can be solved faster using branching steps only, because adding cuts are also used to cut off fractional solutions and that may be helpful as well.

In summary our choice should be guided by the following trade off: If we add more cuts we can (on average) expect to solve the problem with fewer nodes. However, separation, minimization and lifting of cuts is computationally costly, and it may thus pay off to save this time at the expense of having to branch, store and restore more nodes.

- Two types of cut separation, minimization and lifting procedures are supported: The "classic" one and one along the lines of Gu et al. (1998) (see pages 192 and 202, respectively). We have the option to use both methods, only one of them or none. Again, we can hope to need fewer nodes if we add more cuts (i. e. use both methods), but this does not necessarily imply that the average computational time decreases.
- We have two types of heuristics as well (see subsection 6.4.4). Like for our two types of cut-methods, we may decide to use both, only one or neither of them (with similar consequences).
- The basic idea of a cutting plane method is to add one or more cuts to an LP, solve the augmented LP, add some more cuts based on the new LP optimum (if it is not already integer), solve this LP again etc. We have already mentioned that in most cases the LP bound does not change much after quite a few iterations; a behavior that is called "tailing off". If we detect tailing off, we will want to make a branching step. Algorithm 6.13 outlines how our program solves and reoptimizes the LP at every node. Note that if and how cuts are separated in step 8 depends on the settings that we have already described, e. g. if no cuts should be added if all y_o are fixed this will be checked in step 8, and no cuts will be added if indeed no y_o is free.

  As we can see from Algorithm 6.13, our method of detecting "tailing off" is based on the two parameters $tailoffGap$ and $maxIter$. An improvement of the upper bound will be considered insignificant if it is smaller than $tailoffGap$, and we will allow for at most $maxIter$ iterations without improvement. $maxIter$ will be reset if there was a significant improvement or if we were able to restore some global cuts – this operation is much less costly than separating new cuts, it thus seems to be safe not to limit this operation.

Furthermore, we have mentioned that we use a "depth first" approach until the gap between the best lower and best upper bound is smaller than or equal to g. We have chosen to set $g = 10\%$ and have not experimented with varying it, because we have noticed that in the

Algorithm 6.13: Iterative Steps of LP-solving Conducted at Every Node

1. Set $noProgress = 0, lastUB = -\infty$.
2. Solve the LP. Denote the LP upper bound by UB. If an optimal solution was found, check if UB is smaller than or equal to the best known lower bound. If so, the actual node can be pruned immediately, otherwise proceed with step 3.
3. If the LP solution is already integer, we are done. Otherwise proceed with step 4.
4. Fix variables based on reduced costs (see Theorem 6.5 on page 210).
5. If $lastUB < 0$ or $(lastUB - UB)/UB > tailoffGap$ reset $noProgress = 0$ and set $lastUB = UB$, else increment $noProgress$ by one and stop here if $noProgress > maxIter$.
6. Remove all cuts that have been slack for the last three iterations from the local cut pool (i. e. from the LP).
7. If some cuts from the global cut pool are violated by the current LP solution, add all of them to the LP, set $noProgress = 0$ and goto 2.
8. If the parameters allow (or demand) it, separate cuts. If some violated cuts have been found, add them to the LP and goto 2. Otherwise stop here.

bulk of instances this gap is already in the order of one to four percent after a few nodes.

It goes without saying that testing each and every possible parameter combination on all 18,000 instances is out of the question. We thus decided to choose an initial set of parameters in a rather "ad hoc" manner mainly based on intuition and observations that we made on a handful of instances. The result is what we call (in reference to Gu et al. 1998) the "default algorithm". The default algorithm uses the following parameters:

- Cuts are added in root and non-root nodes of the tree, but not if all y_o are already fixed.
- Both types of cut-methods and heuristics are used.
- Tailing off detection uses the parameters $tailoffGap = 0.001$ (0.1 %) and $maxIter = 2$.

This default algorithm has been tested on all 18,000 instances. Based on the results we then selected a sample of around 500 instances and investigated the impact of various parameter settings in great detail. This led to other sets of parameters – "non-default" algorithms – which were then tested again on a large sample of instances.

Performance Using Default Settings

Recall that for $|B| = 10$ we ran and reran our instance generator until ten examples that could be solved by AMPL/CPLEX within 60 seconds had been generated for each of the 360 parameter combinations. We thus focus on instances with 15, 20, 50 and 100 breaks and compare the ability of our default algorithm to obtain optimal solutions with that of CPLEX. We will later compare the running times of CPLEX, the default and the non-default algorithms.

15 Breaks

With a time limit of 60 seconds we obtained the results as depicted in the upper half of Table 6.14. Our default algorithm solved 71.5 % of all instances, among them 68 where CPLEX was stopped by the time limit before an optimal solution was found. On the other hand, CPLEX solves slightly more instances, and it solved 145 instances to proven optimum where our own implementation could not succeed within 60 seconds. 744 instances (23.9 %) have neither been solved by CPLEX nor by our method, so we decided to increase the time limit to 300 seconds. As we in the lower half of Table 6.14, our method caught up with respect to the number of solved instances, but still more than one fifth of all instances remain unsolved. We therefore decided to increase the running time to 900 seconds, but using the full sample of over 600 instances was of course out of the question. So we carefully selected 148 instances (with small NLFs, large qs etc.) and tried to solve them to optimality using CPLEX within 900 seconds. The average time per instance was more than 880 seconds, so the whole effort took more than 36 hours, and only 9 instances (ca. 6 %) were solved.

For the default algorithm, we considered the same 148 instances. It turned out that one of these had already been solved by the default algorithm. Given the poor performance of CPLEX we decided to enlarge the sample in the hope to be able to solve some more instances and to thus retrieve some reasonable results. We therefore added another 91 carefully selected instances to the sample (i. e. we had 238 instances in total) and tried to solve these within 900 seconds. The average time per instance was more than 870 seconds, so the total running time was about 58 hours. The result was similar: 33 instances (ca. 14 %) were solved; out of the 147 instances we tackled both with both procedures, CPLEX solved 9 and the default algorithm solved 7. There was no overlap in these solutions, i. e. the 7 instances solved by the our own B&C-implementation have not been solved by CPLEX and vice versa.

In light of these results it did not seem to make sense to increase the running time beyond five minutes.

Table 6.14: 15 Breaks: Optimal Solutions after 60 and 300 seconds

After 60 seconds:

		Default *time limit*	*Default* *solved*	
CPLEX	*time limit*	744 23.9 %	68 2.2 %	812 26.1 %
CPLEX	*solved*	145 4.7 %	2,158 69.3 %	2,303 73.9 %
		889 28.5 %	2,226 71.5 %	3,115

After 300 seconds:

		Default *time limit*	*Default* *solved*	
CPLEX	*time limit*	639 -105 20.5 %	122 +54 3.9 %	761 -51 24.4 %
CPLEX	*solved*	136 -9 4.4 %	2,218 +60 71.2 %	2,354 +51 75.6 %
		775 -114 24.9 %	2,340 +114 75.1 %	3,115

20 Breaks

Using a running time of 300 seconds we obtained the results that are shown in Table 6.15. Note that the number of solved instances dropped dramatically for both methods compared to problems with 15 breaks (see Table 6.14).

Table 6.15: 20 Breaks: Optimal Solutions after 300 seconds

		Default *time limit*	*Default* *solved*	
CPLEX	*time limit*	1,670 60.0 %	128 4.6 %	1,798 64.6 %
CPLEX	*solved*	138 5.0 %	847 30.4 %	985 35.4 %
		1,808 65.0 %	975 35.0 %	2,783

Why did the problem get so seriously tough stepping from 15 to 20 Breaks? This can be attributed to our choice of the number of breaks $|B_s|$ where each spot can be scheduled: We defined $|B_s| = \lfloor \alpha \cdot |B| \rfloor$ where $\alpha \in \{0.1, 0.2\}$. So for $|B| = 15, \alpha = 0.1$, each spot can only be scheduled in a single break, and scheduling is trivial, while for $|B| = 15, \alpha = 0.2$ and $|B| \geq 20$ we have $|B_s| \geq 2$ and scheduling becomes a crucial part of the problem. To demonstrate this fact we have prepared Table 6.16 which highlights the differences for instances with $|B| = 15$ (the aggregated results have appeared in Table 6.14). Note that there are 1,800 instances for both $\alpha = 0.1$ and $\alpha = 0.2$. Somewhat surprisingly 24.1 % of the instances with $\alpha = 0.2$ have been solved optimally by the heuristics, but only 2.8 % for $\alpha = 0.1$ such that 1,366 resp. 1,749 instances remain. We see that both CPLEX and the default algorithm have practically solved each and every instance with $\alpha = 0.1$ but a little more than half of all instances with $\alpha = 0.2$ remain unsolved. We note that our default algorithm is slightly behind for $\alpha = 0.1$ but slightly ahead for $\alpha = 0.2$.

Table 6.16: 15 Breaks: Optimal Solutions after 300 seconds by α

Instances	$\alpha = 0.1$	$\alpha = 0.2$
solved by CPLEX	1,747 99.9 %	607 44.4 %
solved by default	1,691 96.7 %	649 47.5 %
total	1,749	1,366

50 and 100 Breaks

Both CPLEX and the default algorithm performed very poorly on the larger instances: CPLEX could optimally solve 365 and 287 instances, and the default algorithm solved 248 resp. 103 instances. Recall that there were both 3,600 instances for $|B| = 50$ and $|B| = 100$, and around 700 of each have already been solved by the heuristics (see Table 6.12), i. e. only one out of ten given instances have been solved by either method and the heuristics have solved twice to three times as many instances. This is though not very surprising because the number of binary variables x_{sb} is given by $|B| \cdot NLF \cdot \alpha \cdot |B|$ – that is in the order of 1,000s for $|B| = 50$ and in the order of 10,000s for $|B| = 100$.

Performance of the Heuristics

For each instance, we have recorded the number of times the deterministic and the random heuristic (see Algorithm 6.12) have improved the bound. It turned out that the latter rarely succeeded, so we have decided to turn it off in our subsequent experiments. Since it does not seem to be useful to use no heuristic at all and merely wait until the LP-solution becomes binary by chance, only the deterministic heuristic has been used in the following experiments.

Evaluating the Parameter Settings

So far we have seen that our default algorithm is competitive with respect to its ability to obtain optimal solutions within a reasonable amount of time. It is thus a suitable basis for further experiments with the aim to investigate the impact of various parameter settings. Since optimally solving instances with 50 or 100 breaks seems to be out of scope of both CPLEX and our implementation we have focused on instances with $|B| \in \{15, 20\}$. For the upcoming experiments, we selected all instances with 15 or 20 breaks that have been solved by the default algorithm in a time that was longer than 30 seconds – if the computational time is smaller, it seems to be useless to tune the parameters to improve the performance. That yielded 265 instances. To investigate whether other parameters could improve our ability to solve instances to optimality we selected all instances that have been solved by CPLEX but not by the default algorithm. These are 136 resp. 138 instances, see Tables 6.14 and 6.15. Note that this is quite a nice distribution, because the fraction of solved and unsolved instances is thus approximately 50 % each. Using these 539 instances we studied the effect of varying some of the parameters. We will discuss our findings in the following.

Adding cuts depending on y_o

Recall that adding cuts cannot improve the LP upper bound if all y_o are fixed (to binary values). Furthermore, it may not be useful to add cuts if some y_o is fractional, because the following branching step will certainly change the values of many fractional variables, possibly rendering the cuts to be added useless. With respect to the values of y_o, three strategies are thus possible:

- Always add cuts regardless of the y_o.
- Add cuts if all y_o are binary, but only if some y_o is still free (this is the default setting).
- Do not add cuts if all y_o are binary (this is especially the case if all y_o are fixed).

Note that a fourth potential strategy "Add cuts if all y_o are fixed, but only if some y_o is still non-binary." is infeasible because if all y_o are fixed, they always attain binary values.

Table 6.17 compares the three strategies with respect to the number of instances that have been solved optimally. The running times for the strategy that "always" added cuts and the strategy that did "not if all

y_o are binary" were practically identical based on the 166 instances that have been solved by both. Thus "always" is clearly to be preferred because it solves more instances. Given the bias in our sample of 539 instances we cannot compare the running times of either method with the default algorithm in a really sensible way, but we note that there were 139 instances which have been solved by all of the methods. For these, the default algorithm needed ca. 97 seconds on average, where it took both other methods around 85 seconds. The running times of the other strategies thus seem to be reasonable.

Table 6.17: Comparison of Strategies to Add Cuts Depending on y_o

Strategy	*Instances solved*	
always	317	58.8 %
default	265	49.2 %
not if all y_o are binary	192	35.6 %

Adding cuts in the root node only

We then addressed the question whether it pays off to add cuts only in the very first node and solve the remaining "tightened" formulation of the problem (with a probably improved LP upper bound) using branching steps only. This method is sometimes called "Cut and Branch". If cuts should be used in the root node only we felt that $maxIter = 2$ may be a bit too small, therefore we tried three different strategies setting $maxIter = 10$ and $maxIter = 10{,}000$ as well (the latter basically implies that there is no "tailing off" detection at all and we only stop to add cuts if we are not able to find any more violated ones). In all these cases we added cuts regardless of the values of y_o; however, these settings should not affect the results because in the root nodes rarely all y_o will be binary, let alone fixed. A further option we considered is not to add cuts at all and solve the problem by a pure Branch and Bound (B&B) approach.

Table 6.18 shows how many instances out of 539 have been solved by each of the four variants and compares the running times with the strategy to "always" of Table 6.17 based on the instances that have respectively been solved by either method. We have also compared the four strategies among each other with respect to average times, but the impression is the same as given by the table: $maxIter = 2$ and pure B&B need ca. 35 seconds, where the other take around 45 seconds.

The default parameter setting ($maxIter = 2$) performed best both with respect to the number of instances solved and the running times compared with "always", thereby evidencing (in a somewhat limited way, though) that our initial choice for $maxIter$ was not too bad. Adding cuts in the root node only leads to a poor performance with respect to the number of instances solved – any of the variants discussed in Table 6.17 solve 50 to 100 % more, and "always" has solved practically all instances that have been solved by the four strategies. On the other hand, all the four strategies are much faster than "always" – this may be attributed to the fact that these four only solve a little more than 100 "easier" instances out of 539, where the additional effort to add cuts in non-root nodes does not pay off indeed. We will investigate this question in some more detail later.

Table 6.18: Comparison of Strategies to Add Cuts in the Root Node

			Comparison with "always"		
Strategy	*solved*		*Instances*	*Avg. time*	*Avg. time "always"*
$maxIter = 2$	127	23.6 %	106	37.4	55.6
$maxIter = 10$	109	20.2 %	94	46.6	63.0
$maxIter = 10{,}000$	113	21.0 %	97	47.5	60.9
pure B&B	112	20.8 %	93	37.0	52.0

Methods to add cuts

Thus far we have always used both the "classic" method and the one due to Gu et al. (1998, the "GNS"-method) to separate, minimize and lift cuts. Using the former method only (and adding cuts regardless of the y_o) we were only able to solve 157 instances in 300 seconds; using only the latter (and disregarding the y_o as well) we solved 225. Compared with the "always" strategy, which solved much more instances, the running times were practically identical, thus we will definitely use both methods in the following. As a final remark, 134 instances have been solved by either strategy, and GNS was much faster on average. This demonstrates the power of this method; on the other hand, the success of "always" demonstrates that it is definitely useful to combine both GNS and the classic method.

Performance Using Non-Default Settings

As we have seen in the last paragraphs the default parameter settings have shown a very satisfactory performance. We have though indicated two potential ways to improve the results: Adding cuts "always" (regardless of the y_o) may help to solve more instances to optimality within a time limit of 300 seconds. It will then be interesting to compare the running times with the default algorithm and with CPLEX as well. Adding cuts in the root node only (using $maxIter = 2$) seems to be promising with respect to time, but thus far we have only been able to compare the running times based on a very small number of instances, because the capability of this strategy – which we call "root2" in the following – to optimally solve instances in a reasonable time seems to be somewhat limited. We will thus compare the performance of the default, the "always" and the "root2" parameter setting with CPLEX based on instances with 15 and 20 breaks first. We have already seen that the ability of both the default algorithm and CPLEX to solve larger instances are very limited, so we defer the evaluation of the other methods on instances with $|B| \in \{50, 100\}$.

Instances with 15 and 20 breaks

Table 6.19 shows how many instances have been solved by each of the four methods for 15 and 20 breaks, respectively (The results for default and CPLEX have already appeared in Tables 6.14 and 6.15). Again, we see that there is a big difference between instances with 15 and 20 breaks because of the scheduling problem. For 15 breaks, CPLEX is just a little ahead to default, always is a little behind both. For 20 breaks, always is clearly ahead, default and CPLEX are tied. root2 is largely behind for 15 breaks and still a little for 20 breaks, but in neither case the gap is as large as we have had to fear in light of the previous comparison to always (see Table 6.18).

Table 6.19: Optimal Solutions after 300 Seconds by Method (15-20 Breaks)

	Number of Instances Solved			
Method	*15 Breaks*		*20 Breaks*	
default	2,340	75.1 %	975	35.0 %
always	2,300	73.8 %	1,056	37.9 %
root2	2,001	64.2 %	926	33.3 %
CPLEX	2,354	75.6 %	985	35.4 %
	3,115		2,783	

Tables 6.20 and 6.21 show that there is a large overlap between the instances that have been solved by the methods or where the time limit

has been reached, respectively. For 15 breaks, over 60 % of all instances have been solved by each of the method, and for 18 % no method found a provably optimal solution within 300 seconds. The next largest group is formed by 224 (7.2 %) instances that have been solved by all methods except root2 (which has solved the least number of instances). The picture is somewhat similar for 20 breaks, where almost 30 % of all instances have been solved by any method, and neither method could solve almost 60 % of them.

Table 6.20: Solved and Unsolved Instances (15 Breaks)

Method				*Instances*	
default	always	root2	CPLEX		
time limit	time limit	time limit	time limit	561	18.0 %
time limit	time limit	time limit	solved	106	3.4 %
time limit	time limit	solved	time limit	17	0.5 %
time limit	time limit	solved	solved	8	0.3 %
time limit	solved	time limit	time limit	55	1.8 %
time limit	solved	time limit	solved	13	0.4 %
time limit	solved	solved	time limit	6	0.2 %
time limit	solved	solved	solved	9	0.3 %
solved	time limit	time limit	time limit	33	1.1 %
solved	time limit	time limit	solved	69	2.2 %
solved	time limit	solved	time limit	4	0.1 %
solved	time limit	solved	solved	17	0.5 %
solved	solved	time limit	time limit	53	1.7 %
solved	solved	time limit	solved	224	7.2 %
solved	solved	solved	time limit	32	1.0 %
solved	solved	solved	solved	1,908	61.3 %
				3,115	

Table 6.22 compares the running times in wall clock seconds for the 1,908 instances with 15 breaks that have been solved by either method. We see that the vast majority of instances is solved very fast. CPLEX is clearly ahead, root2 is a little faster than always and default, which have a very similar performance. root2 is, however, not as fast as we have expected in light of Table 6.18. We have also examined the running times of each method on the 2,000+ instances that have respectively been solved. These times are of course not comparable – so we omit a corresponding table –, but we note that the overall picture remains: CPLEX is fastest, and the other methods nevertheless solve the bulk of instances in one second or less.

Table 6.21: Solved and Unsolved Instances (20 Breaks)

Method				*Instances*	
default	always	root2	CPLEX		
time limit	time limit	time limit	time limit	1588	57.1 %
time limit	time limit	time limit	solved	66	2.4 %
time limit	time limit	solved	time limit	14	0.5 %
time limit	time limit	solved	solved	9	0.3 %
time limit	solved	time limit	time limit	64	2.3 %
time limit	solved	time limit	solved	40	1.4 %
time limit	solved	solved	time limit	4	0.1 %
time limit	solved	solved	solved	23	0.8 %
solved	time limit	time limit	time limit	30	1.1 %
solved	time limit	time limit	solved	10	0.4 %
solved	time limit	solved	time limit	6	0.2 %
solved	time limit	solved	solved	4	0.1 %
solved	solved	time limit	time limit	23	0.8 %
solved	solved	time limit	solved	36	1.3 %
solved	solved	solved	time limit	69	2.5 %
solved	solved	solved	solved	797	28.6 %
				2,783	

Table 6.22: Running Times (15 Breaks)

Time (seconds)	*Instances (Absolute and Cumulative %) Solved by Method* default		always		root2		CPLEX	
up to 1	1,574	82.5 %	1,591	83.4 %	1,608	84.3 %	1,844	96.6 %
1 to 2	120	88.8 %	108	89.0 %	125	90.8 %	24	97.9 %
2 to 5	95	93.8 %	94	94.0 %	88	95.4 %	23	99.1 %
5 to 10	51	96.4 %	54	96.8 %	42	97.6 %	4	99.3 %
10 to 30	50	99.1 %	45	99.2 %	27	99.1 %	4	99.5 %
30 to 60	9	99.5 %	6	99.5 %	7	99.4 %	3	99.7 %
60 to 120	5	99.8 %	6	99.8 %	5	99.7 %	3	99.8 %
120 to 240	4	100.0 %	4	100.0 %	5	99.9 %	3	100.0 %
240 to 300	0	100.0 %	0	100.0 %	1	100.0 %	0	100.0 %
	1,908		1,908		1,908		1,908	

Table 6.23 shows that the results for 20 breaks are somewhat similar: Most instances are solved very fast. CPLEX is fastest, way ahead of root2, which is before always and default. The ranking of the last three is as before, but the differences are clearly larger. Again, we note that the picture is similar if all instances that have been solved are considered respectively for each method.

Table 6.23: Running Times (20 Breaks)

Time (seconds)	*Instances (Absolute and Cumulative %) Solved by Method* default		always		root2		CPLEX	
up to 1	290	36.4 %	314	39.4 %	363	45.5 %	618	77.5 %
1 to 2	111	50.3 %	95	51.3 %	143	63.5 %	49	83.7 %
2 to 5	143	68.3 %	161	71.5 %	147	81.9 %	76	93.2 %
5 to 10	125	83.9 %	112	85.6 %	77	91.6 %	17	95.4 %
10 to 30	96	96.0 %	90	96.9 %	51	98.0 %	16	97.4 %
30 to 60	16	98.0 %	15	98.7 %	8	99.0 %	10	98.6 %
60 to 120	11	99.4 %	7	99.6 %	7	99.9 %	8	99.6 %
120 to 240	4	99.9 %	3	100.0 %	1	100.0 %	1	99.7 %
240 to 300	1	100.0 %	0	100.0 %	0	100.0 %	2	100.0 %
	797		797		797		797	

Instances with 50 and 100 breaks

Despite our discouraging results using default and CPLEX for instances with 50 and 100 breaks we nevertheless tried to solve them using always. The results for all three methods are compiled in Table 6.24. We see that all methods have been largely outperformed by the heuristics. In light of these results, and given the fact that the running time for the 5,500+ instances using root2 can be expected to be ca. 18 days we refrained from testing root2 on the larger instances. Since the performance of all methods was very poor and the number of instances that have been solved was very small, it does not seem reasonable to examine the running times, so we omit them as well.

Table 6.24: Optimal Solutions after 300 Seconds by Method (50-100 Breaks)

Method	*Number of Instances Solved* *50 Breaks*		*100 Breaks*	
default	248	8.7 %	103	3.5 %
always	290	10.2 %	124	4.2 %
CPLEX	365	12.8 %	287	9.7 %
	2,842		2,949	
Best heuristic	758		651	
	3,600		3,600	

Summary

To obtain optimal solutions for the RM problem in the broadcasting industry we implemented a B&C-approach. We tested a "default" parameter set on all 18,000 instances and found that it was competitive compared to AMPL/CPLEX 8. Both our method and CPLEX were not able to satisfactorily solve instances with 50 or 100 breaks, so we focused on instances with 15 and 20 breaks. We evaluated the impact of various parameters on the performance of our method based on a carefully selected sample of over 500 instances. Based on our findings, we have developed two improved parameter sets, "always" and "root2". The former adds cuts in each and every node of the tree, regardless of the values of y_o (the default algorithm refrains from doing so if all y_o are fixed), and the latter does add cuts in the root node only (the default settings demand that cuts are added in non-root nodes as well). CPLEX, default and always could solve ca. three quarters of the instances with 15 breaks, where it was only around two thirds for root2. The latter was a little faster than default and always, though, but if an optimal solution was found for an instance, this was a matter of a few seconds for any method and the vast majority of instances. For 20 breaks, root2 solved one third of the instances, default and CPLEX mastered ca. 35 %, and for always it was even around 38 %. root2 was clearly faster than default and always, but again the running times of all methods have been in the order of seconds for the majority of instances that have been solved.

6.6 Some Remarks on RM in Broadcasting Companies Under Uncertainty

Up to now, we have assumed a deterministic setting where the set of orders O and all related parameters where given with certainty. In this section we will sketch models and methods dealing with the planning situation under uncertainty.

The TV program that has been published by the broadcasting company in Spain is valid for a limited amount of time only. Bollapragada et al. (2002) report that the programming schedules in the US cover a year. So we can safely assume a finite time horizon. As before, we will denote the set of breaks over this horizon by B. Our experience with Spanish broadcasting companies suggests that the vast majority of customers sends their orders by fax – this seems to be similar to NBC (cf. Bollapragada et al. 2002) where a standardized request form is used –, so that immediate notification of customers whether their order is accepted or rejected is not necessary. Thus orders can be "batched" over one day, for instance, and customers are notified at the beginning of the next business day. So the time horizon is naturally partitioned into $T < \infty$ discrete periods (e. g. days). Time is counted backwards from T to 0. We do neither explicitly model counteroffers made by Spanish broadcasting companies if an order cannot be accommodated, nor resubmissions of rejected orders by customers (a usual practice at NBC). Once an order has been rejected, however, and is resubmitted to the company in a modified form, it can be treated as a completely new order, so that the difference between a "really new" and a "modified" order is not important in our model.

Our objective function is the revenue-to-go $R(t, O)$ where t is the number of remaining periods and O is the set of orders that have already been accepted. The expected revenue over the complete time horizon is thus given by $R(T, \emptyset)$; or by $R(T, O)$ if some orders are already accepted at the beginning of the planning horizon – this may e. g. be the case if long term contracts are also made, or if a rolling horizon is used (in this case O is the set of orders that have been accepted in previous planning "rolls"). We denote the set of orders that arrives in period t by O_t. An order $o \in O_t$ is a tuple $o = (v_o, S_o, \{(l_s, B_s), s \in S_o\}, \mathcal{C}_o)$ where $v_o > o$ is the revenue, $S_o \neq \emptyset$ is the set of spots (characterized by the lengths l_s and the sets of admissible breaks B_s), and $\mathcal{C}_o$ is the set of conflict sets. A conflict set $C \in \mathcal{C}_o$ is a subset of the set of already accepted and new spots $\bigcup_{o \in O} S_o \cup \bigcup_{o \in O_t} S_o$. We allow that $O_t = \emptyset$.

Given a set of new orders O_t, we will need to know whether it is feasible or not to accept a subset $O' \subseteq O_t$ of them. For that purpose we need a variant of Model 6.1. To simplify the notation define

$$S(O') := \bigcup_{o \in O} S_o \cup \bigcup_{o \in O'} S_o$$

$$S(O', b) := \{s \in S(O') : b \in B_s\}$$

$$BC(O') := \left\{(b, C) \in B \times \left(\bigcup_{o \in O} \mathcal{C}_o \cup \bigcup_{o \in O'} \mathcal{C}_o\right) : |S(O', b) \cap C| \geq 2\right\}$$

Using that notation a set of new orders O' can be accepted if and only if Model 6.2 has got a feasible solution. Note that we have intentionally omitted the minimum break length restrictions, because early in the planning horizon the set of orders $O \cup O'$ will be small, such that a feasible schedule obeying minimum length restrictions may not exist although we clearly have the opportunity to fill up breaks with spots in later stages of the decision process. It is thus sufficient to ensure that the minimum break length restrictions are satisfied at $t = 0$ – this can be enforced by defining:

$$R(0, O) = \begin{cases} -\infty & \text{if a feasible schedule of the accepted spots } s \in S_o, o \in O \text{ such that the minimum break length restrictions are satisfied does not exist} \\ 0 & \text{otherwise} \end{cases}.$$

If we allow the violation of some restrictions (minimum break lengths or conflicts, for instance) at a penalty cost, we can e. g. define:

$$R(0, O) = \begin{matrix} \text{minimum penalties s. t. that all accepted spots} \\ s \in S_o, o \in O \text{ are scheduled} \end{matrix}$$

Model 6.2: Accept New Orders: Feasibility Check

$$\text{find } x_{sb}, s \in S(O'), b \in B_s$$

s. t.

$$\sum_{b \in B_s} x_{sb} = 1 \qquad s \in S(O')$$

$$\sum_{s \in S(O', b)} l_s x_{sb} \le d_b^{\max} \qquad b \in B$$

$$\sum_{s \in C \cap S(O', b)} x_{sb} \le 1 \qquad (b, C) \in BC(O')$$

$$x_{sb} \in \{0, 1\} \qquad s \in S(O'), b \in B_s$$

Define $a(O, O') = 1$ if Model 6.2 is feasible for a given set of accepted orders O and a given set of new orders O' (and 0 otherwise). At time t it is thus optimal to accept a subset of orders that is a maximizer of

$$\max_{O' \subseteq O_t} \left\{ a(O, O') \cdot \left(R(t - 1, O \cup O') + \sum_{o \in O'} v_o \right) \right\}$$

We now have to describe a stochastic process that creates the arrivals of orders – that is, we have to define the probability $P(O_t)$ that O_t is the set of orders collected on day t. In the classic passenger airline case, in hotels or rental car companies, defining an arrival process is not too difficult, because the number of products n is clearly finite. If we assume independent demand, we can just use n different arrival processes where an arrival from process $j \in \{1, \ldots, n\}$ is equivalent to a request of product j (see chapter 5 for an in-depth description of such processes). If we consider choice-based RM (see section 3.2) we can use m different arrival processes and define $P_{ij}(t, S)$ be the probability that a customer arriving from stream $i \in \{1, \ldots, m\}$ chooses product $j \in S$ at time t if $S \subseteq \{1, \ldots, n\}$ is the set of products that is available. In both cases we an use a compound process to describe that a arriving customer may request a random quantity of a product: Let $X_{ij}(t)$ be the random variable denoting the quantity of product j that is demanded by a customer arriving from process i at time t and define a – continuous or discrete – probability distribution on $X_{ij}(t)$ (see e. g. Ross 2003, p. 321-326 for an introduction to the compound Poisson process).

The problem at hand, however, is similar to cargo-RM or RM in make-to-order (MTO) environments, where the characteristics of an order – revenue, number of spots, their lengths, conflicts etc. – allow for such a large number of combinations that the number of potential "products" is practically infinite. A description of $P(O_t)$ has to include many of the aspects we have covered in subsection 6.5.1 (distribution of spot lengths, conflicts, order size, admissible breaks etc.) where we described our instance generator. Taking the complexity of the instance generation procedure into account, even a definition of $P(O_t)$ that only approximates the variety of characteristics – let alone one that leads to a useful model – seems to be impossible. Such a situation where the stochastic aspects of a dynamic model are hard to describe formally is called the "curse of modeling" in the context of dynamic programming. In his paper related to demand modeling, van Ryzin (2005) states that in complex demand settings "*modelling itself* becomes the obstacle" (p. 208, emphasis of the original).

So not surprisingly, to the best of our knowledge only models with a limited focus on the uncertainty involved in the cargo-/MTO RM problems have appeared in the literature: Kasilingam (1996) deals with the air cargo-RM problem, but assumes that all requests can be grouped into a limited number of categories (i. e. products), so basically the same arrival processes like in air passenger RM problems can be used. This is certainly not applicable for the broadcasting industry, and – as Pak and Dekker (2004, p. 3) point out – it does not seem to suit the cargo RM problem very well. In their conceptual paper, Campbell and Morlok (1994) outline an approach where it is analogously assumed that demand can be partitioned into a limited number of "demand classes". Pak and Dekker (2004) roughly outline a dynamic programming-approach to cargo RM, but do not go into the details (much like we do here) – namely they do not specify the arrival process as well. We agree with Pak and Dekker (2004) who report that a dynamic programming approach is intractable and less suited for a practical use. Bartodziej and Derigs (2004) follow – technically speaking – an approach similar to ours, in the sense that they use forecasted values of future demands in a deterministic air cargo model. In their paper, demand is given as a unidimensional measure (weight per origin/destination pair).

Somewhat related to this area of research are stochastic knapsack problems, where items of (possibly random) size and random profit arrive over time, and items can be accepted or rejected to maximize overall profit with respect to the limited size of the given knapsack; see Kleywegt (1996) for an overview. Kleywegt and Papastavrou (1998) and van Slyke and Young (2000) consider variants of the problem where all items have the same size. Papastavrou et al. (1996) and Kleywegt and Papastavrou (2001) come closer to our problem by allowing for random sized items, but like all aforementioned references they only cover the problem with a single, one-dimensional knapsack. Young and van Slyke (1994) consider both the unidimensional and the multidimensional cases, but again in a "passenger airline"-like setting with a limited number of demand classes.

Spengler et al. (2007) consider RM problems in MTO manufacturing. They develop an exact model based on the assumption that the number of orders $n^{\max}$ to arrive over the finite planning horizon as well as the characteristics of the j-th order $j = 1, \ldots, n^{\max}$ are given. The finite time horizon is divided into micro periods such that at most one order arrives in period t. The stochastic process of the arrivals is then given by the probabilities P_{jt} that order j arrives in period t, where it is allowed that $1 - \sum_{j=1}^{n^{\max}} P_{jt} < 1$ (i. e. no order arrives in period t). So technically speaking, we are again dealing with $n^{\max}$ different types of orders (where $n^{\max}$ is in the order of 10,000s per year), and in period t an order of type j appears with probability P_{jt}. This does not seem to appropriate for the RM-problem in broadcasting companies; and as the authors point out, an exact solution approach based on that model is impossible due to the computational burden anyway.

Pak and Dekker (2004) and Spengler et al. (2007) come closest in spirit to the situation encountered here. Pak and Dekker (2004) have suggested a bid price-approach to cargo RM, Spengler et al. (2007) have used a similar method in the MTO context. We briefly outline a method for the broadcasting problem under uncertainty along the lines of these references. However, our approach will be considerably more complicated, because we will also have to deal with the manufacturer's flexibility to schedule orders – Spengler et al. (2007) dealt with the situation of a specific company without flexibility, and Pak and Dekker (2004) neglect the possibility of (re-)routing cargo based on the present circumstances.

A bid price is nothing but an estimate of the opportunity costs of accepting an order (see section 2.3). We will consider additive bid prices here, i. e. the bid price of a given order is the weighted sum of the opportunity costs of the resources it consumes. In our problem, the only resources we are dealing with are the breaks B, which are of limited length $d_b^{\max}$. The potential use of a resource $b \in B$ is further narrowed by conflicts. We will neglect the minimal break length restrictions because – as mentioned before – they only play a minor role in practice. Therefore, we need an estimate λ_b of the opportunity cost of a second of time in break $b \in B$, and analogously an estimate γ_b for the opportunity cost of placing a spot that may conflict with other spots arriving later.

Like in Pak and Dekker (2004) and Spengler et al. (2007) such estimates can be obtained by simulation: A variant of our instance generator (see subsection 6.5.1) could be used to generate set of orders O. A classic way to compute bid prices is then to solve the LP-relaxation of Model 6.1 and use the averaged optimal shadow prices of restrictions (6.3) and (6.4) as estimates λ_b and γ_{bC} , respectively (cf. Talluri and van Ryzin 1999). γ_b may then be defined as the average of the γ_{bC}. Note that Pak and Dekker (2004) and Spengler et al. (2007) develop much more elaborate and efficient methods to compute bid prices.

Given λ_b, γ_b, the bid price of a single order o' will certainly depend on how the spots are finally scheduled (Pak and Dekker 2004 and Spengler et al. 2007 do not have to deal with this problem, because their products are inflexible). We therefore try to find a schedule of the spots S_o that minimizes the order's bid price (see Model 6.3). In this model, π_s is an estimate of the probability that a spot will conflict with spots arriving in the future. Each spot can certainly be unique, however the conflict mainly depends on the product being advertised, and on the desired (first or last) position. If s advertises a sports shoe, π_s can e. g. be set to the observed fraction of spots that also advertise sportive clothing. As before, O is the set of already accepted orders.

Model 6.3: Minimal Bid Price of a New Order o'

$$bp\left(o'\right) = \min \sum_{s \in S_{o'}} \sum_{b \in B_s} \lambda_b x_{sb} + \gamma_b \pi_s x_{sb}$$

s. t.

$$\sum_{b \in B_s} x_{sb} = 1 \qquad s \in S\left(\{o'\}\right)$$

$$\sum_{s \in S(\{o'\},b)} l_s x_{sb} \leq d_b^{\max} \qquad b \in B$$

$$\sum_{s \in C \cap S(\{o'\},b)} x_{sb} \leq 1 \qquad (b, C) \in BC\left(\{o'\}\right)$$

$$x_{sb} \in \{0, 1\} \qquad s \in S\left(\{o'\}\right), b \in B_s$$

Note that our cutting plane approach can be used to optimally solve this problem without any change because cutting planes are independent of the objective function.

We will accept order o' if $v_o \geq bp\left(o'\right)$ (and reject otherwise). In the problem at hand, however, we are not dealing with one order at a time (and immediate notification), but with a set of orders O_t. It is of course possible to extend the idea of Model 6.3 to cases with two or more orders. Model 6.4 is such an extension, where we maximize the revenue of all accepted orders, and the first restriction ensures that only orders o are accepted where the difference between revenue v_o and bid price $bp\left(o\right)$ is greater than € $1/M$.

Using Model 6.4, however means to solve a considerably larger integer problem. It may thus be sensible to consider each order $o \in O_t$ separately, according to a carefully selected ordering of the orders in O_t. Such an ordering may be based on an estimate of yield, e. g. defined by

$$\frac{v_o}{\sum_{s \in S_o} \frac{1}{|B_s|} \sum_{b \in B_s} \lambda_b + \gamma_b \pi_s}$$

– in the denominator, the opportunity costs of placing the spot $s \in S_o$ in break b is estimated by averaging over all breaks B_s.

The bid price approaches by Pak and Dekker (2004) and Spengler et al. (2007) were very successful in the respective contexts. The method we have just outlined is therefore worth considering, but other heuristic methods e. g. based on principles of Neuro-Dynamic Programming or Reinforcement Learning (cf. Bertsekas and Tsitsiklis 1996, Sutton and

Model 6.4: Bid Price Policy for a Set of New Orders O'

$$\max \sum_{o \in O'} v_o y_o$$

s. t.

$$y_o \leq M \cdot \left(v_o - \sum_{s \in S_o} \sum_{b \in B_s} \lambda_b x_{sb} + \gamma_b \pi_s x_{sb} \right) \quad o \in O'$$

$$\sum_{b \in B_s} x_{sb} = 1 \quad s \in S_o, o \in O$$

$$\sum_{b \in B_s} x_{sb} = y_o \quad s \in S_o, o \in O'$$

$$\sum_{s \in S(O',b)} l_s x_{sb} \leq d_b^{\max} \quad b \in B$$

$$\sum_{s \in C \cap S(O',b)} x_{sb} \leq 1 \quad (b, C) \in BC(O')$$

$$x_{sb} \in \{0, 1\} \quad s \in S(O'), b \in B_s$$

$$0 \leq y_o \leq 1 \quad o \in O'$$

Barto 1998), or other methods of stochastic search and optimization (cf. Spall 2003) can also be used to overcome the "curse of modeling".

6.7 Concluding Remarks

Based on a case study of Spanish broadcasting companies we developed a rigorous mathematical model of the RM problem. Bollapragada et al. (2002) describe a similar situation for NBC, thus we conclude that our findings are widely applicable to broadcasting companies in Europe and the US. Albeit there is a large body on the broadcasting industry in general, we are the first to develop RM models and methods for this business. Somewhat unique for the broadcasting RM problem is the predominance of flexible products. This greatly increases the problem's complexity, because we have not only to decide on the acceptance or rejection of orders but also on the schedule of accepted spots. Both problems are clearly interdependent, because if we manage to schedule spots of a given order to some less demanded breaks, the opportunity costs of accepting this order decreases and it becomes (more) profitable to accept it. RM problems with flexible products have only recently attracted attention in the literature.

We have dealt with the RM problem in broadcasting companies under certainty in great detail. We have developed various heuristics as well as a B&C approach to obtain optimal solutions. We have used a tailored instance generator to generate 18,000 problem instances of various sizes to test our heuristics and the B&C procedure. Both the heuristics and various parametrizations of the exact method performed very satisfactory.

Although our exact methods were able to solve the deterministic problem in a few seconds, we have seen that many of the larger instances cannot be solved within a reasonable amount of time. This is not surprising, because the problem at hand is NP-hard, but we nevertheless tried to push the boundary between solvable and unsolvable instances a little further. For instance, we have tried to find better upper bounds by Lagrangian relaxation. Trying various formulations we found, though, that relaxations which can be solved efficiently do not help to speed up the B&C procedure.

We also considered reformulating Model 6.1, aiming at column generation approaches. One was based on the observation that for each order $o \in O$ the number of assignments of spots $s \in S_o$ to breaks (i. e. the number of feasible values for the $x_{sb}, s \in S_o, b \in B_s$) is clearly finite. We might say that for each order o, there are at most T_o *schedules* of the spots $s \in S_o$. We can thus equivalently formulate Model 6.1 by using the decision variable $y_{ot}, o \in O, t \in T_o$ where $y_{ot} = 1$ if schedule t is used for order o (and 0 otherwise). Similarly, the number of possibilities to assign spots $s \in \{1, \ldots, S\}$ to any break $b \in B$ is clearly finite; for break b the number of such *patterns* is P_b, say. We can then use the decision variable z_{bp} to model the problem at hand, where $z_{bp} = 1$ if pattern p is used for break b (and 0 otherwise). Since both the number of "schedules" and "patterns" is large, column generation methods are in order to solve the LP relaxation of the resulting problem formulation. However, preliminary computational experience suggested that the LP bound obtained in this way was not better than the upper bound given by the LP relaxation of Model 6.1 (augmented by cutting planes).

We have finally outlined exact and heuristic approaches to the RM problem in broadcasting companies under uncertainty. We have seen that our treatment of the deterministic problem serves as a necessary foundation for models and methods for this problem. The applicability of the B&C procedure to the stochastic problem is facilitated by the fact that a Branch and Cut approach is largely independent of the objective function. Working out the details of an approach for the RM problem under uncertainty seems to be a fruitful area for future research. We are convinced that our findings will prove to be very useful for that task, and for the solution of other RM problems with flexible products in general.

7

Conclusion

7.1 Summary and Results

The first chapters of this book contain a comprehensive introduction to the field of RM. In chapter 1, we have characterized a typical RM problem based on the four prerequisites necessity to integrate external factors, limited operational flexibility, heterogeneous valuations and behavior and standardized product range. We have illustrated that RM concepts can be applied to a wealth of industries. Based on the defining characteristics and various example applications we have presented a structure of the field demonstrating the relationship of capacity control, overbooking, dynamic pricing and auctions. We have seen that not every application from those four areas satisfy the prerequisites; we have thus focused on "RM in the strict sense", i. e. capacity control and overbooking.

We have reviewed the state of the art of capacity control and overbooking in chapter 2. This chapter concentrated on already well-established models and methods, but we also covered some rather novel approaches, e. g. approximate dynamic programming or simulation optimization. In the subsequent chapter we highlighted recent advances of the field. At the center of our discussion were RM problems with customer- or supplier-driven substitution and multimodal products. Our analysis was based on a thorough categorization of such problems (see Table 3.1), and we highlighted the relationship of those problems to the field of RM in the strict and in the broad sense. We have also briefly mentioned some references on alliance RM, RM under competition and callable products.

Chapter 4 and 5 outlined necessary steps to evaluate RM models and methods, i. e. how to generate instances of RM problems. Up to now, issues related to instance generation have not yet been treated in a rigorous way; and while many authors conduct simulation studies and computational experiments to test their methods we have got the feeling that this is still be done in a rather "ad hoc" way. To facilitate the comparison between different RM methods a standard test bed would be highly desirable. To the best of our knowledge, we are the first to address this problem in a comprehensive and systematic way. In chapter 4, we have outlined and categorized the relevant aspects of instance generation. The following chapter focused on one of the most difficult parts, namely the simulation of stochastic demand data streams. An extensive review of the literature helped to structure existing models with respect to assumptions related to the arrival process (see Figure 5.1). The remainder of the chapter covered the simulation of a single and multiple demand data streams and the parameter estimation problem. Independent demand, choice-based RM and RM with flexible products have been taken into account.

We have seen in chapter chapter 3 that there are only a few references that cover RM problems with flexible products. Furthermore, in the existing approaches it is assumed that a large fraction of all products is unimodal and a flexible product is a "menu" of certain specific ones. In the broadcasting industry, however, specific products are practically not existent such that the existing approaches cannot easily be transferred. Actually, the broadcasting industry has not received much attention at all from the RM community; our extensive treatment in chapter 6 thus is one of the very first attempts to address this area of application in a rigorous way. We have conducted an in-depth case study of the business environment of Spanish broadcasting companies. The results served as a basis for a rigorous formal description and a mathematical model. We have developed various heuristics for that problem as a well as an exact approach based on Branch and Cut. Those methods have been evaluated on a test bed of 18,000 instances and performed quite well. We have finally outlined approaches to the RM problem in broadcasting companies under uncertainty and seen that our model and methods are a necessary and useful prerequisite to tackle the stochastic problem as well.

7.2 Future Research Opportunities

The two major contributions of this book can be found in chapters 4, 5 and 6: We are the first two approach the instance generation problem in a rigorous way. Furthermore, we are among the few authors who consider RM problems with flexible products and an application of RM to the broadcasting industry. Our findings build a useful basis for future research. For instance, we have outlined the relevant aspects of instance generation in chapter 4. We have intentionally disregarded the deterministic/static aspects, but we have roughly indicated how resource and product data could be generated for instances from the airline industry. It would be useful for the RM community to work out the many details of such an airline instance generator, to implement it and to make an executable file of this implementation publicly available. This would be a preliminary step towards a standard test bed for airline RM problems. It should be followed by the phases which we have already mentioned in section 5.5:

1. Identify what characteristics of resources, products, capacities etc. make RM problems hard or easy to solve.
2. Develop an instance generator that creates instances (i. e. resources, products, capacities etc.) with given characteristics, especially a given degree of "difficulty".
3. Generate a systematical set of test-instances to establish a standard test-bed for future work.

Our detailed description of the RM problem in broadcasting companies brings an area of application into play which has not yet been considered by the RM community. We have seen that our model and methods can be used gainfully for the problem under uncertainty. However, we have intentionally made only brief remarks on the stochastic setting in this book, thus it will be fruitful to study this problem in some more detail. Additional findings and results for the RM problem in broadcasting companies will have impact for other areas of applications as well, especially for those where flexible products are prevalent as well (e. g. the cargo industry).

Somewhat related (but obviously not identical) are RM problems with flexible customers (see Table 3.1) which have been indicated in this book for the first time. Practical applications with flexible customers do clearly exist (e. g. German Railways); and it seems to be rather challenging to develop a capacity control strategy if flexible customers are involved. Such problems will thus provide a fruitful field of future research as well.

A

Demand Distribution of the Beta-Gamma-Arrival Process

In this part of the appendix, we will present some details about the non-homogeneous Poisson process (NHPP) over the interval $[0, T]$ with rate function (5.3):

$$\lambda(t) = D \cdot \beta(t)$$

where we have dropped the index j to simplify the notation, $D \sim \Gamma(\gamma, \delta)$ and $\beta(t)$ is the density function of the Beta distribution standardized on the interval $[0, T]$.

Denote the number of arrivals up to time t from this process by $N(t)$. We have already seen that the conditional expectation of $N(T)$ is given by:

$$E(N(T) | D = d) = d$$

As mentioned previously, the marginal distribution of $P(N(T))$ is a negative Binomial, and the posterior distribution of D is a Gamma as well. This will be shown in section A.1 and section A.2, respectively.

A.1 Marginal Distribution of $N(T)$

$N(T)$ follows a Poisson distribution with intensity $\Lambda(T) = \int_0^T \lambda(t)\, dt$, i. e. the conditional distribution of $N(T)$ is given by:

$$P(N(T) = n | D = d) = e^{-d} \frac{d^n}{n!} \tag{A.1}$$

D follows a Gamma-distribution with parameters γ, δ, i. e. the density is given by:

$$f(d) = \frac{\delta^{-\gamma}}{\Gamma(\gamma)} e^{-d/\delta} d^{\gamma-1} \tag{A.2}$$

By the definition of the conditional probability, we have:

$$\begin{aligned} P(N(T)=n) &= \int_0^\infty P(N(T)=n\,|D=u)\,f(u)\,du \\ &= \int_0^\infty e^{-u}\frac{u^n}{n!}\cdot\frac{\delta^{-\gamma}}{\Gamma(\gamma)}e^{-u/\delta}u^{\gamma-1}du \\ &= \frac{\delta^{-\gamma}}{\Gamma(\gamma)\cdot n!}\int_0^\infty e^{-u(1+1/\delta)}u^{n+\gamma-1}du \end{aligned}$$

We substitute:

$$z = g(u) = u(1+1/\delta)$$

$$\Rightarrow u = \frac{z}{1+1/\delta} = z\cdot\frac{\delta}{1+\delta}, \quad du = \frac{dz}{g'(u)} = \frac{dz}{1+1/\delta} = \frac{\delta}{1+\delta}\cdot dz$$

Thus:

$$\begin{aligned} P(N(T)=n) &= \frac{\delta^{-\gamma}}{\Gamma(\gamma)\Gamma(n+1)}\int_0^\infty e^{-z}\left(z\cdot\frac{\delta}{1+\delta}\right)^{n+\gamma-1}\frac{\delta}{1+\delta}dz \\ &= \frac{\delta^{-\gamma}}{\Gamma(\gamma)\Gamma(n+1)}\left(\frac{\delta}{1+\delta}\right)^{n+\gamma-1}\frac{\delta}{1+\delta}\int_0^\infty e^{-z}z^{n+\gamma-1}dz \\ &= \frac{1}{\Gamma(\gamma)\Gamma(n+1)}\left(\frac{1}{1+\delta}\right)^{\gamma}\left(\frac{\delta}{1+\delta}\right)^{n}\Gamma(n+\gamma) \end{aligned}$$

Let $p=(1+\delta)^{-1}$:

$$P(N(T)=n) = \frac{\Gamma(n+\gamma)}{\Gamma(\gamma)\Gamma(n+1)}p^{\gamma}(1-p)^n \tag{A.3}$$

This is the probability mass function of the negative Binomial distribution, somewhat generalized by allowing that γ is not integer.

A.2 Posterior Distribution of *D*

Using (A.3) crucially depends on knowing the parameters γ, δ defining the exact distribution of D. In a typical application, these values will not be known exactly, i. e. γ, δ are random quantities themselves and forecasted values have to be used. Formally, we have forecasted values γ^0, δ^0 and thus assume that the a priori distribution of D is Gamma with parameters γ^0, δ^0. We then observe $N(t)$, the number of arrivals up to time t, and ask for the posterior distribution of D, $P(D \,|N(t))$. Since we know both the prior distribution of D and the conditional distribution $P(N(t)\,|D)$, this can be easily be done using Bayes' Theorem, which can be stated in the following form:

Theorem A.1 (Bayes' Theorem) *Consider a sample* $X_1, \ldots, X_n$. *Let the random variables* $X_i, i = 1, \ldots, n$ *be i.i.d. with distribution* $f(x\,|\,\theta)$. *The parameter* $\theta \in \Theta$ *is unknown and to be estimated. We consider* θ *as a random variable and assume that it follows the prior distribution* $\xi(\theta)$. *We can "update" this distribution in light of our sample* $X_1, \ldots, X_n$ *using* Bayes' Theorem*:*

$$\xi(\theta|\, X_1, \ldots, X_n) = \frac{f(X_1, \ldots, X_n\,|\,\theta)\,\xi(\theta)}{\int_\Theta f(X_1, \ldots, X_n\,|\,\theta)\,\xi(\theta)\,d\theta} = \frac{f(X_1\,|\,\theta)\cdot \ldots \cdot f(X_n\,|\,\theta)\,\xi(\theta)}{g(X_1, \ldots, X_n)} \tag{A.4}$$

where $g(X_1, \ldots, X_n) = \int_\Theta f(X_1\,|\,\theta) \cdot \ldots \cdot f(X_n\,|\,\theta)\,\xi(\theta)\,d\theta$ *and we have used the fact that* $f(X_1, \ldots, X_n\,|\,\theta) = f(X_1\,|\,\theta) \cdot \ldots \cdot f(X_n\,|\,\theta)$, *since the random variables* $X_1, \ldots, X_n$ *are independent.*

We will first consider updating the distribution of D in light of the total demand $N(T)$ to derive the fundamental result. How to use $N(t)$ – the more realistic case – is treated afterwards. The extension to $N(t)$ is straightforward, only the notation gets a little more complicated.

Posterior distribution of D given a sample of $N(T)$

For the ease of notation, let X be the random variable $N(T)$ and $X_1, \ldots, X_n$ be a sample of X – that is, we have simulated/observed the NHPP n times and recorded the total demand X_i of the i-th replication/observation. We start by computing $g(X_1, \ldots, X_n)$. Define $y = \sum_{i=1}^n X_i$ and use (A.1) and (A.2) to obtain:

$$\begin{aligned} g(X_1, \ldots, X_n) &= \int_0^\infty P(X_1\,|\,D = u) \cdot \ldots \cdot P(X_n\,|\,D = u)\,f(u)\,du \\ &= \int_0^\infty \frac{u^y}{\prod_{i=1}^n X_i!} e^{-nu} \frac{\delta^{-\gamma}}{\Gamma(\gamma)} u^{\gamma-1} e^{-u/\delta} du \\ &= \frac{\delta^{-\gamma}}{\Gamma(\gamma)\prod_{i=1}^n X_i!} \int_0^\infty u^{y+\gamma-1} e^{-u(n+1/\delta)} du \end{aligned}$$

Upon substituting $t = u(n + 1/\delta)$, we obtain:

$$g\left(X_1,\ldots,X_n\right)=\frac{\delta^{-\gamma}}{\Gamma\left(\gamma\right)\prod_{i=1}^{n}X_i!}\cdot\frac{\Gamma\left(y+\gamma\right)}{\left(n+1/\delta\right)^{y+\gamma}}$$

Thus:

$$\begin{aligned}f\left(D=u\left|X_1,\ldots,X_n\right.\right)&=\frac{\dfrac{u^y}{\prod_{i=1}^{n}X_i!}e^{-nu}\dfrac{\delta^{-\gamma}}{\Gamma\left(\gamma\right)}u^{\gamma-1}e^{-u/\delta}}{\dfrac{\delta^{-\gamma}}{\Gamma\left(\gamma\right)\prod_{i=1}^{n}X_i!}\cdot\dfrac{\Gamma\left(y+\gamma\right)}{\left(n+1/\delta\right)^{y+\gamma}}}\\&=\frac{\left(n+1/\delta\right)^{y+\gamma}}{\Gamma\left(y+\gamma\right)}u^{\gamma-1}e^{-u(n+1/\delta)}\end{aligned}$$

The posterior distribution of D in light of the sample $X_1,\ldots,X_n$ is thus a Gamma with parameters $\gamma+y,\left(n+1/\delta\right)^{-1}$.

Posterior distribution of D given an observation of $N\left(t\right)$

Updating the distribution of D depending on a sample of $N\left(T\right)$ is not particularly helpful in practice. Therefore, we consider now the case that a single observation of some $N\left(t\right)$ is given, i. e. we have simulated/observed the arrival process up to time t and counted the arrivals. We will make use of the following proposition:

Proposition A.1 (Linear Transformation) *Let X be a continuous random variable and $Z=a+bX$ where a,b are constants and $b>0$. Let G and g be the distribution and density function of X, respectively. The distribution and density function of Z, F and f are then:*

$$F\left(x\right)=G\left(\frac{x-a}{b}\right)\qquad f\left(x\right)=\frac{1}{b}g\left(\frac{x-a}{b}\right)$$

Proof. Consider the distribution function first. We have

$$X=\left(Z-a\right)/b$$

For the event $Z\leq x$ the following holds:

$$\begin{aligned}&Z\leq x\Leftrightarrow\left(Z-a\right)/b=X\leq\left(x-a\right)/b\\&\Rightarrow P\left(Z\leq x\right)=P\left(X\leq\left(x-a\right)/b\right)\\&\Rightarrow F\left(x\right)=G\left(\left(x-a\right)/b\right)\end{aligned}$$

Since f and F are intimately related, it is sufficient to check that the following holds:

$$\int_{-\infty}^{x} \frac{1}{b} \cdot g\left(\frac{u-a}{b}\right) du = \frac{1}{b} \int_{-\infty}^{(x-a)/b} b \cdot g(y)\, dy$$
$$= G((x-a)/b) = F(x)$$

Proposition A.2 *If $X \sim \Gamma(\gamma, \delta)$ and $Z = cX$ where c is a constant with $c > 0$, then $Z \sim \Gamma(\gamma, c\delta)$.*

Proof. By the previous proposition, the density of Z is:

$$f(x) = \frac{1}{c} \frac{\delta^{-\gamma}}{\Gamma(\gamma)} e^{-\frac{d}{c\delta}} (d/c)^{\gamma-1} = \frac{(c\delta)^{-\gamma}}{\Gamma(\gamma)} e^{-\frac{d}{c\delta}} d^{\gamma-1}$$

– indeed the density of a Gamma random variable with parameters $\gamma, c\delta$.

Consider now a subinterval $(s,t) \subset [0,T]$. The number of arrivals in that interval follows a Poisson distribution with parameter $\int_s^t D \cdot \beta(u)\, du$, i. e. the parameter is a random variable $D' = c \cdot D$ where $c = \int_s^T \beta(u)\, du \in (0,1)$. By the proposition, $D' \sim \Gamma(\gamma, c\delta)$. Suppose we have a single observation X_1 of the number of arrivals in the interval (s,t). As we have seen, the posterior distribution of D' in light of X_1 is a Gamma with parameters $\gamma + X_1, \left(1 + \frac{1}{c\delta}\right)^{-1}$. Since $D = c^{-1}D'$, its posterior distribution is a Gamma with parameters $\gamma + X_1, (c + 1/\delta)^{-1}$. This result is intuitive, since we saw that for a sample of $N(T)$ of size n, we obtained a Gamma with parameters $\gamma + \sum_{i=1}^{n} X_i, (n + 1/\delta)^{-1}$. In this case, we just have a "sample" of $N(T)$ of "size" $c < 1$, and obtain an equivalent formula.

B

Implementation of the Combo Algorithm: Technical Details

To separate the most violated cover for a given break b and the corresponding maximum length restriction $\sum_{s \in S(b)} l_s x_{sb} \leq d_b^{\max}$ we have to solve the following knapsack problem (see our discussion starting on page 193):

$$\zeta = \min \sum_{s \in K_1} (1 - x_{sb}^*)\, z_s$$

s. t.

$$\sum_{s \in K_1} l_s z_s \geq d + 1$$

$$z_s \in \{0, 1\} \qquad\qquad s \in K_1$$

Since every break $b \in B$ is treated in isolation the index b is fixed anyway, we thus drop it in the following to improve readability.

We solve this knapsack problem using the COMBO algorithm by Martello, Pisinger, and Toth (1999). A C-implementation of this algorithm can be downloaded from Pisinger's website (`http://www.diku.dk/~pisinger/codes.html`).

COMBO cannot be applied directly to our problem for various reasons. The first issue is that COMBO deals with knapsack problems with a max objective and a $\leq$ restriction. It is however very easy to transform the min problem with a $\geq$ restriction into that form (see e. g. Martello and Toth 1990, p. 15) by complementing the decision variables, i. e. by substituting $y_s = 1 - z_s$:

$$\zeta = \min \sum_{s \in K_1} (1 - x_s^*)\,(1 - y_s) = \min \sum_{s \in K_1} (1 - x_s^*) - \sum_{s \in K_1} (1 - x_s^*)\, y_s$$

The new objective function is thus:

$$z = \max \sum_{s \in K_1} (1 - x_s^*)\, y_s$$

and we have $\zeta = \sum_{s \in K_1} (1 - x_s^*) - z$. Analogously we obtain for the restriction:

$$\sum_{s \in K_1} l_s (1 - y_s) = \sum_{s \in K_1} l_s - \sum_{s \in K_1} l_s y_s \geq d + 1$$

$$\Leftrightarrow \qquad \sum_{s \in K_1} l_s y_s \leq \sum_{s \in K_1} l_s - d - 1$$

Two minor technical restrictions remain to be solved:

1. COMBO assumes that both the "weights" l_s and "profits" $1 - x_s^*$ are integers. While l_s are integer by assumption, $1 - x_s^* \in (0, 1)$ by the definition of K_1 – see (6.23). We therefore multiply x_s^* by 10^6 and truncate the remaining decimal places. Thus at most 10^{-6} is lost for each item s, i. e. 10^6 items would be necessary to wrongly conclude that a violated cover inequality existed.
2. Every item has to fit into the knapsack, i. e. $l_s \leq \sum_{s \in K_1} l_s - d - 1$ has to hold. This restriction may be violated in our application. Consider the following (artificial) example: Let $K_1 = \{1, 2, 3, 4\}, l_1 = 1, l_2 = 20, l_3 = 4, l_4 = 3, d = 25$. Then $\sum_{s \in K_1} l_s = 28$ and the knapsack's capacity in the max formulation is $28 - 25 - 1 = 2$, i. e. the items $\{2, 3, 4\}$ do not fit. In the min problem the restriction reads:

$$1x_1 + 20x_2 + 4x_3 + 3x_4 \geq d + 1 = 26$$

We conclude that the items which to do not fit into the knapsack in the max formulation *have to be inserted* into the knapsack in the min variant of the problem. This follows from the fact that $z_s = 1 - y_s$. For the sake of completeness, we also show this result formally: Let $big = \left\{ s \in K_1 : l_s > \sum_{i \in K_1} l_i - d - 1 \right\}, small = K_1 \backslash big$. We show that each and every element $k \in big$ has to be part of the cover in the min formulation, i. e. we show that:

$$k \in big \Rightarrow \sum_{s \in small} l_s + \sum_{s \in big \backslash \{k\}} l_s < d + 1$$

Recall that $\sum_{s \in K_1} l_s \geq d + 1$ holds. Choose an arbitrary $k \in big$. We have:

$$\sum_{s\in small} l_s + \sum_{s\in big\setminus\{k\}} l_s = \sum_{s\in K_1} l_s - l_k$$

$$< \sum_{s\in K_1} l_s - \left(\sum_{s\in K_1} l_s - d - 1\right) = d + 1$$

The knapsack problem thus simplifies to:

$$\zeta = \sum_{s\in big} (1 - x_s^*) + \min \sum_{s\in small} (1 - x_s^*)\, z_s$$

s. t.

$$\sum_{s\in small} l_s z_s \geq d + 1 - \sum_{s\in big} l_s$$

$$z_s \in \{0, 1\} \qquad\qquad s \in small$$

If $\sum_{s\in big} (1 - x_s^*) \geq 1$, no violated cover exists and we can stop here. If $d + 1 - \sum_{s\in big} l_s \leq 0$ the problem is trivial. Otherwise we transform as before:

$$\zeta = \sum_{s\in big} (1 - x_s^*) + \left(\sum_{s\in small} (1 - x_s^*) - z'\right) = \sum_{s\in K_1} (1 - x_s^*) - z'$$

$$z' = \max \sum_{s\in small} (1 - x_s^*)\, y_s$$

s. t.

$$\sum_{s\in small} l_s y_s \leq \sum_{s\in small} l_s - \left(d + 1 - \sum_{s\in big} l_s\right) = \sum_{s\in K_1} l_s - d - 1$$

$$y_s \in \{0, 1\} \qquad s \in small$$

References

M. Adler, P. B. Gibbons, and Y. Matias. Scheduling space-sharing for internet advertising. *Journal of Scheduling*, 5:103–119, 2002. (Cited on page 173.)

C. C. Aggarwal, J. L. Wolf, and P. S. Yu. A framework for the optimizing of WWW-advertising. In W. Lamersdorf, editor, *Trends in Distributed Systems for Electronic Commerce, Lecture Notes in Computer Science*, pages 1–10. Berlin: Springer, 1998. (Cited on page 173.)

N. Agrawal and S. A. Smith. Optimal retail assortments for substitutable items purchased in sets. *Naval Research Logistics*, 50(7): 793–822, 2003. (Cited on page 96.)

S. Algers and M. Beser. Modelling choice of flight and booking class - a study using stated preference and revealed preference data. *International Journal of Services Technology and Management*, 2:28–45, 2001. (Cited on page 110.)

S. Algers, S.-E. Andersson, and J. Köhler. Impact of deviation and recapture upon class allocations. In *Proceedings of the 33rd AGIFORS Symposium*, 1993. (Cited on page 110.)

J. Alstrup, S. Boas, O. B. G. Madsen, and R. V. V. Vidal. Booking policy for flights with two types of passengers. *European Journal of Operational Research*, 27:274–288, 1986. (Cited on pages 64, 88 and 137.)

J. Alstrup, S.-E. Andersson, S. Boas, O. B. Madsen, and R. V. V. Vidal. Booking control increases profit at Scandinavian Airlines. *Interfaces*, 19(4):10–19, 1989. (Cited on pages 8, 81 and 88.)

K.-D. Altmeppen and M. Karmasin. *Medien und Ökonomie, Band 2: Problemfelder der Medienökonomie.* Wiesbaden: VS Verlag für Sozialwissenschaften, 2004. (Cited on page 173.)

K. Amaruchkul, W. L. Cooper, and D. Gupta. Single-leg air-cargo revenue management. Technical report, Department of Mechanical Engineering, University of Minnesota, 2006. (Cited on pages 10 and 89.)

C. K. Anderson and M. Blair. Performance monitor: The opportunity costs of revenue management. *Journal of Revenue and Pricing Management*, 2(4):353–367, 2004. (Cited on page 13.)

C. K. Anderson and J. G. Wilson. Wait or buy? the strategic consumer: Pricing and profit implications. *Journal of the Operational Research Society*, 54:299–306, 2003. (Cited on page 12.)

S.-E. Andersson. Passenger choice analysis for seat capacity control: A pilot project in Scandinavian Airlines. *International Transactions in Operational Research*, 5(6):471–486, 1998. (Cited on pages 97, 98 and 110.)

A. Ansari and C. F. Mela. E-Customization. *Journal of Marketing Research*, 40:131–145, 2003. (Cited on page 173.)

R. Anupindi, M. Dada, and S. Gupta. Estimation of consumer demand with stock-out based substitution: An application to vending machine products. *Marketing Science*, 17(4):406–423, 1998. (Cited on page 96.)

L. M. Ausubel. An efficient ascending-bid auction for multiple objects. *The American Economic Review*, 94(5):1452–1475, 2004. (Cited on page 28.)

A. N. Avramidis, A. Deslauriers, and P. L'Ecuyer. Modeling daily arrivals to a telephone call center. *Management Science*, 50(7):896–908, 2004. (Cited on pages 150 and 158.)

R. D. Badinelli. An optimal, dynamic policy for hotel yield management. *European Journal of Operational Research*, 121:476–503, 2000. (Cited on page 11.)

R. Balachandra. A simulation model for predicting the effect of advertisement schedules. In *Proceedings of the 9th Conference on Winter Simulation, Gaitersburg*, pages 581–589, 1977. (Cited on page 172.)

N. Bandla. Optimal seat allocation in an aircraft using a reinforcement learning approach. Master's thesis, Dept. of Industrial and Management Systems Engineering, College of Engineering, University of South Florida, December 1998. (Cited on pages 80 and 89.)

G. L. Barlow. Capacity management in the football industry. In A. Ingold, U. McMahon-Beattie, and I. Yeoman, editors, *Yield Management: Strategies for the Service Industries*, pages 303–314. London: Thomson, 2nd edition, 2005. (Cited on page 14.)

R. S. Barr, B. L. Golden, J. P. Kelly, M. G. Resende, and W. R. Stewart. Designing and reporting on computational experiments with heuristic methods. *Journal of Heuristics*, 1:9–32, 1995. (Cited on page 161.)

P. Bartodziej and U. Derigs. On an experimental algorithm for revenue management for cargo airlines. In C. C. Ribeiro and S. L. Martins, editors, *3rd Workshop on Efficient and Experimental Algorithms (WEA 2004)*, volume 3059 of *LNCS*, pages 57–71. Berlin, Heidelberg: Springer, 2004. (Cited on pages 10, 116 and 239.)

P. Barwise and C. Strong. Permission-based mobile advertising. *Journal of Interactive Marketing*, 16:14–24, 2002. (Cited on page 173.)

C. Barz and K.-H. Waldmann. Risk-sensitive capacity control in revenue management. Technical report, Institut für Wirtschaftstheorie und Operations Research, Universität Karlsruhe, 2006. (Cited on page 57.)

Y. Bassok, R. Anupindi, and R. Akella. Single-period multiproduct inventory models with substitution. *Operations Research*, 47(4):632–642, 1999. (Cited on page 95.)

M. J. Beckmann and F. Bobkoski. Airline demand: An analysis of some frequency distributions. *Naval Research Logistics Quarterly*, 5:43–51, 1958. (Cited on page 150.)

D. E. Bell. Incorporating the customer's perspective into the newsvendor problem. Technical report, Harvard Business School, 2001. (Cited on page 96.)

A. Belloch Egea, A. Kimms, and M. Müller-Bungart. Auftragsannahmeentscheidungen für preisdifferenzierte Werbeblöcke im spanischen Fernsehen. *Betriebswirtschaftliche Forschung*, to appear, 2007. (Cited on page 163.)

P. Belobaba and J. Darot. RM coordination and bid price sharing in airline alliances: PODS simulation results. Presentation at the AGIFORS YM Study Group Meeting, 2001. (Cited on page 96.)

P. Belobaba and L. Weatherford. Comparing decision rules that incorporate customer diversion in perishable asset management situations. *Decision Sciences*, 27(2):334–364, 1996. (Cited on pages 60, 97, 100, 135 and 136.)

P. P. Belobaba. Optimal vs. heuristic methods for nested seat allocations. Presentation to the AGIFORS Yield Management Study Group, May 1992. (Cited on pages 59, 100 and 135.)

P. P. Belobaba. Airline yield management: An overview of seat inventory control. *Transportation Science*, 21:63–73, 1987a. (Cited on page 31.)

P. P. Belobaba. *Air Travel Demand and Airline Seat Inventory Management*. PhD thesis, Flight Transportation Laboratory, Massachusetts Institute of Technology, Cambridge, MA, 1987b. (Cited on pages 56, 57, 58, 60, 89, 97, 98, 99, 100, 135 and 136.)

P. P. Belobaba. Application of a probabilistic decision model to airline seat inventory control. *Operations Research*, 37(2):183–197, Mar.-Apr. 1989. (Cited on pages 56, 57, 58, 59, 89, 97, 98, 99, 100, 135, 136 and 139.)

P. P. Belobaba and J. L. Wilson. Impacts of yield management in competitive airline markets. *Journal of Air Transport Management*, 3(1):3–9, 1997. (Cited on pages 60, 96 and 135.)

M. E. Ben-Akiva and S. R. Lerman. *Discrete Choice Analysis: Theory and Application to Travel Demand.* Cambridge: MIT Press, 1985. (Cited on page 109.)

N. Ben-Khedher, J. Kintanar, C. Queille, and W. Stripling. Schedule optimization at SNCF: From conception to day of departure. *Interfaces*, 28(1):6–23, 1998. (Cited on page 9.)

L. Bertsch and O. Wendt. Yield Management. In J. Weber and H. Baumgarten, editors, *Handbuch Logistik*, pages 469–483. Stuttgart: Schäffer-Poeschel, 1998. (Cited on pages 3 and 31.)

D. Bertsekas and D. Castanon. Rollout algorithms for stochastic scheduling problems. *Journal of Heuristics*, 5(1):89–109, 1999. (Cited on page 79.)

D. P. Bertsekas. *Dynamic Programming and Optimal Control*, volume I. Belmont, Massachusetts: Athena Scientific, 2nd edition, 2000. (Cited on page 175.)

D. P. Bertsekas and J. N. Tsitsiklis. *Neuro-Dynamic Programming.* Belmont, Mass.: Athena Scientific, 1996. (Cited on pages 78 and 241.)

D. P. Bertsekas, J. N. Tsitsiklis, and C. Wu. Rollout algorithms for combinatorial optimization. *Journal of Heuristics*, 3:245–262, 1997. (Cited on page 80.)

D. Bertsimas and S. de Boer. Simulation-based booking limits for airline revenue management. *Operations Research*, 53(1):90–106, 2005. (Cited on pages 42, 47, 48, 49, 64, 79, 130, 139, 140, 141, 147 and 151.)

D. Bertsimas and I. Popescu. Revenue management in a dynamic network environment. *Transportation Science*, 37(3):257–277, August 2003. (Cited on pages 67, 68, 69, 74, 79, 80, 87, 133, 139 and 175.)

D. Bertsimas and R. Shioda. Restaurant revenue management. *Operations Research*, 51(3):472–486, May-June 2003. (Cited on page 14.)

D. Bertsimas and J. N. Tsitsiklis. *Introduction to Linear Optimization*, volume 6 of *Athena Scientific Series in Optimization and Neural Computation.* Belmont, Mass.: Athena Scientific, 1997. (Cited on pages 74, 183 and 186.)

C. R. Bhat. Flexible model structures for discrete choice analysis. In D. A. Hensher and K. J. Button, editors, *Handbook of Transport Modelling*, pages 71–90. Amsterdam: Pergamon, 2000. (Cited on page 109.)

S. Biller and J. Swann. Pricing for environmental compliance in the auto industry. *Interfaces*, 36(2):118–125, 2006. (Cited on page 25.)

E. K. Bish and Q. Wang. Optimal investment strategies for flexible resources, considering pricing and correlated demands. *Operations Research*, 52(6):954–964, 2004. (Cited on page 96.)

G. Bitran and R. Caldentey. An overview of pricing models for revenue management. *Manufacturing & Service Operations Management*, 5 (3):203–229, Summer 2003. (Cited on pages 19, 26 and 27.)

G. Bitran, R. Caldentey, and R. Vial. Pricing policies for perishable products with demand substitution. Technical report, MIT/New York University/Universidad de los Andes, 2006. (Cited on page 99.)

G. R. Bitran and S. Dasu. Ordering policies in an environment of stochastic yields and substitutable demands. *Operations Research*, 40(5):999–1017, 1992. (Cited on page 95.)

G. R. Bitran and S. M. Gilbert. Managing hotel reservations with uncertain arrivals. *Operations Research*, 44(1):35–49, Jan.–Feb. 1996. (Cited on pages 11, 60 and 136.)

G. R. Bitran and S. V. Mondschein. An application of yield management to the hotel industry considering multiple day stays. *Operations Research*, 43(3):427–443, May–June 1995. (Cited on pages 11, 62 and 139.)

M. Blair and C. K. Anderson. Performance monitor. *Journal of Revenue and Pricing Management*, 1(1):57–66, 2002. (Cited on page 13.)

S. E. Bodily and P. E. Pfeifer. Overbooking decision rules. *Omega*, 20 (1):129–133, 1992. (Cited on page 85.)

S. E. Bodily and L. R. Weatherford. Perishable-asset revenue management: Generic and multiple-price yield management with diversion. *Omega*, 23(2):173–185, 1995. (Cited on page 100.)

R. J. Boik and J. F. Robison-Cox. Derivatives of the incomplete beta function. *Journal of Statistical Software*, 3(1):1–20, 1998. URL `http://www.jstatsoft.org/index.php?vol=3`. (Cited on page 159.)

S. Bollapragada and M. Garbiras. Scheduling commercials on broadcast television. *Operations Research*, 52(3):337–345, May-June 2004. (Cited on pages 172, 177 and 212.)

S. Bollapragada, H. Cheng, M. Phillips, M. Garbiras, M. Scholes, T. Gibbs, and M. Humphreville. NBC's optimization systems increase revenues and productivity. *Interfaces*, 32(1):47–60, 2002. (Cited on pages 164, 171, 174, 186, 235 and 242.)

S. Bollapragada, M. R. Bussieck, and S. Malik. Scheduling commercial videotapes in broadcast television. *Operations Research*, 52(5):679–689, 2004. (Cited on page 172.)

T. C. Botimer and P. P. Belobaba. Airline pricing and fare product differentiation: A new theoretical framework. *Journal of the Operational Research Society*, 50(11):1085–1097, 1999. (Cited on page 100.)

A. Boyd. Airline alliances. *OR/MS Today*, October 1998. (Cited on page 96.)

E. A. Boyd and I. Bilegan. Revenue Management and E-Commerce. *Management Science*, 49(10):1363–1386, October 2003. (Cited on pages 24, 25, 27 and 31.)

P. Bratley, B. L. Fox, and L. E. Schrage. *A Guide to Simulation*. New York: Springer, 2nd ed., 1987. (Cited on pages 143 and 144.)

A. R. Brown. Selling television time: An optimization problem. *Computer Journal*, 12:201–206, 1969. (Cited on page 172.)

S. Brumelle and D. Walczak. Dynamic airline revenue management with multiple semi-markov demand. *Operations Research*, 51(1):137–148, 2003. (Cited on page 89.)

S. L. Brumelle and J. I. McGill. Airline seat allocation with multiple nested fare classes. *Operations Research*, 41(1):127–137, Jan.–Feb. 1993. (Cited on pages 58, 59, 60, 135, 136 and 139.)

S. L. Brumelle, J. I. McGill, T. H. Oum, K. Sawaki, and M. W. Tretheway. Allocation of airline seats between stochastically dependent demands. *Transportation Science*, 24(3):183–192, Aug. 1990. (Cited on pages 56, 57, 60, 97, 100, 135 and 136.)

S. Calder. *No Frills – The Truth Behind The Low-Cost Revolution In The Skies*. London: Virgin Books, 2003. (Cited on pages 9 and 22.)

K. Campbell and E. Morlok. Rail freight service flexibility and yield management. *Transportation Research Forum Proceedings*, 2:529–548, 1994. (Cited on pages 10 and 238.)

M. Cancian, A. Bills, and T. Bergstrom. Hotelling location problems with directional constraints: An application to television news scheduling. *The Journal of Industrial Economics*, 43:121–124, 1995. (Cited on page 172.)

J. Cao. Evaluation of advertising effectiveness using agent-based modeling and simulation. In *Proceedings of 2nd UK Workshop of SIG on Multi-Agent Systems (UKMAS 1999), Bristol*, 1999. (Cited on page 173.)

W. J. Carroll and R. C. Grimes. Evolutionary change in product management: Experiences in the car rental industry. *Interfaces*, 25(5): 84–104, Sept.–Oct. 1995. (Cited on pages 2 and 13.)

L. M. A. Chan, D. Simchi-Levi, and J. Swann. Pricing, production, and inventory policies for manufacturing with stochastic demand and discretionary sales. *Manufacturing & Service Operations Management*, 8(2):149–168, 2006. (Cited on page 138.)

S. Chapman and J. Carmel. Demand/capacity management in health care: An application of yield management. *Health Care Management Review*, 17(4):45–53, 1992. (Cited on page 83.)

R. E. Chatwin. Multi-period airline overbooking with a single fare class. *Operations Research*, 46:805–819, 1998. (Cited on pages 65, 66 and 87.)

R. E. Chatwin. Continuous-time airline overbooking with time-dependent fares and refunds. *Transportation Science*, 33(2), 1999. (Cited on pages 87 and 88.)

D. Chen. Network flows in hotel yield management. Working Paper TR1225, Cornell University, School of Operations Research and Industrial Engineering, 1998. (Cited on pages 11 and 55.)

D. Chen. *Revenue Management – Competition, Monopoly and Optimization*. PhD thesis, Cornell University, 2000. (Cited on page 96.)

V. C. P. Chen, D. Günther, and E. L. Johnson. Routing considerations in airline yield management. In T. A. Ciriani, G. Fasano, S. Gliozzi, and R. Tadei, editors, *Operations Research in Space and Air*, pages 333–350. Boston: Kluwer, 2003. (Cited on page 117.)

S. Cheung. Rose Bowl vs. Hong Kong: The economics of seat pricing. In K. Clarkson and D. Martin, editors, *Economics of Nonproprietary Organizations*, pages 27–43. Greenwich: Jai Press, 1980. (Cited on page 14.)

A. Ciancimino, G. Inzerillo, S. Lucidi, and L. Palagi. A mathematical programming approach for the solution of the railway yield management problem. *Transportation Science*, 33(2):168–181, May 1999. (Cited on page 9.)

G. M. Coldren, F. S. Koppelman, K. Kasturirangan, and A. Mukherjee. Modeling aggregate air-travel itinerary shares: logit model development at a major US airline. *Journal of Air Transport Management*, 9(6):2003, November 2003. (Cited on page 109.)

T. M. Cook. SABRE soars. *OR/MS Today*, June 1998. (Cited on page 14.)

W. L. Cooper. Asymptotic behavior of an allocation policy for revenue management. *Operations Research*, 50(4):720–727, 2002a. (Cited on page 74.)

W. L. Cooper. Asymptotic behavior of some revenue management policies: Examples and counterexamples. Technical report, Department of Mechanical Engineering, University of Minnesota, 2002b. (Cited on page 74.)

W. L. Cooper and T. H. de Mello. A class of hybrid methods for revenue management. Technical report, University of Minnesota/Northwestern University, 2006. (Cited on page 80.)

W. L. Cooper, T. H. de Mello, and A. J. Kleywegt. Models of the spiral-down effect in revenue management. *Operations Research*, 54 (5):968–987, 2006. (Cited on page 98.)

H. Corsten and S. Stuhlmann. Yield Management – Ein Ansatz zur Kapazitätsplanung und -steuerung in Dienstleistungsunternehmen. Schriften zum Produktionsmanagement Nr. 18, Universität Kaiserslautern, 1998. (Cited on pages 3 and 31.)

J. Coughlan. Airline overbooking in the multi-class case. *Journal of the Operational Research Society*, 50(11):1098–1103, 1999. (Cited on pages 85 and 136.)

Council of the European Communities. Council Directive of 3 October 1989 on the coordination of certain provisions laid down by law, regulation or administrative action in Member States concerning the pursuit of television broadcasting activities (89/552/EEC). Office for Official Publications of the European Communities, October 1989. URL `http://europa.eu.int/eur-lex/en/consleg/pdf/1989/en_1989L0552_do_001.pdf`. (Cited on page 169.)

D. R. Cox. Some statistical methods connected with series of events. *Journal of the Royal Statistical Society, Series B (Methodological)*, 17(2):129–164, 1955. (Cited on page 149.)

D. R. Cox and V. Isham. *Point Processes*. London: Chapman & Hall, repr. 1992, 1980. (Cited on page 149.)

P. Cramton, Y. Shoham, and R. Steinberg, editors. *Combinatorial Auctions*, 2006. MIT Press. (Cited on page 28.)

R. G. Cross. *Revenue Management: Hard-Core Tactics for Market Domination*. New York: Broadway Books, 1998. (Cited on page 8.)

R. G. Cross. *Ressourcen erkennen – Umsätze steigern: Mit Revenue Management neue Einnahmequellen erschließen*. Wien: Ueberreuther, 2001. (Cited on page 8.)

H. Crowder, E. L. Johnson, and M. Padberg. Solving large-scale zero-one linear programming problems. *Operations Research*, 31(5):803–834, September-October 1983. (Cited on page 193.)

R. E. Curry. Optimal airline seat allocation with fare classes nested by origins and destinations. *Transportation Science*, 41(3):193–204, Aug. 1990. (Cited on pages 59, 64, 135, 136 and 139.)

M. Czygan. *Wettbewerb im Hörfunk in Deutschland – Eine industrieökonomische Analyse.* Baden-Baden: Nomos, 2003. (Cited on page 173.)

D. J. Daley and D. Vere-Jones. *Elementary Theory and Methods*, volume I of *An Introduction to the Theory of Point Processes.* New York: Springer, 2nd ed., 2003. (Cited on page 149.)

G. B. Dantzig. Discrete-variable extremum problems. *Operations Research*, 5:266–277, 1957. (Cited on page 197.)

A. Dasci. Dynamic pricing of perishable assets under competition: A two-period model. Technical report, School of Business, University Alberta, Canada, 2003. (Cited on page 96.)

S. Daudel and G. Vialle. *Yield Management.* Campus: Frankfurt/Main, New York, 1992. (Cited on page 31.)

S. Daudel and G. Vialle. *Yield Management: Applications to air transport and other service industries.* Paris: Les Presses de l'Institut du Transport Aérien, 1994. New English version published with additional material and updated statistics by Barry K. Humphreys. (Cited on page 31.)

M. Dawande, S. Kumar, and C. Sriskandarajah. Performance bounds of algorithms for scheduling advertisements on a web page. *Journal of Scheduling*, 6:373–393, 2003. (Cited on page 173.)

M. Dawande, S. Kumar, and C. Sriskandarajah. Scheduling web advertisements: A note on the minspace problem. *Journal of Scheduling*, 8:97–106, 2005. (Cited on page 173.)

S. V. de Boer, R. Freling, and N. Piersma. Mathematical programming for network revenue management revisited. *European Journal of Operational Research*, 137:72–92, 2002. (Cited on pages 71, 72, 75, 130, 141, 147, 150 and 151.)

B. de Reyck and Z. Degraeve. Broadcast scheduling for mobile advertising. *Operations Research*, 51(4):509–517, July-August 2003. (Cited on page 173.)

S. de Vries and R. V. Vohra. Combinatorial auctions: A survey. *INFORMS Journal on Computing*, 15(3):284–309, 2003. (Cited on page 28.)

B. C. Dean and M. X. Goemans. Improved approximation algorithms for minimum-space advertisements scheduling. In J. C. M. Baeten, J. K. Lenstra, J. Parrow, and G. J. Woeginger, editors, *Automata, Languages and Programming*, pages 1138–1152. Berlin: Springer, 2003. 30th International Colloquium, ICALP 2003. Eindhoven, The Netherlands, June 30 - July 4, 2003, Proceedings. Lecture Notes in Computer Science, Vol. 2719. (Cited on page 173.)

F. Defregger and H. Kuhn. Revenue management in manufacturing. In D. Ahr, R. Fahrion, M. Oswald, and G. Reinelt, editors, *Operations Research Proceedings 2003*, pages 17–22. Berlin: Springer, 2004. (Cited on page 14.)

M. H. DeGroot. *Optimal Statistical Decisions.* New York: McGraw-Hill, 1970. (Cited on page 150.)

L. Devroye. *Non-Uniform Random Variate Generation.* New York: Springer, 1986. (Cited on page 143.)

W. Domschke and R. Klein. Bestimmung von Opportunitätskosten am Beispiel des Produktionscontrolling. *Zeitschrift für Planung und Unternehmenssteuerung*, 15:275–294, 2004. (Cited on page 74.)

W. Domschke, R. Klein, and A. Petrick. Revenue Management in Unternehmensnetzwerken. Presentation at the Symposium des Instituts für Betriebswirtschaftslehre: "Gestaltung und Koordination von Unternehmensnetzwerken", 2005. (Cited on page 96.)

R. Dörband. *Vermarktung von Leitungs- und Speicherkapazitäten in der Gaswirtschaft.* PhD thesis, Fakultät für Energie- und Wirtschaftswissenschaften, Technische Universität Clausthal, 2005. (Cited on page 14.)

R. Dörband, K. Homann, and P. Reichetseder. Nutzungsentgelte Gas - Produkte und differenzierte Preisgestaltung für die Vermarktung von Leistungs- und Speicherkapazitäten. Technical report, TU Clausthal, 2003. (Cited on page 14.)

P. Dube, Y. Hayel, and L. Wynter. Yield management for IT resources on demand: analysis and validation of a new paradigm for managing computing centres. *Journal of Revenue and Pricing Management*, 4 (1):24–38, 2004. (Cited on page 14.)

H. Dunleavy and D. Westermann. Future of airline revenue management. *Journal of Revenue and Pricing Management*, 3(4):380–383, 2005. (Cited on page 21.)

S. El-Haber and M. El-Taha. Dynamic two-leg airline seat inventory control with overbooking, cancellations and no-shows. *Journal of Revenue and Pricing Management*, 3(2):143–170, 2004. (Cited on page 90.)

W. Elmaghraby and P. Keskinocak. Dynamic pricing in the presence of inventory considerations: Research overview, current practices, and future directions. *Management Science*, 49(10):1287–1309, October 2003. (Cited on pages 26 and 27.)

W. J. Elmaghraby. Multi-unit auctions with complementarities: Issues of efficiency in electricity auctions. *European Journal of Operational Research*, 166:430–448, 2005. (Cited on page 28.)

P. Erdös, A. L. Rubin, and H. Taylor. Choosability in graphs. In *Proceedings of the West Coast Conference on Combinatorics, Graph Theory and Computing*, pages 125–157. Congressus Numerantium XXVI, 1979. (Cited on page 180.)

M. M. Etschmaier and M. Rothstein. Operations research in the management of airlines. *Omega*, 2:160–175, 1974. (Cited on page 83.)

L. M. Falkson. Airline overbooking: Some comments. *Journal of Transport Economics and Policy*, III(3):352–354, 1969. (Cited on page 84.)

J. Feller. Optimal threshold policies in revenue management with multidimensional resources. Diskussionsbeiträge des Fachgebietes Operations Research und Wirtschaftsinformatik 24, Universität Dortmund, Wirtschafts- und Sozialwissenschaftliche Fakultät, 2002. (Cited on page 67.)

Y. Feng and G. Gallego. Perishable asset revenue management with Markovian time dependent demand intensities. *Management Science*, 46(7):941–956, 2000. (Cited on page 134.)

Y. Feng and G. Gallego. Optimal starting times for end-of-season sales and optimal stopping times for promotional fares. *Management Science*, 41(8):1371–1391, Aug. 1995. (Cited on page 134.)

J. A. Fitzsimmons and M. J. Fitzsimmons. *Service Management. Operations, Strategy, and Information Technology.* New York: McGraw-Hill, 3rd edition, 2001. (Cited on page 3.)

P. Forsyth. Low-cost carriers in Australia: experiences and impacts. *Journal of Air Transport Management*, 9(5):277–284, September 2003. (Cited on page 22.)

A. Freund and J. Naor. Approximating the advertisement placement problem. *Journal of Scheduling*, 7:365–374, 2004. (Cited on page 173.)

A. Fréville. The multidimensional 0-1 knapsack problem: an overview. *European Journal of Operational Research*, 155(1):1–21, 2004. (Cited on page 55.)

L. Froeb and S. Tschantz. Competitive revenue management: Evaluating mergers among cruise lines. Technical report, Vanderbilt University, 2003. (Cited on pages 11 and 96.)

S. Fuchs. Managing the seat auction. *Airline Business*, pages 40–44, 1987. (Cited on pages 8 and 46.)

G. Gallego. Flexible and callable revenue management. Presentation at the 4th Annual INFORMS Revenue Management and Pricing Section Conference, 2004. (Cited on page 97.)

G. Gallego and R. Phillips. Revenue management of flexible products. *Manufacturing & Service Operations Management*, 6(4):321–337, 2004. (Cited on pages 60, 92, 114, 115, 117, 118 and 136.)

G. Gallego and G. van Ryzin. Optimal dynamic pricing of inventories with stochastic demand over finite horizons. *Management Science*, 40(8):999–1020, Aug. 1994. (Cited on page 134.)

G. Gallego and G. van Ryzin. A multiproduct dynamic pricing problem and its applications to network yield management. *Operations Research*, 45(1), Jan.–Feb. 1997. (Cited on page 134.)

G. Gallego, G. Iyengar, R. Phillips, and A. Dubey. Managing flexible products on a network. Technical report, IEOR Department, Columbia University, Stanford University, School of Operations Research and Industrial Engineering, Cornell University, 2004a. (Cited on pages 95, 111, 112, 113, 118, 119 and 134.)

G. Gallego, S. G. Kou, and R. Phillips. Revenue management of callable products. Technical report, Department of Industrial Engineering and Operations Research, Columbia University, New York, 2004b. (Cited on page 97.)

N. Gans and S. Savin. Pricing and capacity rationing in rentals. Technical report, The Wharton School/Columbia Business School, 2005. (Cited on pages 13 and 27.)

M. R. Garey and D. S. Johnson. *Computers and Intractability: A guide to the Theory of NP-Completeness.* San Francisco: Freeman, 1979. (Cited on pages 179 and 180.)

J. G. Geer and J. H. Geer. Remembering attack ads: An experimental investigation of radio. *Political Behavior*, 25:69–95, 2003. (Cited on page 173.)

M. K. Geraghty and E. Johnson. Revenue management saves National Car Rental. *Interfaces*, 27(1):107–127, Jan.–Feb. 1997. (Cited on pages 2 and 13.)

D. Gillen and W. Morrison. Bundling, integration and the delivered price of air travel: are low cost carriers full service competitors? *Journal of Air Transport Management*, 9(1):15–23, Jan. 2003. (Cited on page 22.)

F. Glover. A multiphase-dual algorithm for the zero-one integer programming problem. *Operations Research*, 13:879–919, 1965. (Cited on pages 190 and 191.)

F. Glover, R. Glover, J. Lorenzo, and C. McMillan. The passenger-mix problem in the scheduled airlines. *Interfaces*, 12(3):73–80, June 1982. (Cited on pages 55, 71, 72, 79 and 133.)

P. Goldman, R. Freling, K. Pak, and N. Piersma. Models and techniques for hotel revenue management using a rolling horizon. *Journal of Revenue and Pricing Management*, 1(3):207–219, 2002. (Cited on page 11.)

R. Gomory. An algorithm for the mixed integer problem. Notes on Linear Programming and Extensions Part 54 (RM-2597), The RAND Corporation, 1960a. (Cited on page 186.)

R. Gomory. Outline of an algorithm for integer solutions to linear programs. *Bulletin of the American Mathematical Society*, 64:275–278, 1958. (Cited on page 186.)

R. E. Gomory. An algorithm for integer solutions to linear programs. In R. L. Graves and P. Wolfe, editors, *Recent Advances in Mathematical Programming*, pages 269–302. McGraw-Hill, 1963. (Cited on page 186.)

R. E. Gomory. Solving linear programming problems in integers. In R. E. Bellmann and M. Hall, Jr., editors, *Combinatorial Analysis*, pages 211–216. Proceedings of Symposia in Applied Mathematics X, American Mathematical Society, Providence, Rhode Island, 1960b. (Cited on page 186.)

T. Gorin and P. Belobaba. Revenue management performance in a low-fare airline environment: Insights from the passenger origin-destination simulator. *Journal of Revenue and Pricing Management*, 3(3):215–236, 2004. (Cited on page 22.)

A. Gosavi. A reinforcement learning algorithm based on policy iteration for average reward: Empirical results with yield management and convergence analysis. *Machine Learning*, 55:5–29, 2004. (Cited on pages 80 and 89.)

A. Gosavi, N. Bandla, and T. K. Das. A reinforcement learning approach to a single leg airline revenue management problem with multiple fare classes and overbooking. *IIE Transactions*, 34:729–742, 2002. (Cited on pages 80 and 89.)

A. Gosavi, A. Ozkaya, and A. F. Kahraman. Simulation optimization for revenue management of airlines with cancellations and overbooking. *OR Spectrum*, 29(1):21–38, 2007. (Cited on pages 64, 90 and 140.)

J. Grammig, R. Hujer, and M. Scheidler. Discrete choice modelling in airline network management. *Journal of Applied Econometrics*, 20 (4):467–486, 2005. (Cited on page 109.)

J. Grandell. *Doubly stochastic Poisson processes.* Berlin: Springer, 1976. (Cited on page 149.)

J. Grandell. *Mixed Poisson Processes.* London: Chapman and Hall, 1997. (Cited on page 149.)

L. Green, S. Savin, and B. Wang. Managing patient service in a diagnostic medical facility. *Operations Research*, 54:11–25, 2006. (Cited on page 82.)

Z. Gu, G. L. Nemhauser, and M. W. Savelsbergh. Lifted cover inequalities for 0-1 integer programs: Computation. *INFORMS Journal on*

Computing, 10:427–437, 1998. (Cited on pages XIX, 192, 202, 203, 205, 207, 223, 224 and 230.)

D. P. Günther, V. C. P. Chen, and E. L. Johnson. Airline yield management: Optimal bid prices for single-hub problems without cancellations. Technical report, School of Industrial and Systems Engineering, Georgia Institute of Technology, 1999. (Cited on page 69.)

K. Hägele, C. . Dúnlaing, and S. Riis. The complexity of scheduling TV commercials. Technical report, Trinity College, Dublin, 2000. (Cited on page 172.)

J. Heinrich. *Medienökonomie, Band 2: Hörfunk und Fernsehen*. Wiesbaden: VS Verlag für Sozialwissenschaften, 1999. (Cited on page 173.)

R. Hendler and F. Hendler. Revenue management in fabulous Las Vegas: Combining customer relationship management and revenue management to maximise profitability. *Journal of Revenue and Pricing Management*, 3(1):73–79, 2004. (Cited on page 11.)

J. L. Higle. Bid-price control with origin-destination demand: A stochastic programming approach. Technical report, Systems and Industrial Engineering, The University of Arizona, 2005. (Cited on page 75.)

C. Hopperstad. Modeling sell-up in PODS. Presentation at the 2000 meeting of the AGIFORS Reservations and Yield Management Study Group, 2000. (Cited on page 100.)

J. H. Horen. Scheduling of network television programs. *Management Science*, 26:354–370, 1980. (Cited on page 172.)

J. Hoseason. Capacity management in the cruise industry. In A. Ingold, U. McMahon-Beattie, and I. Yeoman, editors, *Yield Management: Strategies for the Service Industries*, pages 289–302. London: Thomson, 2nd edition, 2005. (Cited on page 11.)

J. Hoseason. Revenue management in visitor attractions: a case study of the EcoTech Centre, Swaffham, Norfolk. In F. Sfodera, editor, *The Spread of Yield Management Practices*, pages 83–100. Heidelberg: Physica, 2006. (Cited on page 14.)

J. Hoseason and N. Johns. The numbers game: the role of yield management in the tour operations industry. *Progress in Tourism and Hospitality Research*, 4:197–206, 1998. (Cited on page 12.)

A. Hsu and Y. Bassok. Random yield and random demand in a production system with downward substitution. *Operations Research*, 47(2):277–290, 1999. (Cited on page 96.)

S. Humair. *Yield Management for Telecommunication Networks: Defining a New Landscape.* PhD thesis, Sloan School of Management, Massachusetts Institute Of Technology, 2001. (Cited on page 14.)

P. Jehiel and B. Moldovanu. An economic perspective on auctions. *Economic Policy*, 18(36):269–308, 2003. (Cited on pages 27 and 28.)

H. Jiang and G. Miglionico. Airline network revenue management with buy-up. Technical report, University of Cambridge/Università della Calabria, 2006. (Cited on page 109.)

M. A. Johnson, S. Lee, and J. R. Wilson. Experimental evaluation of a procedure for estimating nonhomogeneous Poisson processes having cyclic behavior. *ORSA Journal on computing*, 6(4), 356-368 1994. (Cited on page 158.)

P. Jones. Yield management in UK hotels: a system analysis. *Journal of the Operational Research Society*, pages 1111–1119, 1999. (Cited on page 11.)

G. Jongbloed and G. Koole. Managing uncertainty in call centres using Poisson mixtures. *Applied Stochastic Models in Business and Industry*, 17:307–318, 2001. (Cited on pages 150 and 158.)

L. P. Kaelbling, editor. *Recent Advances in Reinforcement Learning*, 1996. Boston, Dordrecht, London: Kluwer. (Cited on page 79.)

L. P. Kaelbling, M. L. Littmann, and A. W. Moore. Reinforcement learning: A survey. *Journal of Artificial Intelligence Research*, 4: 237–285, 1996. (Cited on page 79.)

I. Karaesmen and G. van Ryzin. Coordinating overbooking and capacity control decisions on a network. Decision, risk & operations working papers series, Columbia Business School, 2004a. (Cited on page 90.)

I. Karaesmen and G. J. van Ryzin. Overbooking with substitutable inventory classes. *Operations Research*, 52(1):83–104, 2004b. (Cited on pages 87, 90, 96 and 137.)

I. Z. Karaesmen. *Three Essays on Revenue Management*. PhD thesis, Columbia University, 2001. (Cited on pages 10 and 90.)

R. G. Kasilingam. Air cargo revenue management: Characteristics and complexities. *European Journal of Operational Research*, 96:36–44, 1996. (Cited on pages 10 and 238.)

H. Kellerer, U. Pferschy, and D. Pisinger. *Knapsack problems*. Berlin, Heidelberg: Springer, 2004. (Cited on page 55.)

S. Kim and R. E. Giachetti. A stochastic mathematical appointment overbooking model for healthcare providers to improve profits. *IEEE Transactions on Systems, Man, and Cybernetics: Part A*, 36(6):1211–1219, 2006. (Cited on page 83.)

S. Kimes. Yield management: A tool for capacity-constrained service firms. *Journal of Operations Management*, 8(4):348–363, 1989a. (Cited on pages 3 and 31.)

S. E. Kimes. The basics of yield management. *Cornell Hotel and Restaurant Administration Quarterly*, 30(3):14–19, 1989b. (Cited on pages 3 and 31.)

S. E. Kimes. Restaurant revenue management: Implementation at Chevys Arrowhead. *Cornell Hotel and Restaurant Administration Quarterly*, 45(1):52–67, 2004. (Cited on page 2.)

S. E. Kimes. Restaurant revenue management: Could it work? *Journal of Revenue and Pricing Management*, 4(1):95–97, 2005. (Cited on page 14.)

S. E. Kimes and L. W. Schruben. Golf course revenue management: A study of tee time intervals. *Journal of Revenue and Pricing Management*, 1(2):111–120, 2002. (Cited on page 14.)

S. E. Kimes and J. Wirtz. Perceived fairness of demand-based pricing for restaurants. *Cornell Hotel and Restaurant Administration Quarterly*, pages 31–37, 2002. (Cited on page 14.)

S. E. Kimes and J. Wirtz. Perceived fairness of revenue management in the US golf industry. *Journal of Revenue and Pricing Management*, 1(4), 2003. (Cited on page 14.)

S. E. Kimes, J. Wirtz, and B. M. Noone. How long should dinner take? Measuring expected meal duration for restaurant revenue management. *Journal of Revenue and Pricing Management*, 1(3):220–233, 2002. (Cited on page 14.)

A. Kimms and R. Klein. Revenue Management im Branchenvergleich. *Zeitschrift für Betriebswirtschaft, Ergänzungsheft 1 "Revenue Management"*, pages 1–30, 2005. (Cited on pages 2, 3, 8, 31, 72 and 124.)

A. Kimms and M. Müller-Bungart. Revenue management for broadcasting commercials: The channel's problem of selecting and scheduling ads to be aired. *International Journal of Revenue Management*, 1(1):28–44, 2007a. (Cited on page 163.)

A. Kimms and M. Müller-Bungart. Revenue Management beim Verkauf auftragsorientierter Sachleistungen. Working paper, Technical University Bergakademie Freiberg, 2003. (Cited on pages 33, 37 and 124.)

A. Kimms and M. Müller-Bungart. Erlössteigernde Verkaufssteuerung durch Absatzgrenzen für Logistikdienste mit mehreren knappen Ressourcen. *at – Automatisierungstechnik*, 52(7):304–312, 2004. (Cited on page 38.)

A. Kimms and M. Müller-Bungart. Simulation of stochastic demand data streams for network revenue management problems. *OR Spectrum*, 29(1):5–20, 2007b. (Cited on pages 130 and 213.)

A. Kimms and M. Müller-Bungart. Revenue Management unter Berücksichtigung des Kundenwahlverhaltens. *Wirtschaftswis-*

senschaftliches Studium, 35(8):434–439, August 2006. (Cited on page 96.)

J. F. C. Kingman. *Poisson Processes*, volume 3 of *Oxford Studies in Probability*. Oxford: Clarendon Press, 1993. (Cited on page 149.)

J. K. Klein. Yield Management als Methode zur ertragsorientierten Kapazitätsnutzung bei Reiseveranstaltern. *Tourismus Journal*, 4(3): 283–307, 2000. (Cited on page 12.)

R. Klein. Quantitative Methoden zur Erlösmaximierung in der Dienstleistungsproduktion. *Betriebswirtschaftliche Forschung und Praxis*, 53:245–259, 2001. (Cited on pages 3 and 31.)

R. Klein. *Revenue Management: Grundlagen und Methoden der Kapazitätssteuerung*. Habilitationsschrift, TU Darmstadt, 2005. (Cited on pages 21, 25, 36, 38, 41, 42, 49, 68, 72, 76, 77, 123, 130, 140, 141, 142 and 146.)

R. Klein. Network capacity control using self-adjusting bid-prices. *OR Spectrum*, 29(1):39–60, 2007. (Cited on pages 23, 28, 76, 77, 140, 141, 142 and 146.)

P. Klemperer. Auction theory: A guide to the literature. *Journal of Economic Surveys*, 13(3):227–286, 1999. (Cited on page 27.)

A. J. Kleywegt. *Dynamic and Stochastic Models with Freight Distribution Applications*. PhD thesis, Purdue University, 1996. URL `http://www.isye.gatech.edu/~anton/thesis.ps`. (Cited on page 239.)

A. J. Kleywegt and J. D. Papastavrou. The dynamic and stochastic knapsack problem. *Operations Research*, 46(1):17–35, Jan.–Feb. 1998. (Cited on page 239.)

A. J. Kleywegt and J. D. Papastavrou. The dynamic and stochastic knapsack problem with random sized items. *Operations Research*, 49:26–41, 2001. (Cited on page 239.)

R. Klophaus. Revenue Management: Wie die Airline Ertragswachstum schafft. *absatzwirtschaft - Zeitschrift für Marketing*, 41:146–155, Oktober/November 1998. (Cited on pages 2, 8 and 81.)

R. Klophaus. Revenue Management: Strategischer Ansatz im globalen Luftfrachtwettbewerb. *Internationales Verkehrswesen*, 51:294–297, 1999. (Cited on page 10.)

D. E. Knuth. *Seminumerical Algorithms*, volume 2 of *The Art of Computer Programming*. Boston: Addison-Wesley, 3rd ed. (9th printing, Jan. 2002), 1998. (Cited on pages 143 and 148.)

A. Köcher. *Controlling der werbefinanzierten Medienunternehmung*. Lohmar: Eul, 2002. (Cited on page 172.)

A. Köcher. Medienmanagement als Kostenmanagement und Controlling. In M. Karmasin and C. Winter, editors, *Grundlagen des Me-*

dienmanagements, pages 219–243. München: Fink, 2000. (Cited on page 172.)

A. Köcher. Was kosten die Medien? – Preise in der Mediengesellschaft. In K.-D. Altmeppen and M. Karmasin, editors, *Medien und Ökonomie, Band 2: Problemfelder der Medienökonomie*, pages 209–248. Wiesbaden: VS Verlag für Sozialwissenschaften, 2004. (Cited on page 172.)

C. Köhler. Erlösmanagement bei der DB AG. Presentation at the 2005 meeting of the GOR group "Revenue Management & Dynamic Pricing", Frankfurt/Main, 2005. (Cited on pages 9 and 92.)

T. Koide and H. Ishii. The hotel yield management with two types of room prices, overbooking and cancellations. *International Journal of Production Economics*, 93-94:417–428, 2005. (Cited on pages 11 and 88.)

F. S. Koppelman and V. Sethi. Closed-form discrete-choice models. In D. A. Hensher and K. J. Button, editors, *Handbook of Transport Modelling*, pages 211–227. Amsterdam: Pergamon, 2000. (Cited on page 109.)

M. E. Kuhl, J. R. Wilson, and M. A. Johnson. Estimating and simulating Poisson processes having trends or multiple periodicities. *IIE Transactions*, 29:201–211, 1997. (Cited on page 158.)

H. Kuhn and F. Defregger. Revenue Management in der Sachleistungswirtschaft. Eine empirische Untersuchung am Beispiel der Papier-, Stahl- und Aluminiumindustrie. Discussion Papers of the Faculty of Business Administration and Economics 171, Katholische Universität Eichstätt-Ingolstadt, 2005. (Cited on page 14.)

S. P. Ladany and A. Arbel. Optimal cruise-liner passenger cabin pricing policy. *European Journal of Operational Research*, 55:136–147, 1991. (Cited on page 11.)

K.-K. Lai and W.-L. Ng. A stochastic approach to hotel revenue optimization. *Computers & Operations Research*, 32:1059–1072, 2005. (Cited on page 11.)

G. A. S. Lambert. *A Radio Advertisement Scheduling Heuristic: A Thesis*. Huntsville, 1983. (Cited on page 173.)

C. J. Lautenbacher and S. Stidham, Jr. The underlying Markov decision process in the single-leg airline yield-management problem. *Transportation Science*, 33(2):136–146, May 1999. (Cited on pages 59, 136 and 139.)

H. Laux. Auftragsselektion bei Unsicherheit. *Zeitschrift für betriebswirtschaftliche Forschung*, pages 164–180, 1971. (Cited on page 137.)

A. M. Law and W. D. Kelton. *Simulation Modelling and Analysis*. Boston: McGraw-Hill, 3rd ed., 2000. (Cited on pages 143, 144 and 148.)

E. Laws. Perspectives on pricing decision in the inclusive holiday industry. In A. Ingold, U. McMahon-Beattie, and I. Yeoman, editors, *Yield Management: Strategies for the Service Industries*, pages 69–84. London: Thomson, 2nd edition, 2005. (Cited on page 12.)

T. C. Lawton. *Cleared for Take-Off. Structure and strategy in the low fare airline business.* Ashgate, 2002. (Cited on pages 9 and 22.)

A. Leask, A. Fyall, and P. Goulding. Revenue management in Scottish visitor attractions. In A. Ingold, U. McMahon-Beattie, and I. Yeoman, editors, *Yield Management: Strategies for the Service Industries*, pages 211–232. London: Thomson, 2nd edition, 2005. (Cited on page 14.)

P. L'Ecuyer. Good parameters and implementations for combined multiple recursive random number generators. *Operations Research*, 47 (1):159–164, January-February 1999. (Cited on page 143.)

P. L'Ecuyer, R. Simard, E. J. Chen, and W. D. Kelton. An object-oriented random-number package with many long streams and substreams. *Operations Research*, 50(6):1073–1075, November-December 2002. (Cited on page 143.)

A. O. Lee. *Airline Reservations Forecasting: Probabilistic and Statistical Models of the Booking Process.* PhD thesis, Flight Transportation Laboratory, Massachusetts Institute of Technology, Cambridge, MA, 1990. (Cited on page 130.)

T. C. Lee and M. Hersh. A model for dynamic airline seat inventory control with multiple seat bookings. *Transportation Science*, 27(3): 252–265, Aug. 1993. (Cited on pages 59, 61, 62, 65, 66, 67, 101, 104, 108, 136, 138 and 139.)

L. M. Leemis. Nonparametric estimation of the cumulative intensity function for a nonhomogeneous Poisson process. *Management Science*, 37(7):886–900, 1991. (Cited on page 158.)

G. Lekakos, D. Papakiriakopoulos, and K. Chorianopoulos. An integrated approach to interactive and personalized TV advertising. In *Proceedings of the Workshop on Personalization in Future TV*, 2001. (Cited on page 173.)

P. A. W. Lewis and G. S. Shedler. Simulation of nonhomogeneous Poisson processes by thinning. *Naval Research Logistics Quarterly*, 26:403–413, 1979. (Cited on page 144.)

M. Z. F. Li and T. H. Oum. A note on the single leg, multifare seat allocation problem. *Transportation Science*, 36(3):349–353, August 2002. (Cited on pages 58 and 135.)

T. Li, E. van Hecka, and P. Vervesta. Dynamic pricing strategies for yield improvement with smart card adoption in the Dutch travel industry. Technical report, Erasmus University, The Netherlands, 2006. (Cited on page 9.)

V. Liberman and U. Yechiali. On the hotel overbooking problem – an inventory system with stochastic cancellations. *Management Science*, 24(11):1117–1126, 1978. (Cited on pages 11 and 88.)

W. H. Lieberman and T. Dieck. Expanding the revenue management frontier: Optimal air planning in the cruise industry. *Journal of Revenue and Pricing Management*, 1(1):7–24, 2002. (Cited on page 11.)

C. Lindemann, M. Lohmann, and A. Thümmler. A unified approach for improving QoS and provider revenue in 3G mobile networks. *Mobile Networks and Applications*, 8:209–221, 2003. (Cited on page 14.)

C. Lindemann, M. Lohmann, and A. Thümmler. Adaptive call admission control for QoS/revenue optimization in CDMA cellular networks. *ACM Journal on Wireless Networks*, 10:457–472, 2004. (Cited on page 14.)

J. Lindenmeier. *Yield-Management und Kundenzufriedenheit. Konzeptionelle Aspekte und empirische Analyse am Beispiel von Fluggesellschaften.* PhD thesis, Universität Freiburg, 2004. Deutscher Universitäts-Verlag. (Cited on page 82.)

J. Lindenmeier and D. K. Tscheulin. Kundenzufriedenheitsrelevante Effekte der Überbuchung im Rahmen des Revenue-Managements. *Zeitschrift für Betriebswirtschaft, Ergänzungsheft 1 "Revenue Management"*, pages 101–123, 2005. (Cited on page 82.)

K. Littlewood. Forecasting and control of passenger bookings. In *AGIFORS Symposium Proceedings*, volume 12, pages 95–112, Oct. 1972. (Cited on pages 55, 56, 58, 59, 135, 136 and 139.)

S. Luo, M. Çakanyıldırım, and R. G. Kasilingam. Two-dimensional cargo overbooking models. Technical report, School of Management, University of Texas at Dallas, 2005. (Cited on pages 10, 85 and 86.)

S. Mahajan and G. van Ryzin. Inventory competition under dynamic consumer choice. *Operations Research*, 49(5):646–657, 2001a. (Cited on page 96.)

S. Mahajan and G. van Ryzin. Stocking retail assortments under dynamic consumer substitution. *Operations Research*, 49:334–351, 2001b. (Cited on page 96.)

G. Maier and P. Weiss. *Modelle diskreter Entscheidungen. Theorie und Anwendung in den Sozial- und Wirtschaftswissenschaften.* Wien, New York: Springer, 1990. (Cited on page 109.)

R. Maleri. *Grundlagen der Dienstleistungsproduktion.* Berlin, Heidelberg: Springer, 4. Auflage, 1997. (Cited on page 3.)

G. Marsaglia and W. W. Tsang. A simple method for generating gamma variables. *ACM Transactions on Mathematical Software*, 26 (3):363–372, September 2000. (Cited on page 148.)

S. Martello and P. Toth. *Knapsack Problems: Algorithms and Computer Implementations.* Chichester: J. Wiley & Sons, 1990. (Cited on pages 55, 178, 190, 191 and 255.)

S. Martello and P. Toth. An upper bound for the zero-one knapsack problem and a branch and bound algorithm. *European Journal of Operational Research*, 1:169–175, 1977. (Cited on page 205.)

S. Martello, D. Pisinger, and P. Toth. Dynamic programming and strong bounds for the 0-1 knapsack problem. *Management Science*, 45(3):414–424, March 1999. (Cited on pages 195 and 255.)

S. Marx and P. Bouvard. *Radio's Advertising's Missing Ingredient: The Optimum Effective Scheduling System.* Washington D. C.: National Association of Broadcasters, 1990. (Cited on page 173.)

W. A. Massey, G. A. Parker, and W. Whitt. Estimating the parameters of a nonhomogeneous Poisson process with linear rate. *Telecommunication Systems*, 5(4):361–387, 1996. (Cited on page 158.)

M. Mayer. Seat allocation, or simple model of seat allocation via sophisticated ones. In *16th AGIFORS Symposium Proceedings*, pages 103–135, 1976. (Cited on pages 63, 64 and 137.)

M. Mayr. Yieldmanagement bei Sixt. Presentation at the 2005 meeting of the GOR group "Revenue Management & Dynamic Pricing", Frankfurt/Main, 2005. (Cited on pages 13 and 20.)

R. P. McAfee and J. McMillan. Auctions and bidding. *Journal of Economic Literature*, 25:699–738, June 1987. (Cited on page 27.)

J. I. McGill and G. J. van Ryzin. Revenue management: Research overview and prospects. *Transportation Science*, 33(2):233–256, May 1999. (Cited on pages 31 and 83.)

R. Metters and V. Vargas. Yield management for the nonprofit sector. *Journal of Service Research*, 1(3):215–226, 1999. (Cited on page 15.)

P. Milgrom. Auctions and bidding: A primer. *Journal of Economic Perspectives*, 3(3):3–22, 1989. (Cited on page 19.)

L. Moussawi and M. Çakanyıldırım. Profit maximization in air cargo overbooking. Technical report, School of Management, University of Texas at Dallas, 2005. (Cited on pages 10 and 86.)

M. Müller-Bungart. Network revenue management: Some issues on upper and lower bounds. In D. Ahr, R. Fahrion, M. Oswald, and G. Reinelt, editors, *Operations Research Proceedings 2003*, pages 23–30. Gesellschaft für Operations Research e. V. (GOR), Heidelberg: Springer, 2004. (Cited on page 38.)

M. Müller-Bungart. Prognose der Passagiernachfrage im Linienluftverkehr. Master's thesis, Universität zu Köln, 2002. (Cited on pages 109, 127 and 132.)

K. V. Nagarajan. On an auction solution to the problem of airline overbooking. *Transportation Research*, 13A:111–114, 1979. (Cited on page 84.)

S. K. Nair and R. Bapna. An application of yield management for internet service providers. *Naval Research Logistics*, 48:348–362, 2001. (Cited on page 14.)

G. L. Nemhauser and L. A. Wolsey. *Integer and Combinatorial Optimization.* New York: John Wiley & Sons, 1988. (Cited on pages 71 and 210.)

S. Netessine and N. Rudi. Centralized and competitive inventory models with demand substitution. *Operations Research*, 51(2):329–335, 2003. (Cited on page 96.)

S. Netessine and R. Shumsky. Introduction to the theory and practice of yield management. *INFORMS Transactions on Education*, 3(1), 2002. (Cited on pages 3 and 31.)

S. Netessine and R. A. Shumsky. Revenue management games: Horizontal and vertical competition. *Management Science*, 51(5):813–831, May 2005. (Cited on pages 96 and 98.)

S. Netessine, G. Dobson, and R. A. Shumsky. Flexible service capacity. optimal investment and the impact of demand correlation. *Operations Research*, 50(2):375–388, 2002. (Cited on pages 95 and 96.)

K. Neumann and M. Morlock. *Operations Research.* München, Wien: Hanser, 1993. (Cited on page 189.)

H. Niederreiter. *Random Number Generation and Quasi-Monte Carlo Methods.* Philadelphia: SIAM, 1992. (Cited on page 143.)

E. D. Norman and K. J. Mayer. Yield management in Las Vegas casino hotels. *Cornell Hotel and Restaurant Administration Quarterly*, 38 (5):28–35, 1997. (Cited on page 11.)

U. Oppitz. Tour Operator vs. Airline: Einflüsse auf Revenue Management Techniken. Presentation at the 2004 meeting of the GOR group "Revenue Management & Dynamic Pricing", Berlin, 2004. (Cited on page 12.)

J. Ortúzar and L. G. Willumsen. *Modelling Transport.* Chichester: Wiley, 2nd edition, 1994. (Cited on page 109.)

A. Ovchinnikov and J. M. Milner. Strategic response to wait-or-buy: Revenue management through last minute deals in the presence of customer learning. Technical report, Joseph L. Rotman School of Management, University of Toronto, 2005. (Cited on page 12.)

M. W. Padberg. A note on zero-one programming. *Operations Research*, 23:833–837, 1975. (Cited on pages XIX and 199.)

K. Pak and R. Dekker. Cargo revenue management: bid-prices for a 0-1 multi knapsack problem. Technical report, Rotterdam School of Management, 2004. (Cited on pages 10, 76, 116, 133, 139, 238, 239, 240 and 241.)

K. Pak and N. Piersma. Airline revenue management: An overview of OR techniques 1982-2001. ERIM Report Series Research in Management ERS-2002-12-LIS, Erasmus Research Institute of Management, Erasmus Universiteit Rotterdam, 2002. (Cited on page 31.)

K. Pak, R. Dekker, and G. Kindervater. Airline revenue management with shifting capacity. Econometric Institute Report EI 2003-46, Erasmus University Rotterdam, 2003. (Cited on pages 79, 88 and 133.)

J. D. Papastavrou, S. Rajagopalan, and A. J. Kleywegt. The dynamic and stochastic knapsack problem with deadlines. *Management Science*, 42(12):1706, 1996. (Cited on page 239.)

M. Parlar. Game theoretic analysis of the substitutable product inventory problem with random demands. *Naval Research Logistics*, 35: 397–409, 1988. (Cited on page 96.)

A. Petrick and R. Klein. Revenue Management mit flexiblen Produkten. Presentation at the 2005 meeting of the GOR group "Revenue Management & Dynamic Pricing", Frankfurt/Main, 2005. (Cited on pages 92, 114 and 116.)

P. E. Pfeifer. The airline discount fare allocation problem. *Decision Sciences*, 20:149–157, 1989. (Cited on page 100.)

R. L. Phillips. *Pricing and Revenue Optimization.* Stanford, California: Stanford University Press, 2005. (Cited on pages 3, 25, 26, 27, 31, 83 and 84.)

D. Pisinger. A minimal algorithm for the bounded knapsack problem. *INFORMS Journal on Computing*, 12:75–84, 2000. (Cited on page 55.)

W. H. Press, S. A. Teukolsky, W. T. Vetterling, and B. P. Flannery. *Numerical Recipes in C. The Art of Scientific Computing.* Cambridge: Cambridge University Press, 2nd ed., 1992. (Cited on page 149.)

G. R. Pugh. *An Analysis of the Lanczos Gamma Approximation.* PhD thesis, University of British Columbia, 2004. (Cited on page 149.)

T. K. Ralphs, L. Ladányi, and L. E. Trotter, Jr. Branch, cut, and price: Sequential and parallel. In M. Jünger and D. Naddef, editors, *Computational Combinatorial Optimization*, pages 223–260. Berlin: Springer, 2001. (Cited on page 211.)

S. K. Reddy, J. E. Aronson, and A. Stam. Spot: Scheduling programs optimally for television. *Management Science*, 44:83–102, 1998. (Cited on page 172.)

S. Rehkopf. *Revenue Management Konzepte zur Auftragsannahme bei kundenindividueller Produktion – konkretisiert anhand der Eisen und Stahl erzeugenden Industrie.* PhD thesis, TU Braunschweig, 2006. (Cited on page 14.)

S. Rehkopf and T. Spengler. Revenue management in a make-to-order environment. In H. Fleuren, D. den Hertog, and P. Kort, editors, *Operations Research Proceedings 2004*, pages 470–478. Berlin, Heidelberg: Springer, 2005a. (Cited on page 14.)

S. Rehkopf and T. Spengler. Revenue Management Konzepte zur Entscheidungsunterstützung bei der Annahme von Kundenaufträgen. *Zeitschrift für Planung*, 16(2):123–146, 2005b. (Cited on page 14.)

R.-D. Reiss. *A course on point processes.* New York: Springer, 1993. (Cited on page 149.)

J. Remmers. Yield Management im Tourismus. In W. Schertler, editor, *Tourismus als Informationsgeschäft*, pages 171–205. Wien: Ueberreuter, 1994. (Cited on page 11.)

H. Richter. The differential revenue method to determine optimal seat allotments by fare type. In *AGIFORS Symposium Proceedings*, volume 22, pages 339–362, October 1982. (Cited on pages 56, 57 and 135.)

S. Ringbom and O. Shy. The "adjustable-curtain" strategy: Overbooking of multiclass service. *Journal of Economics*, 77:73–90, 2002. (Cited on page 88.)

L. W. Robinson. Optimal and approximate control policies for airline booking with sequential nonmonotonic fare classes. *Operations Research*, 43(2):252–263, Mar.–Apr. 1995. (Cited on pages 58, 59, 135, 136 and 139.)

S. M. Ross. *Introduction to Probability Models.* Amsterdam: Academic Press, 8th ed., 2003. (Cited on pages 125, 138, 144, 145 and 238.)

M. H. Rothkopf and S. Park. An elementary introduction to auctions. *Interfaces*, 31(6):83–97, 2001. (Cited on page 27.)

M. Rothstein. Hotel overbooking as a Markovian sequential decision process. *Decision Sciences*, 5:389–404, 1974. (Cited on pages 11 and 85.)

M. Rothstein. Airline overbooking: The state of the art. *Journal of Transport Economics and Policy*, V(1):96–99, January 1971a. (Cited on pages 83 and 84.)

M. Rothstein. An airline overbooking model. *Transportation Science*, 5:180–192, 1971b. (Cited on page 85.)

M. Rothstein. OR and the airline overbooking problem. *Operations Research*, 33(2):237–248, Mar.–Apr. 1985. (Cited on page 83.)

R. T. Rust and N. V. Eechambadi. Scheduling network television programs: A heuristic audience flow approach to maximizing audience share. *Journal of Advertising*, 18:11–18, 1989. (Cited on page 172.)

S. V. Savin, M. A. Cohen, N. Gans, and Z. Katalan. Capacity management in rental businesses with two customer bases. *Operations Research*, 53(4):617–631, 2005. (Cited on page 13.)

M. Scheidler. *Discrete Choice Models for Airline Network Management*, volume 168 of *Volkswirtschaftliche Beiträge*. Idstein: Schulz-Kirchner, 2003. (Cited on page 109.)

A. Scholl. *Robuste Planung und Optimierung. Grundlagen – Konzepte und Methoden – Experimentelle Untersuchungen*. Heidelberg: Physica, 2001. (Cited on page 71.)

A. Schrijver. *Theory of Linear and Integer Programming*. Chichester: John Wiley & Sons, reprint April 2000, 1986. (Cited on pages 71, 184 and 186.)

A. Schrijver. *Polyhedra and Efficiency*, volume A of *Combinatorial Optimization*. Berlin, Heidelberg, New York: Springer, 2003. (Cited on page 71.)

E. Shlifer and Y. Vardi. An airline overbooking policy. *Transportation Science*, 9:101–114, 1975. (Cited on page 89.)

R. A. Shumsky and F. Zhang. Dynamic capacity management with substitution. Technical report, University of Rochester/University of California, 2004. (Cited on page 96.)

J. Si, A. Barto, W. Powell, and D. Wunsch, editors. *Handbook of Learning and Approximate Dynamic Programming*, 2004. John Wiley & Sons. (Cited on page 79.)

J. L. Simon. An almost practical solution to airline overbooking. *Journal of Transport Economics and Policy*, II(2):201–202, 1968. (Cited on page 84.)

J. L. Simon. Airline overbooking: A rejoinder. *Journal of Transport Economics and Policy*, IV(2):212–213, 1970. (Cited on page 84.)

J. L. Simon. Airline overbooking: The state of the art – a reply. *Journal of Transport Economics and Policy*, 6(3):254–256, 1972. (Cited on page 84.)

I. Simonson and A. Tversky. Choice in context: Tradeoff contrast and extremeness aversion. *Journal of Marketing Research*, XXIX:281–295, August 1992. (Cited on page 106.)

R. W. Simpson. Using network flow techniques to find shadow prices for market and seat inventory control. Memorandum M89-1, Massachusetts Institute of Technology, Cambridge, MA, 1989. (Cited on page 72.)

B. Slager and L. Kapteijns. Implementation of cargo revenue management at KLM. *Journal of Revenue and Pricing Management*, 3(1): 80–90, 2004. (Cited on page 10.)

B. C. Smith and C. W. Penn. Analysis of alternative origin-destination control strategies. In *AGIFORS Symposium Proceedings*, volume 28, 1988. (Cited on pages 46, 47, 48 and 49.)

B. C. Smith, J. F. Leimkuhler, and R. M. Darrow. Yield management at American Airlines. *Interfaces*, 22(1):8–31, Jan.–Feb. 1992. (Cited on pages 2, 8, 47 and 81.)

G. E. Smith and T. E. Nagle. Frames of reference and buyers' perception of price and value. *California Management Review*, 38(1): 98–116, 1995. (Cited on page 106.)

S. A. Smith and N. Agrawal. Management of multi-item retail inventory systems with demand substitution. *Operations Research*, 48(1):50–64, 2000. (Cited on page 96.)

J. C. Spall. *Introduction to Stochastic Search and Optimization – Estimation, Simulation and Control.* New Jersey: John Wiley & Sons, 2003. (Cited on pages 78 and 242.)

T. Spengler, S. Rehkopf, and T. Volling. Revenue management in make-to-order manufacturing – an application to the iron and steel industry. *OR Spectrum*, 29(1):157–172, 2007. (Cited on pages 14, 76, 133, 139, 239, 240 and 241.)

S. Strasser. The effect of yield management on railroads. *Transportation Quarterly*, 50(2):47–55, 1996. (Cited on page 10.)

A. Stuart and J. K. Ord. *Distribution Theory*, volume 1 of *Kendall's Advanced Theory of Statistics.* London: Charles Griffin & Co., 5th ed., 1987. (Cited on page 150.)

X. Su. Inter-temporal pricing with strategic customer behavior. Technical report, Haas School of Business, University of California, Berkeley, 2005. (Cited on page 12.)

J. Subramanian, S. Stidham, Jr., and C. J. Lautenbacher. Airline yield management with overbooking, cancellations, and no-shows. *Transportation Science*, 33(2):147–167, May 1999. (Cited on pages 62, 65, 66, 67, 89, 90 and 139.)

R. S. Sutton and A. G. Barto. *Reinforcement Learning.* London, Cambridge: MIT Press, 1998. (Cited on pages 78, 80 and 241.)

Y. Suzuki. The net benefit of airline overbooking. *Transportation Research Part E: Logistics and Transportation Review*, 42:1–19, 2006. (Cited on pages 81 and 98.)

Y. Suzuki. An empirical analysis of the optimal overbooking policies for US major airlines. *Transportation Research*, 38E:135–149, 2002. (Cited on page 81.)

J. L. Swann. Flexible pricing policies: Introduction and a survey of implementation in various industries. Technical report, Northwestern University/GM Research & Development Center, 1999. (Cited on page 3.)

J. L. Swann. *Dynamic Pricing Models to Improve Supply Chain Performance.* PhD thesis, Northwestern University, 2001. (Cited on page 27.)

K. Talluri and G. van Ryzin. Revenue management under a general discrete choice model of consumer behavior. *Management Science*, 50(1):15–33, 2004a. (Cited on pages 63, 66, 67, 102, 104, 106, 107, 108, 113 and 139.)

K. T. Talluri. Airline revenue management with passenger routing control: a new model with solution approaches. *International Journal of Services Technology and Management*, 2(1/2):102–115, 2001. (Cited on pages 116, 117 and 119.)

K. T. Talluri and G. J. van Ryzin. A randomized linear programming method for computing network bid prices. *Transportation Science*, 33:207–216, 1999. (Cited on pages 74, 75, 76, 79, 133 and 240.)

K. T. Talluri and G. J. van Ryzin. An analysis of bid-price controls for network revenue management. *Management Science*, 44(11):1577–1593, 1998. (Cited on pages 69, 70, 74, 75 and 77.)

K. T. Talluri and G. J. van Ryzin. *The Theory and Practice of Revenue Management.* Boston: Kluwer, 2004b. (Cited on pages 3, 8, 25, 27, 31, 42, 48, 49, 68, 83, 84 and 127.)

G. Thomas. Serving up data for enhanced DTV programs. In *Proceedings of the 142nd SMPTE Technical Conference, Pasadena*, 2000. (Cited on page 173.)

B. Titze and R. Griesshaber. Realistic passenger booking behaviour and the simple low-fare/high-fare seat allotment model. In *AGIFORS Symposium Proceedings*, volume 23, pages 197–223, 1983. (Cited on page 56.)

S. Tontsch and N. Hoehl. Bottom-Up Methode zur Messung der Effekte von Erlösmanagement. Presentation at the 2005 meeting of the GOR group "Revenue Management & Dynamic Pricing", Frankfurt/Main, 2005. (Cited on page 110.)

K. E. Train. *Discrete Choice Methods with Simulation.* Cambridge University Press, 2003. (Cited on page 109.)

M. W. Tretheway. Distortions of airline revenues: why the network airline business model is broken. *Journal of Air Transport Management*, 10(1):3–14, January 2004. (Cited on page 22.)

D. K. Tscheulin and J. Lindenmeier. Yield-Management – Ein State-of-the-Art. *Zeitschrift für Betriebswirtschaft*, 73(6):629–662, 2003. (Cited on page 31.)

B. Urgaonkar, P. Shenoy, and T. Roscoe. Resource overbooking and application profiling in shared hosting platforms. In *Proceedings of Operating Systems Design and Implementation (OSDI 2002)*, 2002. (Cited on page 83.)

J. A. Van Mieghem and N. Rudi. Newsvendor networks: Inventory management and capacity investment with discretionary activities. *Manufacturing & Service Operations Management*, 4(4):313–335, Fall 2002. (Cited on page 96.)

B. Van Roy. Neuro-dynamic programming: Overview and recent trends. In E. A. Feinberg and A. Shwartz, editors, *Handbook of Markov Decision Processes: Methods and Applications*, volume 40 of *International Series in Operations Research and Management Science*, pages 431–460. Kluwer, 2001. (Cited on page 79.)

B. Van Roy and J. N. Tsitsiklis. Neuro-dynamic programming overview and a case study in optimal stopping. In *Proceedings of the 36th Conference on Decision & Control*, pages 1181–1186, 1997. (Cited on page 79.)

G. van Ryzin and Q. Liu. On the choice-based linear programming model for network revenue management. Technical report, Columbia Business School, 2004. (Cited on pages 111, 112, 113 and 139.)

G. van Ryzin and J. McGill. Revenue management without forecasting or optimization: An adaptive algorithm for determining seat protection levels. *Management Science*, 42(6):760–775, 2000. (Cited on pages 60 and 136.)

G. van Ryzin and G. Vulcano. Simulation-based optimization of virtual nesting controls for network revenue management. Technical report, Columbia University, New York University, 2005. (Cited on pages 47, 48, 49, 64, 139 and 140.)

G. van Ryzin and G. Vulcano. Computing virtual nesting controls for network revenue management under customer choice behavior. Technical report, Graduate School of Business, Columbia University, 2006. (Cited on pages 47, 48, 64, 110, 135 and 140.)

G. J. van Ryzin. Models of demand. *Journal of Revenue and Pricing Management*, 4(2):204–210, 2005. (Cited on pages 131 and 238.)

R. van Slyke and Y. Young. Finite horizon stochastic knapsacks with applications to yield management. *Operations Research*, 48(1):155–172, 2000. (Cited on page 239.)

P. C. Verhoef and B. Donkers. The effect of acquisition channels on customer loyalty and cross-buying. *Journal of Interactive Marketing*, 19(2):13–43, 2005. (Cited on page 173.)

P. C. Verhoef, J. C. Hoekstra, and M. van Aalst. The effectiveness of direct response radio commercials – results of a field experiment in the Netherlands. *European Journal of Marketing*, 34:143–155, 2000. (Cited on page 173.)

W. Vickrey. Airline overbooking: Some further solutions. *Journal of Transport Economics and Policy*, 6:257–270, September 1972. (Cited on page 84.)

B. Vinod. Alliance revenue management. *Journal of Revenue and Pricing Management*, 4(1):66–82, 2005. (Cited on page 96.)

J. T. Virtamo and S. Aalto. Stochastic optimization of reservation systems. *European Journal of Operational Research*, 51:327–337, 1991. (Cited on page 134.)

L. J. Volpano. A proposal to rationalise entertainment pricing using price discrimination. *Journal of Revenue and Pricing Management*, 1(4):379–382, 2003. (Cited on page 14.)

C. Voss, C. Armistead, B. Johnston, and B. Morris. *Operations Management in Service Industries and the Public Sector.* Chichester: John Wiley, 1985. (Cited on page 3.)

L. R. Weatherford. EMSR versus EMSU: Revenue or utility? *Journal of Revenue and Pricing Management*, 3(3):277–284, 2004. (Cited on page 57.)

L. R. Weatherford and S. E. Bodily. A taxonomy and research overview of perishable-asset revenue management: Yield management, overbooking and pricing. *Operations Research*, 40(5):831–844, 1992. (Cited on pages 3 and 31.)

L. R. Weatherford, S. E. Bodily, and P. E. Pfeifer. Modelling the customer arrival process and comparing decision rules in perishable asset revenue management situations. *Transportation Science*, 27(3):239–251, Aug. 1993. (Cited on pages 130, 139, 141, 147 and 150.)

J. G. Webster. Program audience duplication: A study of television inheritance effects. *Journal of Broadcasting & Electronic Media*, 29:121–133, 1985. (Cited on page 172.)

O. Wendt. Optimal pricing of airfreight capacity. In R. Behrendt and L. Bertsch, editors, *Advanced Software Technology in Air Trans-*

port, pages 161–178. Halbergmoos: AIT-Verl.-GmbH, 1991. (Cited on page 10.)

G. Whelan and D. Johnson. Modelling the impact of alternative fare structures on train overcrowding. *International Journal of Transport Management*, 2(1):51–58, 2004. (Cited on page 9.)

E. L. Williamson. *Airline Network Seat Inventory Control: Methodologies and Revenue Impacts.* PhD thesis, Department of Aeronautics and Astronautics, Massachusetts Institute of Technology, June 1992. (Cited on pages 31, 35, 48, 72, 75, 138 and 146.)

J. G. Wilson, C. K. Anderson, and S.-W. Kim. Optimal booking limits in the presence of strategic consumer behavior. *International Transactions in Operational Research*, 13:99–110, 2006. (Cited on page 12.)

W. L. Winston. *Operations Research: Applications and Algorithms.* Belmont: Duxbury, 3rd ed., 1994. (Cited on pages 74, 183, 184 and 210.)

J. Wirtz, S. E. Kimes, J. H. P. Theng, and P. Patterson. Revenue management: Resolving potential customer conflicts. *Journal of Revenue and Pricing Management*, 2(3):216–226, 2003. (Cited on pages 3 and 82.)

R. D. Wollmer. An airline seat management model for a single leg route when lower fare classes book first. *Operations Research*, 40(1):26–37, Jan.–Feb. 1992. (Cited on pages 58, 59, 135, 136 and 139.)

L. A. Wolsey. *Integer Programming.* New York: John Wiley & Sons, 1998. (Cited on pages 180, 187, 188, 189 and 210.)

S. Würll. Implementierung eines Revenue Management-Systems bei Thomas Cook UK. Presentation at the 2004 meeting of the GOR group “Revenue Management & Dynamic Pricing”, Berlin, 2004. (Cited on page 12.)

R. Wysong. A simplified method for including network effects in capacity control. In *AGIFORS Symposium Proceedings*, volume 28, 1988. (Cited on page 47.)

J. K. Xylander. *Kapazitätsmanagement bei Reiseveranstaltern.* PhD thesis, Universität Frankfurt am Main, 2003. Deutscher Universitäts-Verlag. (Cited on page 12.)

R. R. Yager. Intelligent agents for world wide web advertising decisions. *International Journal of Intelligent Systems*, 12:379–390, 1997. (Cited on page 173.)

P.-S. You. Dynamic-pricing in airline seat management for flights with multiple flight legs. *Transportation Science*, 33(2):192–206, May 1999. (Cited on page 139.)

P.-S. You. Airline seat management with rejection-for-possible-upgrade decision. *Transportation Research Part B*, 35:507–524, 2001. (Cited on pages 101, 102, 103, 104, 105 and 110.)

Y. Young and R. van Slyke. Stochastic knapsack models of yield management. Technical Report 94-76, Polytechnic University, New York, 1994. (Cited on page 239.)

E. Zemel. Easily computable facets of the knapsack polytope. *Mathematics of Operations Research*, 14(4):760–764, November 1989. (Cited on pages XIX, 200 and 201.)

Zentralverband der deutschen Werbewirtschaft. *Werbung in Deutschland 2004*. Berlin: Edition ZAW, 2004. (Cited on page 173.)

D. Zhang and W. L. Cooper. Revenue management for parallel flights with customer choice behavior. *Operations Research*, 53(3):415–431, 2005a. (Cited on page 110.)

D. Zhang and W. L. Cooper. Pricing substitutable flights in airline revenue management. Technical report, University of Chicago, University of Minnesota, 2005b. (Cited on pages 99 and 110.)

W. Zhao and Y.-S. Zheng. A dynamic model for airline seat allocation with passenger diversion and no-shows. *Transportation Science*, 35 (1):80–98, 2001. (Cited on pages 63, 88, 97, 100, 101 and 134.)

Index

Lecture Notes in Economics and Mathematical Systems

For information about Vols. 1–507
please contact your bookseller or Springer-Verlag

Vol. 508: K. Neumann, C. Schwindt, J. Zimmermann, Project Scheduling with Time Windows and Scarce Resources. XI, 335 pages. 2002.

Vol. 509: D. Hornung, Investment, R&D, and Long-Run Growth. XVI, 194 pages. 2002.

Vol. 510: A. S. Tangian, Constructing and Applying Objective Functions. XII, 582 pages. 2002.

Vol. 511: M. Külpmann, Stock Market Overreaction and Fundamental Valuation. IX, 198 pages. 2002.

Vol. 512: W.-B. Zhang, An Economic Theory of Cities.XI, 220 pages. 2002.

Vol. 513: K. Marti, Stochastic Optimization Techniques. VIII, 364 pages. 2002.

Vol. 514: S. Wang, Y. Xia, Portfolio and Asset Pricing. XII, 200 pages. 2002.

Vol. 515: G. Heisig, Planning Stability in Material Requirements Planning System. XII, 264 pages. 2002.

Vol. 516: B. Schmid, Pricing Credit Linked Financial Instruments. X, 246 pages. 2002.

Vol. 517: H. I. Meinhardt, Cooperative Decision Making in Common Pool Situations. VIII, 205 pages. 2002.

Vol. 518: S. Napel, Bilateral Bargaining. VIII, 188 pages. 2002.

Vol. 519: A. Klose, G. Speranza, L. N. Van Wassenhove (Eds.), Quantitative Approaches to Distribution Logistics and Supply Chain Management. XIII, 421 pages. 2002.

Vol. 520: B. Glaser, Efficiency versus Sustainability in Dynamic Decision Making. IX, 252 pages. 2002.

Vol. 521: R. Cowan, N. Jonard (Eds.), Heterogenous Agents, Interactions and Economic Performance. XIV, 339 pages. 2003.

Vol. 522: C. Neff, Corporate Finance, Innovation, and Strategic Competition. IX, 218 pages. 2003.

Vol. 523: W.-B. Zhang, A Theory of Interregional Dynamics. XI, 231 pages. 2003.

Vol. 524: M. Frölich, Programme Evaluation and Treatment Choise. VIII, 191 pages. 2003.

Vol. 525: S. Spinler, Capacity Reservation for Capital- Intensive Technologies. XVI, 139 pages. 2003.

Vol. 526: C. F. Daganzo, A Theory of Supply Chains. VIII, 123 pages. 2003.

Vol. 527: C. E. Metz, Information Dissemination in Currency Crises. XI, 231 pages. 2003.

Vol. 528: R. Stolletz, Performance Analysis and Optimization of Inbound Call Centers. X, 219 pages. 2003.

Vol. 529: W. Krabs, S. W. Pickl, Analysis, Controllability and Optimization of Time-Discrete Systems and Dynamical Games. XII, 187 pages. 2003.

Vol. 530: R. Wapler, Unemployment, Market Structure and Growth. XXVII, 207 pages. 2003.

Vol. 531: M. Gallegati, A. Kirman, M. Marsili (Eds.), The Complex Dynamics of Economic Interaction. XV, 402 pages, 2004.

Vol. 532: K. Marti, Y. Ermoliev, G. Pflug (Eds.), Dynamic Stochastic Optimization. VIII, 336 pages. 2004.

Vol. 533: G. Dudek, Collaborative Planning in Supply Chains. X, 234 pages. 2004.

Vol. 534: M. Runkel, Environmental and Resource Policy for Consumer Durables. X, 197 pages. 2004.

Vol. 535: X. Gandibleux, M. Sevaux, K. Sörensen, V. T'kindt (Eds.), Metaheuristics for Multiobjective Optimisation. IX, 249 pages. 2004.

Vol. 536: R. Brüggemann, Model Reduction Methods for Vector Autoregressive Processes. X, 218 pages. 2004.

Vol. 537: A. Esser, Pricing in (In)Complete Markets. XI, 122 pages, 2004.

Vol. 538: S. Kokot, The Econometrics of Sequential Trade Models. XI, 193 pages. 2004.

Vol. 539: N. Hautsch, Modelling Irregularly Spaced Financial Data. XII, 291 pages. 2004.

Vol. 540: H. Kraft, Optimal Portfolios with Stochastic Interest Rates and Defaultable Assets. X, 173 pages. 2004.

Vol. 541: G.-y. Chen, X. Huang, X. Yang, Vector Optimization. X, 306 pages. 2005.

Vol. 542: J. Lingens, Union Wage Bargaining and Economic Growth. XIII, 199 pages. 2004.

Vol. 543: C. Benkert, Default Risk in Bond and Credit Derivatives Markets. IX, 135 pages. 2004.

Vol. 544: B. Fleischmann, A. Klose, Distribution Logistics. X, 284 pages. 2004.

Vol. 545: R. Hafner, Stochastic Implied Volatility. XI, 229 pages. 2004.

Vol. 546: D. Quadt, Lot-Sizing and Scheduling for Flexible Flow Lines. XVIII, 227 pages. 2004.

Vol. 547: M. Wildi, Signal Extraction. XI, 279 pages. 2005.

Vol. 548: D. Kuhn, Generalized Bounds for Convex Multistage Stochastic Programs. XI, 190 pages. 2005.

Vol. 549: G. N. Krieg, Kanban-Controlled Manufacturing Systems. IX, 236 pages. 2005.

Vol. 550: T. Lux, S. Reitz, E. Samanidou, Nonlinear Dynamics and Heterogeneous Interacting Agents. XIII, 327 pages. 2005.

Vol. 551: J. Leskow, M. Puchet Anyul, L. F. Punzo, New Tools of Economic Dynamics. XIX, 392 pages. 2005.

Vol. 552: C. Suerie, Time Continuity in Discrete Time Models. XVIII, 229 pages. 2005.

Vol. 553: B. Mönch, Strategic Trading in Illiquid Markets. XIII, 116 pages. 2005.

Vol. 554: R. Foellmi, Consumption Structure and Macroeconomics. IX, 152 pages. 2005.

Vol. 555: J. Wenzelburger, Learning in Economic Systems with Expectations Feedback (planned) 2005.

Vol. 556: R. Branzei, D. Dimitrov, S. Tijs, Models in Cooperative Game Theory. VIII, 135 pages. 2005.

Vol. 557: S. Barbaro, Equity and Efficiency Considerations of Public Higer Education. XII, 128 pages. 2005.

Vol. 558: M. Faliva, M. G. Zoia, Topics in Dynamic Model Analysis. X, 144 pages. 2005.

Vol. 559: M. Schulmerich, Real Options Valuation. XVI, 357 pages. 2005.

Vol. 560: A. von Schemde, Index and Stability in Bimatrix Games. X, 151 pages. 2005.

Vol. 561: H. Bobzin, Principles of Network Economics. XX, 390 pages. 2006.

Vol. 562: T. Langenberg, Standardization and Expectations. IX, 132 pages. 2006.

Vol. 563: A. Seeger (Ed.), Recent Advances in Optimization. XI, 455 pages. 2006.

Vol. 564: P. Mathieu, B. Beaufils, O. Brandouy (Eds.), Artificial Economics. XIII, 237 pages. 2005.

Vol. 565: W. Lemke, Term Structure Modeling and Estimation in a State Space Framework. IX, 224 pages. 2006.

Vol. 566: M. Genser, A Structural Framework for the Pricing of Corporate Securities. XIX, 176 pages. 2006.

Vol. 567: A. Namatame, T. Kaizouji, Y. Aruga (Eds.), The Complex Networks of Economic Interactions. XI, 343 pages. 2006.

Vol. 568: M. Caliendo, Microeconometric Evaluation of Labour Market Policies. XVII, 258 pages. 2006.

Vol. 569: L. Neubecker, Strategic Competition in Oligopolies with Fluctuating Demand. IX, 233 pages. 2006.

Vol. 570: J. Woo, The Political Economy of Fiscal Policy. X, 169 pages. 2006.

Vol. 571: T. Herwig, Market-Conform Valuation of Options. VIII, 104 pages. 2006.

Vol. 572: M. F. Jäkel, Pensionomics. XII, 316 pages. 2006

Vol. 573: J. Emami Namini, International Trade and Multinational Activity. X, 159 pages, 2006.

Vol. 574: R. Kleber, Dynamic Inventory Management in Reverse Logistics. XII, 181 pages, 2006.

Vol. 575: R. Hellermann, Capacity Options for Revenue Management. XV, 199 pages, 2006.

Vol. 576: J. Zajac, Economics Dynamics, Information and Equilibnum. X, 284 pages, 2006.

Vol. 577: K. Rudolph, Bargaining Power Effects in Financial Contracting. XVIII, 330 pages, 2006.

Vol. 578: J. Kühn, Optimal Risk-Return Trade-Offs of Commercial Banks. IX, 149 pages, 2006.

Vol. 579: D. Sondermann, Introduction to Stochastic Calculus for Finance. X, 136 pages, 2006.

Vol. 580: S. Seifert, Posted Price Offers in Internet Auction Markets. IX, 186 pages, 2006.

Vol. 581: K. Marti; Y. Ermoliev; M. Makowsk; G. Pflug (Eds.), Coping with Uncertainty. XIII, 330 pages, 2006.

Vol. 582: J. Andritzky, Sovereign Default Risks Valuation: Implications of Debt Crises and Bond Restructurings. VIII, 251 pages, 2006.

Vol. 583: I.V. Konnov, D.T. Luc, A.M. Rubinov† (Eds.), Generalized Convexity and Related Topics. IX, 469 pages, 2006.

Vol. 584: C. Bruun, Adances in Artificial Economics: The Economy as a Complex Dynamic System. XVI, 296 pages, 2006.

Vol. 585: R. Pope, J. Leitner, U. Leopold-Wildburger, The Knowledge Ahead Approach to Risk. XVI, 218 pages, 2007 (planned).

Vol. 586: B.Lebreton, Strategic Closed-Loop Supply Chain Management. X, 150 pages, 2007 (planned).

Vol. 587: P. N. Baecker, Real Options and Intellectual Property: Capital Budgeting Under Imperfect Patent Protection. X, 276 pages , 2007.

Vol. 588: D. Grundel, R. Murphey, P. Panos , O. Prokopyev (Eds.), Cooperative Systems: Control and Optimization. IX, 401 pages , 2007.

Vol. 589: M. Schwind, Dynamic Pricing and Automated Resource Allocation for Information Services: Reinforcement Learning and Combinatorial Auctions. XII, 293 pages , 2007.

Vol. 590: S. H. Oda, Developments on Experimental Economics: New Approaches to Solving Real-World Problems. XVI, 262 pages, 2007.

Vol. 591: M. Lehmann-Waffenschmidt, Economic Evolution and Equilibrium: Bridging the Gap. VIII, 272 pages, 2007.

Vol. 592: A. C.-L. Chian, Complex Systems Approach to Economic Dynamics. X, 95 pages, 2007.

Vol. 593: J. Rubart, The Employment Effects of Technological Change: Heterogenous Labor, Wage Inequality and Unemployment. XII, 209 pages, 2007

Vol. 594: R. Hübner, Strategic Supply Chain Management in Process Industries: An Application to Specialty Chemicals Production Network Design. XII, 243 pages, 2007

Vol. 595: H. Gimpel, Preferences in Negotiations: The Attachment Effect. XIV, 268 pages, 2007

Vol. 596: M. Müller-Bungart, Revenue Management with Flexible Products: Models and Methods for the Broadcasting Industry.XXI, 297 pages, 2007

Vol. 597: C. Barz, Risk Averse Capacity Control in Revenue Management. Approx. 180 pages, 2007

Vol. 598: A. Ule, Partner Choice and Cooperation in Networks: Theory and Experimental Evidence. Approx. 200 pages, 2007

Printing: Krips bv, Meppel
Binding: Stürtz, Würzburg